CONFRONTING 9-11, IDEOLOGIES OF RACE, AND EMINENT ECONOMISTS

RESEARCH IN POLITICAL ECONOMY

Series Editor: Paul Zarembka

RESEARCH IN POLITICAL ECONOMY   VOLUME 20

CONFRONTING 9-11, IDEOLOGIES OF RACE, AND EMINENT ECONOMISTS

EDITED BY

PAUL ZAREMBKA

Department of Economics, State University of New York, Buffalo, USA

2002

JAI
An Imprint of Elsevier Science

Amsterdam – Boston – London – New York – Oxford – Paris
San Diego – San Francisco – Singapore – Sydney – Tokyo

ELSEVIER SCIENCE Ltd
The Boulevard, Langford Lane
Kidlington, Oxford OX5 1GB, UK

First edition 2002

Library of Congress Cataloging in Publication Data
A catalog record from the Library of Congress has been applied for.

British Library Cataloguing in Publication Data
A catalogue record from the British Library has been applied for.

ISBN: 0-7623-0984-9
ISSN: 1061-7230 (Series)

⊗The paper used in this publication meets the requirements of ANSI/NISO Z39.48-1992 (Permanence of Paper).
Printed in The Netherlands.

CONTENTS

LIST OF CONTRIBUTORS

Babacar Camara	Miami University, Middletown, OH, USA
Massimo De Angelis	University of East London, Dagenham, Essex, UK
Andy Denis	City University, London, UK
Victor Kasper, Jr.	Buffalo State College, Buffalo, NY, USA
David MacGregor	King's College, University of Western Ontario, London, Ontario, Canada
Guido G. Preparata	University of Washington, Tacoma, WA, USA
Peter Dale Scott	University of California at Berkeley, Berkeley, CA, USA
Turan Subasat	The University of Bath, Bath, UK

FOREWORD

This editor has not typically provided Forewords for volumes in this series, feeling that titles and abstracts speak well enough for themselves. While this volume is not different in that respect, the importance of 9-11 and its inclusion here in Part I suggests some remarks.

Many web sites and a few publications have developed which contest in one way or another the official interpretations of 9-11 and the role of the U.S. government in the event and its aftermath. This is very healthy. Critics are far ahead of where they were after the Kennedy assassination in being able to address probing questions. Nevertheless, we must continue to press ahead in exploring all evidence for there is so much at stake.

The most common charitable interpretation of the role of the U.S. government in 9-11 is incompetence of the security services in handling forewarnings of many sorts before the event happened, and in not stopping events as they were unfolding. Certain reported failures border on the ridiculous. If people in the U.S. are being taxed billions of dollars for a service, they expect the agencies to perform.

Step two up the ladder says: "look at the evidence, sections of U.S. security agencies actually were in the know that 9-11 was going to happen". They had nothing to do with the planning and execution of the plot. But they let it happen (avoiding, say, a single act of grounding all flights for that day). This critique does not question that there were indeed nineteen hijackers of Middle Eastern descent who took over the four planes (exactly how is still unclear).

Step three argues actual, albeit partial, participation by sections of the U.S. government in planning and execution of the attacks on the World Trade Center, the Pentagon and/or whatever the target of the plane which crashed in Pennsylvania. For example, the WTC attacks could have occurred similar to the official explanation of al-Qaeda responsibility, but knowing of those plans certain individuals or groups within the U.S. government *added on* an attack on Washington, D.C. Promoters of this theory argue that the collapse of the towers may have been unexpected and destruction of merely several floors in each tower would have been insufficient to justify 'big plans' to be undertaken by the U.S. government.

The highest step of the ladder argues that sections of U.S. government fully and completely planned and executed the attacks, including focusing the blame elsewhere to their advantage. Just as Lee Harvey Oswald himself said before his own murder that he was a "patsy", the reasoning would seem to argue that named hijackers were also "patsies".

How should we resolve such competing interpretations and analyses of the events? Evidence should be the guide. Yet evidence itself is often being suppressed. Nevertheless, major issues are emerging including the following:

(1) Very large increases in put options against American and United Airlines and for certain insurance companies in the days before 9-11 clearly indicate financial killings (no pun) to be anticipated on their soon-to-follow falling stock prices. Widely reported shortly after 9-11, finding out who placed those options would be major evidence. Whatever investigation took place has not been reported to the public, nor has the mass media demanded answers.

(2) Atta and Alomari are stated to have used a close connecting flight from Portland, Maine (Colgan Air, scheduled arrival time about 6:50 a.m.) to get to Boston for American Flight 11 (scheduled departure, 7:45 a.m.). Why, when surely the danger of a mis-connection would be in calculations of hijackers? No videos of any of the hijackers have been released showing them boarding any of the hijacked planes (the video from Maine is no contradiction). The alleged hijackers' behavior in days and hours before the flights seems inconsistent with disciplined terrorists. Reporting of Atta's personal belongings left behind, his passport found on a Manhattan street a couple of blocks from the WTC debris, and Jarrah's partial passport at the crash site in Pennsylvania invite questions of plants. There are also reports that Atta's passport was earlier stolen and that his father has said that Atta called him on September 12, 2001.

(3) The wife of a man killed at the South Tower asked on the Phil Donahue show why wasn't the Pentagon protected by 9:41 a.m. – 55 minutes after the first tower was hit and even more time after that hijacking was first discovered (around 8:20 a.m.). Kristen Breitweiser, as co-Chairperson, September 11th Advocates, then took her questions to the U.S. Senate and House Joint Select Committee on Intelligence (September 18, 2002), questions which resonate with those of quite a few independent investigators and have not been satisfactorily answered. A military stand-down particularly for protecting the Pentagon, perhaps also for the second (or even first) tower to be hit, has been suggested by some as an explanation. In any case, Breitweiser herself is demanding a truly independent, thorough investigation of 9-11.

(4) The government has not released flight and data recorders, except that portion heard by families for Flight 93 downed in Pennsylvania. Even for Flight 93, the last minutes were not released nor accounted for, although those last minutes would almost certainly be definitive regarding speculations that the plane was shot down by a military jet in the vicinity. In other words, important evidence is being suppressed.

(5) Did the impact and fires resulting from the crashed planes cause the towers to collapse or is there another reason for their total destruction? The WTC towers coming straight down in virtual free fall, certain reports of explosions or flashes of light on lower floors (were these demolition explosions?), quick removal of relevant physical evidence on the ground, and the issue of whether the towers should have collapsed at all invite further questions. The South Tower was hit second but collapsed first, yet the plane failed to go directly into that tower and consequently released much fuel into the outside air. In fact, a few minutes before the South Tower's collapse, two firefighters are reported to have reached the 78th floor (the 78th to 84th being the floors immediately damaged) and radioed that they could see "two pockets of fire", had a "coherent plan for putting out the fires", and were not panicked (*New York Times*, August 4, 2002). There was no mention of any intense heat endangering the firefighters, let alone the building structure.

(6) The hole in the Pentagon and the surrounding damage have been analyzed as too small to be associated with a Boeing 757, the plane for Flight 77. There is also lack of much physical evidence of a plane (supposedly due to the heat of the explosion, but which would contradict claims that DNA evidence was available to identify all but one person on the flight). If so, what struck the Pentagon and what truly happened to Flight 77? There is also a very unusual five-minute, unexplained, deviation by Flight 77 from its flight path west out of Dulles airport while under the control of the original pilot. Why was there only one reported phone call from this plane by any flight attendants or passengers (this reported call itself from passenger Barbara Olson to her husband, high Bush appointee Ted Olson[1]), even as they are reported to have been told by the hijackers that they were going to die and should make phone calls to family?

Could certain sections inside the U.S. government have played a role in planning and executing the events of September 11th similar to the way many believe evidence points to parts of the government being involved in the assassinations of an elected President (JFK) or would-be President (RFK)?

Peter Dale Scott's *Deep Politics and the Death of JFK* (University of California Press, 1993) is a background for the first two chapters of this volume.

'Deep politics' has the status of a concept in his work. What 'deep politics' might be going on today inside the United States? And how can our under-standings of class analysis of the United States be integrated into the results of these investigations, however unpleasant the results might well be? Might not those using class analysis benefit from 'deep politics' and vice versa? By the inclusion of the first two chapters here, the *Research* hopes to promote such analysis and theoretical development.

NOTE

1. U.S. Solicitor General Olson, who had been Bush's lawyer in the U.S. Supreme Court against Gore, actually told that court on a later occasion that it is "easy to imagine an infinite number of situations . . . where government officials might quite legitimately have reasons to give false information out", *Washington Post*, March 21, 2002).

Paul Zarembka
Editor

October 6, 2002

PART I:
9-11 AND DEEP POLITICS

THE DEEP POLITICS OF SEPTEMBER 11: POLITICAL ECONOMY OF CONCRETE EVIL

David MacGregor

ABSTRACT

This paper offers a deep political analysis of September 11 drawing upon Peter Dale Scott's concept of deep politics and the Hegelian-Marxist political economy of evil. Concrete evil concerns outbreaks of malevolence in history and their connection with ruling social groups; deep politics extends this by investigating hidden forces lying beneath the surface of conventional political processes. The deep politics of September 11 and intervention in Afghanistan points to covert U.S. reliance on warlords, holy warriors and drug traffickers to secure American interests, including Caspian oil resources and the limitation of Russian influence over its former republics and satellites.

INTRODUCTION

The sacrifice is a gift, a gift to the gods which is directed to the flow of power, to keeping the life force moving there where it has been blocked by sin. With the sacrifice man feeds the gods to give them more power so that he may have more. The sacred food has the strength of life. The sacrifice of living things adds visible life power to the stream of life; the more living things sacrificed, the more extravagant release of power . . . Ernest Becker, *Escape from Evil* (1975).

Confronting 9-11, Ideologies of Race, and Eminent Economists,
Research in Political Economy, Volume 20, pages 3–61.
ISBN: 0-7623-0984-9

It is first to be noted that where in other principalities one has only to contend with the ambition of the nobles and the arrogance of the people, the Roman emperors had a third problem: they had to endure the cruelty and avarice of the soldiers. This was such a difficult thing that it was the cause of the downfall of many of them, since it was hard to satisfy both the soldiers and the populace; for the people loved peace and quiet and because of this loved modest princes, while the soldiers loved the prince who had a military character and was arrogant, cruel and rapacious; they wanted him to practice such qualities on the people so that they might double their salary and unleash their avarice and cruelty (Machiavelli, 1979, pp. 140–141).

The Afghans are divided into clans, over which various chiefs exercise a sort of feudal supremacy. Their indomitable hatred of rule, and their love of individual independence, alone prevents their becoming a powerful nation; but this very irregularity and uncertainty of action makes them dangerous neighbours, liable to be blown about by the wind of caprice, or to be stirred up by political intriguers, who artfully excite their passions (Engels, 1857).

The calamities in Washington and New York City of September 11, 2001 and their geopolitical ramifications present troubling problems, and thus unrivalled opportunities, for an understanding of Western democracy. The origin of the attacks, and the inadequate response of U.S. security agencies during the crisis, are in question. No event since the 1963 shooting of President John F. Kennedy in Dallas has had a comparable impact on a world scale. In terms of erosion of civil liberties and deliberate reversal of political freedoms in the American homeland (Knox, 2002), the aftermath of September 11 exhibits disturbing resemblances to the Nazi response to the Reichstag Fire of 1933.[1] U.S. military installations in significant geostrategic sites once belonging to, or invested by, the former Soviet Union[2] recall initial stages of the Vietnam War, when after the French defeat in 1954, America advisors supported the Diem regime.

In *Deep Politics and the Death of JFK*, Peter Dale Scott sketches a political theory that undermines standard views of modern democracy, and illuminates, as I argue in this paper, the gruesome events of September 11. Scott's concept also returns in a reflexive mood to earlier notions about the arrangement of politics.

Scott's theory of government pushes the dialectic of malevolence, initially presented by Hegel and Marx, into the forefront of social inquiry. These classic writers originated a project I shall call the political economy of concrete evil. The study of concrete evil centers on corruption at the highest levels of global political power, a phenomenon mostly unexplored in contemporary social science.

This paper offers a deep political analysis of September 11 that draws upon Scott's concept and the political economy of evil put forward by Hegel and Marx. The paper proposes no final conclusions about the identity of the magus of terror in New York and Washington. However, there are many reasons to doubt the official story of September 11.

The first three sections discuss the concept of evil and Nixon's Watergate; and the so-called American Taliban, John Walker Lindh. Section IV outlines the political economy of concrete evil initiated by Hegel and Marx. Scott's concept of deep politics, originally developed to explain the Kennedy shooting, is introduced in Section V.

Section VI investigates ties between U.S. investment firm the Carlyle Group and the Saudi Binladin Group. Section VII explores the Islamist ideology of bin Laden and its spread by holy warriors, the "free electrons of jihad." The role of the CIA's drug trafficking proxies in the 1979–1989 Afghan jihad occupies Section VIII, and political chaos in Afghanistan preceding the 1994 Taliban victory is the focus of Section IX. Prime Minister Benazir Bhutto's creation, the Taliban, and its victorious sweep of most of Afghanistan provides the focus of Section X; the next section concerns an "evil triangle" of drugs, terrorism and human rights abuses described by Tajik leader Ahmed Shah Massoud. Section XII examines the deep politics of contemporary Afghanistan, including U.S. reliance on killers and drug lords. The final sections spotlight the possible motives for September 11, including the race for Caspian Sea oil resources, and America's geopolitical quest to cage the Russian bear.

I. CONTESTING EVIL

In his television statement on the night of September 11, President George W. Bush called the suicide attacks on the World Trade Center and the Pentagon an act of "evil" demanding massive U.S. retribution. Evil became a Washington buzzword. *New York Times* columnist Thomas Friedman (2002, p. 15) proposed an "'Office of Evil,' whose job would be to constantly sift all intelligence data and imagine what the most twisted mind might be up to." Bush's bellicose rhetoric about "evildoers" frightened NATO allies, especially his "axis of evil" reference to Iran, Iraq and North Korea in the January 2002 State of the Union Address, which announced a $50 billion increase in defense spending and vowed to eradicate "weapons of mass destruction" in the hands of states that support terrorism.

Evil may be more appropriately employed to describe corrupt activities of the powerful rather than of those on the margins such as Afghan cave-dwellers targeted by the Administration as perpetrators of September.

The comprehension of malevolence recommended in this paper stands in direct opposition to the puerile view of evil and American values that informs a recent statement, addressed to the world Muslim community called, "What

Are We Fighting For?", signed by 60 U.S. academic stars (Walzer, 2001). The signatories identify Islamist terror as "a world-threatening evil that clearly requires the use of force to remove it," and proclaim "support [of] our government's, and our society's, decision to use force of arms against [it]." Widely circulated in Europe this text is mostly unknown in America. It reinforces the thesis put forward alike by those strange ideological bedfellows, Samuel Huntington and Osama bin Laden, that a fresh division of the world has erupted between Western democracy and a newly arisen, militant Muslim world (Said, 2002).

An emerging field of study called the sociology of evil indulges a worldview similar to "What Are We Fighting For?" and ends up approving orthodox, but distorted, narratives of momentous political events. For example, Jeffrey Alexander's (1990, p. 215; 2001) neo-Durkheimian interpretation of Watergate, in which Richard Nixon becomes "the very personification of evil," might have been lifted from the feel-good screenplay of *All the President's Men*. Omissions in the conventional account of Watergate foreshadow similar lacunae in the official version of September 11.

II. EVIL AT WATERGATE

According to the received version, President Richard Nixon masterminded two bungled mid-1972 break-ins at the Democratic National Committee (DNC) headquarters in the Watergate complex, and covered up White House links to the crime. Washington police interrupted the second burglary attempt, arresting the perpetrators. "Within twenty-four hours, police and FBI agents established links between the arrested men, the Committee to Re-elect the President (CRP) and the Nixon White House" (Hougan, 1984a, p. 1). Evidently, the anxious Chief Executive and his men aimed to de-rail the Democrat's campaign for the November, 1972 Presidential election, which Nixon won by a landslide.

An alternative theory suggests that Nixon had no prior knowledge of the burglaries, and, in any case, never would have sanctioned the amateur proceedings at the DNC. Elite actors, including the U.S. Joint Chiefs of Staff and the CIA, may have orchestrated the president's exit on August 9, 1974. This argument was offered at the time by leading Administration figure, Charles Colson, but not seriously pursued (Hougan, 1984a, pp. 270–275).

U.S. intelligence agencies and the Joint Chiefs bitterly opposed White House foreign policy, including Nixon's opening to China, nuclear arms talks with the Soviets, and peace efforts in Vietnam. These initiatives may have provoked a poisonous scheme against the Administration. Certainly, Watergate involved a number of untimely deaths, including a mysterious Chicago plane crash in

December 1972 that killed Dorothy Hunt (the wife of one of the imprisoned Watergate burglars) and dozens of others (Oglesby, 1976).

Bob Woodward, who along with Carl Bernstein whipped up the scandal in the *Washington Post* with timely messages from a supposed White House informer called Deep Throat, had an interesting earlier career in U.S. naval intelligence. In 1969–1970, Naval Lieutenant Woodward occupied a highly unusual "oversite position" at the Pentagon and the White House "*vis-à-vis* a broad spectrum of interagency intelligence operations" that brought him into intimate contact with Admiral Thomas Moorer (then head of the U.S. Navy) and Admiral Robert O. Welander (Hougan, 1984b, p. 295). As communications liaison officer between the Pentagon and the White House, Woodward would often brief Admiral Moorer and then "travel to the West Basement offices of the White House [to] brief Alexander Haig about the same matters he had earlier conveyed to Moorer" (Colodny & Gettlin, 1991, p. 85).

A few months after Woodward's tour of secret military duty in Washington, Admiral Moorer and Admiral Welander ran a notorious 1971 Joint Chiefs' spy operation targeting the President himself and National Security Advisor, Henry Kissinger. "It was an unprecedented case of espionage that pitted the nation's top military commanders against their civilian commander in chief during wartime" (Rosen, 2002).

Nixon learned of a plot against him through the inadvertent testimony of a Naval stenographer, Yeoman Charles Edward Radford. Radford pilfered top secret documents from Henry Kissinger's briefcase while acting as an assistant for General Alexander Haig.

Partly to avoid a major wartime crisis, Nixon chose to keep the Moorer-Radford affair confidential. Besides he was never quite convinced of the brazen pervidy of his closest advisors. "I understand [INAUDIBLE] and so forth over at the Joint Chiefs," said Nixon to his advisors. "However, but taking stuff out of Henry's briefcase! I'm sure Haig would never approve of that" (Nixon Era Library, 2002). Nixon finessed the scandal by having a few of the villains transferred out of Washington. He re-appointed Moorer as Chairman of the Joint Chiefs, confident he could now control the remorseful admiral. "By allowing a cast of characters he distrusted, and who distrusted him, to remain in place in the White House and in the Pentagon, Nixon virtually ensured that the culture of secrecy and paranoia that infused his first term would persist until the Watergate scandal prematurely ended his presidency" (Rosen, 2002).

Watergate thieves included Cuban exile Rolando Martinez and CIA operative Frank Sturgis, who played shadowy roles in events surrounding the assassination of John F. Kennedy. Burglars E. Howard Hunt (also connected with the Dallas shooting) and James McCord had recently occupied senior ranks in the CIA.

The infamous break-in likely targeted a sexual blackmail operation based in the Columbia Plaza apartment complex, situated close to DNC headquarters, and covertly overseen by the CIA. According to Jim Hougan's (1984a) landmark investigation, call girls at Columbia Plaza communicated with DNC headquarters via a private telephone network. Prospective clients were taken to the desk of the DNC secretary. "They were told that the telephone would ring, and that, when they answered it, they'd be speaking with . . . (here a photograph would be taken from [the secretary's] desk and shown to the visitor.) They could make whatever arrangements they liked" (Hougan, 2001, p. 34). Watergate burglars may have been looking for documents concealed in the DNC secretary's locked desk.

Len Colodny's and Robert Gettlin's *Silent Coup* (1991) argues that White House counsel John Dean – who gave crucial insider testimony against the beleaguered president – and Alexander Haig, White House chief of staff, may have been at the core of the plot to unseat Richard Nixon. No charges were laid against the disgraced president; nor was he convicted of any illegal acts. A trial might have revealed secrets damaging to Nixon's enemies and threatening to the case against him. Nixon requested a full investigation of Watergate, which never took place. Attention focused on the question, "What did the President know, and when did he know it?" No one inquired about the reason behind the burglaries (Hougan, 1984a, p. xvi).

Vice President Gerald Ford supplanted Nixon, pardoning the errant chief of state in an extraordinary document that mentioned "no specific acts or offenses" (Colodny et al., 1991, p. 429). This was not the first time Ford played a role in the sudden departure of a president. In 1964, he conspicuously served on the blue ribbon panel that authored the Warren Report, the official record of JFK's assassination. President Lyndon Johnson chose him for the Warren Commission specifically because of Ford's close ties to the CIA (Hecht, 2001).

III. JOHN WALKER LINDH

Nixon's unseemly exit, without the awkwardness of a trial, is reminiscent of the fate of a contemporary figure of evil, the "American Taliban" John Walker Lindh. In Lindh's case, as in Nixon's, presidential intervention was required to offer the guilty party a lenient alternative to a mooted heavy sentence. Moreover, as with Nixon, the nature of the alleged crime committed by Lindh was somewhat obscure. Lindh accepted a sentence of ten years for "rendering services to the Taliban" in contravention of a 1999 federal statute; and an additional ten years for carrying a firearm while committing a felony (Andrews, 2002).

In January 2002, "Attorney General John Ashcroft pronounced [the charges against Lindh] a critical case in the nation's fight against terrorism" (Johnston, 2002). Following Lindh's July 15, 2002 surprise guilty plea to being a "Taliban foot-soldier," however, his case was downgraded. According to *The Wall Street Journal* (Bravin, 2002), the guilty plea "relieves the government of a complicated criminal prosecution involving evidence from the battlefields of Afghanistan, testimony from intelligence officers and possibly even the appearance of Taliban and al Qaeda fighters brought from their prison at the U.S. Guantanamo Bay Naval Base in Cuba."

A Congressional investigation of Watergate might have shaken the foundations of the American political system (Hougan, 1984a, pp. 302, 313). Similarly, the Lindh case might have submitted the U.S. terror war itself to trial by jury. Compromising details, successfully hidden from the American public, might have been revealed – such as the November 2001, Northern Alliance massacres of hundreds of surrendering Afghan Army soldiers at Kanduz and Mazar-I-Sharif, where Lindh, a 21 year old native Californian, was captured, interrogated and tortured, first by the blood thirsty forces of Northern Alliance Uzbek warlord, General Dostum (who were accompanied by two CIA agents, including one – since murdered – named Johnny Michael Spann[3]) and later by U.S. Special Forces (West & Cummings, 2002).

Hougan (1984a, p. 313) notes that Richard Nixon's "pardon . . . seems almost a contradiction in terms. For how does one forgive and forget what has not been committed or what remains unknown?" John Lindh received two consecutive 10 year prison terms for joining the Afghan Army in the first week of September, 2001. Before September 11 the Taliban maintained an exchange program with the University of Nebraska, and Leila Helms, niece of the ex-CIA Director Richard Helms, was an envoy for the Taliban in the U.S. (Andrews, 2002). Someone once said that patriotism is a matter of dates.

IV. POLITICAL ECONOMY OF CONCRETE EVIL

A. New Breed of Terrorist

"Bin Laden," claimed an influential U.S. government report, "is the prototype of a new breed of terrorist – the private entrepreneur who puts modern enterprise at the service of a global terrorist network" (Hudson, 1999, p. 11). From the beginning, however, some commentators doubted the deadly attack on New York City and Washington was the work solely of Osama bin Laden and his al Qaeda network, as the Administration contended. The finely-tuned, simultaneous multiple hijackings must have involved years of planning and cooperation of dedicated organizations spanning half the globe. For almost five years U.S. authorities had meticulously tracked bin Laden's communications and financial networks. He could not have lifted a finger without triggering an alarm in the American intelligence community. (*Stratfor.com*, 2001a). Critics pointed out that the hi-jackers' satanic achievement depended on an appalling series of U.S. government security lapses that suggested negligence or outright complicity.

President Musharraf of Pakistan, surely a privileged (though not disinterested) observer, revealed his own doubts about the official story in an interview with *The New Yorker*: "I didn't think it possible that Osama sitting up there in the mountains could do it. He was perhaps the sponsor, the financier, the motivating force. But those who executed it were much more modern. They knew the U.S., they knew aviation. I don't think he has the intelligence or the minute planning. The planner was someone else" (Hilton, 2002a, p. 54).

Spring and summer 2002 brought revelations of key intelligence failures that seemed to justify dissenters from the received version. Nevertheless, the July 2002 (Associated Press) report from the House Intelligence subcommittee on terrorism, while documenting problems at the CIA, FBI and the National Security Agency, found nothing requiring "disciplinary actions against anyone."

The official bin Laden story evolved considerably after September 11, perhaps to address a plausibility gap. On one hand, estimates of bin Laden's wealth were scaled down (Bergen, 2002, p. 105), and speculation grew that the al Qaeda leader was dead. Meanwhile, media attention switched from bin Laden himself to the global terrorist organization he founded.

Contrary to official accounts of September 11, ability and inclination to inflict a massive blow on such a formidable antagonist likely functions in direct proportion to power well beyond the scale that might be achieved by a single individual, or a private network. This is one of the lessons of the Hegelian-Marxist political economy of **concrete evil**, outlined below, and a clue to the events of September 11.

The 1993 bombing of the World Trade Center, which may have been the work of the "Blind Sheikh" Omar Abdel Rahman, currently in prison for plotting to kill Egyptian President Mubarak during the latter's 1994 visit to New York, might be cited against the thesis of concrete evil. Rahman possessed nothing like the combined resources of the United States (Kepel, 2002, p. 302). However, the accused Sheikh, like his colleague Osama bin Laden, was a recipient of CIA training and financing during the 1979–1989 Afghan war (Cooley, 2001, p. 223). He may have relied on subverted U.S. and other intelligence networks (including Israel's Mossad) to deliver his bombs in New

York (Friedman, 1993). Sheikh Omar's connections to the Afghan jihad (discussed below) were never mentioned at the time.

B. The Devil's Bargain

Neither Hegel nor Marx explicitly proposed a political economy of concrete evil. Nevertheless, it is possible to construct a theory of evil, mostly from Hegel's writings. Hegel's conception of wickedness may be assimilated into the Marxist outlook as an addendum to Marx's perspective. Marx wrote about evil at least as much as Hegel did, and the concept is present in his earliest writings. For example, in the *Paris Manuscripts* (1963, pp. 190–191), written in the mid-1840s, Marx alludes to an "evil spirit tempting men to a devil's bargain" (Prawer, 1976, p. 83) The relationships of money in a market economy reminded the young Marx of "the role that Mephistopheles plays *vis-à-vis* Faust." The concept of evil and its perverted presence in capitalism fascinated Marx. Few works receive multiple citations in *Capital*; Goethe's chronicle of deviltry *Faust* appears six times.

Hegel (1975, p. 43) maintained that theory could assist in understanding "all the ills of the world, including the existence of evil, so that thinking spirit may be reconciled with the negative aspects of existence; and it is in world history that we encounter the sum total of concrete evil."

The concept of concrete evil implies a condensation of evil, the appearance and massing of evil at significant points, a dialectical leap or transformation manifested in an evil occurrence, or a corrupt social arrangement. At certain times in history evil is kept at bay, even though the world is saturated with the existence of evil.

Hegel (1975, pp. 78–79, 91) insisted that history as *Zeitgeist*, as chronicle of the human spirit, "is not the soil in which happiness grows". History deals chiefly with the negative, with evil. Periods of "harmony" are only "blank pages." One side of history, in the Hegelian-Marxist vision, is the progress of freedom; the other, equally potent aspect, concerns the diabolical ascent of evil. This facet of malevolence occupies an important space in the framework of deep politics.

Hegel (1989, p. 820) spoke of an "undisclosed realm of darkness" that lies beyond our consciousness in the external manifold of reality. This darkness, resistant to the illumination of thought, and beyond the reach of the good, comprises the shaded social world of concrete evil, the tenebrous cave Plato also spoke of, where hidden controllers manipulate chained prisoners with a show of puppets and streaks of fire. The sunlit towers of the World

Trade Center on the morning of Tuesday, September 11 stood in such terrifying darkness (Vidal, 2002, p. 1).

The word "concrete" for Hegel has a peculiar meaning, also highlighted in Marx's writings (MacGregor, 1984, pp. 15–16, 138–139, 186–187). The term refers to a unity of diverse characteristics that must be encountered conceptually before the whole can be understood. Concrete evil is not solely a property of subjective consciousness but a complex characteristic of the social world. Accordingly, Hegel (1975a, p. 245) subscribes to a definition of "concrete reality" or "concrete *external* existence" resembling Marx's discussions of the material world confronted by the human individual. Concrete, on this reading, includes the natural environment within which human action occurs; the mode of production and distribution characteristic of a particular society, and "the actual world of spiritual [social – DM] relations . . . the different modes of command and obedience, of family, relatives, possession, country and town life, religious worship, the waging of war, civil and political conditions, sociability, in short the whole variety of customs and usages in all situations and actions."

A cartoonish fiend like Osama bin Laden (Ahmad, 2001, pp. 22–26), branded product of a U.S. propaganda factory that eclipses Disney Studios, hardly qualifies under the Hegelian-Marxist rubric of concrete evil. Ahmed Rashid (2001, p. 135) writes that since the mid-1990s the Bin Laden myth has provided the U.S. government with "an all-purpose, simple explanation for unexplained terrorist acts. Bin Laden became the center of what was promulgated by Washington as a global conspiracy against the USA." With bin Laden and al Qaeda to blame, there was no incentive to examine or challenge the socio-political environment of violence. "What Washington was not prepared to admit was that the Afghan jihad, with the support of the CIA, had spawned dozens of fundamentalist movements across the Muslim world which were led by militants who had grievances, not so much against the Americans, but their own corrupt, incompetent regimes."

Concreteness in the Hegelian-Marxist framework indicates the outcome, sometimes unintended, of thought and action. Concrete evil is not a result of fully reflexive human action – as for instance in a work of art – since evil necessarily reveals a flaw or distortion that violates rationality. Wickedness has little place in aesthetic representation, however accurate its portrayal. Henry James warned writers against centering a narrative on a purely evil character for without moral responsibility, "there was no true tale to tell" (Vidal, 2002, p. 46).

Perhaps this explains the propaganda failure of Osama bin Laden's amateurish videos, released in stages through a series of pratfalls in late 2001 and spring 2002. "Luckily for us," wrote the *Toronto Star*'s Thomas Walkom (2002) about the al Qaeda production studio, "these fanatic anti-modernists make plenty of videos. They video each other plotting, video attack plans, video their dinner parties, then leave the videos lying about. Luckily also, they write down many of their schemes in English." The uncovered tapes, badly translated by U.S. Middle East experts and mostly ignored in the Arab world, contrasted with bin Laden's earlier "carefully crafted" media efforts (Esposito, 2002, p. 21). Offering dubious ammunition for Islamists, the Osama videos did not have the requisite chilling effect on the Western public. Something about them may have smacked of SCTV's Bob and Doug McKenzie,[4] with Afghan gear and Kalashnikov in place of tuques, plaid shirts and bottles of beer. Certainly bin Laden, like Bob and Doug, favored coarse representations. "In fact, one of the signatures of bin Laden's thought is his crude and vulgar discourse regarding his enemies" (AbuKhalil, 2002, pp. 92, 69).

C. Displacing Evil

Thomas Cushman (2001, p. 84) and Jeffrey Alexander (2001, p. 160) observe that social science has "displaced evil," and favors an optimistic understanding of human agency, or social action. Habermas's "ideal speech act," for example, does not include nefarious conspiracies like September 11. In this cheerful sociology, "reflexive human activity produces only gratifying results, never wicked ones."

From our perspective, individuals certainly perpetrate heinous acts informed by profound intelligence and closely held value commitments. Indeed, concrete evil always depends ultimately on value-oriented will. Conspiracy, for example, is a heightened instance of value-vested action. "Anyone who conspires," said Hegel (1995, p. 200), "has overcome aversion to crime, and has strengthened his will by using people who serve him rather as a means; and the action is that of a more intensive will." Rational action, in the Hegelian-Marxist framework, only may be action for the good, since irrational or wicked acts cannot endure holistic, dialectical contemplation (Amin, 1998, p. 103). The 19 Muslim hijackers who, according to the official story, simultaneously commandeered four aircraft, interrupted flight paths, eluded stringent U.S. flight security measures, and brought three planes down with uncanny accuracy on the World Trade Center and the Pentagon may have acted out of a profound sense of injustice. But their action was not rational in the sense used here.

Evil springs from a will determined by exclusive self-love, whether that of an individual or a nation. As we shall see in the final sections of this paper, Mr. Bush's War on Terror exemplifies the danger of national arrogance, which may yet draw the U.S. into a quagmire perhaps rivaling Vietnam (*Stratfor.com*, 2001).

Machiavelli observed that evil is a function of contingency and time. "One day in an unpredictable fashion, man will fall, as into a trap that closes upon him. Man abandoned to time is man abandoned to evil in all its forms" (Sfez, 1996, p. 129). Wickedness, as opposed to good, is a nullity, an inconsequence, an accident of fate. Since evil belongs to the character of human existence, then any slip, any contingency may produce its manifestation. George W. Bush's fraudulent defeat of Al Gore in November 2000 demanded extensive groundwork by Republican Party elites, but it also hinged on a result close enough to involve oversight by dishonorable judges on the U.S. Supreme Court.

Capitalist society provides a pure model for the Hegelian-Marxist concept of malevolence, insofar as it combines unlimited potential for self-understanding with a reign of hazard and contingency. "Evil is nothing but the incompatibility between what is and what ought to be," Hegel (1971, p. 232) wrote. And capital has little respect for what ought to be. "Where the rewards justify the risks," notes a perceptive article in *Harper's Magazine* (Fishman, 2002, p. 34), "money will brave any hellhole."

D. Concrete Evil and the World Historical Individual

The structure of capitalism itself, the basic relationships of property, derive from arbitrariness and injustice. The core of Hegel's concept of concrete evil lies in the wage contract, outlined in two critical paragraphs (§§ 62, 195) in the *Philosophy of Right* (MacGregor, 1998, pp. 157–168). Hegel argued that the flawed deal between capitalist and worker enriched the former while leaving the worker without a recognized claim to property.

A landmark essay by A. O. Hirschman (1973, 1981) notes striking similarities between the theory of imperialism developed by J. A. Hobson and Rosa Luxemburg in the early twentieth century and Hegel's lucid discussion in the *Philosophy of Right* (MacGregor, 1992, pp. 1–2). Hegel offered a theory of socioeconomic crisis and imperialism grounded on underconsumption (or overproduction), which depended on his concept of the wage contract (MacGregor, 1984, pp. 34–35, 228–230). Economic turbulence, springing from social inequality, threatened the modern state with internal conflict, or forced it aggressively to seek opportunities outside its own borders. "Not only do peoples emerge from war with added strength," Hegel (1991, p. 362) said, "but nations troubled by civil dissension gain internal peace as a result of wars with their external enemies." Industrial societies, on Hegel's reckoning, may be more prone to instability and war than earlier modes of social organization.

In the Hegelian-Marxist framework, relations between states are formed by their limited national principle, and are dictated by self-interest of the governing classes (Marx & Engels, 1972, p. 60). As a result, interaction between nations, noted Hegel (1991, p. 371), "encompass the ceaseless turmoil not just of external contingency, but also of passions, interests, ends, talents and virtues, violence, . . . wrongdoing and vices in their inner particularity." Mostly dominated by irrational and malign forces – "the manifest dialectic of finitude" – every national entity becomes an object of inexorable, pitiless fate.

State leaders, blinded by the maelstrom Hegel describes, are more apt to choose evil than good – a predisposition originally explained by Machiavelli (1979, p. 141). "[I]f a prince wishes to maintain the state, he is often obliged not to be good; because whenever that group which you believe you need to support you is corrupted, whether it be the common people, the soldiers, or the nobles, it is to your advantage to follow their inclinations in order to satisfy them; and then good actions are your enemy."

Hegel (1991, pp. 375, 477–479) invented the concept of the world-historical individual to capture the fertile nexus between action and personality. Such individuals are living instruments of the progress of freedom in human history. The notion of the world historical actor, as we shall see, is critical for Peter Dale Scott's argument that President Kennedy's death unleashed forces ultimately threatening the global landscape.

Marx (1973, pp. 147–148) shared Hegel's concept, suggesting, for example, that within France after 1789, Napoleon "created the conditions which first made possible the development of free competition, the exploitation of the land by small peasant property, and the application of the unleashed productive power of the nation's industries."

The full meaning of their own action is hidden from world historical individuals. Their accomplishments may appear in the guise of a bygone era, just as Napoleon draped himself in the raiment of the Roman world and Oliver Cromwell concealed his bourgeois purposes even from himself, noted Marx (1973, p. 148), "with the language, passions and illusions of the Old Testament." Following his death, pundits celebrated Kennedy's presidency, not as an exuberant mode of democratic governance (Gabel, 2000, pp. 74–75), but as a return to a mythical Camelot.

World-historical individuals are controversial by nature; they may enjoy fame, but are rarely credited for contributing to freedom – either by their contemporaries or by "public opinion of subsequent generations" (Hegel, 1991, pp. 375, 478–479). They commonly suffer intense personal tragedy in a vortex of malevolence. There are exceptions. South Africa's Nelson Mandela survived torture and imprisonment to lead his country toward freedom; Fidel Castro lasted at the helm of the Cuban Revolution; Rosa Parks, champion of the 1955 Montgomery bus boycott, received the U.S. Congressional Medal of Honor forty-four years later. More often great leaders, such as Patrice Lumumba, Rosa Luxemburg, Malcolm X, Ruth First, Salvador Allende, and Martin Luther King are brought down early, or snuffed out in dreadful circumstances. President Kennedy's ultimate accomplishments are under debate, though the slain President may have been the harbinger of a new form of politics cruelly, if perhaps only momentarily, extinguished on Dealey Plaza.

Noam Chomsky (1993, p. 147) compares grassroots enthusiasm for the Kennedy years with "cargo cults of the South Sea Islanders who await the return of the great ships with their bounty." Seymour Hersh (1997) devoted a tendentious volume to *The Dark Side of Camelot*, detailing Kennedy's moral turpitude (four pages of photographs of Kennedy girlfriends); JFK's vicious Cold War rhetoric; his defeat at the Bay of Pigs; close relations with crime lords; vendettas against Castro; and cowardly capitulation to the Soviets during the Cuban Missile Crisis. Many on the left, convinced of Kennedy's reactionary politics, have joined conservative and liberal writers in ridiculing assassination theorists who admire the New Frontier (Parenti, 1996, pp. 175–176).

There may be, nevertheless, compelling reasons to view President Kennedy as a world-historical figure, in the Hegelian-Marxist sense.

Few could have predicted the Dallas murder would sharpen understanding of government, and the critical function of intelligence agencies in democratic politics. This was a contribution made inadvertently by Kennedy and those who conspired to kill him. More than any other single event in recent U.S. history the assassination encouraged doubt about motives of the powerful. It sparked an entire field of research and investigative journalism exposing the extraordinary role of secret state organizations like the CIA (Ramsay, 2000, pp. 40, 86). The presidential killing also established that a threatened elite is easily capable of extreme measures.

Regardless of Kennedy's actual politics he was viewed with "anger and contempt" by powerful elements of the ruling circle, especially the military and the CIA (May & Zelikow, 1997, p. 26). JFK's decision after the Bay of Pigs to abandon plans to invade the island; cancel sporadic raids on Cuban targets; and root out armed anti-Castro bases in the United States, inflamed the right (Oglesby, 1976, p. 73). "He fired [the CIA's] most powerful and insubordinate leaders, Director Allen Dulles, Deputy Director Charles Cabell, and Deputy Director for Plans Richard Bissell. He tried to reduce its powers and jurisdiction and set limits as to its future actions, and he appointed a high-level committee to investigate the CIA's past misdeeds" (Parenti, 1996, p. 179). The President opposed a ground war in Vietnam, and likely would have disengaged from Indochina (Logevall, 1999, pp. 395–399). Unlike his successor, President Lyndon Johnson, Kennedy never accepted the premise that there was no alternative to war in Vietnam (Kaiser, 2000, pp. 289–290; Newman, 1992). During the Cuban Missile Crisis, when the slightest miscalculation could have sparked a nuclear exchange, Kennedy avoided armed conflict with the Soviet Union. "It is hard to imagine that any president would have adopted a more peaceful course than the one Kennedy chose" (May et al., 1997, p. 696).

The theory of concrete evil describes a dialectic opposed to the more familiar and optimistic ascent associated with Hegel and Marx. History can move in such a way that conditions become much worse, not as a stage towards something better, but as an unfolding of sheer malevolence. There are periods when social forces coalesce to create a point of transformation toward an era of social advance. Equally, there are disjunctions where irrationality coalesces to create a qualitative leap to a new form of evil.

The public execution of Kennedy prepared the ground for the Indochina wars, and a novel and deadly series of post-colonial firestorms, including murderous rampages in Brazil, Indonesia, Chile, the Dominican Republic, El Salvador, Nicaraugua and Iraq, to name only a few. Tony Blair (2002) claimed that the first session of the NATO-Russia Council in May 2002, formed to allay Russian fears of an aggressive American emperium, "genuinely marks the end of the Cold War." Perhaps, but the demise of the Cold War does not bode well for the world. Without its checks and balances, and with apparent EU surrender to the United States, the world may have embarked on a more treacherous stage of capitalist malignancy. "The most dangerous characteristic of the current period," writes Islamic scholar Eqbal Ahmad (2001, p. 50), "is that a single power dominates the world militarily and dominates international institutions of peacekeeping and law without countervailing forces."

V. DEEP POLITICS

In keeping with Hegel's universal class, which locates teachers and bureaucrats at the core of the ideal state, it may not be surprising that a foremost chronicler and analyst of concrete evil is an unassuming professor of English literature named Peter Dale Scott. Scott confers a systematic theory of concrete evil in democratic society that he calls, "deep politics."

In the aftermath of September 11, establishment liberal and left-wing writers, such as David Corn (2002) in *The Nation* and Edward Herman on ZNet.org (Albert & Shalom, 2002), leveled a barrage of invective against critics of the Administration's account of events in New York and Washington (McMurtry, 2002; Brissard, Corn & Ruppert, 2002). The unprovoked assaults echoed earlier forays against Scott, and other assassination investigators, and underline the parallels between the Dallas events and the September terrorist attacks.

Scott briefly became a Hegelian at Oxford in the early 1950s, studying under Michael Foster, who wrote a 1935 masterpiece called, *The Political Philosophies of Plato and Hegel*. A substantial difference between the two thinkers, Foster (1984, p. 196) wrote, is that Plato had no conception of human greatness, or of historical importance. These two notions, so central for the Hegelian-Marxist concept of concrete evil, figure in Scott's writings as well. *Deep Politics* asserts that the Dallas execution flowed from an ill-fated President's stubborn determination to curb secret abuses of American power. Kennedy's death assured success and malignant growth for hidden networks that poison and may yet destroy the U.S. political system.

Scott makes a large claim about the nature of governance. McCarthyism, the serial assassinations of the 1960s starting with JFK's murder, Watergate, and Iran-Contra, he (1993a, pp. 6–7) contends, are only the most visible domestic extrusions of a corrupt political system. These recall my earlier discussion of the dialectical condensation of evil, the sudden eruptions of malevolence in history. For Scott, the government of the United States, like the regimes of other Western countries, is shaped by what he calls, "deep politics" – "political practices and arrangements that are usually repressed rather than acknowledged." Scott's book delves "beneath public formulations of policy issues to the bureaucratic, economic, and ultimately covert and criminal activities that underlie them."

Deep politics is a revision of Scott's original concept of parapolitics first developed in *The War Conspiracy* (1972a). It responds to criticism that political conspiracies, like the murder of Kennedy, are too difficult to arrange and keep hidden. Parapolitics (1993a, pp. xi, 6–7) is a form of "traditional conspiracy theory" which assumes "conscious secret collaborations toward shared ends." This conventional model, a popular staple in cinema, posits a single control point or center – like the camel-coated villain of *The French Connection* or various arch-fiends in the Bond movies. Scott came to see parapolitics as "too narrowly conscious and intentional to describe the deeper irrational movements which culminated collectively in the murder of the President." In contrast deep political analysis presupposes "an open system with divergent power centers and goals." The collapse of the First Italian Republic in the mid-1990s, involving large-scale criminal influence in government, offers a telling example (Stille, 1995; Ginsborg, 2001, pp. 179–212). It originated as an American parapolitical operation to suborn the threat of communism which parachuted prominent U.S. Mafia hoods into power in post-war Italy "[B]y the 1980s this . . . strategem had helped spawn a deep political system of corruption exceeding Tammany's, and (as we know from the Andreotti trial of 1995) beyond the ability of anyone to call it off" (Scott, 1993a, p. xi). Another example, discussed further below, is the CIA-financed *jihad* against Russian occupiers in Afghanistan that flooded Europe with opium and helped create Osama bin Laden, a modern version of the Old Man of the Mountains, whose 11th Century followers – the Assassins – "sacrificed for him in order to perpetuate his crimes" (Hegel, 1975, pp. 42–43; Esposito, 2002, p. 42).

Scott probes manifold and chaotic connections between U.S. business and government leaders, and the murky world of drug smuggling, secret intelligence agencies, prostitution, organized crime, and murder. Scott (1993a, p. xii) challenges the political science paradigm in which law enforcement and crime are in constant battle, with the police struggling to contain the forces of evil.

Secret government alliances with the criminal underworld, documented by Scott, echoes Hegel's (1995, p. 212) dark observations on the dangers of over-zealous and compromised police work.

> In London use is made of people who have no official role to go after criminals, but anyone who brings a criminal in is rewarded. These people, or police spies, hunt around, without being officials, out of subjective interest, and they seek themselves to make criminals or to impute crimes falsely. For example poor Irishmen were made counterfeiters without knowing what they were doing, and then arrested. This can give rise to the abyss of depravity.

Deep politics – "the abyss of depravity" – flourishes whenever national sovereignty shrinks and private forces emerge to subordinate public power. This process accelerates with "the move toward larger sovereign political conglomerates" exemplified by the history of the United States, though it may also result from shrinkage and demolition of national boundaries as in the case of the former Soviet Union. The result is a strange alliance between the mob and government aimed at protecting the interests of corporations and the rich "who prefer[ ] endemic corruption to the enforcement of laws against themselves" (Scott, 1993a, pp. xxii, xiv). Deep politics depends on psychological repression, the reluctance of many to accept that irrational and contingent forces have an enormous field of play within the state.

The deep political system erupts and becomes visible in times of crisis, when structural shifts are occurring in the U.S. elite system. Though possible exposure is dangerous for ruling groups, as in the Kennedy shooting or Iran-Contra, the stakes are high enough to justify the risk.

If human agency and history are critical to Scott's argument, so too are the factors of irrationality and accident emphasized by the political economy of evil. Scott (1993a, p. 16) quarrels with Marxist and mainstream models that omit these four vital determinants of human affairs.

> What is at stake here is a competition between paradigms of how politics works. One is the establishment paradigm, codified in textbooks and taught in universities as "political science," whether pluralist or Marxist; this sees politics as a system of overtly identified interactive forces, and offers an inclusive chart of political behavior in which, for example, there is no room for assassinations.

Notoriously, Machiavelli (1979, p. 357) insisted on the prominence of conspiracy and assassination in politics. "More princes have lost their lives and positions through them than through open war." Contemporary resistance to theorizing assassinations and other forms of irrationality, arises from under-estimation of human agency in the hyperstructural political science model of politics. Dealey Plaza is hardly an exceptional case. Recent history is studded with high profile political killings reminiscent of the tumultuous Roman experience chronicled by the Italian political theorist. The 1960s assassinations (Ben Barka, Martin Luther King, Medger Evers, Malcolm X, Bobby Kennedy, and many others) offer a sensational epic of blood. Many political murders followed, including (to name only a few) Chilean President Salvador Allende's death on September 11, 1973; the brutal 1977 killing of South African political activist Steve Biko; Indira Ghandi's 1984 execution by her Sikh bodyguards; the murder in 1986 of Swedish Prime Minister Olaf Palme; the twin 1992 Mafia bombings that killed Giovanni Falcone and Paolo Borsellino; the shooting of Israeli leader Yitzhak Rabin in 1995 and the 1994 killing of Luis Donaldo Colosio, presidential candidate of Mexico's then-ruling Institutional Revolutionary Party (PRI).

In Scott's (1993a, p. 313) perspective, Kennedy's death helped weaken U.S. democratic institutions. Each manifestation of deep politics, from the 1950s Red Scare to Iran-Contra, revealed that "the real power centers [are] institutions like the CIA or the National Security Council, which the Constitution never contemplated and arguably cannot survive."

VI. THE CARLYLE GROUP AND SBG

Samuel Huntington's (1996) black and white portrait of world struggle between militant Islam and the West ignored common histories and socioeconomic struc-tures that bind his presumed antagonists. Perhaps most salient here are the shared interests of Osama bin Laden's family and those of the Bush clan, united until recently in the Carlyle group, one of the world's largest military contrac-tors. The *Wall Street Journal* (Golden, Bandler & Walker, 2001) reported that through its investments in the Carlyle Group,

> and its ties to Saudi royalty, the bin Laden family has become acquainted with some of the biggest names in the Republican Party. In recent years, former President Bush, ex-Secretary of State James Baker and ex-Secretary of Defense Frank Carlucci have made the pilgrimage to the bin Laden family's headquarters in Jeddah, Saudi Arabia. Mr. Bush makes speeches on behalf of Carlyle Group and is senior adviser to its Asian Partners fund, while Mr. Baker is its senior counselor. Mr. Carlucci is the group's chairman.

The *Journal* opined that President's Bush's war on terror would be especially profitable for the Carlyle Group and hence for the bin Laden family.

According to a special *Fortune* (Warner, 2002) investigation, which insists that most conspiracy theories about the firm "are amusingly overblown," the Carlyle Group raised a total of $14 billion from investors in the last half-decade. "Not counting the standard 20% cut that goes to Carlyle's partners and managing directors, the firm's average annual rate of return has been 36%." By coincidence, Shafig bin Laden "one of Osama's many brothers and a Carlyle investor, was in attendance at a Carlyle meeting in a Washington hotel on that infamous day." Given its lucrative connections with luminaries such as U.S. Secretary of Defense Donald Rumsfeld, *Fortune* wondered whether Carlyle has "stepped over the line into an ethical twilight zone in which the public trust is broken." Marx's (1976, p. 926) famous comment may aptly describe the Group's activities. "If money, according to Augier, 'comes into the world with a congenital blood-stain on one cheek,' capital comes dripping from head to toe, from every pore, with blood and dirt."[5]

Bin Laden and Bush interests go beyond the Carlyle Group. After the death of Osama bin Laden's father in a 1967 plane crash, his elder brother Salem took over the family business, now called Saudi Binladin Group (SBG). In 1976 Salem arranged a profitable connection with Houston magnate James Bath, a close friend of George W. Bush, whose father was Director of the CIA and about to be vice presidential running mate of Ronald Reagan (Bergen, 2002, p. 49). The bin Laden's were not the Bush family's only Saudi friends. As CIA chief, Bush Sr. "helped to strengthen ties between the CIA and Saudi intelligence," a spy outfit with intimate connections to the fraudulent Bank of Credit and Commerce International, later a major funder of the Afghan jihad (Truell & Gurwin, 1992, p. 130). Like his father, Salem bin Laden died in an airplane crash (in San Antonio Texas in 1988), but Salem's death did not prevent family members from maintaining ties with America. "Several have resided in the country (although they fled within days of the September 11 attack)" (Bergen, 2002, p. 49).

The $5 billion Saudi Binladin Group works closely with the Americans in Saudi Arabia, and in the 1990s helped construct Saudi-financed U.S. military installations in the desert kingdom worth over $200 billion (Armstrong, 1993). Binladin Group repaired or replaced U.S. facilities destroyed by terrorist attacks, including black sheep Osama bin Laden's bombing of the Khobar Towers military complex in Dharan, Saudi Arabia (Golden et al., 2001). As if to snub Huntington's "clash of civilizations" thesis, American planners later used this SBG installation to "coordinate[ ] airstrikes against bin Laden's Afghan hideouts" (Bergen, 2002, p. 50). In another turn of the screw, many of these high-tech Afghan cave complexes were built by Osama bin Laden himself in the 1980s as joint projects with SBG.

VII. FREE ELECTRONS OF JIHAD

Spreading rapidly across the Islamic world since the 1970s, and nourished by Saudi petrodollars, the Islamist ideology of al Qaeda, Egypt's Islamic Jihad and Saudi Arabia's Wahhabi movement, relies heavily on medieval and pre-modern Islamic revivalism, which urged religious war against fellow Muslims "according to the Quranic mandate to 'command the good and forbid evil' " (Esposito, 2002, pp. 42, 108). Early Islamic movements believed in the inter-connectedness of religion, state and society – a key aspect of modern political Islam. In the Islamist view, evil amounts to whatever violates its "puritanical, militant mentality," including television, music, unveiled women, and the religious productions of other faiths. Thus the Taliban, under Saudi influence, detonated Buddhist shrines in Afghanistan. Similarly, Saudi-assisted Islamist terror groups destroyed "historic mosques, libraries, Quran schools, and cemeteries in Bosnia and Kosovo because their Ottoman architecture, decorations, frescoes, and tombstones did not conform to Wahhabi iconoclastic aesthetics that regard statues, tombstones, or artwork with human representations as idolatry and polytheism."

Saudi Arabia's Wahhabi version of Sunni Islam, founded in the eighteenth century, opposes secular Arab nationalism and communism. It has little disagreement with Western capitalism (Amin, 2001, p. 3). Nor does Wahhabism eschew advanced technology, unless it poses a security threat (Esposito, 2002, p. 109).

From the 1970s onwards, Saudi leaders forged alliances with non-Wahhabi sectors of radical Sunni Islam, such as Egypt's Islamic Jihad, the Palestinian group Hamas, and Islamic opposition movements in Russia, the Caucasus, Chechnya, Dagestan and Central Asia. Abhoring the Shiite form of Islam practiced by geostrategic rival Iran, Saudi foreign policy makers specifically targeted Iran and its political allies in Lebanon, Shiite Hizbollah.

Militant Islam has its roots not only in cash-rich Saudi Wahhabism but also social and community service movements like the Muslim Brotherhood of Egypt and Algeria's Islamic Salvation Front. Palestine's Hamas provides a wide range of similar assistance, in the absence of a Palestinian state capable of adequately serving its citizens. Across the Muslim world, radical Islamic community efforts compelled loyalty from the poor as well as from an alienated middle class.

The influence of radical Islam exploded during the decade-long holy war against the USSR in Afghanistan, financed largely by Saudi Arabia. "In the eyes of the Saudi establishment . . . the sacred cause of the Afghan jihad offered a chance to enroll potential troublemakers, divert them from the struggle against the powers that be in the Muslim world and their American allies, and above all keep them away from the subversive influence of Iran" (Kepel, 2002, p. 315). After toppling the Russian-backed Kabul regime in 1992, thousands of holy warriors dispersed, spreading Islamist ideology to every corner of the Muslim world.

These "free electrons of jihad," according to Gilles Kepel's (2002, pp. 219–220) study of the rise of political Islam, subscribe to a radicalized version of Wahhabism called "jihadist-salafism." This is a religious ideology, composed in magnificent isolation from actual political communities or social groups, "whose first doctrinal principle was to rationalize the existence and behavior of militants." Adherents of the faith such as bin Laden combine respect for literal interpretation of sacred texts "with an absolute commitment to jihad" and hatred for America "perceived as the greatest enemy of the faith." They constructed a form of thought uniquely comfortable with the smuggler fiefdom or terrorist encampment, a nightmare version of Karl Mannheim's free-floating intellectuals. Islamist fanatics, bred in the Afghan wars, "constituted a kind of demobilized army of several thousand seasoned warriors, all without passports, in search of a place to fight or hide. As combatants they were ready to serve anyone willing to fund them and help them travel from one place to another around the globe" (Kepel, 2002, p. 300).

Osama bin Laden contributed a geopolitical gloss to Islamist thought (Kepel, 2002, pp. 315–319). Invoking his sometime teacher and theorist of the Afghan jihad, Palestinian professor Abdallah Azzam, bin Laden argued in 1996 that the key areas for Islamist liberation are Palestine under the heel of U.S.-supported Israel, and the holy land of Saudi Arabia, ruled by the corrupt al-Saud regime, and occupied (since 1990) by U.S. troops. Azzam was "mysteriously assassinated" in 1989, the year of the Soviet defeat, and shortly after he had broken with bin Laden, perhaps because the latter had wider ambitions for jihad than his erstwhile teacher.

Bin Laden's fiery critique of the House of Saud was supposedly fueled by the events of August 7, 1990, a year after Azzam's murder, when 540,000 troops were stationed in Saudi Arabia (Mackey, 2002, p. 19).

The Gulf War split the Islamist movement and may have done permanent damage to Saudi Arabia's conservative Wahhabism. Islamist ideology amounts to a reactionary thrust for power hardly justified by social or theological critique, guaranteed by ethnic and religious exclusion, and resting on oppressive violence against women and those who stray from the faith (Amin, 2001). After a thirty year run, its "violent and corrupt political traditions" (Kepel, 2002, pp. 374,

219) may now have limited appeal in the Muslim world. A veneer of anti-Americanism masks political Islam's partnership with market liberalism, and its accommodation with organized crime and intelligence agencies of the U.S. and its partners. Islamists "constitute[] a pool of manpower that could be used by the secret services of a number of states who might find it opportune to manipulate unattached extremist militants."

VIII. THE U.S., BCCI, AND THE AFGHAN JIHAD

Osama bin Laden, and others who might have been involved in September 11, are complicated, human personalities, but mostly they are a symbol of ingenious and bountiful capacities possessed by American and allied secret service establishments that created them. The notorious Afghan jihad, and the holy warriors or Mujaheddin, along with the religious schools or madrassas that dot Pakistan and the Middle East, are certainly homegrown. But they prospered mightily under the CIA and its Saudi Arabian and Pakistani intelligence allies, which in their effort to defeat Soviet invaders in Afghanistan between 1979 and 1989, lavishly funded "an army of Muslim zealots" and supplied a sophisticated flotilla of propagandists and expert advisors on terror and assassination. Trade in opium and heroin, with money laundering services provided by the murky CIA-connected Bank of Credit and Commerce International (BCCI), funneled additional billions to holy warriors (Cooley, 2001, pp. 5, 23).

Inflammatory Islamist school texts, printed in the United States and shipped to Afghanistan, assisted the effort to defeat the Russians (Stephens & Ottaway, 2002) "The primers, which were filled with talk of jihad and featured drawings of guns, bullets, soldiers and mines, have served since then [i.e. since the violent destruction of the Afghan socialist government in 1992] as the . . . school system's core curriculum. Even the Taliban used the American-produced books . . ." Versions of these U.S.-printed pamphlets continue to flow into the country, where they are distributed by U.S. troops.

In cooperation with Pakistan's Interservices Intelligence (ISI) and Saudi Arabia's General Intelligence Service (SOR), the CIA trained "more than 50,000 Muslim mercenaries", and tapped Osama bin Laden, offspring of a fabulously wealthy Yemeni contracting family, for a leading role (Cooley, 2001, pp. 4, 23). The ISI desired a Saudi royal to spearhead the so-called "Arab Afghans" – the Saudi Arabian contingent in Afghanistan – and demonstrate the Arabian kingdom's commitment to the Muslim anti-Soviet crusade None, however, qualified for, or desired, the rough assignment in Afghanistan. "Bin Laden, although not a royal, was close enough to the royals and certainly wealthy enough to lead the Saudi contingent" (Rashid, 2001, p. 121). Using U.S. Army

Special Forces personnel and Navy SEALS (Sea/Air/Land/Commando teams), both veterans of paramilitary operations in Indo-China, the CIA "would train a huge mercenary army; one of the largest ever seen in American military history." This legion of salaried fanatics and thugs offered an early glimpse of September in New York and Washington.

> Virtually all would be Muslims. They would fervently believe God had commanded them to fight His enemies, the Godless Communists and foreign Russian invaders. Their earthly rewards would be glory and generous pay. For those who died as martyrs rewards would be in heaven (Cooley, 2001, p. 23).

The Carter administration launched support for Pakistan, which felt threatened by the pro-Soviet government installed in Kabul in 1978. "The Reagan administration was much more generous, seeing a chance to fight the Soviet 'evil empire' by aiding Pakistan as well as the Mujaheddin rebels in Afghanistan." Reagan's CIA chief, William Casey, enjoyed especially close relations with Pakistan's General Zia, and Saudi intelligence chief, Prince Turki bin Faisal, a BCCI shareholder who "distributed more than $1 billion in cash to Afghan guerillas during the late 1980s." The BCCI helped transfer funds from the CIA and the National Security Council "to supply arms discretely to allies like the Mujaheddin" (Truell et al., 1992, pp. 132–133).

Casey's CIA stickhandled a series of astonishing moves that wrecked the Soviet offensive in Afghanistan. Together with Pakistan's ISI and the Saudi General Intelligence Service, the CIA lavishly funded the most radical Mujaheddin groups, led by Gulbuddin Hekmatyar and Ahmed Shah Massoud. Pakistan figured these heavily-armed, heroin-dealing Islamists would destroy the age-old religious accommodation that marked Afghanistan, and terminate Kabul's chances for uniting the country's disparate groups. The extremists would be useful also to attack the USSR's soft southern underbelly in Central Asia, the Muslim Soviet republics of Tajikistan and Uzbekistan (Rashid, 2001, p. 129).

Casey stepped up the war in 1986 by persuading "the U.S. Congress to provide the Mujaheddin with American-made Stinger anti-aircraft missiles to shoot down Soviet planes and provide U.S. advisers to train the guerillas. Until then no U.S.-made weapons or personnel had been used directly in the war effort" (Rashid, 2001, p. 129).

Casey and President Reagan may have taken the advice of French intelligence supremo Count Alexandre de Marenches, who recommended that the Americans supply cheap drugs to the Soviets. According to the French superspy, Reagan secretly ordered that drugs seized by the Drug Enforcement Agency should be diverted to Afghanistan and supplied to invading Russian forces. Black operations would include false editions of "Russian newspapers, with demoralizing articles and exhortations to desert the Red Army" (Cooley, 2001, p. 129). Large quantities of hashish, opium, and heroin showed up in Kabul "all made easy for the Soviet personnel to buy for nominal prices or 'find' as free gifts."

Casey joined Pakistan's ISI in encouraging radical Muslims from across the globe "to come to Pakistan and fight with the Afghan Mujaheddin" (Rashid, 2001, p. 129). Pakistan and the U.S. government made visas easy to obtain by Muslim radicals. Embassies fielded welcome committees for tired Islamist travelers. Militants were housed and trained and "encouraged to join the Mujaheddin groups, usually [Hekmatyar's] Hizb-e-Islami. The money was good. "[A] full time fighter's pay . . . could range from $100 to as much as $300 a month; sometimes considerably more for commanders and their deputies. For the majority of young Afghanis, Pakistanis, Algerians, Egyptians, Filipinos and others, these were huge sums" (Cooley, 2001, p. 108).

Drug smuggling to provide weapons for Afghan holy warriors, facilitated by ISI and the CIA (Rashid, 2001, p. 121), flooded the U.S. with heroin, imported from Afghanistan by the Corsican Mafia in an operation labeled, the Pizza Connection (Cooley, 2001, p. 133). By late 1980 Afghanistan supplied the U.S. with 60% of its heroin (McCoy, 1991, p. 439).

Casey secretly engineered "an exemption, sparing the CIA from a legal requirement to report drug smuggling by CIA officers, agents or other 'assets.'" A few months later, in June 1982, Nancy Reagan, the First Lady, began her own crusade, "Just Say No to Drugs." Pay for the Afghan rebels, as for the Nicaraguan Contras, was arranged by the CIA and ISI with drug money laundered by the giant Bank of Credit and Commerce International, founded in 1972 by Pakistani financier Agha Hasan Abedi (Cooley, 2001, p. 134; Beaty & Gwynne, 1993, pp. 304–315).

Governments across the globe were aware of BCCI's noxious drugs and weapons deals, but the rogue bank, which benefited from feckless auditing by Price Waterhouse, was never prosecuted. Indeed, there is evidence that BCCI, and its founder Abedi, were creations of the CIA, which may have concealed BCCI's trickery and spent the stolen money (Truell et al., 1992, p. 432).

Conditions for the Afghan jihad and its horrific consequences were prepared by a 14 year communist interregnum that followed the 1978 overthrow of President Daoud Khan, the last member of the Durrani dynasty that ruled Afghanistan for more than two hundred years.

Following sections explore the turbulent history that led to the 1992 victory of the Mujaheddin and the arrival of the Taliban in 1994. The malignant deep political influence of the two superpowers and their allies destroyed government and civil society in Afghanistan.

IX. CHAOS IN AFGHANISTAN

A. Daoud and the Communists, 1973–1975

Perhaps dazzled by gold and red stars on his Soviet Marshal's uniform, Moscow's military chief Dmitri Ustinov promised in December 1979 that "a limited contingent" of the Red Army "will remain a year or a year and a half in Afghanistan until full stabilization is achieved" (Lourie, 2002, p. 301). Soviet dissident Andrei Sakharov called the Russian invasion "expansionism," a statement for which the world-famous nuclear physicist and winner of the Nobel Peace Prize was exiled and tortured. But the brutal and reckless Soviet attack, suddenly ordered by the Politburo on Christmas Eve 1979, had its own deep political rationale.

Daoud Khan overthrew his first cousin King Zahir Shah in 1973 during an economic depression caused by reductions in foreign aid and unfair trade terms with Afghanistan's biggest market, the Soviet Union. Unrest in the universities brought support for leftists Nur Mohammed Taraki, Babrak Karmal and Hafizullah Amin, all of whom "were to be future Presidents of Afghanistan" (Ewans, 2002, p. 122).

Taraki founded the Peoples Democratic Party of Afghanistan (PDPA) and three years later, in 1968, the radical journal *Khalq*. After falling out with the Khalq faction, Babrak Karmal started his own group called Parcham. The Parcham party had working relations with King Zahir before his fall.

Taraki's Khalq faction belonged to the Ghilzai Pashtuns from the east. Khalq dominated the police and the officer corps, "and was more purely Pashtun, with a particular accent on its rural, more 'proletarian' origins" (Griffin, 2001, pp. 18–19). Married into the royal Mohammedzai branch of the Durrani Pashtuns, Karmal hailed from Kabul. Unlike Khalq, his Parcham group was broad-based and thoroughly urbanized.

B. Daoud Spurns the Soviets, 1975–1978

At first welcomed, communists found themselves frozen out of Daoud's government. After an abortive 1975 coup attempt, supported by Pakistan, Daoud confronted Islamist leaders Gulbuddin Hekmatyar, Burhanuddin Rabbani (who each fled to Pakistan) and Ahmed Shah Massoud. These highly educated Muslim radicals shared the same urban and university base as their communist opposition.

Kabul angered Pakistan by reviving the Pashtunistan issue, an old argument regarding Pakistan's North West Frontier Province, coveted by Afghanistan, which Britain had handed to Islamabad in 1947. Fixed by the British in 1892, the Durand line separating Afghanistan from British India, divided the Pashtun tribal area in two. (The North West Province is now patrolled by U.S. troops hoping to flush out bin Laden.)

Moscow resented Daoud's 1975 sidelining of its preferred Afghan communist, Parchum head Babrak Karmal. A year later Daoud limited the number of Russian advisors and turned to Egypt and India for military training. The Afghan president opened negotiations with U.S. allies Iran and the newly oil-rich Gulf states. He showed interest in reconciling with Pakistan, now a partner with China.

Before the 1970s, when assistance programs were stripped, the Soviets and Americans vied with one another for the most generous Afghan aid package, so that the country "became a peaceful battleground of the Cold War" (Magnus & Naby, 2002, p. 62). Foreign funding was substantial, amounting to almost half of state revenue (Rashid, 2001, p. 13).

Seeking to justify Soviet support for Afghanistan in the 1950s, former Soviet Premier Nikita Khrushchev struck a prophetic note. "The amount of money we spent in gratuitous assistance to Afghanistan," he wrote, "is a drop in the ocean compared to the price we would have to pay in order to counter the threat of an American military base on Afghan territory. Think of the capital we would have to lay out to finance the deployment of our own military might along our side of the Afghan border, and it would have been an expense that would have sucked the blood of our people without augmenting our means of production one whit" (Krushchev, 1970, pp. 561–562).

On a visit to Moscow in April 1977, Daoud walked out in the middle of a harangue by Soviet President Leonid Brezhnev, who "warned . . . that Afghanistan was allowing too many foreign specialists, some from member states of the North Atlantic Treaty Organization (NATO), even in northern Afghanistan, an action not sanctioned by past Afghan governments. He claimed that these foreign experts were mere imperialist spies" (Ewans, 2002, p. 133). The die may have been cast for Daoud.

Following the April 17, 1978 assassination of a PDPA militant, and subsequent rioting at the U.S. embassy by angry crowds who blamed the CIA, a frightened Daoud arrested the entire PDPA organization. Rival communist factions, the Khalq and Parcham, had reconciled a year earlier (with Soviet prompting) and now found themselves together in prison. On April 27 Afghan airplanes bombed the royal palace, toppling the regime. Daoud, his entire extended family (including women and children) "and the Presidential Bodyguard were all massacred" (Rashid, 2001, p. 13).

C. Communist Self-Criticism in Kabul, 1978–1979

Following the April military coup, civilian communists quickly took over, declaring a social revolution. Taraki became President and Prime Minister of the Democratic Republic of Afghanistan. Taraki's Khalq viciously attacked the Parcham faction, arresting, torturing and killing communist political rivals. The President implemented a program of rapid change which included land reform; abolition of usury and bride price; an end to gender discrimination in education, and compulsory use of the Russian language. Conservative mullahs rebelled in the countryside; mass arrests and executions became common (Ewans, 2002, p. 142).

An uprising in Herat in March 1979 exposed government officials, and Soviet advisors and their families to the wrath of the populace. Hundreds of Russians, including women and children, were killed, their bodies placed on spikes and paraded through the city. "Moscow, fearing copycat uprisings in other Afghan cities," reports Ahmed Rashid (2001, p. 37), "sent 300 tanks from Soviet Turkmenistan to crush the revolt and began to bomb one of the oldest cities in the world indiscriminately. Fifteen years later, large tracts of the city still looked like a lunar landscape with rubble stretching to the horizon. More than 20,000 Heratis were killed during the next few days."

Hafizullah Amin nudged Taraki out of the Prime Minister's office, appointing his own nephew head of the security service. The Soviets suspected Amin, perhaps responsible for the most provocative aspects of the disastrous government reform program, of being a U.S. agent (Cooley, 2001, p. 13). Amin was friendly with the American embassy in Kabul; while at university during the 1960s he was trained by American experts (Magnus et al., 2002, p. 106). In September 1979 Soviet officials advised Taraki to eliminate his Prime Minister. Warned of the plot, Amin survived a September 14 Palace ambush, and returned to murder the hapless Afghan head of state. Amin made himself President a few days later; Kabul announced that Taraki had left for medical reasons.

The Soviet Politburo worried that Amin would deliver Afghanistan to the Islamists, already being armed and supported by Pakistan and the U.S.-backed Gulf states. Claiming that "President Karmal" had requested assistance (Karmal was living in the Soviet Union at the time) the Red Army subdued Kabul on 27 December 1979. A Speznatz unit (Soviet Special Forces) butchered President Amin in his fortified palace at Darulaman.

D. "A Criminal Adventure" 1979–1989

Finally grasping power in Kabul, the Soviets fulfilled Khruschev's prophecy. Russia would bleed on the desolate battlefields of Afghanistan and its means of production would wither under the strain. Khrushchev did not dream that the price would include the fall of the USSR and addiction to heroin of large numbers of Russians.

The anti-imperialist credentials of the USSR died with President Amin. With two-thirds of the country occupied by its enemies, Babrak Karmal's new government searched for legitimacy while sitting atop a Soviet tank.

The "bear trap" set by the U.S. and its allies could now do its work (Adkin & Yousaf, 2001). Six months before Marshal Ustinov ordered his troops into Afghanistan, the CIA and its Pakistani and Gulf allies were supplying Islamists with arms and money (Bloom, 2002). The Soviet invasion was, after all, a response to American intervention. Pakistan was for years arming exiled Islamists from among 3 million Afghan refugees in camps surrounding Peshawar. They returned to fight the Russians. Everywhere in the refugee camps there was a heady mixture of guns, money and heroin.

The Russians employed ruthless forms of combat some of which are increasingly familiar from revelations concerning U.S. actions in Afghanistan. The Red Army depopulated the countryside "by attacking civilians in the villages in which they lived" (Ewans, 2002, p. 153). They bombed hospitals and schools. "They sent armoured columns, supported by artillery, aircraft and helicopters, into areas where the *mujahidin* might be present. When the population fled into the hills to escape them, they employed a 'scorched earth' policy, destroying buildings, animals, crops and irrigation systems, and killed anyone who had been left behind. When they departed, they left booby traps . . . Sometimes they simply carpet bombed villages and valleys." The Russians dropped "butterfly-bombs," anti-personnel mines "meant to maim rather than kill" which often looked like children's toys.

In 1986 President Gorbachev announced an initial withdrawal of Red Army forces. Karmal was replaced in 1987 by his former Pashtun bodyguard Mohammed Najibullah, who like Karmal, had taken refuge nine years before in the Soviet Union.

The final official casualty list claimed that 15,000 Soviet soldiers died and 37,000 were wounded. "The true numbers were possible of the order of three times those figures" (Ewans, 2002, pp. 169–170). But Afghanistan's losses were much higher. More than a million lost their lives. Towns and cities were turned to rubble; the countryside was strewn with landmines and other unexploded bombs. The war was a "criminal adventure," remarked Sakharov. "And that's what lies upon us as a terrible sin, terrible reproach. We must cleanse ourselves of this shame that lies on our leadership."

E. Najibullah's End, 1989–96

Soviet troops withdrew from Afghanistan in February 1989 but the pro-Soviet government survived until April 1992. The besieged leader in Kabul succeeded in "buying the support of disaffected groups among the Tajik, Uzbek, Turkmen, Hazara and Ismaili minorities, turning them into ethnic militias to fight against their former comrades" (Griffin, 2001, pp. 2, 64).

The U.S. may have kept Najibullah in power to thwart the Pakistan-supported Mujaheddin. (Adkin et al., 2001, pp. 233–235). President Zia and ISI head General Akhtar, both keen to see an Islamist Kabul, died in a mysterious August 1988 plane crash that most Pakistanis believed was arranged by the Americans (even though the U.S. ambassador perished along with Zia). The CIA's military assistance dwindled while Najibullah's forces inherited the gigantic store of military equipment abandoned by the retreating Red Army.

An unusual alliance joined General Rashid Dostum, the Uzbek warlord, and Ahmed Shah Massoud, leader of the Tajik *Jamiat-I-Islami* party, and brought about Najibullah's fall from power. Massoud inserted his own candidate, Professor Burhannudin Rabbani, into the Presidential palace in Kabul. But Rabbani's term was not auspicious. He failed to unite warring Mujaheddin factions, including those of Pashtun commander and ISI favorite Gulbuddin Hekmatyar, Massoud himself, and Shia leader (and Iran's Afghan stalking horse) Abdul Ali Mazari. In the battle for power, Hekmatyar, even while he was prime minister of Afghanistan, daily shelled the country's capital from 1992 until 1995 (Bergen, 2002, p. 73).

Najibullah repaired to a UN compound where he stayed "in pampered imprisonment" (Griffin, 2001, p. 2) until 28 September 1996, when the ex-President's UN protectors abandoned him to the Taliban, who promptly tortured and hanged him. While under guard, Najibullah was often consulted by General Fahim, his former secret service chief, and minister of security under the new government of President Rabbani. A man with obviously gifted political instincts, General Fahim is now (August 2002) security chief for President Hamid Karzai.

Najibullah's death marked the final gasp of traditional moderation in inter-ethnic and religious relations in "immensely tolerant" Afghanistan (Rashid, 2001, pp. 82–83). By providing a foil for its multiple enemies, the government fostered solidarity in the countryside. When the state crumbled, divisions that festered beneath fragile Mujaheddin alliances broke into open civil war. Ahmed Rashid rehearses the grotesque record that existed even before the U.S. campaign of 2001 which unleashed, as we shall see, similar evils. "Masud's massacre of the Hazaras in Kabul in 1995, the Hazaras' massacre of the Taliban in Mazar in 1997 and the Taliban massacres of Hazaras and Uzbeks in 1998 has no precedent in Afghan history and perhaps has irreparably damaged the fabric of the country's national and religious soul."

X. BHUTTO'S TALIBAN FOLLIES

The Taliban, led by Mullah Mohammad Omar, suddenly emerged in October 1994, and its fighters eventually drove the Rabbani government from Kabul, liberating much of Afghanistan from lawless Mujaheddin groups. According to legend, Mullah Omar and his ethnic Pushtun holy warriors started their triumphal advance by riding shotgun for a Pakistani transport caravan from Islamabad destined for Turkmenistan. The Taliban spontaneously appeared from over the border in Pakistan and gallantly defended the marooned convoy from attack in Kandahar. After three days of bitter fighting the city fell to the new rulers (Griffin, 2001, p. 39).

More likely, however, the Taliban was a fabulously successful geopolitical creation by Prime Minister Benazir Bhutto's interior minister, General Babar, who dispatched the Islamabad truck convoy, which probably was filled with hardened Pakistani troops disguised as Mullah Omar's Taliban warriors (Griffin, 2001, p. 37). In a devilish twist, given the Taliban's misogynist ethos, Pakistan's Harvard-educated Bhutto – "whose face had graced the covers of countless women's magazines in the West ... encouraged a movement that was to imprison Afghan women behind their veils" (Kepel, 2002, p. 226).

Pakistan had had enough anarchy in what was fast becoming another of its provinces, Afghanistan. The collapse of the Soviet Union "reopened the old trade routes between Central Asia and the Indian Ocean that had been blocked by the Russians since Czarist times" (Kepel, 2002, p. 228). But fractious Mujaheddin groups monopolized vital truck routes, charged fantastic fees, and looted and ransomed undefended travelers.

Following their Kandahar triumph, the Taliban wrested Kabul from the Mujaheddin in September 1996. "The same happened in predominantly Shiite regions of Western Afghanistan, where they devoutly massacred the 'ungodly,' notably at Mazar-e-Sharif in 1998" (Kepel, 2002, p. 229). This could be no band of fanatic student amateurs fighting blooded and ruthless Mujaheddin (Ewans, 2002, p. 183). They operated with "a degree of skill and organization" beyond the ken of mere novices. The Taliban likely contained "former members of the Afghan armed forces," i.e. Najibullah's men, trained by the Soviets. Nevertheless, "the speed and sophistication with which their offensives were conducted, and the quality of such elements as communications, air support and artillery bombardments, leads to the inescapable conclusion that they must have owed much to a Pakistani military presence, or at least professional support."

The Taliban was recruited from Afghan refugee camps in Pakistan, educated in Pakistani madrassas (religious schools) and trained in fighting by Pakistani Mujaheddin parties (Rashid, 2002, p. 7). Crudely misogynist, the Taliban worsened the condition of Afghan women, which was already in crisis thanks to 20 years of warfare, and the equally woman-hating dominion of some sections of the Mujaheddin. The Taliban's gender oppression was "shaped by their own internal dynamic and the nature of their recruiting base." Most of the Taliban's members were orphans or belonged to "the rootless lumpen proletariat from the war and the refugee camps." The madrassa milieu was an entirely male society that honored the degradation of women as a proud mark of manhood "and a reaffirmation of the student's commitment to jihad" (Rashid, 2001, pp. 23, 111; Hilton, 2002).

The offensive gender code of the Taliban led to a 1997 about-face in American policy, apparently driven by an effective feminist campaign in the U.S. (Griffin, 2001, p. 180). But the Taliban was not unique in its treatment of women. The Taliban's infamous Vice and Virtue police were modeled after their counterparts in Saudi Arabia (Kepel, 2002, p. 230). Scarcely an Afghan indigenous movement, the Taliban was created by Pakistan, where similar fanatical groups, tolerated by the state, flourish.

After taking Kabul in 1996, the Taliban formed a fateful alliance with Osama bin Laden. The Taliban did not at first share the geopolitical analysis of its Arab ally. Given Mullah Omar's support from Riyadh and Islamabad, both supposedly hostile to bin Laden, the Taliban chief's friendship with the Saudi terrorist seemed bizarre.

Until September 11, the U.S. sent conflicting signals about its attitude to the Taliban. As late as May, 2001 the U.S. pledged bin Laden's friend, the Taliban regime, $43 million, in appreciation of its support for the War on Drugs (*Washington Post*, 2001).

XI. AHMED SHAH MASSOUD'S "EVIL TRIANGLE"

Alarmed by the success of the Taliban, Russia and its partner Iran began secretly to support the Northern Alliance in Afghanistan, headed by Tajik warlord Ahmed Shah Massoud, the only Mujaheddin leader then strong enough to oppose the Taliban. (The Tajiks are Afghanistan's second-largest ethnic group, numbering 5 million compared to 9 million Pashtuns.) Funding for Massoud may have come in part from the opium and heroin trade (Orth, 2002, p. 177). Massoud received pledges of military support from Russian and Iranian officials in October, 2000, in order for him to hold Badakhshan "the last northern Afghan province under his control, which also bordered Tajikistan" (Rashid, 2002, p. 110).

Massoud was assassinated on the eve of September 11, apparently by al Qaeda (Gannon, 2002), who sent two Arabs posing as journalists to his encampment. Ignored by the U.S. media until after his death, Massoud was a celebrity in Europe, invited to speak at the European Parliament in Strassbourg (Anderson, 2002).

Unusual among Mujaheddin leaders, Massoud sought to reduce suffering and loss of life among civilians in Afghanistan. The Tajik leader also "created the only faction in the country run by civilians rather than warlords . . . Massoud was the only Afghan commander in 22 year of war to cultivate a younger generation of educated, competent Afghans for future leadership" (Rashid, 2001a).

"Conspiracy theories are given credence in Afghanistan," says *The New Yorker*, "not least because there have been, historically, a lot of conspiracies" (Anderson, 2002). Abdul Sayyaf could easily figure in any number of conspiracies. Sayyaf is an Afghan Islamic scholar who was sent by the Saudis to Peshawar in the 1980s as part of their effort to spread Wahhabism. Along with Gulbuddin Hekmatyar, Sayyad was one of Massoud's bitterest rivals among Mujaheddin chiefs in 1992 when the Rabbani government was formed (Rashid, 2001, pp. 131–133). Sayyaf possesses a reputation as a savage killer. His specialty . . . "was to take one of the metal shipping containers that litter Afghan cities, fill it with Shia captives, and then light a fire around it" (Griffin, 2001a).

Sayyaf has a theory about Massoud's assassination – one widely held in Kabul (Anderson, 2002) "[T]he Americans, with the aid of Pakistan, supported the Taliban and Osama bin Laden so that they could justify an invasion and take over the country."

Before his death in 1996 due to UN negligence, former communist President Mohammed Najibullah prophesied, "[i]f fundamentalism comes to Afghanistan, war will continue for many years. Afghanistan will turn into a center of world smuggling for narcotic drugs. Afghanistan will be turned into a centre of terrorism" (Griffin, 2001, p. 5). Two years later, in a letter to the U.S. Senate, Najibullah's nemesis Ahmed Shah Massoud talked about "an evil triangle" (Griffin, 2001, p. 208) The Mujaheddin caused the fall of the Soviet Union, but the people of Afghanistan did not benefit from this famous victory. "Instead, they were thrust in a whirlwind of foreign intrigue, deception, great-gamesmanship and internal strife." The Afghans were not blameless, Massoud admitted. "Our shortcomings were as a result of political innocence, inexperience, vulnerability, victimisation, bickering and inflated egos. But by no means does this justify what some of our so-called Cold War allies did to undermine this just victory and unleash their diabolical plans to destroy and subjugate Afghanistan."

Massoud was convinced that a "dark accomplishment" had delivered "his country over to fanatics, extremists, terrorists, mercenaries, drug mafias and professional murderers." He might well have quoted Hegel on the appearance of concrete evil in Afghanistan at the turn of the 21st Century. "Three major concerns," he wrote to U.S. Senators, "– namely terrorism, drugs and human rights – originate from Taliban areas but are instigated from Pakistan, thus forming the inter-connecting angles of an evil triangle. For many Afghans, regardless of ethnicity or religion, Afghanistan, for the second time in one decade, is once again an occupied country."

Perhaps if he had lived past September 11, Massoud would have included the United States in his roster of "dark accomplishment."

XII. DEEP POLITICS IN AFGHANISTAN

A. Warlords and Drugs

There are implausible and overly convenient elements in the official story of September 11. Beneath the received version lurk deep political factors typically ignored or downplayed in most mass media and mainstream academic accounts. The following sections consider hidden and unacknowledged political forces that may be responsible for the U.S. invasion of Afghanistan and the catastrophe of September 11.

Many Northern Alliance leaders who expected a place in the interim government of Afghanistan appointed on December 5 in Bonn are drug kingpins, including bin Laden's old friend, former President Burhanuddin Rabbani (who was exiled by the Taliban), and General Rashid Dostum, the Uzbek warlord. Hamid Karzai, interim Afghan leader (who was anointed President in June 2002) lived in the United States until 2001. He represents the powerful Pashtun Popalzi tribe.

Dostum was given a seat in the December conference in Bonn, but left in protest, citing bias in favor of Tajik leaders and Pashtuns. Since then Dostum has received "increasingly important appointments from the leader of the interim government, Hamid Karzai. He first became deputy defense minister, and then, last month [July 2002], was named Mr. Karzai's personal representative in the north." Dostum's leading Tajik rival, General Ostad Atta Mohammed has received offsetting favors from the Karzai regime. While both are powerful in the north, General Mohammed maintains the most formidable military contingent in

Mazar-I-Sharif, the biggest northern city. His troops engage in "looting, thieving and kidnapping" aimed at Pashtun communities (Gall, 2002). By late September 2002, Dostum appeared to be in considerable danger. " 'The noose is tightening around my neck,' he told a visitor recently" (Gall, 2002b).

Notorious drug czar and Mujaheddin chief Gulbuddin Hekmatyar, remains at large in eastern Afghanistan, despite U.S. efforts to kill him in May 2002. Hekmatyar claims he has Stinger missiles that he will use against Karzai. (MacKinnon, 2002b).

The June 2002 loya jirga in Kabul, meant to legitimize Hamid Karzai's administration, "was rocked by allegations that death threats and murder were being used to keep delegates in line." One delegate fled "after receiving a death threat because he angered a warlord with his speech from the floor, and the wife of another member was raped and killed" (MacKinnon, 2002c). Loya jirga rules forbidding delegates with a record of human rights violations were ignored.

Karzai's win in June was Afghanistan's first democratic election in forty years. "He will lead a transitional government that is to oversee general elections in 2004, according to the road map outlined in the United Nations-brokered Bonn agreement last December" (Rashid, 2002b). It was an odd election since "no final list of delegates was ever published." The national security directorate, mainly Tajik thugs from the Panjshiri valley, maintained order during deliberations. Warlords Rashid Dostum, Ismail Khan and Gul Agha Sherzai took front row seats at the assembly.

In July, Afghan security officials announced "that they had thwarted a Qaeda-linked car-bomb assassination attempt on Mr. Karzai" (Burns, 2002a). The same month, one of Afghanistan's three Vice Presidents, Abdul Qadir, an ally of famed Mujaheddin warlord Maulawi Yunis Khalis, was assassinated in Kabul. "He was the second Cabinet minister assassinated since the Taliban collapsed last year. On Feb. 14, Civil Aviation and Tourism Minister Abdul Rahman was killed at Kabul airport under mysterious circumstances." (Associated Press, 2002b).

Karzai blamed Rahman's February murder on incompetent police and security personnel. Following Vice President Qadir's fatal shooting in July 2002 the Afghan President gave up any pretence of autonomous authority. U.S. troops were assigned to defend the Presidential Palace, and Karzai's Tajik bodyguards (complete with Soviet-style uniforms) were replaced by "United States Special Forces soldiers trained in 'close protection' of public officials" (Burns, 2002a).

Reports of easy U.S. victories were premature.[6] By August 2002 even Kabul was subject to bomb attacks and shootings (Shah, 2002). A huge explosion in Jalalabad on August 9 killed more than 80 people (Fisher, 2002a). U.S. soldiers have been ambushed in the countryside as pro-Taliban and pro-al Qaeda units began regrouping in the south and east.

The U.S. war has been fought mostly with air strikes guided on the ground by a small contingent (possibly around 350) of Special Forces and CIA personnel (Ignatieff, 2002) while "[s]everal thousand American troops" patrol the country "on the ground and in the air" (Fisher, 2002C). Recently the U.S. increased the number of ground troops, but the U.S. air war has killed many civilians, causing says *The New York Times*, "an erosion of support" (Fisher, 2002c). But American officials attribute the altered strategy "less to concerns about civilian casualties than to the need to hunt smaller, and more active, enemy groups." According to U.S. officials, Afghanis support the American campaign but "the reality of having aircraft and special forces teams combing their villages, especially along the border of Pakistan, can be deeply disturbing."

American soldiers "have killed dozens of Afghans" and local leaders have urged the U.S. "to consult more closely with them on operations" (Shah, 2002). According to *The Guardian* "U.S. special forces have also begun to train and fund separate 'anti al-Qaida' units, often associated with local warlords, to act as American proxies and seek out al-Qaida fugitives in the Pashtun regions of southern Afghanistan" (Steele, 2002a).

In Kabul where powerful ministries are held by the non-Pashtun Northern Alliance, hundreds of Pashtun commanders, mostly members of the previously strong fundamentalist Mujaheddin group, Hizb-i-Islami, were arrested in April, 2002 (Hizb-Islami was founded by Mujaheddin warlord Maulawi Yunis Khalis, who now lives in Peshawar). Taliban spiritual leader Mullah Omar Mohammad reportedly visits U.S.-occupied Kandahar every week to worship at the Sufi shrine, accompanied by convoys of Toyota SUVs.[7] Meanwhile the Northern Alliance is splintering, as the return of former monarch Zahir Shah,[8] an 87 year-old proponent of the Pashtun nation, has threatened warlords from other ethnic groups, including Hazars, Tajiks, and Uzbeks (Shahzad, 2002).

Originally, U.S. operations in Afghanistan took a different approach from that of Russia, which committed tanks and large numbers of ground troops to defeating the Mujaheddin. With the switch to a battle strategy that puts more troops on the ground, this phase of the war may match the toll on civilians lives taken by the Russian invasion, especially if "American forces begin to be drawn into factional fighting" when and if the Karzai regime crumbles (Fisher, 2002c).

"There is growing skepticism," reported *The New York Times* in late August, "among Afghans about the government's stability, and its ability to sustain a political climate supportive of the American war effort" (Burns, 2002). Defense Minister Muhammad Fahim, the most powerful ethnic Tajik leader (who consulted frequently with former communist President Najibullah in his UN

compound) is seeking, after American prompting, to reduce friction between
Tajiks and Karzai's Pashtun-dominated government. In a deliberate display of
military strength Fahim "keeps an estimated arsenal of 300 tanks and 500
armoured personnel carriers north of the city and in the Panjshir valley. In
Kabul he has 10,000 troops" (Steele, 2002a).

General Fahim (who escaped an April 2002 assassination attempt) contends
that "Westerners have misjudged military strongmen like Ismail Khan in
the west, Gen. Abdul Rashid Dostum in the north, and Gul Agha Shirzai in the
south" (Burns, 2002a). Fahim denies "news reports linking him to the Qadir
killing." Instead, he suggested, the assassination was carried out by "drug lords
and Hajji Qadir's political rivals in Jalalabad, the eastern city where Qadir, in
April, sent 300 troops to raid Afghanistan's opium and heroin market in the
town of Ghanikhel. 'Nobody had dared to do anything like that for years and
the drug mafia decided to take their revenge,' he said."

In Khost, once the site of Osama bin Laden's camps, warlord Padsha Khan
Zadran openly mocks the Karzai government and its American benefactors.
Khost is also "where American forces have been most active in recent months.
Indeed Mr. Zadran and his men have played several roles in the American hunt
for Taliban and Qaeda forces here. He says 600 of his 6000 men are in the
direct pay of the Americans." Zadran was offered the post of governor in of
Paktia Province but another warlord disputed his appointment. "Then in April
Mr. Zadran sought his revenge, carrying out a rocket attack on Gardez that
killed 36 people, including women and children" (Fisher, 2002b).

Zadran figures in the December 2001 U.S. attack on a convoy of tribal elders
heading to Kabul "for the inauguration of the new interim government."
Zadran's men halted the caravan at Khost and "demanded that the elders pressure Mr. Karzai to appoint Mr. Zadran the governor of Paktia, Paktika and
Khost Provinces. The elders, Afghans in Gardez say, refused." Shortly after,
the procession "was hit by a succession of American attacks, which killed most
of the occupants. The survivors scrambled up a hill, toward the villages of
Smani and Pokharai, and the American planes, circling back, struck both
villages, destroying about 20 homes" (Filkins, 2002).

Some of Zadran's troops are likely supported by U.S. money. Bag loads of
U.S. dollars *The Observer* disclosed, "have been flown into Afghanistan, sometimes on RAF planes, to be given to key regional power brokers who could
cause trouble for Prime Minister Hamid Karzai's administration" (Burke &
Beaumont, 2002). The U.S. told relief workers in Afghanistan to wait for
financial assistance while buying off warlords, or "renting" them for astro-
nomical sums. The Bush administration's argument that "rebuilding a stable
Afghanistan was the only way to prevent it from again being a breeding ground

for terrorists" (Fisher, 2002d) has been reversed. As the country slides into a humanitarian crisis, the goal may be to prevent stability in Afghanistan by financing terrorists.

An extraordinary report in *The New York Times* (Burns, 2002a) documents how the U.S. vainly attempts to control opium production in Afghanistan's four eastern provinces by paying local warlords to obliterate poppy fields. "Many of the crops the warlords claim to have destroyed continue to yield opium gum, and farmers mill about every day at the warlords' gates complaining that they have been denied the money that is their due." Three or four times weekly, U.S. and British military helicopters "land at Jalalabad airport with strongboxes carrying cash for the drug eradication program." By May 2002, US$80 million supposedly had been distributed to poppy farmers. Most of the money was siphoned off by warlords who used it to recruit new followers, pay soldiers and acquire weapons. "One reason this is possible is that warlords and Afghan relief officials under their domination, have been left in control of the eradication program. The United Nations drug control agency, after years of experience in Afghanistan, has been frozen out of the operation." A serious attempt by the U.S. to halt the opium trade would encounter bitter resistance, and turn Afghanis decisively against the Karzai government. As one poppy farmer related, following ill-fated Vice President Abdul Qadir's May 2002 raid on the market town of Ghanikhel, where raw opium and heroin are freely traded, "now we are not happy, because the governments that control Karzai, the American and the British, are cruel. They freed us from one evil [the Taliban], and now they have delivered us into another one."

Carl Trocki (1999, pp. 7, 9) suggests there are parallels between Asian drug epidemics sponsored by imperialist powers in the nineteenth century in order to defray the cost of empire, and those "that now appear almost endemic in the Americas and Europe." Britain forced open China's borders with the mid-century Opium Wars, and funnelled enormous profits from drug trafficking into colonial administration and astounding infrastructure development. "Opium came to be an essential element, indeed the cash cow, in the finances of every Asian state structure during the nineteenth century and even during the first part of the twentieth." A revived drug trade in Afghanistan may furnish the U.S. with willing allies among the Mujaheddin, replenish stocks of cheap heroin in Europe and North America, and help fund global anti-terrorist warfare.

Unsuccessful in restraining bitter rivalry among drug lords and Mujaheddin, America's strategy may be to open up Afghanistan to favored armed factions (some recently formed by the U.S.), while exerting control over others. The U.S. may want to keep the situation fluid in order to maintain Islamist pressure on the Central Asian Republics that ring the northern border of Afghanistan.

Certainly, U.S. policy does not lean toward reducing drug traffic in Afghanistan. *The Wall Street Journal* (Levine & Pearl, 2001) reported in late November 2001 that the ouster of the Taliban prompted farmers to re-plant fields of poppies. *Vanity Fair* (Orth, 2002, p. 178) revealed that "[t]he Taliban ban on poppy growing was the largest, most successful interdiction of drugs in history, resulting in a 91% reduction in the cultivation of opium poppies." Since the U.S. invasion, opium production has soared and is likely to reach and surpass peak levels obtained before the Taliban ban. The attempted assassination of Defense Minister Mohammad Fahim may have been in response to the new ban on poppy growing proclaimed by the Kabul government.

Much of the 1990s exodus from Afghanistan to Pakistani refugee camps was caused by the Taliban prohibition. One returning Afghan farmer said, "No Taliban meant no ban. It was an opportunity for us to get out of Peshawar [Pakistan]. I'm so glad" (Chipaux, 2002). Poppy farmers who came back to Afghanistan after the fall of the Taliban are determined to harvest their crop, and are not attracted by Karzai's offer of US$250 per acre to stop planting, which is far less than the US$12,000 return on poppy growing (MacKinnon, 2002).

The U.S. revived old drug circles in the southern Pashtun provinces of Afghanistan, presumably to offset Northern Alliance influence. These maneuvers may amount to a revival of U.S.-Soviet rivalry, in which both sides sought to assert control over drug trafficking in order to fund their activities, while cutting off their antagonist's access to the trade. Control over trafficking provides intelligence and security authorities with personnel assets who are not bound by the rules of war. *The Observer* reported on August 11, 2002 that "three heroin laboratories" have been set up "in the lawless hills southeast of Jalalabad, close to the border with Pakistan. There are believed to be several more." Each heroin lab is "capable of producing £400,000 [US$600,000] worth of heroin a week" (Burke, 2002).

The Afghan heroin business now involves Russian and Ukrainian mafia figures based in Israel. Researchers speculate that U.S. anti-drug efforts to investigate suspected mafia leaders have been "blocked internally for years by higher-ups in the U.S. government, or have been hindered by negative publicity asserting that the investigations were motivated by anti-Semitism." The U.S. invasion of Afghanistan provided an opening for these groups to export large quantities of heroin from Afghanistan, through Turkey and the former Central Asian republics of the USSR, into Russia (*Stratfor.com*, 2002a).

The U.S. proxy war in Afghanistan created a drug crisis in both the former Soviet Union and Pakistan. Pakistan had almost two million heroin addicts in 1997, "up from virtually none before" the Soviet invasion (Cooley, 2001, p. 138). Afghanistan supplies 75% of the world's opium, which is refined into heroin, and Pakistan contributed an eager market. Pakistani social workers found close to 200,000 child opium addicts. Eqbal Ahmad (2001, p. 36), the late columnist for the Pakistani newspaper, *Dawn*, observes that opium from Afghanistan has become the dominant trade item in Pakistan, worth some $4 billion. Before the drug era, the country's total foreign exports amounted to only $6 billion.

Just as returning Vietnam veterans brought heroin from the Golden Triangle into the United States, defeated and demoralized Soviet troops imported the heroin habit. Drugs flowed from the Golden Crescent countries of Iran, Pakistan and Afghanistan into Russia and its territories, and then to Europe. Weakened by an unpopular war, the Soviet military lost much of its effectiveness. When the Central Asian states, which contain some of the world's richest sources of oil and gas, left the FSU after 1991, Moscow did not respond with invasion forces, as it had during the height of the Cold War in East Germany, Hungary, and Czechoslovakia.

Almost a decade later, in 1998, the Russians were back with "peace keeping" troops in Central Asia to ward off the Islamists who threatened the independent republics of Turkmenistan, Uzbekistan, Kyrgyzstan and Tajikistan. Russian Army Division 201, stationed in Dushanbe, Tajikistan, helped to facilitate the drug trade, the richest source of income in the country. "In 1997 a Division 201 plane flying to Moscow was found to have eight kilos of drugs aboard, including three kilos of heroin. Twelve soldiers were arrested" (Orth, 2002, p. 172).

Cheap heroin, smoked like cigarettes, and flooding from Afghanistan may destroy the countries of Central Asia which "are in real danger of becoming narco-societies, unstable, lawless tinder-boxes where, despite the fall of the Taliban, radical Islamist groups still control large areas" (Orth, 2002, pp. 168–172). There are only hazy differences between Islamist terror groups, arms smugglers, narcotics traffickers, and government officials in these areas. Tajikistan, for example, debilitated by civil war and economically weakened since separation from the former Soviet Union, features a government partially composed of former drug lords. Its ambassador to Kazakhstan, "who was apprehended crossing the border in May 2000 with 60 kilos of heroin, was not charged."

Tajik writer Muhibulloh Siddiqzoda observed that "the law is like a spider-web. Strong people simply tear through it, but weak people get caught in it" (Orth, 2002, pp. 168–172). Uzbek Islamist Juma Namangami ran terrorist campaigns and military assaults while controlling most of the narcotics routes joining Tajikistan and Kyrgyzstan. "[M]any on the Tajikistan side of the border felt that the purpose of any battle Namangani fought was at least as much to secure drug routes as to claim territory of an Islamic caliphate state." Saodat Olimova, an expert on narcotics in Central Asia, offers an alternate version of Massoud's evil triangle: "terrorism is an equilateral triangle of violence, drugs, and the intelligence services."

The upshot of military intervention in the former republics may be an epidemic of drug-related HIV in Russia. "Illegal drug users might now be between 3 and 4 million, 20 times the official figure." Most are aged between 15 and 29; many start at 13 or 14. The drug calamity arises from "a huge rise in trafficking in central Asia. Inexpensive heroin flooded into Tajikistan and Uzbekistan "where heroin use doubled between 1998 and 2000." Last year on the Tajik-Afghan border, there was a five-fold increase in heroin seizures alone" (Walsh, 2002). The successful Taliban shut-down of poppy-growing in 2001 may have exacerbated the crisis. Opium smokers in Afghanistan, Iran and Pakistan switched to heroin. The ban on Afghan opium caused a price rise, but stockpiled heroin was plentiful and relatively cheap. A shot of heroin in Pakistan and other areas of central Asia has dropped to around 10 cents (U.S.).

B. Human Rights

A cartoon entitled "Wishful Thinking, American Style" by Ted Rall (Rall, 2002, p. 32) describes official U.S. attitudes toward life and politics in Afghanistan. Two Afghans are warming their hands over a wood fire in a bombed-out town. One says to the other, "Sure – the Americans dropped a bomb that killed my wife and maimed my kid. But hey – no biggie." The other replies, "You know what would be really cool? A repressive, corrupt, U.S.-backed puppet dictatorship. That would totally rock!"

The American media's most accomplished war-monger, Thomas Friedman of *The New York Times*, said it best, on November 23, 2001: "It turns out many of those Afghan 'civilians' were praying for another dose of B-52s to liberate them from the Taliban, casualties or not" (Scott, 2002).

B-52s dropped America's most powerful non-nuclear weapon, the 15,000-pound "daisy cutter" on populated areas, including the city of Kanduz. A daisy-cutter obliterates everything within a few hundred yards when it explodes (*Guardian* Staff & Agencies, 2001). American policy seemed to be the same as that adopted by the Russians twenty years earlier: kill anyone who might provide support for the enemy. Cities in Northern Alliance territory were carpet-bombed (Rall, 2002, pp. 77, 81). During the siege of Kanduz, U.S. F-16 fighters destroyed vehicles travelling on roads held by the Northern Alliance, "just for the hell of it."

July 2002 attacks on civilians by U.S. troops and U.S. AC-130 gunships turned four villages in remote Oruzgan Province of southern Afghanistan into charnel houses. The inhabitants of one village, Kakrak, were celebrating an engagement when the bombs struck (Gall, 2002a). The U.S. blamed "faulty intelligence" but the attack, which killed at least 54 civilians, resembled those carried out by occupying Soviet forces. "This is the home province of the Taliban leader, Mullah Mohammed Omar, and remnants of Taliban and Queda forces are thought to have retreated to this hard to reach area." The U.S. has carried out at least four deadly attacks on civilian areas in the province; in January an American attack killed 25 soldiers loyal to the government of Hamid Karzai. While promising closer cooperation with local officials, the U.S. continues to bomb and invade villages without warning. "What angered Afghans . . . and Westerners working in the area, is the trigger-happy American approach. No Americans entered [Kakrak] before the planes opened fire. Once called in, the American AC-130 gunship, which employs machine guns and heavy cannons, strafed four villages" (Filkins, 2002).

U.S. and British military planners promised there would be an insignificant number of civilian deaths, not even worth computing. However, bombing from the air inevitably kills many civilians, and instilling terror in the population is often the intent. Marc Herold (2002) estimates that "between 3,125 and 3,620 Afghan civilians were killed between October 7 and July 31." These casualties occurred, he writes, "because U.S. military and political elites chose to carry out a bombing campaign using extremely powerful weaponry in civilian-rich areas (the isolated training camps were largely destroyed during the first week)." Authorities have hidden evidence of the carnage for obvious political reasons. "Given that many of the bombing attacks – such as those on civilian infra-structure (cars, clinics, radio stations, bridges) and those during November and December on anything rolling on the roads of southern Afghanistan – violated the rules of war, there are war crimes that need to be investigated."

An unforgettable image in the 2001 film "Kandahar" shows one-legged men hobbling desperately to catch artificial legs dropped by parachute from a Red Cross helicopter. The U.S. air war will create many more Afghani victims without arms and legs, especially among children, who are more likely to wander and pick up unexploded devices. Live bomblets litter the countryside, adding to an already huge assortment of unexploded anti-personnel devices planted by the Russians. "The cheerful yellow-coloured devices – called bomblets – parachuted to earth from the mother bomb 202 at a time. They are a highly effective killer, deploying, in military parlance, three "kill mechanisms" to slice through the thick armour of tanks, and injure and burn humans" (Goldenberg, 2002). *The Washington Post* reported on 16 March 2002 that "[b]etween 50 and 100 people are injured or killed every week in Afghanistan in incidents involving land mines and unexploded ordnance. . . . Experts estimate that Afghanistan has more than 300 square miles of uncleared mine fields – mostly in agricultural and grazing areas – and that as many as 14 million antipersonnel and antitank mines might be present in those and other, undiscovered fields."

According to UN officials, "another 190 square miles of Afghanistan have been littered with unexploded bombs, shells and mortar rounds, including about 25,000 "bomblets" from cluster bombs, since the start of the U.S. military campaign" (Scott, 2002a).

In October 2001, Ahmed Rashid (2001a) warned of the "Jekyll-and-Hyde reality of the Northern Alliance." Enthusiastic liberators were also efficient killers, looters and rapists. As Rall reported, Alliance and Taliban soldiers were usually hard to tell apart, especially when victorious Alliance ranks were swelling with opportunistic ex-Taliban reinforcements. Defense Secretary Donald Rumsfeld's portentous witticism of late November 2001 provided the rationale for war crimes committed against captured prisoners. "Well, the president's policy is 'dead or alive,' Rumsfeld joked with reporters. 'I have my preferences'" (Diebel, 2001). Jamie Doran's (2002) documentary "Massacre at Mazarr," showing the torture and murder of thousands of Taliban prisoners at Mazar-I-Sharif, was partly corroborated in August 2002 by a leaked UN report (Teather, 2002). Soldiers under the command of Uzbek warlord Abdul Rashid Dostum, accompanied by U.S. troops, stuffed hundreds of Taliban prisoners into metal shipping containers, where they suffocated.

Thousands of prisoners, including Pakistanis, are languishing in Hamid Karzai's jails, "many of them in pitiable conditions, crammed into dark underground cells with buckets for sanitation, no medical care and scraps of food" (Burns, 2002b). On August 7, 13 tried to escape from prison in Kabul but were mowed down "by Afghan forces a few miles south of Kabul, as they made a last stand in a roadside trench." Public opinion in Pakistan, enraged by the treatment of prisoners, is creating problems for Karzai. Similar concerns are being voiced by Pakistani critics of the U.S. incarceration of almost 600 Taliban prisoners from 38 countries in Guantanamo Bay, Cuba. Officially, these men are supposed to be former al Qaeda operatives, but leaks suggest that no Qaeda members have been found. According to Bush officials, the wretched Guantanamo prisoners are not POWs entitled to certain rights under the Geneva Convention, but "enemy combatants."

Granting itself extraordinary powers under the USA Patriot Act of October 26, 2001, the Bush administration has committed a range of acts that offend the Constitution, including holding civilian prisoners without trial, arresting individuals on the basis of their ethnic and religious background, pursuing criminal cases against defendants without adequate cause, mooting the use of torture to capture and convict terrorists, and encouraging neighbors and workers to report on suspected al Qaeda sympathizers. It remains to be seen whether U.S. courts will defer to the Bush agenda (Chang, 2001).

Both Clinton and Bush used women's rights to fan righteous anger against the Taliban. But Sima Samar, the champion of women's rights in Kabul, now lives behind "protective razor wire erected around her house ... by soldiers from the U.S.-led military coalition" (York, 2002). Named to Karzai's interim government in December, "she became one of the new government's vice-presidents." During the June 2002 loya jirga she was attacked by Islamists and dismissed from cabinet. The strict Islamic sharia law requiring the burqa remains in place, as it did under the Taliban.

XIII. DID BIG OIL KILL MASSOUD?

Operation Enduring Freedom may be an excuse to occupy former Soviet spheres of influence and undercut Russia's monopoly on world oil supplies in Central Asia. Fundamental to the U.S. economy, oil is also the means for America to control its European and Japanese allies, which are equally dependent on a stable supply (Ahmad, 2001, p. 33). The Bush administration is dominated to an extraordinary degree by U.S. oil and gas interests (Van Natta Jr. & Banerjee, 2002), who favor these foreign policy goals. The Afghan adventure involves a large gamble. According to *Business Week* (2002), "[t]he game the Americans are playing has some of the highest stakes going. What they are attempting is nothing less than the biggest carve-out of a new U.S. sphere of influence since the U.S. became engaged in the Middle East fifty years ago."

Afghanistan offers a potential pipeline route from energy-rich landlocked countries of Central Asia, through to ports in Pakistan. The Caspian region (which includes Kazakhstan, Turkmenistan, Azerbaijan and Uzbekistan) "has more than 6% of the world's proven oil reserves and almost 40% of its gas reserves." In the past decade it has created much excitement among international oil companies. Secretary of State Colin Powell estimated that U.S.$200 billion "could flow into Kazakhstan over the next 5 to 10 years" (Van Natta Jr. et al., 2002). Often compared to the Middle East of the 1920s, the Caspian region comprises much more complex and bitter rivalries with a long lineage. "Arabs, Persians, Mongols and Greeks invaded Afghanistan. The Great Game pitted the United Kingdom against imperial Russia for control of Afghanistan's trade and transit routes" (*Stratfor.com*, 2001a). What Ahmed Rashid called, "The New Great Game," includes "[b]ig powers such as Russia, China, and the USA; the neighbours Iran, Pakistan, Afghanistan and Turkey; the Central Asian States themselves, and the most powerful players of all, the oil companies." (Rashid, 2001, p. 147).

In the mid-1990s, with U.S. policy guided by Russophile Deputy Secretary of State Strobe Talbott, the U.S. seemed willing to form a partnership with Russia to arrange export of oil and gas from the Caspian region to markets in Europe and Southeast Asia. But this policy changed as the Russian economy disintegrated and U.S. oil companies grew impatient with Russian interference.

The Russians are reluctant to give U.S. and other foreign oil companies carte blanche in developing the country's reserves (Banerjee & Tavernise, 2001).

By 1997 new policy emerged that would allow big oil "to exploit the Caspian resources, help the Caspian states assert their independence from Russia and enlist them in the Western camp" (Rashid, 2001, pp. 162, 169). The impact was immediate. "[O]utside interference in Afghanistan," said the UN Undersecretary for Humanitarian Affairs, "is now all related to the battle for oil and gas pipelines. The fear is that these companies and regional powers are just renting the Taliban for their own purposes" (Rashid, 2001, pp. 162, 169).

The Taliban victory in the western Afghanistan city of Herat in 1995 was celebrated by the U.S. as a step toward further isolating Iran and securing a pipeline base for UNOCAL. The Taliban would be America's bet for securing stability in Central Asia. Meanwhile, its most dangerous competitors in the region, Iran and Russia, locked out of pipeline deals by the U.S., were concerned to destabilize Afghanistan by aiding the Northern Alliance (Rashid, 2001, pp. 178–179).

The pipeline was originally the brainchild of Argentinian oil company, Bridas, which had painstakingly negotiated a 1995 deal with Turkmenistan, the Taliban and Northern Alliance warlords. Bridas's option collapsed when Turkmenistan's President Saparmurad Niyazov reneged in favor of an offer from UNOCAL, in October 1995. "It was the triumph of hope over experience," quipped UNOCAL consultant Henry Kissinger.[9] Bridas took its case to court but "[o]n 5 October 1998, the Texas District Court dismissed Bridas's US$15 billion suit against Unocal – on the grounds that the dispute was governed by the laws of Turkmenistan and Afghanistan, not Texas law" (Rashid, 2001, p. 175).

The Argentinian oil company redoubled efforts to secure a pipeline route, teaming up with a Saudi partner called Ningharco. The Gulf firm had ties to Prince Turki bin-Faisal, the head of Saudi intelligence, "who was widely credited with having financed the Taliban phenomenon in the first place" (Griffin, 2001, p. 181). In September 1996 Bridas invited "the Taliban's energy mullahs to Buenos Aires to negotiate a deal". Bridas was too late. The following month, a consortium called Central Asia Gas Pipeline (CentGas) was formed, headed by UNOCAL, and including Saudi Arabia's Delta Oil Company and the Turkmen government. "The group planned to build a 790-mile pipeline from the Turkmen-Afghan border to Multan, Pakistan" (Watson, 2002).

In September 1998, when Russia supplied Ahmed Shah Massoud's anti-Taliban forces with "heavy weapons, training and logistical support," (Risen, 1998), UNOCAL's pipeline proposals dimmed. The Taliban could not eject Massoud and his allies from their northern redoubt. President Clinton bombed bin Laden's Afghan camps in October, and UNOCAL withdrew from the field.

Bridas (now part of BP Amoco/Pan American Energy) was caught up in the 2001 Argentine financial crisis, the dates of which straddled September 11.

In early 2001 Washington revived the UNOCAL plan. Bush representatives bargained with the Taliban from February 2001, when it offered to extradite bin Laden, until August. The Taliban hired Laili Helms, niece of former CIA Director Richard Helms and a relative of King Zahir Shah, to develop their publicity (Walkom, 2001).

But Massoud's resistance in the north, made possible by alliances with Russia and Iran, showed that the Taliban might never be able to guarantee pipeline security.

The death of Massoud, perhaps the only leader in Afghanistan with the charisma and credibility to maintain an independent stance versus the Americans, may have set the stage for September 11. The Tajik warlord, whose death was likely expedited by someone in his inner circle, was replaced by a triumvirate, including General Fahim, "who have played their cards well over the past two months, going along with changing U.S. priorities" (Rashid, 2001a). Massoud's Uzbek ally, General Dostum, originally opposed to the interim government of Hamid Karzai, changed his mind after Karzai visited him at Mazar-I-Sharif. The Afghan president put one of Dostum's commanders at the head of the Ministry of Mines and Industries, "responsible for what could be one of the country's most important development projects, the newly reborn trans-Afghanistan pipeline" (Watson, 2002).

Hamid Karzai, Pakistan's President Musharraf and Turkmen President Niyazov signed an agreement in Islamabad to build a pipeline, just before the June 2002 loya jirga. The word in Kabul is that UNOCAL maintains its interest in a pipeline. "Bush named a former Unocal consultant Zalmay Khalilzad, as his special envoy to Afghanistan late last year" (Chin, 2002). Khalilzad, who reports to Condoleeza Rice, has a fascinating background. He was present "in Unocal's talks with the Taliban in 1997. In fact, it was Khalilzad who drew up the risk analysis of the pipeline. Khalizad was a special advisor to the State Department during the Reagan administration, where he was instrumental in arming the mujahadeen during the 1980s."

XIV. STRANGLING RUSSIA

The British East India Company acted as a "cat's paw of London's imperial ambitions during the early years of the Raj" (Griffin, 2001, p. 118). Leaders of the British government and the East India Company were interchangeable, much as with the George W. Bush administration and big oil interests. Similar industry-government relationships have appeared in Russia, where "Prime

Minister Viktor Chernomyrdin made a personal fortune as head of Gazprom's board of directors until mid-1996." In the mid-1990s, Russia deliberately destabilized the oil-rich new republics around the Caspian Sea "whenever they tried to forge independence from Boris Yeltsin's Russian Federation." State-sponsored civil conflicts, disguised as ethnic revolt, "served the dual purpose of reasserting Russia's dominance in the 'troubled' Caucasus and undermining the feasibility of alternative pipeline routes which did not pass through Russian territory."

The United States now may be in a similar hunt, with Russia as prey. "Already the United States has established a military presence in Uzbekistan, Kyrgyzstan and Georgia, neatly bracketing the region [around Russia] . . . Washington may also be planning deployments to Azerbaijan and Kazakhstan, moves which would insert the United States firmly into the region's politics" (*Stratfor.com*, 2002b). The Americans claim they have sent 200 crack troops to Georgia in order to fight Islamic terrorism. "Observers see ulterior motives to the U.S. deployments – a strong signal to the Russians to keep their hands off post-Soviet Georgia, a longer-term role protecting the billion dollar pipeline projects that will transport the hydrocarbon riches of the Caspian basin west to Turkey via Georgia, or more immediately a preparation for war on Saddam Hussein's Iraq, 500 km to the south" (Traynor, 2002b).

In the 1990s the Islamist contagion, sponsored by the U.S. and its Saudi Arabian and Pakistani allies, spread into other regions once dominated by Moscow, including Chechnya, Bosnia and Kosovo, where the Albanian mafia linked to the Islamist Kosovo Liberation Army controls the $400 billion Balkans drug trade and lucrative prostitution rackets (Junger, 2002, p. 117). Osama bin Laden, along with top Iranian and Pakistani intelligence officials, purportedly attended "a secret summit of HizbAllah International held in 1996" to plan the war in Chechnya, which resulted in Russia's destruction of Grozny. The war helped disrupt the main Russian oil pipeline route through Chechnya and Dagestan and provided succor to "the Anglo-American oil conglomerates which are vying for control over oil resources and pipeline corridors out of the Caspian Sea basin" (Chossudovsky, 2001, p. 4).

Holy warriors appeared in Bosnia and Kosovo, where they fought the Yugoslav army of Slobodan Milosevic, now on trial in the Hague for war crimes (Fisher & Simons, 2002). Heavily armed Mujaheddin warriors, fresh from Kabul in 1992, arrived in Bosnia. "They were just as cruel as their opponents, and the photographs of grinning Arab warriors brandishing the freshly severed heads of 'Christian Serbs' or crushing them with their boot heels created such furor that the Bosnian army had to regain control over them before their excessive zeal did any more harm to the Muslim image" (Kepel, 2002, p. 250).

The Bosnian war involved Pentagon secret intelligence, rather than the CIA (Norton-Taylor, 2002). "Agents from Iran and Turkey worked together with the U.S. to import Mujaheddin fighters and supply Saudi Arabian-financed arms to the Muslim faction in Bosnia led by Alijah Izetbegovic ... a Muslim fundamentalist who began his political career supporting the Nazis during World War II." The Western press christened Izetbegovic's faction, "the government of Sarejevo, while anti-Izetbegovic Muslims allied with the Bosnian Serbs were called "rebels" (Israel, 2002a). The embargo was monitored by U.S. intelligence on behalf of the UN, and manipulated to overlook a massive infusion of weapons through Croatia. "Initially aircraft from Iran Air were used, but as the volume increased they were joined by a mysterious fleet of black C-130 Hercules aircraft." Norwegian officials alarmed by the shipments were threatened into silence. In 1995 the first CIA head of station at Sarajevo was marked for assassination by the Iranians and quickly withdrawn (Aldrich, 2002).

A massive terrorist attack in 1999 on civilian apartments and military housing in Moscow killed almost three hundred people and injured thousands. The explosions, which facilitated the rise of former KGB officer Vladimir Putin to the Presidency, were blamed on Osama bin Laden and his followers (Cooley, 2001, pp. 177–178). Persistent rumors suggested the bombings were actually the work of Russian intelligence (Globe & Mail, 2002), seeking to justify Russia's second intervention in Chechnya. Moscow sent 90,000 troops into Chechnya, as many as the former Soviet Union committed against the Mujaheddin. The war has devastated the Caucasian republic, causing tens of thousands of civilian casualties, leveling cities, depopulating the countryside, and inflicting unsustainable losses on the Russian armed forces (Cheterien, 2002). In August 2002 a Chechen rebel missile brought down a Russian helicopter, killing 122 (Associated Press, 2002a).

Terrorists in Uzbekistan received support from Pakistan's Inter-Services Intelligence agency. They met with Afghan Arabs, bin Laden himself, and Taliban officials; Saudi Arabia offered large donations. Tashkent's authoritarian head of state, Islam Karimov, presented a tempting target. Jumaboi Namangani and other Islamists deliberated provoked security forces to take hard measures, and inspired incidents that created inevitable conflict between neighboring states. Predictably, most funding for Namangami's Islamic Movement of Uzbekistan (IMU) "came from the lucrative opium trade from Afghanistan" (Rashid, 2002, p. 165). In 2001, Namangani built facilities in Tajikistan for refining opium into pure heroin.

The march on Afghanistan and the widening war on terrorism fits well with U.S. geostrategic objectives delineated by foreign policy luminary, Zbigniew Brzezinsky (1997, pp. 123–124). The unstable nations of Central Asia, he writes, "tempt and invite the intrusion of more powerful neighbours." While U.S. hegemony dominates the Middle East, no comparable Central Asian hegemony exists that could grasp this "potential geopolitical prize." If a rival power such as Russia or China seized control of Central Asia this would threaten "the American-dominated security of the Persian Gulf region." Oil politics are only part of the story in Central Asia. The Central Asian Republics comprise a potential transportation bridge between eastern and western Eurasia, and an area rich in many natural resources besides petroleum.

The U.S. may be preparing to strangle Russia, as it did Yugoslavia in the 1990s, by squeezing its borders and setting up conflict and rivalry among its closest neighbours. Brzezinski (1997, p. 121) singles out Uzbekistan as "a major obstacle to any renewed Russian control over the region." Under strongman President Islam Karimov, Uzbekistan has become America's chief proxy in Central Asia, benefiting from $160 million in U.S. aid and security promises against its neighbors, Krygyzstan and Tajikistan. "So far," reports *Stratfor.com* (2002a) "at least 1,500 U.S. Air Force and Special Operations personnel are stationed at Uzbekistan's Khanabad Air Base, just over 90 miles from the Afghan border."

Sharing America's distaste for Islamist terror, Karimov is prepared to welcome U.S. intervention within Uzbekistan itself, including bombing campaigns aimed at Qaeda cells on its territory. Karimov's chief opposition, the Islamic Movement of Uzbekistan, controls most of the opium and heroin exiting Afghanistan. America, like Russia before it,[10] may be playing a double game, supporting the IMU while offering Uzbekistan military assistance to fight off the terrorists.

Whatever the motives of U.S. military operations in Afghanistan, they are not likely to bring peace. American forces have mostly withdrawn from northern Afghanistan, where rivalries are stormy between Tajiks and General Dostum's Uzbeks (Gall, 2002). The U.S. has ignored Hamid Karzai's and UN experts' pleas for an upgraded peace effort. The U.S. may be repeating its previous lacklustre performance in peacekeeping. After 1989, the U.S. appeared to walk away from Afghanistan and let Saudi Arabia and Pakistan gather up loose ends. "The U.S. strategic absence allowed all the regional powers, including the newly independent [Central Asian Republics], to prop up competing war lords, thereby intensifying the civil war and guaranteeing its prolongation" (Rashid, 2001, p. 176).

Allied peacekeeper are deployed only in Kabul, and their limited numbers are far below the 5000 originally established in the Bonn agreement of December 5, 2001 (Scott, 2002b). The U.S. has pledged $297 million to assist the new government in rebuilding the country, only 7% of the $4.5 billion it has already spent on the war (MacKinnon, 2002a).

As with the Afghan jihad, Qaeda terrorism may be serving the interests of the United States. Terrorism destabilizes the countries of the Caspian basin, prevents any kind of détente between the competing regional forces, and provides an opening for intense U.S. military engagement in the region, which now includes American military forays into Pakistan. "One year after the September attacks," writes Ahmed Rashid (2002b) ". . . there is growing instability and domestic crisis in every country in Central and Southern Asia." Whatever the real source of the September terror attacks on New York and Washington, this horrific assault provided the excuse that Zibigniew Brzezinski (1997, pp. 35–36) argued in *The Grand Chessboard* was required to obtain unquestioning public support for massive U.S. military mobilization in the Caspian region.

XV. EVIL AND SEPTEMBER 11

The model provided by the political economy of evil suggests there are good reasons to suspect some kind of U.S. complicity in the multiple crashes of September 11. Outbreaks of malevolence, like the events of September 11, are generally connected to the actions of ruling groups, relying on hidden forces unacknowledged by conventional political analyses. The deep politics of September 11 and intervention in Afghanistan point to dangerous U.S. dependence on warlords, holy warriors and drug traffickers to secure American interests, including Caspian oil resources and the limitation of Russian influence over its former republics and satellites. Achieving these goals presents considerable political risks for the Bush Administration, and threatens to exacerbate tensions in the Caspian region and the Middle East, increasing the chances of a wider war. Already there are reports that the U.S. is taking much heavier casualties in Afghanistan than admitted, and may consider bombing Pakistan's border regions (*Stratfor.com*, 2002b).

Instead of a quickly arranged response to an unexpected attack, the war in Afghanistan appears to be part of a strategy developed well before September, 2001. Similar to the aftermath of the Kennedy assassination,[11] establishment media in North America have closed off speculation that might undermine the approved version.[12] A cascade of reports carried by major U.S. media in the spring and summer 2002, showing that the Bush administration was warned early and often about the possibility of a terrorist attack, but did nothing, has led only to a toothless Congressional inquiry which does not include the role of the White House (Cloud & Rogers, 2002). Even this toothless investigation "touched nerves at the" CIA and FBI, and apparently provoked President Bush "to drop his opposition to an independent commision, created by Congress, to conduct a broader inquiry" (Johnston & Risen, 2002).

In those few places where alternative accounts of September are aired, they are quickly doused with ridicule.[13] Cynthia McKinney of Georgia, who spoke out against the Bush deception, failed to keep her seat in Congress.

The ease with which the terrorists of September eluded U.S. armed response[14] is reminiscent of the security lapses at Dealey Plaza in 1963. Jets at nearby airbases failed to scramble, despite plenty of warning.[15] Nineteen hijackers penetrated security readily, suggesting that they and their mission may have had support from within the U.S. deep political system. The tiresome joke about hijackers learning their trade in rustic Florida flying schools, while avoiding lessons in take-off and landing, hardly accounts for the impressive flight skills demonstrated by supposed suicide pilots. The immobility of President Bush, sitting before a class of grade school pupils in a highly publicized Florida visit during the crucial events of September 11, prompts serious questions about his competence, if not his Administration's complicity, in the attacks. Criminal investigations of the four air crashes have been delayed; flight recorder information for the plane that went down in Pennsylvania has not been released; and the ruins of the WTC towers were removed before a proper investigation could be conducted on the cause of the collapse. Official recalcitrance has led to wide spread rumors. In France, a book that claims no jet hit the Pentagon became an overnight best-seller (Ruppert, 2002).[16]

Persistent international reports of massive share trading in the airlines and financial interests hit hard by the September attacks suggest prior knowledge. U.S. intelligence agencies ignored warnings from reputable sources about a raid on New York and Washington (Ruppert, 2002). A spate of anthrax assaults on media outlets and liberal U.S. politicians turned out to have used spores "identical to the stocks of the deadly bacteria maintained by the U.S. Army since 1980" (Weiss & Schmidt, 2001). Well after September 11, prominent Saudi billionaire families, with financial ties to the Osama bin Laden terror network through Muslim charitable foundations, "continue[d] to engage in major oil deals with leading U.S. corporations" (Boston Herald, 2001) unhindered by U.S. investigators.

September 11 accomplished a dramatic shift in U.S. policy toward military incursions in many countries supposedly harboring al Qaeda remnants, and to what *Business Week* (2002) called "an accidental empire."[17] The outcome of this move cannot be predicted. It represents an ominous new form of concrete evil with possible horrendous consequences on a world scale.

NOTES

1. Kenneth Maxwell – Nelson and David Rockefeller fellow at the Council of Foreign Relations – takes exception to this interpretation of September 11. "Talk about blaming the victim. Three days after 9/11 the eminent economist Celso Furtado suggested in one of Brazil's most influential newspapers that there were two explanations for the attack. One possibility, Furtado implied, was that this savage assault on America was the work of foreign terrorists, as the Americans suspected. But a more plausible explanation, he asserted, was that this disaster was a provocation carried out by the American far right to justify a takeover. He compared the attacks on the Twin Towers and the Pentagon to the burning of the Reichstag in 1933 and the rise of the Nazis to power in Germany" (2002). Furtado's reaction was widely shared in Brazil and elsewhere in Latin America.

2. "The past six months have seen an extraordinary projection of American power into a vast region dominated by Moscow for the last two centuries, installing U.S. firepower at Soviet-built bases in four countries in a 3,200 km arc from near the Chinese border to the eastern shores of the Black Sea" (Traynor, 2002a).

3. Spann was killed by escaping Taliban prisoners in November 2001.

4. Bob and Doug McKenzie are stereotyped Canadian characters from Second City Television, played respectively by Rick Moranis and Dave Thomas (http://www.secondcity.com/02_02.asp?pid=02_01_03).

5. Marx's (1976, p. 230) quote from Sophocles's *Antigone* may also be applicable to the Carlyle Group. "Nothing so evil as money ever grew to be current among men. This lays cities low, this drives men from their homes, this trains and warps honest souls till they set themselves to works of shame; this still teaches folk to practice villainies, and to know every godless deed."

6. Stan Goff offered one of the best critical analyses of the U.S. war in Afghanistan (2001). See also, Tom Carew (2001), "There's no way to win in the death zone."

7. According to President Hamid Karzai, speaking in New York in September 2002, Mullah Omar is a man of many tricks. "[I]t was difficult to trace Mullah Omar in part because 'nobody recognizes him. This is a man nobody has seen. He goes and hides in houses' " (Brooke, 2002).

8 The ex-king left Kabul for Paris in September 2002 to seek medical treatment.

9. Kissinger is not the only famous American personality involved in Central Asia. Zbigniew Brezezinski, a chief planner of the Afghan jihad of 1979–1989, represents Amoco; former National Security Advisor Alexander Haig is employed as a lobbyist by Turkmenistan. CEO of Halliburton Oil before becoming Vice President, Dick Cheney served on the U.S.-Azerbaijan Chamber of Commerce. National Security Advisor Condoleezza Rice is a former member of Chevron, which was a player in the CentGas deals. "Rice made an impression on her old colleagues at Chevron. The company has named one of their supertankers the SS Condoleezza Rice" (Madsen, 2002). Robert Oakley, UNOCAL's key envoy in Central Asia and former ambassador to Pakistan, reports Larry Chin (2002), "was a 'counter-terrorism' specialist for the Reagan administration who armed and trained the mujahadeen during the war against the Soviets in the 1980s . . . Richard Armitage, the current Deputy Defense Secretary . . . [and] director with the Carlyle Group . . . is allegedly deeply linked to terrorist and criminal networks in the Middle East, and the new independent states of the former Soviet Union (Chin, 2002).

10. Among Tajik officials many believed that Russia tolerated IMU raids on Uzbekistan "because Moscow was trying to pressure {Uzbek dictator] Karimov into accepting Russian troops and greater Russian influence in Uzbekistan. The fact that since 1999 the Russian army had three times helped evacuate IMU guerillas to Afghanistan is undeniable" (Rashid, 2002).

11. See, for example, Barbie Zelitzer's astonishing study, *Covering the Body: The Kennedy Assassination, the Media, and the Shaping of Collective Memory*, Chicago: The University of Chicago Press, 1992.

12. There are exceptions to this, especially in Canada, where *Toronto Star* columnist Tom Walkom questioned the September 11 story in a series of articles in September and October, 2001. Also Vision TV, another Canadian media outlet, has featured the intrepid reporting of Jared Israel on the Emperor's Clothes website (www.emperors-clothes.com), and highlighted Mike Ruppert (www.copvcia.com) in a panel discussion that questioned the Bush administration account of September 11.

13. An informative website on "the unanswered questions of September 11th" is www.unansweredquestions.org

David Corn in *The Nation* mocks writers who have the temerity to raise questions about September. He suggests that U.S. intelligence would be incapable "of such a foul deed." American spies and special agents "are not good enough, evil enough, or gutsy enough to mount this operation." Interestingly, Corn's criticism would suggest that the Afghan jihad of 1979–1989 was itself out of reach of U.S. intelligence operations, though, of course, it was not. "The most basic understanding of how government functions realizes that the national security bureaucracies of Washington do not work well together." The September conspiracy "to execute the simultaneous destruction of the two towers, a piece of the Pentagon, and four airplanes and make it appear as if it all was done by another party – is far beyond the skill level of U.S. intelligence. It would require dozens (or scores or hundreds) of individuals to attempt such a scheme. They would have to work together, and trust one another not to allow their part or reveal the conspiracy." Corn claims that no American intelligence agent would ever murder another, and certainly not thousands of innocents. "Not evil enough: This is as foul as it gets – to kill thousands of Americans, including Pentagon employees, to help out oil companies. This is a Hollywood-level of dastardliness, James Bond (or Dr. Evil) material." Corn rehearses for September 11 all the old arguments still used to smother questions about the Kennedy assassination, and the complicity of government officials in his death. "At the start of such a conspiracy, no one could be certain it would work and remain a secret. CIA people – and those in other government agencies – do care about their careers. Would George W. Bush take the chance of being branded the most evil president of all time by countenancing such wrongdoing? Oil may be in his blood, but would he place the oil industry's interests ahead of his own?"

14. One can imagine Russian Cold War hawks slapping their foreheads. If only we had known it would be so easy to penetrate U.S. air space!

15. See the remarkable series of articles by Illarion Bykov and Jared Israel, "Guilty For 9–11: Bush, Rumsfeld, Myers" on the website, www.emperors-clothes.com See also, Barry Zwicker, "The Great Deception, 9/11, Part 1: What Really Happened on Sept. 11th?" January 21, 2002, Insight Mediafile Vision TV. Transcript of Mon., Jan. 21 2002 Broadcast, www.visiontv.ca

16. The book by Thierry Meyssan is called *L'Effroyable Imposture (The Frightening Fraud)*. See Michael Ruppert, "Incoming!", *From the Wilderness*, April 4, 2002.

Ruppert's website www.copvcia.com is a valuable source of information on September 11. Other important sites, from which this paper benefited, are www.emperors-clothes.com; www.onlinejournal.com; and Peter Dale Scott's al Qaeda website, http://socrates.berkeley.edu/~pdscott/q.html

17. This radical foreign policy shift was confirmed by *The National Security Strategy of the United States*, released in late September 2002. Amidst sabre-rattling directed at Iraq's Saddam Hussein, the National Security paper reminded some of the nineteenth century Manifest Destiny. *Business Week* (Nussbaum, 2002) worried that the Bush Doctrine would elicit "a global backlash against perceived unilateralism and arrogance."

ACKNOWLEDGMENTS

The author wishes to acknowledge encouragement and assistance generously offered by Paul Zarembka, Alan Pomfret, Thomas Walkom, Kathryn Kopinak, Joseph Hermer, Robin Ramsay and Peter Dale Scott.

REFERENCES

Books and Articles

AbuKhalil, A. a. (2002). *Bin Laden, Islam and America's New "War on Terrorism"*. New York: Seven Stories Press.

Adkin, M., & Yousaf, M. (2001). *The Bear Trap*. Havertown, PA: Casemate.

Ahmad, E. (2001). *Terrorism: Theirs and Ours*. New York: Seven Stories Press.

Alexander, J. C. (1990). Culture and Political Crisis: "Watergate" and Durkheimian Sociology. In: *Durkheimian Sociology: Cultural Studies* (pp. 187–224). Cambridge: Cambridge University Press.

Alexander, J. C. (2001). Toward a Sociology of Evil, pp. 153–172. In: *Rethinking Evil*. Berkeley: University of California Press.

Amin, S. (1998). *Spectres of Capitalism: A Critique of Current Intellectual Fashions*. New York: Monthly Review Press.

Amin, S. (2001). Political Islam. *Covert Action Quarterly, 71*(3–6.71)(Winter).

Beaty, J., & Gwynne, S. (1993). *The Outlaw Bank: A Wild Ride into the Secret Heart of BCCI*. New York: Random House, Inc.

Becker, E. (1975). *Escape from Evil*. New York: Collier Macmillan Publishers.

Bergen, P. L. (2002). *Holy War, Inc: Inside the Secret World of Osama bin Laden*. New York: Simon and Schuster.

Browning, C. (1998). *Ordinary Men: Reserve Police Battalion 101 and the Final Solution in Poland*. New York: HarperCollins.

Brzezinski, Z. (1997). *The Grand Chessboard: American Primacy and its Geostrategic Imperatives*. New York: Basic Books.

Chang, N. (2001). The USA Patriot Act. *Covert Action Quarterly*, (Winter).

Chomsky, N. (1993). *Rethinking Camelot*. Montreal: Black Rose Books.

Chomsky, N. (2001). *9-11*. New York: Seven Stories Press.

Chossudovsky, M. (2001). Who Is Osama Bin Laden? *Global Outlook, 1*.

Cockburn, A., & St. Clair, J. (1998). *Whiteout: The CIA, Drugs and the Press*. New York: Verso.
Colodny, L., & Gettlin, R. (1991). *Silent Coup: The Removal of a President*. New York: St. Martin's Press.
Cooley, J. K. (2001). *Unholy Wars* (new ed.). London: Pluto Press.
Cushman, T. (2001). The Reflexivity of Evil: Modernity and Transgression in the War in Bosnia. In: *Evil After Postmodernism: History, Narratives and Ethics*. New York: Routledge.
Engels, F. (1857). *Afghanistan*. www.marxists.org
Esposito, J. L. (2002). *Unholy War: Terror in the Name of Islam*. Oxford: Oxford University Press.
Ewans, M. (2002). *Afghanistan: A Short History of Its People and Politics*. New York: HarperCollins.
Foster, M. (1984). *The Political Philosophies of Plato and Hegel*. New York: Garland Publishing Inc.
Gabel, P. (2000). *The Bank Teller and Other Essays on the Politics of Meaning*. San Francisco: Acada Books.
Ginsborg, P. (2001). *Italy and Its Discontents: Family, Civil Society, State 1980–2001*. London: Allen Lane The Penguin Press.
Goff, S. (2001). The Story We Hear Is Simply Not Believable. *Global Outlook, 1*
Griffin, M. (2001). *Reaping the Whirlwind: The Taliban Movement in Afghanistan*. London: Pluto Press.
Hegel, G. (1971). *Philosophy of Mind: Being Part Three in the Encyclopaedia of the Philosophical Sciences*. Oxford: Oxford University Press.
Hegel, G. (1975a). *Aesthetics*, Vol. 1. Oxford: Oxford University Press.
Hegel, G. (1975). *Lectures on the Philosophy of World History: Introduction*. Oxford: Oxford University Press.
Hegel, G. (1989). *Hegel's Science of Logic*, J. N. Findlay (foreword). Atlantic Highlands, N.J.: Humanities Press International, Inc.
Hegel, G. (1991). *Elements of the Philosophy of Right*. A. W. Wood (Ed.). Cambridge: Cambridge University Press.
Hegel, G. (1995). *Lectures on Natural Right and Political Science: The First Philosophy of Right*. Berkeley: University of California Press.
Hersh, S. (1997). *The Dark Side of Camelot*. New York: Little, Brown and Company.
Hirschman, A. O. (1973). On Hegel, Imperialism, and Structural Stagnation. Discussion Paper 280. Cambridge: Harvard Institute of Economic Research, Harvard University.
Hirschman, A. O. (1981). *Essays in Trespassing: Economics to Politics and Beyond*. Cambridge: Cambridge University Press.
Hougan, J. (1984). *Secret Agenda: Watergate, Deep Throat and the CIA*. New York: Random House.
Hougan, J. (2001). The Alternative Theory of Watergate on Trial. *Lobster, 41*(Summer), 33–34.
Hudson, R. A. (1999). *The Sociology and Psychology of Terrorism: Who Becomes a Terrorist and Why?* Washington: Federal Research Division, Library of Congress.
Huntington, S. (1996). *The Clash of Civilizations and the Remaking of World Order*. New York: Touchstone.
Kaiser, D. (2000). *American Tragedy: Kennedy, Johnson, and the Origins of the Vietnam War*. Cambridge, Mass.: Harvard University Press.
Kepel, G. (2002). *Jihad: The Trail of Political Islam*. Boston: Harvard University Press.
Krushchev, N. (1970). *Kruschev Remembers*. Boston: Little, Brown and Company.
Logevall, F. (1999). *Choosing War: The Lost Chance for Peace and the Escalation of the War in Vietnam*. Berkeley: University of California Press.
Lourie, R. (2002). *Sakharov: A Biography*. London: Brandeis University Press.

MacGregor, D. (1984). *The Communist Ideal in Hegel and Marx*. Toronto: University of Toronto Press.

MacGregor, D. (1992). *Hegel, Marx and the English State*. Boulder, Colorado: Westview Press.

MacGregor, D. (1998). *Hegel and Marx After the Fall of Communism*. Cardiff: University of Wales Press.

Machiavelli, N. (1979). The Portable Machiavelli. In: *The Portable Machiavelli*. Harmondsworth, Middlesex: Penguin Books.

Mackey, S. (2002). *The Reckoning: Iraq and the Legacy of Saddam Hussein*. New York: W. W. Norton and Company.

Magnus, R. H., & Naby, E. (2002). *Afghanistan: Mullah, Marx, and Mujahid*. Boulder, CO: Westview Press.

Marx, K. (1963). *Early Writings*. Toronto: McGraw-Hill Book Company.

Marx, K. (1973). *The Eighteenth Brumaire of Louis Bonaparte. Surveys from Exile: Political Writings*, Vol. 2. Harmondsworth, Middlesex: Penguin Books.

Marx, K. (1976). *Capital: A Critique of Political Economy*, Vol. 1. Harmondsworth, Middlesex, England: Penguin Books.

Marx, K., & Engels, F. (1972). *The Revolution of 1848–1949, Articles from the Neue Rheinische Zeitung*. Moscow: Progress Publishers.

May, E. R., & Zelikow, P. D. (1997). *The Kennedy Tapes: Inside the White House during the Cuban Missile Crisis*. Cambridge, Massachusetts: Harvard University Press.

McCoy, A. W. (1991). *The Politics of Heroin: CIA Complicity in the Global Drug Trade*, Completely Revised and Expanded Edition of *The Politics of Heroin in Southeast Asia*. Chicago: Lawrence Hill Books.

Newman, J. (1992). *JFK and Vietnam: Deception, Intrigue and the Struggle for Power*. New York: Warner Books.

Nixon Era Library (2002). *Oval Office Conversation 639-30*, December 21, 1971. Beckley, West Virginia: Mountain State University.

Novick, P. (1999). *The Holocaust in American Life*. Boston: Houghton Mifflin.

Oglesby, C. (1976). *The Yankee and Cowboy War*. Kansas City: Sheed Andrews and McMeel, Inc.

Parenti, M. (1996). *Dirty Truths: Reflections on Politics, Media, Ideology, Conspiracy, Ethnic Life and Class Power*. San Francisco: City Lights.

Prawer, S. (1976). *Karl Marx and World Literature*. Oxford: Oxford University Press.

Rall, T. (2002). *To Afghanistan and Back*. New York: Nantier, Beall, Minoustchine Publishing Inc.

Ramsay, R. (2000). *Conspiracy Theories*. Harpenden, Herts: Pocket Essentials.

Rashid, A. (2001). *Taliban: Militant Islam, Oil and Fundamentalism in Central Asia*. New Haven: Yale University Press.

Rashid, A. (2002). *Jihad: The Rise of Militant Islam in Central Asia*. New Haven: Yale University Press.

Scott, P. D. (1972). Vietnamization and the Drama of the Pentagon Papers. In: *The Pentagon Papers*. Boston: Beacon Press.

Scott, P. D. (1972a). *The War Conspiracy: The Secret Road to the Second Indochina War*. Indianapolis: Bobbs-Merrill.

Scott, P. D. (1993a). *Deep Politics and the Death of JFK*, Paperback Edition with a New Preface. Berkeley: University of California Press.

Scott, P. D. (1993). *Deep Politics and the Death of JFK*. Berkeley: University of California Press.

Sfez, G. (1996). Deciding Upon Evil. In: *Radical Evil* (pp. 126–149). London: Verso.

Stille, A. (1995). *Excellent Cadavers: The Mafia and the Death of the First Italian Republic*. New York: Pantheon Books.

Truell, P., & Gurwin, L. (1992). *False Profits: The Inside Story of BCCI, the World's Most Corrupt Financial Empire*. Boston: Houghton Mifflin Company.

Vidal, G. (2002). *Perpetual War for Perpetual Peace*. New York: Thunder's Mouth Press/Nation Books.

West, T., & Cummings, W. B. (2002). Proffer of Facts in Support of Defendent's Suppression Motions. In: Crim. No. 02-37-A, In the United States District Court for Eastern Division of Virginia Alexandria Division.

Newspapers, Magazines and Web Sites

Aldrich, R. J. (2002). America Used Islamists to Arm Bosnian Muslims. *The Guardian*, April 22.

Albert, M., & Shalom, S. R. (2002). Conspiracies Or Institutions: 9-11 and Beyond. *Znet.org*, June 2.

Anderson, J. L. (2002). The Assassins: Who Was Involved in the Murder of Ahmed Shah Massoud? *The New Yorker*, June 10.

Andrews, J. (2002). Legal Witch Hunt of John Walker Lindh Ends With Plea Bargain. *World Socialist* Web Site, July 18.

Armstrong, S. (1993). The Arming of Saudi Arabia. *FRONTLINE*, (February 16).

Associated Press (2002b). Afghan Vice President Assassinated by Two Gunmen, July 8.

Associated Press (2002). Study on Sept. 11 Intelligence Failures.

Finds Rampant Problems at CIA, FBI. *The Wall Street Journal*, July 18.

Associated Press (2002). Russia Points to Rebel Fire As Cause of Helicopter Crash. *The Wall Street Journal*. August 21.

Banerjee, N., & Tavernise, S. (2001). As the War Shifts, Oil Deals Follow. *The New York Times*, December 15.

Blair, T. (2002). PM Hails New NATO-Russia Council. 10 Downing Street Newsroom. London, May 28.

Bloom, W. (2002). The Grand Chessboard: The CIA's Intervention in Afghanistan – An Interview with Zbigniew Brzezinski. *Global Outlook*, *1*(Spring).

Boston Herald (2001). December 10.

Bravin, J. (2002). Lindh Agrees to Serve Twenty Years in a Plea Deal Approved by Bush. *The Wall Street Journal*, July 16.

Brissard, J.-C., Corn, D., & Ruppert, M. (2002). Debating September 11. *The Nation*, (July 12).

Brooke, J. (2002). Taliban Founder Still Eludes Search. *The New York Times*, September 19.

Burke, J. (2002). Afghan Warlords Set Up Heroin Labs. *The Observer*, August 11.

Burke, J., & Beaumont, P. (2002). West Pays Warlords to Stay in Line. *The Observer*, July 21.

Burns, J. F. (2002) Afghan Warlords Squeeze Profits from the War on Drugs, Critics say. *The New York Times*, May 5.

Burns, J. F. (2002a). Afghan Defense Chief Acts to Counter Talk of a Rift. *The New York Times*, August 18.

Burns, J. F. (2002b). Foreign Prisoners Becoming a Problem for Karzai. *The New York Times*, August 23.

Business Week (2002). The Next Oil Frontier, May 27.

Carew, T. (2001). There's No Way to Win in the Death Zone. *The Guardian Weekly*, September 27.

CBC News (2002). Opium Production Rises in Afghanistan, May 14.

Cheterien, V. (2002). The Other "Anti-Terrorist" War: Chechnya: Russia, get out now. *Le Monde Diplomatique*, (April).

Chin, L. (2002). Players On A Rigged Chessboard: Bridas, Unocal and the Afghanistan Pipeline. *Online Journal*, March 5.

Chipaux, F. (2002). Afghan Farmers Defy Ban on Poppy Growing. *Le Monde*, April 10.

Cloud, D. S. (2002). CIA Catching up with War on Terror. *The Wall Street Journal*, April 19.

Cloud, D. S., & Rogers, D. (2002). Congressional Panel Faces Pressure to Hold Tough Public Probe on 9/11. *The Wall Street Journal*, June 5.

Corn, D. (2002). The September 11 X-Files. *The Nation*, May 30.

Diebel, L. (2002). Rage Grows Over War Atrocities. *The Toronto Star*, November 28.

Doran, J. (2002). Afghanistan's Secret Graves, A Drive to Death in the Desert. *Le Monde Diplomatique*, September.

Dow Jones Newswires (2002). Turkmenistan Leader Appears to Reject President for Life. August 9.

Filkins, D. (2002). Flaws in U.S. Air War Left Hundreds of Civilians Dead. *The New York Times*, July 21.

Fisher, I. (2002). Warlord Pushes for Control of a Corner of Afghanistan. *The New York Times*, August 6.

Fisher, I. (2002a). Big Blast Kills 21 Afghans; Link to Terror Is Suspected. *The New York Times*, August 10.

Fisher, I. (2002b). GI's Are Taking Care Not to Offend Afghan Hosts. *The New York Times*, August 21.

Fisher, I. (2002c). Ready to Rebuild, Afghans Await Promised Aid. *The New York Times*, August 25.

Fisher, I., & Simons, M. (2002). Defiant, Milosevic Begins His Defense by Assailing NATO. *The New York Times*, Feburary 14.

Fishman, T. C. (2002). Making a Killing: The Myth of Capital's Good Intentions. *Harper's Magazine*, (August).

Friedman, R. I. (1993). "Israeli Intelligence Connection to WTC Bombing". *The Village Voice*, (August 3).

Friedman, T. L. (2002). Op-Ed: A Failure of Imagination. *The New York Times*, 15, May 19.

Gall, C. (2002). Two Afghan Rivals Co-Exist, but Hardly Hand-in-Hand. *The New York Times*, April 28.

Gall, C. (2002a). Expecting the Taliban, but Finding Only Horror. *The New York Times*, July 8.

Gall, C. (2002b). Afghan Warlord, With a New Job and Suit to Match, Bears Fresh Burdens. *The York Times*, September 29.

Gannon, K. (2002). Bin Laden Ordered Killing, ex-Taliban Minister Says. *The Globe and Mail*, August 16.

Globe and Mail (2002). February 12.

Globe and Mail (2002a). April 17.

Godov, J. (2001). U.S. Policy on Taliban Influenced by Oil – Authors. *Asia Times*, November 20.

Goldenberg, S. (2002). Long After the Air Raids, Bomblets Bring More Death. *The Guardian*, January 28.

Golden, D., Bandler, J., & Walker, M. (2001). Bin Laden Family Could Profit From a Jump in Defense Spending Due to Ties to U.S. Bank. *The Wall Street Journal*, September 27.

Griffin, M. (2001). A Gruesome Record. *The Guardian*, November 16.

Guardian Staff and Agencies (2001). Al-Qaida Flout Second Surrender Deadline. *The Guardian*, December 13.

Hecht, J. (2001). Ford and the Agency. *CounterPunch.org*, October 18.

Herold, M. (2002). Counting the Dead. *The Guardian*, August 8.

Hilton, I. (2002). Personal and Political in Afghanistan. *The New York Times*, April 28.

Hilton, I. (2002a). Letter from Pakistan: The General in His Labyrinth. *The New Yorker*, August 12.

Ignatieff, M. (2002). Nation-Building Lite. *The New York Times Magazine*, July 28.

Israel, J. (2002A). Dutch Report: U.S. Sponsored Foreign Islamists in Bosnia. The New Emperors Clothes: Piercing A Fog of Lies, April 29.

Johnston, D. (2002). A Plea Suited to Both Sides. *The New York Times*, July 16.

Johnston, D., & Risen, J. (2002). Panel's Findings Take Intelligence Officals by Surprise. *The New York Times*, September 29.

Junger, S. (2002). Slaves of the Brothel. *Vanity Fair*, (July).

Knox, P. (2002). Rights Trampled in U.S., Report Says. *Globe and Mail: A*, 12, August 15.

Lapham, L. H. (2002). Notebook: Innocents Abroad. *Harper's 304*(1825), 7–9; *304*(1825)(June).

Levine, S., & Pearl, D. (2001). Until Afghanistan Gets a New Government, Opium Growers Are Planting Crops Again. *The Wall Street Journal*, November 26.

MacKinnon, M. (2002). Afghan Bomb Kills 4, May Show Farmers' Anger at Poppy Ban. *The Globe and Mail*, April 9.

MacKinnon, M. (2002a). Fresh Calls for Jihad Arise in Afghanistan. *The Globe and Mail*, April 27.

MacKinnon, M. (2002b). Afghan Warlords Bide Their Time. *The Globe and Mail*, May 13.

MacKinnon, M. (2002c). Warlords Tactics Cloud Summit. *The Globe and Mail*, June 17.

Madsen, W. (2002). Afghanistan, the Taliban and the Bush Oil Team. Centre for Research on Globalisation, January 23.

Maxwell, K. (2002). Anti-Americanism in Brazil, Council of Foreign Relations.

McMurtry, J. (2002). What Did Bush Know? Reply to ZNet Commentary of May 22, 2002. *ZNet.org*, June 8.

Molson, B. (2002A). September 11: The Circumstantial Case. Part 1 of a four-part series. *On Line Journal*, OnLineJournal.com, April 17.

Nordland, R., Yousafzai, S., & Dehghanpisheh, B. (2002). How Al Qaeda Slipped Away. *Newsweek*, August 19.

Norton-Taylor, R. (2002). Offical Dutch Report Says that Pentagon Broke UN Embargo. *The Guardian*, April 22.

Nussbaum, B. (2002). Foreign Policy: Bush is Half Right. *Business Week*, October 7.

Omicinski, J. (2001). General: Capturing bin Laden is Not Part of the Mission. *U.S. News and World Report*, November 8.

Orth, M. (2002). Afghanistan's Deadly Habit. *Vanity Fair*, (March).

Rashid, A. (2001). Jekyll-and-Hyde Reality of Northern Alliance Creates Tough Task for Antiterror Coalition, *November 15*. November 15.

Rashid, A. (2002a). Freedom Isn't Easy. *Far Eastern Economic Review*, June 27.

Rashid, A. (2002b). September 11, One Year On, New Wars to Fight. *Far Eastern Economic Review*, September 12.

Risen, J. (1998). Russians Are Back in Afghanistan, Aiding Rebels. *The New York Times*, July 27.

Rosen, J. (2002). Nixon and the Chiefs. *The Atlantic Monthly*, (April).

Ruppert, M. (2002). Incoming. *From the Wilderness Publications*. April 4.

Ruppert, M. (2002a). The Case for Bush Administration Advance Knowledge of the 9-11 Attacks. *From the Wilderness Publications*. April 22.

Said, E. (2002A). Clash of Ignorance. *ZNet.org*, Boston.

Said, E. (2002). Thoughts About America. *Al-Ahram Weekly*, March 02.

Scott, P. D. (2002b). U.S. Must Get Serious About Peace in Afghanistan. *Pacific News Service*, February 8.

Scott, P. D. (2002c). FLASH 31: An Ignored Crisis: Afghan Civilian Deaths Continue from Unexploded U.S. Cluster Bombs. *Peter Dale Scott's Website. On War 9/11, Afghanistan, Al-Qaeda, Drugs, Oil, and Osama bin Laden*, March 30.

Scott, P. D. (2002). FLASH 5: Pre-1990 Drug Networks Being Restored Under New Coalition? *Peter Dale Scott's Website. On War 9/11, Afghanistan, Al-Qaeda, Drugs, Oil, and Osama bin Laden*, December 9.

Shah, A. (2002). Gunmen Attack Afghan Army Post. *Associated Press*, August 7.

Shahzad, S. S. (2002). Winds of Trouble Sweep Across Afghanistan. *Asia Times*, April 10.

Steele, J. (2002A). Arms and the Warlords. *The Guardian*, July 16.

Stephens, J., & Ottaway, D. B. (2002). From U.S., the ABCs of Jihad. *The Washington Post*, March 23.

Stratfor.com (2001). U.S. Faces Islamic Radical Network. *Strategic Forecasting LLC*, September 16.

Stratfor.com (2001a). Conflict Will Follow Taliban's Fall. *Strategic Forecasting LLC*, October 8.

Stratfor.com (2002). Russian, Ukrainian Crime Groups Set to Control Global Drug Market. *Strategic Forecasting LLC*, April 8.

Stratfor.com (2002a). High Stakes Future for Caspian Oil and Gas Development. *Strategic Forecasting LLC*, April 26.

Stratfor.com (2002b). Situation Deteriorating Rapidly in Afghanistan. *Strategic Forecasting LLC*, August 28.

Teather, D. (2002). Leaked Report Says 960 Died in Sealed Containers. *The Guardian*, August 19.

The Economist (2002). Know Thine Enemy, pp. 48–50, February 2.

The New York Times (2001). December 10.

Traynor, I. (2002). War on Terror Extended to the Gorges of Georgia. *The Guardian Weekly*, March 29–April 3.

Traynor, I. (2002). Jostle to Plunder Caspian Sea's Riches Turns Nasty. *The Guardian Weekly*, May 5.

Van Natta Jr., D., & Banerjee, N. (2002). High Administration Officials Have Linksto Energy Industry. *The New York Times*, April 21.

Walkom, T. (2001). Did Bin Laden Have Help From U.S. Friends? *The Toronto Star*, November 27.

Walkom, T. (2002). Bush Counts on the War Without End. *The Toronto Star*, February 5.

Walsh, N. P. (2002). Russia's Rise in Addicts Leads to Rampant HIV. *The Guardian*, August 7.

Walzer, M., E. (2001). What Are We Fighting For: Letter from America. Institute for American Values, New York.

Warner, M. (2002). The Big Guys Work For the Carlyle Group. *Fortune*, Monday, March 18.

Washington Post (2001). May 25.

Watson, P. (2002). Afghanistan Aims to Revive Pipeline Plans. *Los Angeles Times*, May 30.

Weaver, M. A. (2000). The Real bin Laden. *The New Yorker*, January 24.

Weiss, R., & Schmidt, S. (2001). Capital Hill Anthrax Matches Army Stocks. *The Washington Post*, December 16.

Wetzel, K. (2002). Utd Defense Gets Pact To Develop Cannon Artillery System. *Dow Jones Newswires*, August 9.

Wright, L. (2002). The Counter-Terrorist. *The New Yorker*, January 14.

York, G. (2002). Holy War Engulfs Afghan Feminist. *The Globe and Mail*, August 7.

U.S. WARS IN THE LIGHT OF THE INTERNATIONAL DRUG TRADE

Peter Dale Scott

ABSTRACT

The United States since World War Two, inheriting the patterns of European colonial systems before it, has collaborated with local drug lords ("drug proxies") to maintain its influence in the Third World, particularly in areas of geostrategic importance because of their proximity to petroleum resources. These alliances have cumulatively strengthened the U.S. presence in the Third World. But they have also progressively strengthened and consolidated the global drug traffic throughout the world. Most recently, in 2001, U.S. armed force has helped restore the drug traffic to Afghanistan, where opium production had been radically curtailed by the Taliban.

I. OIL, DRUGS, AND AMERICAN THIRD WORLD INTERVENTIONS

In the half century since the Korean War the U.S. has been involved in four major wars in the Third World: in Vietnam (1961–1975), in the Persian Gulf

---

The material in this article is more extensively discussed in my book *Drugs, Oil, and War: The United States in Afghanistan, Colombia, and Indochina* (Lanham, MD: Rowman & Littlefield, forthcoming in 2003); and in my chapter in M. Selden and A. So, (Eds), *War and State Terrorism: The U.S. and the Asia-Pacific in the Modern Era* (Lanham, MD: Rowman & Littlefield, forthcoming in 2003).

Confronting 9-11, Ideologies of Race, and Eminent Economists,
Research in Political Economy, Volume 20, pages 63–81.
ISBN: 0-7623-0984-9

(1990–1991), in Colombia (1991–present), and in Afghanistan (2001–2002).[1] All four wars have been fought in or near significant oil-producing areas. All four involved reliance on proxies who were also major international drug-traffickers.[2] The American habit of training, arming, and financing its drug-trafficking allies, in order to help secure oil resources abroad, has been a major factor in the huge increase in global illicit drug-trafficking since World War Two.

This pattern is further reinforced when we consider two of America's major indirect interventions of the same period: support for the Nicaraguan Contras (1981–1988) and the Afghan *mujahedin* (1979–1991). The CIA contracted for Contra support in Central America with an airline owned by a ringleader of the largest cocaine network in the region (Scott, 2000, p. 30).[3] By providing funds for Gulbuddin Hekmatyar, a drug-trafficker selected for support by Pakistani intelligence (the Interservices Intelligence Directorate, or ISI), the CIA helped propel Hekmatyar into becoming, for a while, the largest heroin trafficker in Afghanistan and perhaps the world (McCoy, 1991, p. 19).

The American dependence on drug proxies can be traced to the CIA decision, in 1949–1950, to provide arms and logistic support to the residual forces of the Chinese Guomindang in Burma.[4] This evolved into the much larger program of support for the opium-growing Hmong tribesmen in northeastern Laos. In the wake of the domestically unpopular Vietnam War, the U.S., in asserting a more and more explicit geostrategic interest in oil reserves throughout the world, has continued to seek out local drug proxies as a supplement or alternative to the use of U.S. armed forces.

I am not suggesting that concerns about oil and gas have dictated every U.S. policy move. On the contrary, when Clinton in 1996 was urged to recognize the Taliban by the U.S. oil company Unocal, which was eager to build a gas pipeline through the country, he declined to do so. Pressure from women's groups, appalled by the Taliban's anti-feminist policies, proved decisive (Rashid, 2001, pp. 173–175, 182).

In general oil is a major factor, not in determining just how or when U.S military engagement occurred in a given area, but rather why the U.S. inclines towards intervention in the first place. Over the long haul, since World War Two, it has been oil interests that have dictated the general disposition of U.S. foreign policy. In Central Asia today, these interests transcend the issue of a single nation or pipeline: the goal is access to and control over the immense oil and gas fields of the Caspian basin.

I propose to show that this recurring convergence between oil and drugs is not a coincidence, but a feature of what I have called the deep politics of U.S. foreign policy – those factors in policy formation which are usually repressed rather than acknowledged. The role of oil in U.S. geostrategic thinking is generally acknowledged. Less recognized has been the role of drug proxies in waging and financing conflicts that would not have been financed by Congress and U.S. taxpayers.

The phenomenon I am describing is sometimes characterized as blowback: the CIA's own term for unintended consequences at home of covert (and usually illegal) programs designed for abroad. But the term, by suggesting an accidental and lesser spin-off, misrepresents the dimensions and magnitude of the drug traffic which the U.S. helped re-launch after World War II. That drug traffic has multiplied and spread through the world like a malignant cancer. It has also branched out into other areas – notably money laundering and people smuggling – which like the drug traffic itself have contributed to the problem of terrorism we now face. Of course the U.S. reliance on drug proxies, at risks which were always clear, was motivated by the desire to secure access to natural resources in the Third World – principally oil.

I prefer to characterize what is happening by a general proposition, which is that covert operations, when they generate or reinforce autonomous political power, almost always outlast the specific purpose for which they were designed. Instead they enlarge and become part of the hostile forces the U.S. has to contend with. To put it in terms I find more precise, *parapolitics*, the exercise of power by covert means, tends to metastasize into *deep politics*, an interplay of unacknowledged forces over which the original parapolitical agent no longer has control.

Other examples could also be put forward. In 1998 the U.S. intervened in Kosovo, on behalf of a Kosovo Liberation Army which shortly earlier the U.S. State Department had described as a drug-financed terrorist force.[5] This was after talk of the Balkans as a route for a Western pipeline to transport oil from the newly exploited oil fields of Central Asia.[6]

In the 1980s, the CIA helped arrange a support network for the Nicaraguan Contras with the help of a drug cartel (the Matta Ballesteros-Caro Quintero-Félix Gallardo cartel) operating through Mexico. DEA, at the same time, had identified this cartel as a major target – accounting for a major share (perhaps a third, perhaps more than half) of all the cocaine moving between Colombia and the United States (McClintick, 1993, pp. 227–228; *Newsweek*, 05/15/85; Scott, 2000, pp. 29–32). The CIA's over-riding of DEA's enforcement priority reflected the CIA's involvement with its Mexican counterpart the DFS, and through them with the chief Mexican drug traffickers, a powerful right-wing force in oil-rich Mexico (Scott & Marshall, 1998, pp. 37–42).

But the clearest and most important case of consequential parapolitics was the decision of the U.S., in April and May 1979, to arm *mujahedin* guerrillas

in Afghanistan, at least one of whom was already known as a drug-trafficker
with his own heroin refineries. In the subsequent years Afghan-Pakistani opium
production soared. Almost no heroin from this area reached the U.S. before
1979, yet according to official U.S. sources it supplied 60% of U.S. heroin by
1980 (Smith, 1982, pp. 2–3; U.S. General Accounting Office, 1988; Scott, 1992,
p. 127; McCoy, 1991).

Yet this scandal was kept out of the mainstream U.S. press until the CIA
support was winding down. Belatedly, in 1990, the *Washington Post* (05/13/90)
reported that U.S. officials had failed to investigate drug trafficking by Pakistan's
intelligence service, the ISI (Inter Services Intelligence), and Gulbuddin
Hekmatyar, the top CIA-ISI client in Afghanistan, "because U.S. narcotics
policy in Afghanistan has been subordinated to the war against Soviet influence
there" (*Washington Post*, 5/13/90; McCoy, 1991, p. 459).

* * * * *

The examples cited above, of drug factors underlying U.S. interventions, illustrate what I mean by deep politics. The point is not to suggest that the increase
in drug consumption was a conscious aim of high-level U.S. planning, but that
it was a direct consequence of policy decisions. There are however grounds for
considering a different question: whether successive crises in the illicit drugs
industry were a factor in promoting the successful pressures and maneuvers of
some U.S. sectors and allies for a U.S. involvement in an Asian war. This is
a question asked in my book, *The War Conspiracy* (Scott, 1972, p. 205).
Although I had partly retreated from this question by the time I finished the
book in 1971, conspicuous recent developments have persuaded me to revive
it today.

I do not believe that the U.S. Government intervened militarily as a conscious means of maintaining control over the global drug traffic. However
conscious decisions were definitely made, time after time, to ally the U.S. with
local drug proxies. The U.S. motives for doing so were usually to minimize
the costs and exposure of direct engagement. However the drug proxies appear
to have exploited these conditions of non-accountability with escalations to meet
their own drug agendas, particularly at moments when the survival of the drug
traffic was threatened.

The whole history of the U.S. in the Far East since World War II has involved
from the beginning a drug-trafficking proxy – the GMD – that from the days
of the China Lobby had obtained or purchased significant support within the
U.S. political establishment. Although the picture is a complex one defying
reduction, one can certainly see the role of the China Lobby as a factor in the
events leading to America's first war on the Asian mainland – the Korean War

in 1950 (Cumings, 1990, pp. 106–117, 599–602). This was right after the victorious armies of Mao Zedong began to eliminate Chinese opium, the source of 85% of the world's heroin.

Furthermore drugs from regions where the CIA has been active have tended to migrate through other countries of CIA penetration, and more importantly through and to agencies and groups that can be classified as CIA assets. In the 1950s opium from Indochina traveled through Iran and Lebanon to the Corsican mafia in Marseille and the Sicilian mafia under Lucky Luciano (Scott, 1980, pp. 14–15). In the 1980s *mujahedin* heroin was reaching the Sicilian mafia via the Turkish Grey Wolves, who "worked in tandem with the Turkish Army's Counter-Guerrilla Organization, which functioned as the Turkish branch of the CIA's multinational 'stay behind' program" (Lee, 1997, p. 202). The routes shifted with the politics of the times, but the CIA denominator remained constant.

The following sections examine two moments when U.S. wars became deeply intertwined with the world drug traffic, beginning with the most recent.[7]

II. RESTORING DRUG FLOWS AFTER THE TALIBAN

In October 2001, a UN Report confirmed that the Taliban had successfully eliminated the year's opium production in Afghanistan, which in recent years had supplied 90% of Europe's heroin. However it appears that what would have been the world's largest curtailment of opium production in half a century has been reversed. Following the defeat of the Taliban, farmers began replanting wheat fields with opium poppy; and it is now anticipated that the 2002, opium may equal about 85% of the 4,500 tonnes harvested in 1999 (*Washington Post*, 12/10/01; *San Francisco Chronicle*, 12/21/01; *Financial Times*, 02/18/02).

On October 16, 2001, the United Nations Office for Drug Control and Crime Prevention (United Nations Office for Drug Control and Crime Prevention, 2001) released its Afghanistan Annual Opium Poppy Survey for 2001. It reported that the Taliban ban on opium in 2000 was almost universally enforced. The estimated 2001 crop of 185 metric tonnes was only 6% of Afghanistan's 2000 total of 3,276 tonnes, which had been more than half the world's output. Over 90% of this year's crop came from provinces under the control of America's eventual allies the Northern Alliance, where the area under cultivation radically increased. Helmand Province under the Taliban, the highest cultivating area in 2000, recorded no poppy cultivation in the 2001 season.

The UNDCP Report further noted that the approximately 3,100 tonne reduction in 2001 opium production in Afghanistan (compared to 2000) was not offset by increases in other countries. As *Jane's Intelligence Review* (10/10/01) noted, "the

ban imposed by Taliban supreme leader Mullah Mohammad Omar in July 2000
. . . resulted in some 70% of the world's illicit opium production being wiped out
virtually at a stroke."

Those skeptical about Mullah Omar's motives for the ban speculated that the
Taliban held substantial reserves of processed opium and wished to drive up
prices. Nevertheless even the U.S. State Department reported (2001) that the
Taliban's ban had been "remarkably successful," reducing total Afghan opium
production from 3,656 tons in 2000 to 74 tons in 2001. More credible explanations stress the Taliban's efforts to gain legitimacy and recognition from the
U.S. and other nations, a policy that proved abortive. Despite the Taliban ban,
Afghanistan remained (in the Report's words) "one of the world's leading opium
producers by virtue of continued cultivation in its northern provinces [controlled
by the Northern Alliance]."

As the Taliban was ousted from province after province in 2001, starving
farmers everywhere started to replant the one lucrative crop available to them,
often at the behest of local commanders. The crop augured a return of
warlordism to Afghanistan – regional commanders and armies financed by the
opium in their area, jealously refusing to relinquish such a lucrative income
source to a central government. Thus there could be a revival of the vicious
internecine feuds that took so many civilian lives in the 1990s, after the Soviet
withdrawal. As of Spring 2002, it appears that there will be a token eradication
campaign only, with ineffective enforcement and an inadequate budget of $50
million (DRCNet, 2002; *New York Times*, 4/01/02).

The London *Observer* (11/10/01) reported that "Western and Pakistani
officials fear that, within a year or two, Afghanistan could again reach its peak
production figures of 60,000 hectares of poppies producing 2,800 tonnes of
opium – more than half the world's output. It reported further on 12/10/01 that,
"With the Taliban gone, Afghanistan's farmers are going back to their old,
lucrative ways. In the tribal areas of Pakistan, where most of the opium is
processed, prices have plummeted in expectation of a bumper crop."

The *Financial Times* (02/18/02), reported: "The U.S. and United Nations
have ignored repeated calls by the international anti-drugs community to address
the increasing menace of Afghanistan's opium cultivation, threatening a rift
between Europe and the U.S. as they begin to reconstruct the country." It
predicted that the Afghan opium crop for 2002 would reach 4,500 tons.

The initial failure of the U.S. press to report or comment on these developments was an ominous sign that the U.S. Government might be prepared to
see its former protégés finance themselves once again through the drug traffic.
More ominous was active disinformation by officials of the U.S. Government.
The Taliban's drastic reduction in opium cultivation was ignored, and indeed

misrepresented, by CIA Director George Tenet (2001) in his report to Congress on 2/7/01, in a speech that threatened retaliatory strikes against the Taliban: "Production in Afghanistan has been exploding, accounting for 72% of illicit global opium production in 2000. The drug threat is increasingly intertwined with other threats. For example, the Taliban regime in Afghanistan, which allows Bin Laden and other terrorists to operate on its territory, encourages and profits from the drug trade."

On January 17, 2002, Afghanistan's new leader Hamid Karzai issued a new ban on opium poppy cultivation, and promised to work with donors to assure it could be implemented. However, as the State Department (2001) reported, "Whether factions will follow a ban on poppy cultivation, issued by the Interim Authority is uncertain. The Northern Alliance, for example, has, so far as the U.S. is aware, taken no action against cultivation and trafficking in the area it controls. There have also been recent reports of farmers cultivating a second opium crop in Northern Alliance-controlled areas."

The result has been that drugs have continued to flow north into Tajikistan and Kyrgyzstan, where they finance Islamist radical groups. Author-journalist Ahmed Rashid (2002, pp. 178, 214–216) has reported the conviction of Tajik officials that the main drug-financed group they faced, the Islamic Movement of Uzbekistan or IMU, was being covertly assisted by Russia, "because Moscow was trying to pressure [Uzbek dictator] Karimov into accepting Russian troops and greater Russian influence in Uzbekistan. . . . Other Tajik officials claimed that the IMU was supported by Saudi Arabia and Pakistan, who were backing Islamic movements in Central Asia in order to gain leverage in the region." Rashid himself confirms both Saudi funds and ISI "discreet support" for the IMU, adding that "senior ISI officials are convinced that the IMU has close intelligence links to Russia."

We are still waiting for a clearer American resolve to deal with the restored drug flows it has created, for adequate funds to restore the shattered Afghan economy, and for a firm commitment to address the problem of warlordism. Until then one has to believe that once again the U.S. is unprepared to challenge the drug politics of its proxies in the region. One can even ask if there are not those in the U.S. Government who, like their Russian counterparts, accept the corruption of the Central Asian States through drugs as a means of increasing influence over politicians there.[8]

III. 1979: DRUG-INDUCED WAR?

The situation in 2001 recreated many elements of the 1980s, when, in the words of the *Washington Post* (05/13/90), U.S. officials ignored heroin trafficking by the *mujahedin* "because U.S. narcotics policy in Afghanistan has been subordinated to the war against Soviet influence there."

The consequences of that official toleration of trafficking have been summarized vividly by Michael Griffin (2001, pp. 145–146):

> By the mid-1980s, the processing and export of heroin had created a black economy in Pakistan of about $8 billion – half the size of the official one – and Pakistan's military administration was showing signs of evolving into a fully-blown narco-government. . . . The number of Pakistani addicts, meanwhile, had spiralled from nil in 1979 to between 1.2 and 1.7 million at the end of 1988. Such a rapid rate would have been impossible without the protection or active collaboration of the ISI which, empowered by CIA funding and arms deliveries, had grown from a small military department into a modern intelligence network with a staff of 150,000 and hundreds of millions of dollars a year at its disposal. . . . The U.S. colluded in the development of this new heroin source for fear of undermining the CIA's working alliance for the *mujahedin*.[9]

Many authors besides Griffin have seen this enormous expansion of the drug trade as a by-product of the anti-Soviet war. The total contraband economy in Pakistan, for example, now amounts to $15 billion (Orth, 2002, p. 178). But there are signs that opium traffickers did more than just profit from the war: they may have helped induce it. It is certain that the build-up of opium and heroin production along the Afghan-Pakistani frontier was not a consequence of the war: it preceded it. What particularly catches our eye is that, in 1979 just as in 2001, the war helped avert what would otherwise have been an acute drop in world opium production from earlier heights.

In his important book *The Politics of Heroin,* Alfred McCoy notes that heroin from Southern Asia had been insignificant in the global market until in the late 1970s there was a two-year failure of the monsoon rains in the Burma-Laos area. In the wake of this drought Pakistan cultivation increased and heroin labs opened in the Northwest Frontier region by 1979 (a fact duly noted by the Canadian *Maclean's Magazine* of April 30, 1979).

McCoy (1991, pp. 447–448; cf. Haq, 2000, p. 194; Griffin, 2001, p. 148) notes the subsequent increase: "By 1980 Pakistan-Afghan opium dominated the European market and supplied 60% of America's illicit demand as well."[10] He also records that Gulbuddin Hekmatyar controlled a complex of six heroin laboratories in the Koh-i-Sultan district of Baluchistan, a region (we are told elsewhere) "where the ISI was in total control."

This timetable raises the same question as events in 2001. What forces led the CIA in May 1979, armed with an NSC authorization from Brzezinski one month earlier, to work with the Pakistani ISI and their protégé Hekmatyar, in the context of an already burgeoning heroin trade (McCoy, 1991, p. 451) that would come to dominate the activities of the ISI-Hekmatyar connection?

Before that time the CIA had already cultivated Pakistani assets that would become an integral part of the Afghan arms pipeline. One was the Gulf Group shipping line of the Gokal brothers, a firm that was heavily involved in shipping goods to Third World countries for American aid programs (Truell & Gurwin, 1992, p. 123). Another, allegedly, was BCCI, the biggest financier of Gulf Group (Kerry & Brown, 1992, pp. 318–319). BCCI's Chairman Agha Hasan Abedi had been suspected of links to U.S. intelligence even before he founded BCCI in 1972. BCCI's inside connection to the CIA appears to have been strengthened in 1976, when under CIA Director George Bush, "the CIA strengthened its relationships with so-called friendly Arab intelligence agencies. One of the most important of these was Saudi Arabia's intelligence service [the Istakhbarat], run by Kamal Adham, Prince Turki [al-Faisal al-Saud], and Abdul-Raouf Khalil, all of whom were BCCI insiders" (Truell & Gurwin, 1992, p. 130).

BCCI's links with the CIA – and more specifically with CIA Director Bush and his eventual successor William Casey, are said to have increased in 1976, after Bush's non-reappointment by Jimmy Carter. At this time the swelling ranks of ex-CIA operatives, dismissed for the sake of a down-sized clandestine service, are said to have combined to create a "shadow" "CIA-in-exile" – an "off-the-books group made up of the old boys" (Trento, 2001, pp. 410, 467). It has been alleged that in 1976 CIA Director Bush acted with British Intelligence and with William Casey (who at the time was campaign manager for Reagan's first presidential campaign) to help set up the Cayman Island affiliate (and intelligence connection) of the BCCI (Loftus & Aarons, 1994, p. 395).[11] The purpose was to establish BCCI as "an intelligence consortium among the British, the Americans, and the Arabs."[12]

According to this theory, the Syrian drug dealer Monzer al-Kassar, who had been recruited by British intelligence, "played a key role in this. . . . He convinced all the terrorist groups, from Abu Nidal to the Marxists, to transfer their accounts to the new BCCI branch in London. There the secret service could easily wiretap and decipher every coded transfer"[13] (Loftus & Aarons, 1994, p. 395). The Kerry-Brown Senate Report on BCCI confirmed that information on the Monzer al-Kassar and Abu Nidal accounts at the London BCCI branch had been passed on to British and American intelligence, by the branch manager who was apparently "a paid informant" (Kerry & Brown, 1992, pp. 68, 611). It also criticized the "casual manner" in which BCCI had been regulated in England, leading to a climax in which "the Bank of England had . . . inadvertently become partner to a cover-up of BCCI's criminality"[14] (Kerry & Brown, 1992, pp. 361–363).

A third firm that became part of the Afghan arms pipeline was Global International Airways of Kansas City, a firm that had already expanded in 1979, thanks to "money borrowed from an Arabian international bank" – allegedly BCCI (Pizzo et al, 1991, p. 89).

From the outset Abedi's entry into U.S. banking was tied to the achievement of personal influence to achieve national policy changes, possibly with the help of pro-Arab elements in the CIA. Some of this personal influence was with President Jimmy Carter, after a number of favors to Carter's embattled Budget Director, Bert Lance. Long after leaving the presidency, Carter continued to tour the world in Abedi's BCCI plane, allowing Abedi to profit from joint appearances with Carter in Kenya, Ghana, Pakistan, Bangladesh, China, Thailand, and the Soviet Union, "all key targets of BCCI business development"[15] (Beaty & Gwynne, pp. 195–196).

However Abedi's efforts with Carter met with only limited success after 1979. In that year the U.S. Government alienated the Saudis by brokering a Camp David settlement which failed to satisfy Saudi demands for the relinquishment by Israel of East Jerusalem and the Temple Mount (Lacey, 1981, pp. 451–455). In April 1979 the U.S. also stopped economic aid to Pakistan, because of its development, financed by BCCI and by drugs, of an atomic bomb (*New York Times*, 7/16/80 4/16/79; *Washington Post*, 4/18/79; Beaty & Gwynne, 1993, pp. 238, 255, 272–277). Meanwhile Saudi intelligence and BCCI continued to have better relations with some CIA personnel than with the White House.[16] BCCI's strenuous efforts to acquire an American bank in Washington, starting in 1978, were unsuccessful as long as Carter was President. However they were unanimously approved in 1981, under the new Reagan-Bush Administration (Adams & Frantz, 1992, pp. 64–72).[17]

In Pakistan, meanwhile, Abedi was extremely close to General Mohammed Zia-ul-Haq, who seized power in 1977. Abedi and Zia also met frequently with Fazle Haq or Huq, the man whom Zia appointed Military Governor of the Northwest Frontier Province, and allegedly the patron of the Pakistani heroin refiners who bought the *mujahedin* opium (Lifschultz, 1992, p. 342; Truell & Gurwin, 1992, pp. 160–161; Labrousse, 1991, p. 110). Like Abedi, Fazle Haq developed a reputation as a CIA asset, as well as a reputation with Interpol by 1982 as an international narcotics trafficker (Beaty & Gwynne, 1993, p. 52; Lifschultz, p. 342).

Drugs may have been at the heart of this relationship from the outset. A BCCI informant told U.S. authorities that Abedi's influence with Zia "benefited from the backing of a Pakistani named Fazle Haq, who was . . . heavily engaged in narcotics trafficking and moving the heroin money through the bank" (Beaty & Gwynne, 1993, p. 48).[18] DEA Headquarters in Washington told reporters they knew nothing about Fazle Haq; but a highly placed U.S. official explained to *Time* correspondent Jonathan Beaty that this was because Haq "was our man . . . everybody knew that Haq was also running the drug trade," and "BCCI was completely involved" (Beaty & Gwynne, 1993, p. 52).

It is well known that Brzezinski subsequently claimed responsibility for the CIA-ISI intervention in Afghanistan. But in a 1989 interview Fazle Haq maintained that it was the Pakistanis (including himself) who pressured Brzezinski to back the ISI clients in Afghanistan: "I told Brzezinski you screwed up in Vietnam and Korea; you better get it right this time" (Lamb, 1991, p. 222).[19] In his book *Drugs in South Asia*, M. Emdad-ul Haq (2000, pp. 185, 187) speculates further that Fazle Haq was the "foreign trained adviser" who, according to *The Hindustan Times*, had suggested to General Zia that he use drug money to meet the Soviet challenge (Goodson, 2001; Amin & Schiltz, 1984, p. 381).[20]

It is clear that in May 1979, months before the Soviet invasion, the ISI put the CIA in contact with Hekmatyar, the ISI protégé who would become the central figure in *mujahedin* drug-trafficking (McCoy, 1991, p. 451; Lifschultz, 1992, pp. 321–323, 326). The CIA did so at a time the international heroin trade had suffered a major drop-off in opium from the Golden Triangle, and thus needed to build up a new source. After Pakistan banned opium cultivation in February 1979, and Iran followed suit in April, the absence of legal controls in the Pashtun areas of Pakistan and Afghanistan "attracted Western drug cartels and 'scientists' [including "some 'fortune-seekers' from Europe and the U.S."] to establish heroin processing facilities in the tribal belt" (Haq, 2000, p. 88).[21] All this new attention from "the international drug syndicates" was apparently *before* either the CIA active intervention in Afghanistan in August 1979 or the Soviet invasion in December.[22]

No one can doubt the importance of drug trafficking to the ISI, both as an asset in support of policy goals, and also (for some) as a source of personal profit. Through the 1980s and 1990s, the ISI clearly allowed Hekmatyar to use drugs to increase his influence vis-à-vis other Afghan commanders over which the ISI had less control (Orth, 2002, pp. 170, 152). (As late as 2001, Orth observes, one ISI general was convicted in Pakistan for having "assets disproportionate to his known sources of income.")

Control of drug flows appears to have become part of the CIA-ISI strategy for carrying the Afghan War north into the Soviet Union. As a first step, Casey appears to have promoted a plan suggested to him by Alexandre de Marenches, that the CIA supply drugs on the sly to Soviet troops (Cooley, 2001, p. 128; Beaty & Gwynne, 1993, pp. 305–306). Although de Marenches subsequently denied that the plan went forward, there are reports that heroin, hashish, and even cocaine from Latin America soon reached Soviet troops; and that the CIA-ISI-linked bank BCCI, along with "a few American intelligence operatives were deeply enmeshed in the drug trade" before the war was over (Beaty & Gwynne, 1993, p. 306; Allix, 1998, pp. 35, 95). Maureen Orth (2002, pp. 170–171) heard from Mathea Falco, head of International Narcotics Control for the State Department under Jimmy Carter, that the CIA and ISI together encouraged the *mujahedin* to addict the Soviet troops.[23]

But the plans went farther. In 1984, during a secret visit by CIA Director Casey to Pakistan, "Casey startled his Pakistani hosts by proposing that they take the Afghan war into enemy territory – into the Soviet Union itself. . . . Pakistani intelligence officers – partly inspired by Casey – began independently to train Afghans and funnel CIA supplies for scattered strikes against military installations, factories and storage depots within Soviet territory. . . . The attacks later alarmed U.S. officials in Washington, who saw military raids on Soviet territory as àn incredible escalation,' according to Graham Fuller, then a senior U.S. intelligence [CIA] official who counseled against any such raids" (*Washington Post*, 7/19/92).

"Thus it was," according to Pakistani Brigadier Mohammed Yousaf (Adkin & Yousaf, 2001, p. 189), "the U.S. that put in train a major escalation of the war which, over the next three years, culminated in numerous cross-border raids and sabotage missions north of the Amu Darya." According to Ahmed Rashid (2002, p. 43; 2001, p. 129), "In 1986 the secret services of the United States, Great Britain, and Pakistan agreed on a plan to launch guerrilla attacks into Tajikistan and Uzbekistan." The task "was given to the ISI's favorite Mujaheddin leader Gulbuddin Hikmetyar," who by this time was already supplementing his CIA and Saudi income with the proceeds of his heroin labs "in the Koh-i-Sultan area [of Pakistan], where the ISI was in total control" (Haq, 2000, p. 189). At this same time the CIA also helped ISI and Saudi Arabia distribute in the Soviet Union thousands of Korans that had been translated into Uzbek, an important contribution to the spread of Islamism in Central Asia today (Adkin & Yousaf, 2001, p. 193; Rashid, 2002, p. 223).

Casey was an oil man, and his Central Asian initiative of 1984 was made at a time when right-wing oil interests in Texas already had their eyes on Caspian Basin oil. His cross-border guerrillas, recruited from ethnic Uzbeks and Tajiks, evolved in time into the heroin-financed Islamist groups like the IMU who are the scourge of Central Asia today (Adkin & Yousaf, 2001; Alix, 1998, p. 100).

There is also a second question: how far back did this use of Hekmatyar and drugs go, and who originated it? Did CIA initiate the May 1979 contact with Hekmatyar as part of Carter's and Brzezinski's national policy? Or did Abedi, Haq and company, enjoying a special relationship with pro-Saudi elements in the CIA, arrange the contact on behalf of drug interests that would soon profit handsomely (Kerry-Brown Report, 1993, pp. 49–51; Truell & Gurwin, 1992,

p. 160)? Or did the CIA strengthen the drug-trafficking position of its friends like BCCI and Fazle Haq, because it feared the Soviet-backed and heroin-financed intelligence activities among Muslims of men like Rifaat Assad, who controlled the drugs and laboratories of Lebanon's Bekaa valley (Loftus & Aarons, 1994, pp. 381–382)?

If that question cannot yet be definitively answered, it is clear that BCCI and its affiliated Gokal shipping interests (and possibly Global International Airways) soon formed the backbone of the CIA-ISI arms pipeline to Gulbuddin Hekmatyar. And the U.S., fully conscious of Hekmatyar's drug-trafficking and anti-Americanism, never exerted pressure to have the ISI deny him U.S. aid (Bergen, 2002, pp. 67, 70). This inaction is the more striking because of Hekmatyar's conspicuous failure to contribute to the *mujahedin* military campaign.

IV. CONCLUSION: U.S. RESPONSIBILITY FOR INCREASES IN GLOBAL DRUG-TRAFFICKING

When the CIA began its covert involvement in Burma in the early 1950s, local opium production was in the order of 80 tons a year. Ten years later, thanks to KMT warlords supported by CIA and Civil Air Transport (later Air America), the region produced 300–400 tons a year (McCoy, 1991, pp. 162, 286–287). During the Vietnam War, production at one point reached 1200 tons a year. By 1971 there were also seven heroin labs in the region, just one of which, close to the forward CIA base of Ban Houei Sai in Laos, was estimated to produce 3.6 tons of heroin a year.

With the waning of the Vietnam War, opium production in the Golden Triangle also declined. In the case of Laos, it plummeted, from 200 tons in 1975 to 30 tons in 1984 (Scott, 1992, pp. 126–127). Heroin consumption in the United States also declined. Although the decline in Laotian production has been attributed to drought conditions, a related factor was clearly the increase in cultivation in the so-called Golden Crescent along the Pakistani-Afghan border, from 400 tons in 1971 to 1,200 tons in 1978 (McCoy, 1991, p. 446). This coincided with a number of political developments in the region, including an increase in Pakistani support for Afghan Islamic resistance movements after a left-wing Afghan coup in 1973 (Haq, 2000, pp. 175–186; Rashid, 2001, pp. 12–13).

The decline in U.S. heroin consumption also occurred in the context of an increase in other areas, notably Europe and Australia. In the case of Australia, the first major drug imports were financed by the Nugan Hand Bank, organized in part by veterans of U.S. Special Forces and CIA in Laos. The bank combined drug financing with arms deals and support for CIA covert operations in other regions such as Africa (Marshall, Scott & Hunter, 1987, pp. 36–40; Marshall,

1991, pp. 55–56; Kwitny, 1987). The Australian surge occurred just as Richard Nixon inaugurated a "war on drugs" to keep opium and heroin from reaching the United States.[24]

The U.S. military intervention in Colombia has also been accompanied, as I (1992, pp. 126–127) predicted in 1991, by a dramatic increase in coca production (from 3.8 to 12.3 thousand hectares between 1991 and 1999). These boosts are cumulative, and up to now not permanently reversible. The U.S. Bureau of Narcotics reported in 1970 that annual illicit opium production at that time amounted to from 1,250 to 1,400 tons, more than half of it coming from the Golden Triangle of Burma, Laos, and Thailand (which before World War II accounted for only about 47 tons) (McCoy, 1991, p. 191). In 1999 the UN put the opium production of Afghanistan alone at 4,600 tons, or 70% of the world's crop (Cooley, 2001, p. 139).

The strengthening of the global narcotics traffic has fueled other smuggling and related criminal activities, leading to the consolidation of an international criminal milieu. Chinese Triads, Japanese yakuza, Russian gangs, and the mafias of Italy, America and Colombia have now combined into a "worldwide criminal consortium" that is, according to experts, "growing exponentially" (Sterling, 1994, p. 44). Delegates to a global crime conference in November 1994 were informed that organized crime generates $750 billion annually; many of these illicit dollars end up corrupting markets, institution, businessmen, and of course politicians (Nicaso & Lamothe, 1995, p. xiii). Writing in 1997 of his experience in exposing BCCI, Senator John Kerry concluded that "today globalized crime can rob us not only of our money but also of our way of life" (Kerry, 1997, p. 18).

We can take his words as a prophecy now fulfilled. Although Al-Qaeda and the Taliban might appear on the surface to exemplify a "clash" of civilizations, their activities were paid for, as noted above, by heroin and other transactions at the very heart of this global crime milieu that transcends religious boundaries.

The United States has shown, once again, that it has still not kicked the habit of using and rewarding drug proxies in order to achieve its goals of domination in oil-producing areas abroad. Until it does, we must fear that the world will become an increasingly unstable and dangerous place.

NOTES

1. There were of course a number of briefer military, paramilitary, and covert involvements. What I am about to say about drugs and/or oil can also be adapted to some of these involvements, notably Indonesia and Panama.

2. In this essay I shall not deal at length with the Iraq War, because the scheduled uprising by Kurdish proxies never really took place. They have however been accused of drug-trafficking. Concerning them, a well-placed Washington source (Cordesman,

1998) observed that "The only military skill the Iraqi Kurds have ever demonstrated is the ability to fight each other over smuggling rights."

3. The ringleader was Juan Ramon Matta Ballesteros.

4. The proposal was first advocated by Gen. Claire Chennault, a friend of Jiang Kaishek and owner of the airline Civil Air Transport, that was later taken over for this purpose by the CIA, and still later renamed Air America.

5. According to the *Washington Times* (5/3/99), "In 1998, the U.S. State Department listed the KLA – formerly known as the Ushtria Clirimtare e Kosoves, UCK – as an international terrorist organization, saying it had bankrolled its operations with proceeds from the international heroin trade and from loans from known terrorists like Osama bin Laden." The *Times* of London (3/24/99) also reported that the Kosovo Liberation Army (KLA) is allegedly funded by profits from narcotics trafficking.

6. *The Guardian* (01/15/01) reported: "During the 1999 Balkans war, some of the critics of Nato's intervention alleged that the western powers were seeking to secure a passage for oil from the Caspian sea. This claim was widely mocked. . . . For the past few weeks, a freelance researcher called Keith Fisher has been doggedly documenting a project which has, as far as I can discover, has been little-reported in any British, European or American newspaper. It is called the Trans-Balkan pipeline, and it's due for approval at the end of next month. Its purpose is to secure a passage for oil from the Caspian sea."

7. In my book *Drugs, Oil and War*, I look also at the examples of Colombia and above all Indochina, where the documentation of U.S. support for drug traffickers is, thanks to Alfred McCoy, most fully documented.

8. In *Deep Politics and the Death of JFK* (1993, p. 203), I reported how a U.S. oil company employed a major Sicilian mafia figure as managing director of a subsidiary, prior to that subsidiary's securing oil leases in Tunisia. I commented then that "It is normal, not unusual, for the entry of major U.S. firms into Third World countries to be facilitated and sustained, indeed made possible, by corruption." Rashid's book *Jihad* (2001, p. 237) corroborates how Western oil company investments are "creating an extremely wealthy, corrupt minority class" in the Central Asian states, thereby "breeding even greater social discontent."

9. Christina Lamb (1991, p. 195)in *Waiting for Allah:* "The Afghan war had made Pakistan the world's largest supplier of heroin, and by 1989 drugs were bringing in at least \$4 billion a year – more foreign exchange than all Pakistan's legal exports combined." Lamb cites Pakistan Narcotics Control Board figures; also Melvyn Levitsky, U.S. Assistant Secretary of States for International Narcotics, before a House Committee, Washington, 8 January 1989. Giovanni Quaglia, the chief of operations for the UN Office of Drug Control, has estimated that the total contraband economy in Pakistan now amounts to \$15 billion (Orth, 2002, p. 178).

10. The estimate of 800 tons for 1979 was originally published in 1986 in the *Review of United States Narcotics Efforts in the Middle East and South Asia* (3). This figure if true would imply that the Soviet-Afghan War of the 1980s was not accompanied by a significant increase in opium production from the Afghan-Pakistan region, a result few would agree with. U.S. State Department statistics actually "claimed that due to climatic conditions opium production in Pakistan and Afghanistan dropped in the 1980s." But these statistics were contested, not only by local observers but by a 1986 U.S. Congressional Report (Haq, 2000, p. 194).

11. The Cayman Islands affiliate was an inner bank, International Credit & Investment Company Ltd. (ICIC). The law firm that established ICIC for BCCI, Bruce Campbell & Company, also acted as a registered agent for the CIA-related Australian drug bank, Nugan Hand. Nugan Hand and BCCI also used the same auditors, Price Waterhouse (Truell & Gurwin, 1992, p. 125).

12. This theory correlates with the widely-held observation that CIA officers let go by Carter's DCI, Admiral Stansfield Turner, regrouped as a "shadow" Agency with outside backing and funding: "The CIA did not like President Jimmy Carter . . . The wolves in Clandestine Services went for the president's jugular, and eventually destroyed his presidency. . . . [The] non-hiring of George Bush [as DCI] gave momentum to the creation of a CIA in exile. This was a group of out-of-work agents. . . . By the time Reagan and Bush took office, they had a choice of two CIA's they could do business with – one that required oversight by Congress, and another off-the books group made up of the old boys" (Trento, 2001, pp. 466–467).

13. Loftus and Aarons refer to various news stories leaked later by Mossad, such as the following: "The CIA had a covert relationship with BCCI in 1976. At the very same time, George Bush was director of the CIA. We are told the late William Casey . . . met secretly and regularly with the BCCI bank's founder, Aga Hassan Abedi" (Fine, 1992).

14. For a more severe account of British passivity in the BCCI case, see Beaty and Gwynne (1993, pp. 105–107).

15. In the end Carter took millions from Abedi, "including $1.5 million long after BCCI was indicted and convicted for laundering drug money" (Beaty and Gwynne, 1993, p. 63).

16. Kerry-Brown Report (1992, p. 300), citing *New York Times*, 12/6/81: "While Adham was still in place as the CIA's liaison [to the Istakhbarat] in 1977, the CIA station chief for Saudi Arabia, Raymond H. Close, chose to go to work for Adham upon leaving the CIA. . . . As Jeff Gerth of the New York Times reported in 1981 . . . 'some think Mr. Close may still be working for the CIA in some capacity, although he officially retired in 1977. They add that a further complicating factor is that some Saudis privately share the same perception.' The Times account describes how Close had actually given approval to weapons sales from Saudi Arabia to Pakistan in the early 1970s, in contravention to the 'official policy' enunciated by the American ambassador." Cf. (Cooley, 2001, pp. 112–113).

17. Until 1977 Financial General had been controlled by General George Olmsted, the head of OSS China during World War II.

18. The informant, named here as "Mirza," is identified by Adams (1992, p. 257) and the Kerry-Brown Report (1992, pp. 348, 226) as Amir Lodhi.

19. General Fazle Haq, (on Pakistan's confidence that Washington would back their decision to support the Afghan resistance);" quoted in Christina Lamb [Haq's interviewer] (1991, pp. 222, 206), cited in M. Emdad-ul Haq (2000, p. 185).

20. Fazle Haq's story (that the U.S. backing of the *mujahedin* was in response to a Pakistani initiative) is corroborated by Robert Gates of the CIA. His memoir speaks of "an approach by a senior Pakistani official to an Agency officer" in March 1979, four months before Carter "signed the first finding to help the Mujahedin covertly" (Gates, 1996, pp. 144, 146). Haq's suggestion might explain the CIA-backed ISI decision to focus aid on Gulbuddin Hekmatyar, whose Hizb i Islami faction was allegedly ignored and "almost non-existent" during the formation of the first organized Afghan resistance

in Pakistan in mid-1978. See M. Emdad-ul Haq, 187 (cf. 185); citing Amin and Schiltz, 1984, p. 381. Cf. Larry Goodson, *Afghanistan's Endless War: State Failure, Regional Politics, and the Rise of the Taliban* (2001, p. 56; Cooley, 2001, p. 64).

21. The transnational drug presence in Afghanistan was even clearer by the 1990s, when a French journalist (Allix, 1998, pp. 33–34) learned "that 'the Pakistanis' – presumably the ISI's clandestine operators . . . – had actually provided seed grains of a new and more productive species of poppy . . . said to have come from Burma . . . and Africa, probably Kenya" (Cooley, 2001, p. 150; Griffin, 2001, p. 148).

22. According to a contemporary account, Americans and Europeans had started to become involved in drug-smuggling out of Afghanistan from the early 1970s; see Catherine Lamour and Michel R. Lamberti, *The International Connection: Opium from Growers to Pushers* (Lamour & Lamberti, 1974, pp. 190–192).

23. A Tajik sociologist added that she knew "drugs were massively distributed at that time," and that she often heard how Russian soldiers were "invited to taste."

24. Among the unanswered questions about Nugan Hand: Why was its regional branch in Chiangmai, Thailand, located down the hall from the local DEA office? Why did so many CIA veterans become Nugan Hand bank officers, despite their lack of training? Why, when Australian officials asked for FBI help when prosecuting the bank, were their requests for Nugan Hand bank documents turned down by the U.S. on grounds of "national security"?

REFERENCES

Adams, J. R., & Frantz, D. (1992). *A Full Service Bank.* New York: Pocket Books.
Adkin, M., & Yousaf, M. (2001). *The Bear Trap.* Havertown, PA: Casemate.
Allix, S. (1998). *La petite cuillère de Schéhérazade, sure la route de l'héroine.* Paris: Editions Ramsay.
Amin, H., & Schiltz, G. B. (1984). *A Geography of Afghanistan.* Kabul: Centre for Afghanistan Studies.
Beaty, J., & Gwynne, S. (1993). *The Outlaw Bank: A Wild Ride into the Secret Heart of BCCI.* New York: Random House, Inc.
Bergen, P. L. (2002). *Holy War, Inc: Inside the Secret World of Osama bin Laden.* New York: Simon and Schuster.
Cooley, J. K. (2001). *Unholy Wars, New Edition.* London: Pluto Press.
Cordesman, A. (1998). *Los Angeles Times.* November 19.
Cumings, B. (1990). *The Origins of the Korean War: II. The Roaring of the Cataract 1947–1950.* Princeton: Princeton University Press.
DRCNet (2002). March 29 (www.drcnet.org/wol/231/html#afghanopium).
Financial Times (Various citations).
Fine, A. (1992). *Jewish Times.* March 6.
Goodson, L. (2001). *Afghanistan's Endless War: State Failure, Regional Politics, and the Rise of the Taliban.* Seattle: University of Washington Press.
Griffin, M. (2001). *Reaping the Whirlwind: The Taliban Movement in Afghanistan.* London: Pluto Press.
Haq, M. E.-u. (2000). *Drugs in South Asia.* New York: St. Martin's Press.
Jane's Intelligence Review (2001). October 10.
Kerry, J. (1997). *The New War.* New York: Simon & Schuster.

Kerry, J., & Brown, S. H. (1992). *The BCCI Affair: A Report to the Committee on Foreign Relations.* Washingtion, D.C.: United States Senate.

Kwitny, J. (1987). *The Crimes of Patriots.* New York: Simon and Schuster.

Labrousse, A. (1991). *La drogue, l'argent et les armes.* Paris: Fayard.

Lacey, R. (1981). *The Kingdom: Arabia and the House of Sa'ud.* New York: Avon.

Lamb, C. (1991). *Waiting for Allah: Pakistan's Struggle for Democracy.* New York: Viking.

Lamour, C., & Lamberti, M. R. (1974). *The International Connection: Opium from Growers to Pushers.* New York: Pantheon.

Lee, M. A. (1997). *The Beast Reawakens.* Boston: Little Brown.

Lifschultz, L. (1992). *Pakistan: The Empire of Heroin. In War on Drugs: Studies in the Failure of U.S. Narcotics Policy.* Boulder, CO: Westview Press.

Loftus, J., & Aarons, M. (1994). *The Secret War Against the Jews.* New York: St. Martin's.

London Observer (Various citations).

Marshall, J. (1991). *Drug Wars: Corruption, Counterinsurgency and Covert Operations in the Third World.* Forestville, CA: Cohen and Cohen.

Maclean's Magazine (1979). April 30.

Marshall, J., Scott, P. D., & Hunter, J. (1987). *The Iran-Contra Connection: Secret Teams and Covert Operations in the Reagan Era.* Boston: South End Press.

McClintick, D. (1993). *Swordfish: A True Story of Amibition, Savagery, and Betrayal.* New York: Pantheon.

McCoy, A. W. (1991). *The Politics of Heroin: CIA Complicity in the Global Drug Trade,* Completely Revised and Expanded Edition of *The Politics of Heroin in Southeast Asia.* New York: Lawrence Hill Books.

Newsweek (1985). May 15.

New York Times (Various citations).

Nicaso, A., & Lamothe, L. (1995). *Global Mafia: The New World Order of Organized Crime.* Toronto: Macmillan.

Orth, M. (2002). Afghanistan's Deadly Habit. *Vanity Fair*, March.

Pizzo, S., Fricker, M., & Muolo, P. (1991). *Inside Job: The Looting of America's Savings and Loans.* New York: Harper Perennial.

Rashid, A. (2001). *Taliban: Militant Islam, Oil and Fundamentalism in Central Asia.* New Haven: Yale University Press.

Rashid, A. (2002). *Jihad: The Rise of Militant Islam in Central Asia.* New Haven: Yale University Press.

San Francisco Chronicle (Various citations).

Scott, P. D. (1972). *The War Conspiracy: The Secret Road to the Second Indochina War.* Indianapolis: Bobbs-Merrill.

Scott, P. D. (1980). Foreword. In *The Great Heroin Coup*, by H. Kruger. Boston: South End Press.

Scott, P. D. (1992). Honduras, the Contra Support Networks, and Cocaine. In: *War on Drugs: Studies in the Failure of U.S. Narcotics Policy.* Boulder, CO: Westview Press.

Scott, P. D. (1993). *Deep Politics and the Death of JFK.* Berkeley: University of California Press.

Scott, P. D. (2000). *Drugs, Contras, and the CIA: Government Policies and the Cocaine Economy.* Sherman Oaks, CA: From the Wilderness Publications.

Scott, P. D., & Marshall, J. (1998). *Cocaine Politics: Drugs, Armies and the CIA in Central America.* Berkeley and Los Angeles: University of California Press.

Smith, W. F. (1982). Drug Traffic Today: Challenge and Response. *Drug Enforcement*, Summer.

Sterling, C. (1994). *Thieves' World: The Threat of the New Global Network of Organized Crime,* New York: Simon & Schuster.

Tenet, G. J. (2001). Statement by Director of Central Intelligence Agency before the Senate Select Committee on Intelligence, February 7.

The Guardian (Various citations).

The Times (Various citations).

Trento, J. J. (2001). *The Secret History of the CIA*. New York: Forum/Crown/Random House.

Truell, P., & Gurwin, L. (1992). *False Profits: The Inside Story of BCCI, the World's Most Corrupt Financial Empire*. Boston: Houghton Mifflin Company.

United Nations Office for Drug Control and Crime Prevention (2001). *Afghanistan Annual Poppy Survey*.

U.S. Department of State (2001). *International Narcotics Strategy Report*.

U.S. General Accounting Office, D.C. (1988). U.S. Supported Efforts in Burma, Pakistan, and Thailand, GAO/NSIAD-88-94, February.

Washington Post (Various citations).

Washington Times (Various citations).

PART II:
IDEOLOGIES OF RACE

IDEOLOGIES OF RACE AND RACISM

Babacar Camara

ABSTRACT

Racism is an ideology in the Marxian sense, which is why it is so pervasive. One needs to find the common thread in all forms of racism and their theories by placing them against capitalist society's goals and hegemonic strategies. Debates over racism are truly ideological mystifications. Questions of race effectively come down to questions of ideology. Racism is an ideology that is inseparable from the national or international socio-economic and political situation. A brief study of the Republics of Haiti and South Africa under apartheid illustrates how racial and racist ideologies are manipulated to cover up the exploitation of the masses.

Race has become a metaphorical way of referring to and distinguishing forces, events, classes, and expressions of social decay and economic division far more threatening to the body politic than biological race ever was. Expensively kept, economically unsound, a spurious and useless political asset in election campaigns, racism is as healthy today as it was during the enlightenment (p. 63).

Toni Morrison (1993)

There seems little doubt that one of the key questions we shall have to confront in the future is how to understand and tackle the social and political impact of racism, both as set of ideas and as form of political mobilization ... Yet, it is precisely on this issue that current research seems to be least enlightening, since researchers have not yet, by and large, had much to say about reasons why we have seen the resurgence of racist ideas in recent time (p. 216).

John Solomos and Les Back (1996)

Confronting 9-11, Ideologies of Race, and Eminent Economists,
Research in Political Economy, Volume 20, pages 85–118.
ISBN: 0-7623-0984-9

INTRODUCTION

Racism has become more pervasive in the sense that its power and "success" reside in its ability to secrete a variety of forms and contents. One can argue the particularities of racism in Hitler's Germany or Europe in general; the USA, South Africa, or even the changes racism may produce or incorporate today. But that diversity is precisely the strength that allows racism to survive. Already existing conflicts feed into various racisms, to produce situations such as black on black crime or ethnic antagonism and profiling, among others, and to fragment *Racism*. As such, they prevent the struggle from precisely stating its object: the target is confused with its shadow.

With Marxian lenses, the differences between the different aspects of racisms or the new forms they take are simply the results of the application/impact of racism on a particular historical, geographical, social, economic and political society. Thus, oppression varies according to historical and geographical conditions, but the victimization of Blacks is one thing that has remained constant. Blacks are plagued by a pervasive racial discrimination whose manifestations, symptoms and consequences may differ from one country to another. In order to explain such a chronicity and diversity, one needs to look into the mechanism that maintains such a status quo and find the common thread in all forms of racism by placing them against capitalist society's goals and strategies. In so doing, one finds that the ideological web that sustains racism is an identical and common one, despite the diverse locations, forms and contents.

Racism is not only social and political but also, it is an ideological force – in the Marxian sense – which explains why it is so pervasive. Moreover, the debate over racism is truly one of concealment of the real object. Questions of race effectively come down to questions of ideology. Therefore, the debate must be global and the questions must necessarily apply to the social and economic structure, which, in the last instance and according to Marxian theory, explains how ideology develops. We argue that race and racism are constructed ideologies and as such, controlled and distributed according to the needs of capitalism, in its conquest of the universe.

Racial and racist ideologies are two sides of the same coin and they are masks, which hide exploitation. No matter how complex and different the mechanisms of racism are, there still are essential characteristics that one can find at the root of any racist society. Therefore, we look for the essential elements in society, to reveal the complex mechanism at work inside a systematized racism. The essentialist approach is a strategy to see through the magma of race theories. Racism has been the subject of endless theories, animated by ideological biases, and one possible way out of this labyrinth of interpretations is to focus on the

elements common to all racist societies. This provides us with a constant
theoretical background for the analysis of any apparently particular racism.

We insert the ideological issues that are addressed into their proper historical
and capitalist contexts, and the Marxist theory allows us to see the common
thread in all forms of racism. Marxist theory is not often seen as relevant
to today's most urgent struggles. In terms of racism, orthodox Marxism is
seen as being useless to the Black struggle because it is economic and class
reductionist and does not recognize the specificities of the African American
oppression.[1] Marxism has even been accused of being racist and an accomplice
to the capitalist exploitation of Black nations.[2] But just as many feminists have
appropriated Louis Althusser's version of Marxist ideology from his essay
"Ideology and Ideological State Apparatuses" (1971), those who undertake the
task to combat racism have much to learn from applying a specifically Marxist
notion of ideology to the interpretation of racism.

Althusser's understanding of ideology as a dynamic, on-going process through
which subjects are created, is understood as a departure from orthodox Marxist
economism, which sees ideology as an epiphenomenal reflection of the base.
For Stanley Aronowitz (1974), Althusser's theory of ideology "has the potential
for overcoming Marxist economism [. . .] and the continuing problems of race,
sex, and ecology" (p. 5). On the other hand, Terry Boswell et al. (1974) explains
how Althusser's theory is marred by a stagnant functionalism, which tends to
reduce ideologies of race, sex and nation to class ideologies and does not come
to grips with social relations outside of production and the state (id.). For me
as well as for Michele Barrett, what is interesting in Althusser's theory is that
he stresses ideology as a lived experience [. . .] and emphasizes that individual
subjects are constructed and reproduced in ideology. In Barrett's words,

> There has been a tendency to locate the oppression [of women] principally at the level of
> ideology, and it is easy to see how feminists, concerned to emphasize the importance
> of gender divisions in the capitalist social formation, have seized on arguments for the
> importance and autonomy of ideological process (p. 31).

In the same order of idea, we re-prioritize ideology, in which racism can be
situated.

Structure of the Analysis

From a Marxian point of view, any discourse is a product of society, which
produces the categories and concepts of our thoughts. In other words, the mental
universe is linked to a determined material and historical basis. In this sense,

our thoughts are the reflection of political, social, and economic conflicts, and racist discourses are no exception. They articulate themselves into an ensemble of categories of thoughts corresponding to a well-determined world and in this case, the capitalist one. We realize that explaining how racist expressions take the forms of oppression, exclusion, persecution, murder or massacre is insufficient. This is why we are looking into the systemized ideology feeding and justifying such acts and situations. We disentangle the web of racism, not only to reveal its intricate process, but also to show that its origin, development and ideas are inseparable from capitalist realities. So far the debate is a-politicized and fragmented, and that is why we seek to reposition the debate where it has always belonged: racism is an ideological invention that serves the dominant class, be it local or global. It has always been about the social structures on which racism rests; therefore, it has always been a political and an ideological question. The role of critical theorists is to help uncover implicit reasons, to explain theoretically the truth, i.e. being able to unmask the contradictions of advanced capitalism. So far, most of them – already seduced by the semiological and structuralist post-modernist approach – ignore essential issues such as money, merchandise, alienation, or ideology. And even when they recognize that racism is a product of capitalism, they still remain caught in the viewpoint of their academic specializations, which refrain from criticizing the totality. Thus, problems are tackled through situations, people and trends that are striving to make up the enunciation. It is a difficult task to find ways to establish necessary distinctions in the formless magma of racist theories from all trends. We hope that the nature of the task will serve as an excuse for the imperfection in our analysis.

Therefore, we start by showing the insufficiency in the humanist position and the postmodernist approach, which tend to look for a plurality of racisms and how culture falls into the ideological sphere. But instead of presenting the various definitions of ideology, we go straight to the Marxist understanding of ideology as a distortion of reality at the service of the dominant class. Then, just to show how racial ideologies can be manipulated by any hegemonic powers, we take a look at the Republic of Haiti as the very example of a victim country, reproducing at the local level the very ideology of "purity" and miscegenation once used by colonial powers, to create and maintain the present-day class structure, which relegates the vast majority of dark Black Haitians to an inferior and exploited mass.

The section on Africa as the ideological "dumping ground" par excellence reveals the mechanism and reasons for a racial ideology. But ideology in Africa is understood as being positive. The adjusted Marxism to the realities of Africa is an instrument of political, social and economic development. At the same time, in the Southern part of the continent, ideology was used to impose racism and to justify the exploitation of Blacks under the system of apartheid. However, the study of South Africa is not a systematic or chronological history. Rather, apartheid is considered one moment of the racist movement, i.e. a mere illustration of racism at work. Our analysis is based on few of the historical and religious myths sustaining racism, which Marianne Cornevin provides in her *Apartheid: Power and Historical Falsification* (1978). Even though apartheid seems to be a thing of the past, nevertheless, South Africa remains the highest illustration and materialization of both the concrete and abstract forms of racism.

The scope of the studies of Haiti and South Africa is severely limited, considering the complexity of their respective history. Nevertheless, in both countries, the ethnic and racial definition is an ideology used to conceal the stark exploitation of the disempowered and disenfranchised Blacks.

I. RACISM AND IDEOLOGY

Racism is often understood as purely emotional and affective. It is like a monster sleeping inside an individual. Therefore, with morale, self-discipline, or will power, racist individuals can control it or rehabilitate themselves. This position is interesting, for it places the problem at an individual level: particular individuals must individually solve the problem. It obviously does not look into the causes of this effect. Questioning the origins of the effect could certainly shed light on how one can be racist in spite of oneself. If one can be racist without meaning it, well, meaning not to be racist should suffice to get rid of it, *once it is conscious*. Such an understanding of the problem falls into some kind of "voluntarism myth". Therefore, the problem is social or collective and an individual solution is a pseudo-solution. On the other hand, however, such a position reveals the psychological aspect of the problem. It does underline the fact that racism is not the consequence of an objective judgment. Racism thus is not the product of an objective reason but rather, an affective, neurotic reaction. That is to say, there is a connection between racism and neurosis and the origin of that connection lies in the frustrations of social life and would consequently trigger aggressive reactions geared to certain minorities and more so, since they are easily recognizable by their common physical traits. This corresponds to the theory of the scapegoat in psychology and comes with a problem: it does not inquire into the social structure, which produces those frustrations and neurotic reactions. Therefore, the insufficiencies reveal themselves in the very way the problem is apprehended: it ignores the social structures that produce racism. Consequently, the situation is rather dramatic as we witness the persistence of racism or its growth, if not its becoming cancerous.

After countless years of assaults by scholars, racism is still holding up. It is present in society more than ever.

The reason for such chronicity is that, the bulk of the criticism against racism does not take into account the capitalist structure, which is the fundamental aspect of the problem, because it sustains racism and feeds on it. Even if some scholars do so, they do not give capitalism its full manipulative power. With the triumph of capitalism, the sphere of communication and its social sciences have secreted a dominant discourse – postmodernism – using a semiologico-symbolico-structuralo-psychoanalytico-linguistic jargon. For this trend, one is no longer dealing with racism as a totality, but just another aspect of the system such as the economic order, education, religion, and art. In John Solomos and Les Back's words (1996), "the goal is to avoid uniform and homogeneous conceptualizations of racism" (p. 17). Quoting David Goldberg (1990), they add: "The presumption of a single monolithic racism is being displaced by the mapping of the multifarious historical formulations of *racisms"* (p. 18).

They may see positive consequences from this broadening of the focus, but for us, such an approach fragments the object of racism and does not aim at any immediate change. It is rather destined to lose itself in reformist aspirations. Therefore, the present-day analyses of racism by postcolonialists and post-modernists are ideological and, as such, limited by a theoretical frame defined by that very ideology, which refrains from questioning the heart of the matter. An objective analysis of the problem must consider racism, as Pierre Paraf (1972) says, "as multiple element problem, which is a skin and blood problem, but which, from the beginning, found itself to be a problem of force between the concurrent needs to satisfy [. . .] and which has become an economic and social problem" (p. 7). Consequently, the fundamental element of our analysis is that the problem is one of force but above all, of concealment of racism. Such an approach does allow us to understand why the birth of modern racism coincided with the European industrial revolution and is stronger today with the global-ization of capitalism. Racism is explained and recognized from very real and spe-cific circumstances, and not only from an idea in a head. Therefore, alongside Wilhelm Reich (1985), I affirm that racism in general has a concrete relation to the economic aims of capitalism, which is finalizing its conquest of the planet. Therefore, humanist or cultural idealism, which considers racism a problem of cultural contact, or clash between differences, is very insufficient.

Racism and Culture

According to Pierre Fougeyrollas (1985), "the difference between racism and cultural prejudices resides in racism's ideological characteristics and that the oldest source of racism resides in cultural prejudices" (p. 74). Therefore an analysis of the dialectic between culture and ideology is necessary to understand racism. Culture can simply be understood as a system of values lived by a society. But if for Alain Tourraine[3] a system of values is a more or less coherent ideology, and Guy Debord[4] considers culture as nothing more than a commodity, it is because capitalist society is based on fierce competitions and on antagonisms between rich and poor. In such a situation, culture cannot be understood out of the total historical movement, which carries it, i.e. the capitalist conquest of the world. This means that neither one aspect of culture nor its totality can claim the innocence of a supra-historicity.

One interesting illustration of culture's role in colonialism is offered by Richard G. Fox in his *Lions of the Punjab* (1985), in which he undertakes the task of revealing culture in the making. His position is that there is no weight of tradition on culture, only a current action. He defines it as:

> A selective construction from the debris and standing structures of the past – contemporary individuals and groups take pieces, not the pattern, of the past and form them into new social arrangements. They do so as they gain consciousness of their material conditions and interests and work to further them (p. 197).

For Fox thus, culture is just a progressive movement and the illustration of his position is the scene of the Punjabi (India) under British colonial rule. Fox sees a new Punjabi culture that he considers totally constructed by the British colonial authority. The British have developed a specific and biological imagery, such as the Punjabi as "lions, martial, courageous and stalwart species of men, women . . ." (p. 2); consequently, "[The British] not only rationalize colonial oppression but also constructed it – they made Europeans see India and act toward her people in particular ways" (p. 3).

However, the Punjabi in turn were able to assimilate that constructed culture and made it theirs. But what really interests me in Fox is that his analysis reveals the connection between culture, ideology and hegemony, and that connection is explained by Raymond Williams (1985):

> Hegemony is a whole body of practices and expectations, over the whole living: our senses and everyday assignment of every energy, our shaping perceptions of our world and ourselves. It is a lived system of meanings and values . . . It thus constitutes a sense of reality for most people in society. It is, that is to say, in the strongest sense a culture but a culture, which has also been seen as the lived dominance and subordination of particular classes (p. 205).

My argument is that if the process of hegemony has a dialectic quality, and that culture can be appropriated or constructed, it is because culture is what Barthes[5] calls mythology and Karl Marx ideology.[6] However, I would be careful not to flatly equate culture with ideology although it is difficult to distinguish between the cultural and the ideological. Ideology as I will explain later – is both conceptual and affective, and part of personal experiences, therefore of culture. In other words, the individual is subjected to the situation of his milieu as well as the general ideology of society. Fougeyrollas expresses it in the following terms: "its [culture] unity is the unity of society or social environment, while its plurality is the plurality of individuals who, by living and playing it, make it so" (p. 38). Therefore, in agreement with Fougeyrollas, I think that ideology is immanent to culture. It dominates culture or better, exercises an influence from within. More precisely, ideology is above and inside culture, which explains its manipulative or structuring power. Emile Durkheim (1912) illustrates it even better, when he explains how in former societies – at the beginning of class and state formation – ethnic religion constantly creates a fusion between what we now call culture and ideology:

> The ancestors' cult and the cult of the cosmo-vital unity was experienced in the sacred dances and constituted great cultural phenomena. By way of ceremonies, society's norms (women's submission to men or youths to elders) were affirmed and reinforced, thereby possessing an ideological character and function in the reproduction of the social order (p. 38).

In such societies, the cultural and the ideological are thus confused as in modern societies where sport, entertainment and politics overlap to form an ideology which, according to Reich, aims at reflecting the economic process of society, and embedding this economic process in the psychic structure of the people who make up society (p. 13).

Our discussion of culture could be more exhaustive, but would be too demanding for this paper. We think that the following exploration of the Marxian understanding of ideology will shed more light on the problem.

II. MARXIAN CONCEPT OF IDEOLOGY

Terry Eagleton finds the term ideology, impossible to define adequately not because scholars are incapable of it, but because ideology has a myriad of meanings that are often incompatible with each other" (p. 1). Indeed the concept of ideology is the most important concept of our epoch, judging by the organization around it of the greatest confusion and the myriad of definitions Eagleton is referring to. Therefore, instead of reviving the quarrel surrounding "ideology," I refer the reader to David McClellan's *Ideology* (1986) and Christopher L. Pine's *Ideology and False Consciousness: Marx and his Historical Progenitors* (1993). I will also not use Guy Debord's understanding of the accumulation of merchandise in capitalist society as the materialization of ideology.[1] Otherwise, as far as writing about Marxism is concerned, there seems to always be a pressure to go back to basics and not to assume that modern readers are familiar with the Marxist theory. Therefore, I am providing a short presentation of Marxian understanding of ideology as a necessary transition to the analysis of the objective and subjective role of racism as an integral part of capitalism. However, my explanations of ideology are twofold: (1) ideology serves the ruling class; it is a state of false consciousness, but also a set of material and subjective conditions which render it indispensable. (2) In the Third World in general and in Africa in particular, Marxism became the panacea for a fast economic recovery after 1960. Ideology was seen as positive and a weapon with which former colonies would accede to a national dignity previously treaded on by colonialism.

For Karl Marx and Frederich Engels, the production of consciousness is directly linked to the material conditions of existence. Therefore, any appreciation of the products of consciousness, therefore of ideology, must be considered in close connection with the social and the political. That is why, in the first part of the *German Ideology* (1983), they affirm:

> We do not set out from what [humans] say, imagine, conceive nor from [humans] as narrated, thought of, imagined, conceived, in order to arrive at [humans] in the flesh. We set out from real, active [humans], and on the basis of their real life process we demonstrate the development of the ideological reflexes and echoes of this life-process (p. 25).

It is from such a perspective that one can see how ideology, while being a specific instance – possessing a relative autonomy to some extent – does not have its proper history or development.

A. Ideology as a Specific Instance

Marx's historical materialism offers two levels of analysis: the social economic structure (the infrastructural level) and its political, moral, legal and religious structure (the superstructural level); in other words, a social existence and a social consciousness, each depending on the other. From such a point of view, the superstructural level coinciding with ideology does appear as a particular instance for any social formation. But Marx and Engels specify, "the production of ideas, of conceptions, of consciousness, is at first directly interwoven with the material activity and the material intercourse of [humans], the language of real life" (p. 24). Such a precision seems to reduce the independence and specificity of the ideological instance, to a reflection, an interpretation of reality. But what is more fundamental for the Marxian approach is the interdependency of the various instances of reality. The ideological instance is a specific instance although an element of social wholeness, which should be understood as a dialectic interaction between the various levels of social reality. Thus, the superstructure, therefore ideology is not the simple reflection of the material basis, but has its proper efficiency, which, combined with the fact that ideology can survive long after the disappearance of the material conditions which gave it birth, provides proof that ideology, while being an element of the totality, while being part of the interaction between the various elements of that totality, has nonetheless a certain (relative) independence. As such, ideology is a specific instance of social reality.

B. The Relative Independence of Ideology

The independence of ideology as explained above – considered in a totality of interactional elements – cannot but be a relative one. Indeed Nicos Poulantzas (1982) states:

> Ideology consists of a specific objective level, of a relatively coherent ensemble of representations, values and beliefs: just as [humans], the agents within a formation participate in an economic and political activity, they also participate in religious, moral, esthetic and philosophical activities (p. 206).

The fact remains that "ideology concerns the world in which [humans] live, their relations to nature, to society, to other [humans] and to their own activity including their own economic and political activity" (p. 206). All this means that ideology is inseparable from the real or society. Moreover, one can say that ideology is omnipresent at all levels of society and even personality. Therefore, an objective analysis of ideology must exclude the idea of considering "ideology in itself." In this order of ideas, ideology is truly the "language of real life" since it reflects the way humans live. Such a position allows us to understand why ideology, being omnipresent and blended into personal experiences, is almost undetectable. That is a difficulty worth mentioning. It remains, as Poulantzas says, that:

> Ideology, as a specific instance of a mode of production and social formation, is constituted within the limits fixed by this mode and this formation in that it offers an imaginary coherence to the unity governing the real contradiction of this formation (p. 208).

It seems, thus, that ideology does not contain in itself its own explanatory principle in the sense "it is constituted within the limits fixed" by a particular mode of production, and consequently by a determined social formation. Such a position finds an echo in Louis Althusser.

> Therefore, the developmental major principle of a particular ideology cannot be found within ideology itself but outside it, in what underlies (l'en-deçà) the particular ideology; its author

as a concrete individual and the *actual story* reflected in this individual development according to the complex ties between the individual and his history (p. 63).

Therefore, the independence, of ideology is indeed a relative independence for "the production of ideas, of conceptions, of consciousness is directly interwoven with the material activity." Because of this, ideology does not allow either an intelligibility of itself or an intelligibility of its development, for all this is determined at the level of actual history.

As Marx explains in the *German Ideology*, consciousness and its activities are interwoven with the material conditions of existence. This tie must be understood as a dialectic one: as the concrete and historical material conditions determine consciousness (its development and restructuration), in the same way, consciousness, in turn, can transform the material conditions, and in so doing, can also transform its content. This Marxian approach necessarily rejects accepting the possibility of an "independent" history of ideas while still allowing one to understand that consciousness and its activities can appear as basic realities, i.e. possessing a full independence. And such a situation is only possible because there is an inadequacy between one's idea of reality and reality itself. As Marx says:

Morality, religion, metaphysics, all the rest of ideology and their corresponding forms of consciousness, thus no longer retain the semblance of independence. *They have no history*, no development; but [humans], developing their material productions and their material intercourse, alter, along with their real existence, their thinking and the product of their thinking (p. 25).

Ideology has no history, which does not mean it has no history at all, but simply does not have a proper history, in the sense that history does not reside inside ideology but rather, outside with the history of concrete individuals. That is what Althusser says: "Ideological history is not its own principle of intelligibility [. . .] Ideological history can only be understood through the real history which explains its formations, deformations and their restructurations" (p. 83).

C. Ideology and Social Antagonisms

The Marxian conception of ideology also considers ideology as having a class function. According to Marx, "the ideas of the ruling class are in every epoch the ruling ideas, i.e. the class that is the ruling material force of society, is at the same time its ruling intellectual force" (p. 172). Here again, Althusser adds:

So when we speak of the class function of ideology it must be understood that the ruling ideology is indeed the ideology of the ruling class and that the former serves the latter not only in its rule over the exploited class, but in its own constitution of itself as the ruling class, by making it accept the lived relation between itself and the world as real and justified (p. 235).

Therefore, one must understand that ideology, if it parts from the real, always comes back to it, seizes reality only to represent it in accordance with the "views" of a determined interest group. According to Bernard Magubane (1987), "[ideology] reflects, above all, objective factors. And the very nature of the distortion of truth in the ideology of the exploiting classes is also objectively determined" (p. 47). That is how one should understand Poulantzas' affirmation: "ideologies fix in a relatively coherent universe not only a real but also an imaginary relation: i.e. [humans'] real relation to their conditions of existence in the form of an imaginary relation" (p. 207). This process of transposition of real relations into imaginary relations shows there is indeed an adequacy/ inadequacy between ideology and reality. Such an inversion allows us to understand that if ideology is necessarily distorted, it is because, as Poulantzas says, "its social function is not to give agents a true knowledge of the social structure but simply to insert them as it were into their political activities supporting this structure" (p. 207).

Ideology, thus, is indispensable to any society because of its efficiency in social strategies, and especially in societies riddled with antagonisms. That is how in all class societies, particularly the capitalist society, the social division of labor appears as one of the possible conditions for ideology. Ideology imposes its force on both material realities and psychological conditions, and operates at all levels of the personality, which is connected to socialization, education and the like, thereby making ideology almost indiscernible from lived experiences. Magubane explains the process by which ideology develops by taking place unconsciously:

> [Ideology] assumes a certain naturalness and compels respect from the society in which it grows, individuals who grow under the influence of education and environments may be filled with the most sincere, most elevated attitudes to the views and forms of social existence which arose historically on the basis of more or less narrow class interests (p. 54).

Ideology thus, is omnipresent and blended into personal experience and therefore difficult to detect. It belongs to the social subconscious and that is why, for Fougeyrollas, "it does not allow itself to be easily flushed out by simple conceptual criticisms" (p. 38). In *Ideology and Utopia* (1939), Karl Mannheim stresses the stimulation and regulation of the collective imaginary by ideology, hence his understanding of ideology as an ensemble of both ideas and feelings, of phenomena inseparably intellectual and affective. Indeed Mannheim's position is influential, since it leads to two major trends in the deconstruction of ideology: those who share Mannheim's view, consider ideology a system of representations, exercising regulatory role on the functioning of a social group or society in its totality, while those who share Marx's, consider ideology as a topsy-turvy representation of fundamental social relation, in peoples consciousness.[8] Both positions complement each other and are conscious of the role of ideology in the functioning and reproduction of order in society.

However, I part from Mannheim when he gets into a fragmented analysis, seeing ideology as a plurality, corresponding to diverse groups: each professional, confessional or political group would have its own ideology. In his approach, ideology can have multiple roles and functions according to each case, which means that there is not one ideology, but many kinds. The various social groups would use their ideologies according to their needs; therefore, ideology is neither alienating nor enlightening. Where Mannheim sees a distorted representation, Marx sees an upside down representation as in a photographic camera, and such a situation is an effect of the exploitation of social labor. Mannheim's identification of mini-ideologies, must be inserted into a global context, otherwise, the notion of ideology is lost in the diversity of ideologies. That is why, for Poulantzas (1974), these mini-ideologies are regions of the dominant ideology. For Marx, to each mode of production corresponds an ideology justifying or hiding the status quo: an ideology for the system of slavery, feudalism or capitalism. He states:

> The class, which has the means of material production at its disposal, has control at the same time over the means of mental production, so that thereby, generally speaking, the ideas of those who lack the means of mental production are subject to it (p. 172).

Furthermore, he explains:

> how the ideologists reproduce at the level of theory, that reality which the rank and file member encounters in his daily life, and which in the final analysis dictates to him a given course of behavior, given strivings and moral standards. The social reality of the dominant strata is justified by its own ideology, which these groups readily accept, while rejecting the one reflecting the objective interests of the subordinate groups (p. 47).

In this same order of ideas, Reich found that "every social order produces in the masses that structure which it needs to achieve its aims" (p. 13). Marx himself observed:

> Upon the different forms of property, upon the social conditions of existence, rises an entire superstructure of distinct and peculiarly formed sentiments, illusions, modes of thought and view of life. The entire class creates and forms them out of its material foundations and out of the corresponding social relations (p. 54).

Thus, once the individual, for instance, is subject to the general ideology of society, racism can be triggered whenever needed: it becomes an instrument, manipulable according to the necessities of concrete historical situations.

III. CLASS AND COLOR IN HAITI

The description of the situation in the Republic of Haiti is very brief and intended to only illustrate how Léopold Senghor's ideology of Négritude[9] spawned both the Noiriste ideology, with its emphasis on Afrocentric essentialism, and Mulâtrism, with its emphasis on metissage; and compounding irony upon irony, it shows how the proponents of metissage in turn, used the essentialist stance to exclude and segregate, rather than integrate and mix; and how all this play and display of color is as blinding as it is revealing, and serves to efface and hide, and yet reinforces and perpetuates, the even more crucial distinctions of class.[10]

> There can never be anything between a peasant and a grand homme. They despise us for our blackness.
>
> (The Storytellers, *Once on This Island*)

If there is race/class dialectic in Haiti, it is because there is a profound coincidence between class and skin color, dating back to the system of slavery and colonialism. As most of the slaves were, so most of the poor are Black today. Throughout its modern history, the color question has played a crucial role in politics as well as in social and economic development. According to David Nicolls (1985), a Haitian was born into one of the following groups: Whites at the top; Blacks at the bottom, the majority of whom were slaves; and the free "people of color" or *affranchis* – most of whom were Mulattoes – in the middle. This last group comprised people of all shades, depending on how much "White blood" and how much "Black blood" they had. One could add another group, "the *maroons* which consisted of slaves that had escaped from the plantations and lived in the hills as outlaws" (p. 23). From the nineteenth century to the present day, partly due to a deep fear and hatred of Blacks, a light skin, which was considered "closer" to Whites, has been an indication of prosperity. It is this dynamic between class and color that animates the Haitian political scenes.

Racial and Ethnic Ideologies and Their Influence on Social and Political Realities

As explained by Alex Dupuy (1985), most of the Black elite in Haiti, even when they came from poor peasant families and have made it via army promotion, shared the rich mulattoes' attitudes. They both were culturally Europeanized and publicly hostile towards African cultural values. In spite of their common objective however, conflicts between *affranchis* and Blacks have continued. The divisions and conflicts were further cultivated in "ethnic ideologies," which in turn instigated antagonism between mulattoes and Black political leaders. According to Dupuy, Haiti has maintained two dominant ethnic ideologies in its social and political scenes. They are the *Noiriste* (Black nationalist) and the *Mulâtriste* (mulatto) ideologies and both were immensely influenced by Léopold S. Senghor's (1964) Négritude theory on race and culture.

Senghor's psychological theory differentiates "Black" and "White" souls. Emphasizing racial specificities pertinent to all people of African descent, Senghor advocates the African's strong emotion, sensuality, and his/her natural inclination to art and rhythm. According to Senghor, Blacks seek harmony with nature through active dialogue with it, while Whites seek to dominate it. This Senghorian view of Blacks became popular in Haiti especially during the ethnological movement led by Price Mars and other intellectuals.[11] It was then incorporated into the *Noiriste* movement, which was initiated around the time of the U.S. occupation (1915–1935). The movement revived people's interest in African ancestry and Black specificities. It raised a new consciousness of ethnic heritage and brought a revisionist look at Mulattoes as substitutes for the White colonizers and thus as responsible for Haiti's ailments. On the other hand, Blacks who maintained or believed in African customs were considered representing the true interests of the majority.

The *Mulâtriste* ideology also developed from Senghorian theories. However, while the *Noiristes* considered the specificities of the Black person, the Mulâtristes utilized Senghor's concept of the Civilization of the Universal. Emphasizing a reconciliation of differences between Blacks and Whites, the *Civilisation de l' universel* envisions the ultimate civilization by incorporating special and unique aspects of all cultures into a new hybrid edifice. This ideology, *métissage* (intermarriage between different races), is viewed not only as a physical and biological phenomenon, but also an ideal one. Understanding culture as the echo of race, Senghor views cultural (and ideal) *métissage* as a natural extension of a racial métissage. The Mulatto is a psychological point of convergence. He attests that *métissage* reconciles seemingly irreconcilable traits of both Black and White: warmth and cold; affection and rationality; and dream and action. Senghor also attributes all great civilizations to *métissage*. For example, the "Greek miracle" was the result of a fecund *métissage*, and the future of the world also depends on *métissage*.[12] As Dupuy explains, Senghor's *mulâtriste* ideology has legitimized the sense of Mulatto superiority: the *mulâtriste* ideology "claimed that all advanced civilizations, most notably European, were the product of racial miscegenation," and that Africa remained "backward because it has always been outside the great currents of immigration" (p. 123). Mulattoes, who are the product of miscegenation, are considered "closer" to Europe, thus are "most capable to rule the black majority who did not benefit from "White blood" and remained "primitive" (p. 123).

Both Black and Mulatto leaders used both *noiriste* and *mulâtriste* ideologies to gain and maintain political powers. However, by resorting to racial and biological differences between Black and White, both ideologies fell short and trapped themselves into racist positions and revealed their power-laden agenda. Both Black and Mulatto leaders failed to locate Haiti's real problems. The debate was not over ethnicity and race, but rather over the social and economic structure of Haiti, which reveals itself in the stark exploitation of Haitian masses. According to Nicholls, the situation in Haiti has not changed for "No Haitian government in living memory has done anything substantial for the peasants" (p. 33). Therefore, *noiristes* leaders and bourgeois *mulâtristes* reduced all socio-political issues to the color question, but only as a strategy to manipulate and control Haitian masses. Thus, the ruling class in Haiti included both Mulattoes and Black elements that fought each other to secure state power, but nevertheless, they were identical in all other respects. The racial theory was simply an ideological concealment of the class system of exploitation in Haiti. In the following quote, Nicholls observes more intricate class divisions hidden beneath the "racial axis" created and propagated in Haitian political paradigms:

> [The] fortunate and the powerful who constituted the ruling class and which included blacks as well as mulattoes, and on the other hand, the immense majority of jobbing laborers, the workers, the non-specialized, the unemployed of all colors, and especially the mass of rural laborers, the mass of peasants . . . constituted the *social question* from 1804 to 1915. For a long time, blacks and mulattoes killed one another to conquer power without success of one or the other fraction having changed in any way the living standard of the unfortunate more or less black, or more or less light skin . . . (p. 126).

IV. RACISM AND THE DENIGRATION OF AFRICA AS AN IDEOLOGY

> It is highly probable that the thinking in terms of race would have disappeared in due time together with other irresponsible opinions of the nineteenth century, if the "scramble for Africa" and the new era of imperialism had not exposed Western humanity to new and shocking experiences. Imperialism would have necessitated the invention of racism as the only possible "explanation" and excuse for its deeds, even if no race thinking had ever existed in the civilized world (pp. 63–64).
>
> Hannah Arendt (1968).

Colonial and imperialist discourses constructed images of the racial other. The other (race i.e. non-Western) is primitive, unsophisticated, and backward. But the ostensible and perpetual "othering" of Africa shows how the constructed imagery of Blacks is an ideological balm for the Western world to soothe the social misery secreted by capitalism.

For Albert Caraco (1983), "the reality of racism is that it is a European invention: and that those very Europeans systematized it" (p. 10). Ideologically, the othering or denigration took the form of historical myths and stereotypes perpetuated worldwide, and for generations. Joseph E. Harris (1972) explains, at length, African inferiority as a concept, starting from antiquity to today. As he notes, the denigration of Africans reached its high point when influential philosophers of the Enlightenment theoretically systematized it. The Scot philosopher David Hume (1898) writes: "I am apt to suspect the Negroes [. . .] to be naturally inferior to the white. [. . .] No ingenious manufacturers amongst them, no arts, no science" (p. 252). Kant (1996), echoing Hume, writes:

> The Negroes of Africa have by nature no feeling that rises above the trifling. Mr. Hume challenges anyone to cite a single example in which a Negro has shown talents and asserts that among the hundreds of thousands of blacks who are transported elsewhere from their countries, although many of them have been set free, still not a single one was ever found who presented anything great in art or science or any other praise-worthy quality . . . (pp. 110–111).

And G. W. F. Hegel writes:

> Africa proper, as far as History goes back, has remained for all purposes of connection with the rest of the world shut up [. . .] It is the land of childhood [. . .] it is manifest that want of self-control distinguishes the character of the Negroes [. . .] (p. 91) [. . .] at this point we leave Africa, not to mention it again, for it is no historical part of the world; it has no movement of development to exhibit (p. 99).

One needs to ask whether this theoretical systematization of racial denigration is a coincidence or a necessity. The answer necessarily leads to the establishment of a connection between the rising Western imperialism and its ideological motivations. In fact, Magubane observes, "stereotype thinking about Africa grew in intensity and viciousness with the growth of imperialism" (p. 28). Here, I do not intend to refute the falsities of Europe's views of Africa, but rather, to explain how economic and political reasons are at the core of the on-going orchestration of the othering of Africa.

Nineteenth century anthropological discourses were justificatory racial ideologies, with a concrete relation to the economic expansion of capitalist Europe. In Reich's terms, "these economic factors constitute the soil in which racism germinates; in short, they constitute the conditions that are indispensable to the genesis of such ideologies" (p. 79). Western imperialism needed to justify the exploitation of Negroes in particular. The strategy was to make people believe that Negroes belonged to an inferior race. Therefore, their domination and exploitation were tolerable and justifiable. As Patrick Brantlinger (1986) explains, the myth of the Dark Continent was a Victorian invention. He says:

> As part of a larger discourse about empire, it was shaped by political and economic pressures and also by a psychology of blaming the victim through which Europeans projected many of their darkest impulses onto Africans (p. 217).

Therefore, racist discourses do have a practical finality and a regulatory power within society. This is probably what W. E. B. Du Bois (1968) perceived when he said: "I began to see the race problem in America, the problem of the people of Africa and Asia, and the political development of Europe as one. I began to unite my economics and politics" (p. 334). Referring to Dubois' description of the changing images of the Black man in his *The Gift of Black Folk, the Negroes in the Making of America* (1970), Magubane states:

> They [the changing images] were the result of ideologies, which justified and made legitimate white rule over blacks and white exploitation of foreign lands. They were part of a hegemonic superstructure, which created crises of personal identity and destiny among many darker peoples of the world. It was precisely this that created the beginnings of common outlooks and efforts among certain black intellectuals to comprehend their own existence as something historically determined and conditioned (p. 16).

These changes were not accidental but rather, fit in the strategy of capitalist dominance. He adds:

> [Those images] were the result of ideologies, which justified and made legitimate white rule over blacks and white exploitation of foreign lands? They were part of a hegemonic superstructure, which created crises of personal identity and destiny among many darker peoples of the people (p. 16).

Similarly, one can ask whether the encounter between the globalization of capitalism and the growing forms of racial denigration, oppression and othering are coincidences or necessities? Only a necessity can explain the ostensible recalcitrance of the media and many researchers to debase the Black race.

Africa and the West

Global studies textbooks and curricula, the media, and Hollywood among others, in concert with the dominant ideology, reinforce the negative portrayal of Africa. When they do not denigrate the continent, they simply omit it from any information or studies. When they do acknowledge Africans, they are represented as helpless victims of natural disasters, or of their own governments for lacking democratic structures. Western textbooks still describe the continent as full of natural barriers, reclusive and unfavorable to human development, or just inhabited by politically unsophisticated tribes, constantly caught in backward antagonisms. Meanwhile, for such an ideology, the danger of overpopulation makes life more miserable as Africans have to compete with animals for space to survive. Omissions and distortions in the history of Blacks and their contributions to the development of the world are still found in the majority of Western textbooks; and one common insinuation is that anything that Blacks have achieved in history is thanks to the Arabs or Europeans. One persistent case is offered by the theory stating that slave trading was already in existence in Africa and that Arabs and Europeans simply followed up. And now, the BBC has begun a debate among scholars on slavery and the part Africa has played in it.[13] This trend, which only sees the negative when it comes to Africa, dominates the mind of most westerners and unfortunately of some Western-educated Africans.

This attitude toward Africa is a variety of what Edward W. Said (1979) calls "Orientalism." Said argues that "Orientalism" was and is a distinctive cultural understanding found in Western Europe and in the United States. It refers to an area of academic specialty, a level of scholarly stereotyping of [Africa] and a way of controlling the regions and the peoples so classified. To paraphrase Said, I say that othering is "the way of dealing with [Africa] by making statements about it, authorizing views of it, describing it, by teaching it, settling it, ruling over it: in short, othering [Africa] is a Western style for dominating, restructuring, and having authority over [Africa]" (p. 3). Such an ideological and imaginative production of Africa provides Euro-America strength and identity by setting itself up against Africa. Thus, those distorted views about underdeveloped Africa, "the other," whom anthropology traditionally studies, serve the purpose of concealing the double nature of capitalist hegemony: it has been exploiting Africa and its Diaspora and, as a capitalist center, has its own antagonisms to camouflage. Therefore, the old scapegoat strategy resurfaces: contradictions are transferred on to the "alien race," i.e. Blacks in the USA, Brazil, the Caribbean and African immigrants in the West, who are relegated in this way to an inferior status. From now on, the depreciation of the "alien race" is a balm that relieves Euro-American masses from all the daily frustrations secreted by their system. The othering of the Third World in general and Africa in particular helps divert attention from the acute social problems the system has created and is incapable of getting rid of.

The success of othering has made racism one of the most constant, reliable and efficient ideologies so far, and this in all domains, including sexuality. Depriving people of sexual freedom has been the primary basis of authoritarian ideology since Puritanism. Sex has become a commodity and is indeed distorted. The oppressive association of sex with bestiality, lasciviousness, and evilness, once used in Euro-America to maintain the patriarchal authoritarian sexual order is now an ideology in full concert with racism. From now on, Black people's sexuality is looked upon as "a cultural degeneration." Otherwise "fornicators" – next to thieves and liars – is one of the major stereotypes associated with Blacks. However, the situation is very complex. While the ideology of Black sexual superiority has produced endless stories of White fantasies over it, it is also dreaded, because now, the source of sexually transmitted diseases are attributed to Blacks. As Sander Gilman (1985) puts it, "Black sexuality, associated with images of sexually transmitted diseases, has become a category of marginalization" (p. 262). She also explains how,

> In the 1980s, after white America was made aware of the intolerable state of blacks in this country through the civil rights movement in the 1960s and 1970s, one could no longer as easily locate the source of disease among American blacks, as had been done in the Tuskegee experiment. Rather, the perceived source of pollution was shifted to foreign blacks [. . .] (p. 263).

Thus Africa and its Diaspora remain the "dumping grounds" of othering ideologies entertained by Euro-America. The AIDS disease is a blatant illustration of othering, as well theorized by Gilman: "It is clear that we need to locate the origin of disease, since its source, always distant from ourselves in the fantasy land of our fears, gives us assurance that we are not at fault, that we have been polluted by some external agent" (p. 262). In this paradigm of Euro-America's racist ideology, the source of AIDS in the 1990s is attributed to Africans and other Blacks of the Diaspora such as Haitians.

V. IDEOLOGIES IN AFRICA: FROM LIBERATION TO OPPRESSION

Ideology in Africa has been seen as a valuable instrument in the rebuilding of former colonies. Its role was not only to put newly independent countries on the road to development, but also to create unity after years of arbitrary colonial divisions. Yet, at the same time, the southern part of the continent was revealing ideology at the service of one of the most ruthless and oppressive system of exploitation.

A. Ideologies of Liberation and Development

Of Marxist background, Fanon's thought developed in the violent setting of the Algerian war (1954–1962). His efforts were devoted to the study of the processes and effects of ideological domination in the historical context of colonialism. J. W. Freiberg (1974) states that "[Fanon] is a critical theorist

[who] comes to understand the profundity of and material efficacy of psycho-logical domination" (p. 88). Thus, Fanon's project was to define the dynamic of the "laws of the psychology of colonization" (id.). His investigation of the human condition under colonialism reveals that "colonialism is a system of guns and capital that is operable profitable *only and through* very complex processes of ideological domination" (id.). For Fanon (1967), racism obeys a flawless logic:

> A country that lives, and draws its substance from the exploitation of other peoples, makes those people inferior. Race prejudice applied to those peoples is normal. Racism is there-fore not a constant of the human spirit. It is, as we have seen, a disposition fitting into a well-defined system (pp. 40–41).

At this point, Fanon understood that the struggle against the colonial ideology – instilling the feeling of inferiority and dependency among Blacks and robbing and falsifying their cultures – was related to if not identical with the struggle for a people's liberation. Fanon attached a psychological and moral value to social revolution. In Paulin Hountondji's words (1996), for Fanon, "the struggle against colonization had meaning not simply as a means to an objective purpose signified by the attainment of political independence, but as a process through which colonized [people] would remake [their] humanity, diminished and distorted by the experience of domination" (pp. 23–24). This position, understood in the context of Marx's strategy for the dictatorship of the prole-tariat, would turn "Fanonism"[14] into one of the most influential ideologies of liberation in Africa.

For Marx, ideology is bourgeois, which means that it must be fought. In order for the proletariat to do so, they have to transcend that ideology – which presents a false reality – and develop a "true" consciousness of their own. Jurgen Habermas (1987) explains:

> The major obstacles to achieving class-consciousness, Marx believed, were ideology, which involves the manipulation of the cultural superstructure for the purpose of legitimizing exploitative class relations, and commodity fetishism, which creates the illusion that social relations among persons are natural and invariant (p. 6).

Thus, ideology has become synonymous with consciousness.

The idea, developed by Vladimir Lenin,[15] is that the proletariat, being divided and inexperienced, needs an ideology to reach its goals. This strategy, for the pro-letariat's need to counter the hegemony of the bourgeoisie by developing an ide-ology of their own, finds echo in Gramsci (1981). He notes: "The party then, is the necessary mediating force which enables the masses to transcend their mystified conditions" (p. 136). Therefore intellectuals, who are supposed to impregnate the masses with ideology and lead them to victory, should undertake the task. This positive understanding of ideology became very popular in the Third World in general and among African intellectuals and leaders in particular.

1960 – the year before Fanon's death – was the official year of independence for the majority of African countries. It was also around that time that a new ideology called African socialism[16] started to circulate in Africa. As far as Fanon was concerned, the next ideological trend was a combination of Marxism and Fanonist praxis, i.e. a new African Marxism that took the form of liberation movements.[17] Thus, for Africans, the role of ideology was to create unity after years of arbitrary colonial divisions. It is the exigencies of certain practical objectives – to get out of underdevelopment and regain a lost political dignity – that have made this understanding of ideology a *sine qua non* for Africans. They have developed ideologies for the particularity of their historical conditions and traditional values. Irvin Markovitz (1969) sees this form of ideology as a strategy "to arouse interest among the population of the newly independent countries – that were crushed under colonial authority, hence the development of a deep apathy-and to create a *prise de conscience*" (p. 5). However, despite all the ideological efforts to establish economic and political relationships between them and to remain original powers, African countries failed in their tasks. They were caught in what Kwame Nkrumah (1965) calls "neo-colonialism,"[18] and eventually created their own antagonism and more economic needs and inequalities. All this, while Southern Africa was the scene of the crudest form of racism: apartheid.

B. Ideological Justifications of Apartheid

> If a nation wishes to deny that a large number of its subject inhabitants can never attain national status and citizenship, it needs a justification which transcends theoretical categories of nationalism ... So racialism then becomes a theory by which one nation can oppress other nations (p. 48).
>
> Bernard Crick (1962)

Every form of racism that Black people – in or out of Africa – have ever experienced was multiplied tenfold by the South African regime. Historically and religiously based ideologies, and an intricate legal apparatus sustained racism in South Africa. The segregationist policy going back to 1948, when apartheid was officially instituted. Aletta Norval (1994) says, "apartheid [. . .] is the most racist of racisms. It is racism par excellence. It can portray itself, in its essence, as self-sufficient, separate, intact, independent" (p. 118). Contrary to Nazism – another manifestation of a racist ideology in "full swing" – which, at the theoretical level, enjoyed important developments, apartheid did not really undergo systematic theoretical elaborations. The reason must be that the phenomenon developed on the political level, which is probably why it is often necessary to invoke statesmen's or politicians' discourses justifying the racist ideology of apartheid.

Here, as well as in the Haitian case, the demarcation line between the races and classes was blurred, or more precisely, the social class division lines over- lapped with the "ethnic" or racial ones. This is how one could find a fundamentally White bourgeoisie next to a fundamentally Black proletariat, resulting from a continuous proletarianization and the obvious "promotion" of the Whites. Andrew Asheron (1973) explains this dialectic of race/class:

> In South Africa, the normal horizontal lines of class stratification are also crossed by a diagonal line of social segregation which places a total barrier on the vertical mobility between whites and blacks and in so doing locks up the country into a closed social system (pp. 6–7).

It is precisely that closure that revealed the "colored" aspect of classes in South Africa. But what was the true role of the "ethnic" division? There certainly was a logic of dividing in order to perpetuate White domination, and this, on two levels. First, it kept in reserve a surplus of cheap and oppressed labor. Second, dividing the local population – which was greater in number – into smaller groups allowed a stricter control of their movements. This idea of establishing "native reserves" for the original inhabitants has existed in other areas and has always been a sign of racism, oppression and exploitation. Barbara Rogers (1980) mentions that "European settlers in the United States, Canada and Australia all confined indigenous people, who regarded the land as rightfully theirs, to small areas" (p. 7). Kant, despite his categorical statements on the inferiority of Negroes, describes the same situation:

> But to this perfection compare the inhospitable actions of the civilized and especially of the commercial states of our part of the world. The injustice that they show to the lands and peoples they visit, (which is equivalent to conquering them) is carried by them to terri- fying lengths. America, the lands inhabited by the Negro, the Spice Islands, the Cape, etc., were at the time of their discovery considered by these civilized intruders as lands without owners, for they counted the inhabitants as nothing (p. 103).

a. Historical Ideology

Historical arguments are intensively used in any racist society. In South Africa, the apartheid regime needed to prove that Blacks' disenfranchisement and disempowerment had always existed in history. The past was thus constructed or reconstructed to justify the racist status quo. Therefore, one was first dealing with the creation of "historical myths" and falsifications as theoretical and ideological elaborations to justify apartheid.

Cornevin's *Apartheid* was part of UNESCO's program of studies for the International Year Against Apartheid, declared by the UN in 1974. The work exposes a variety of "historical myths," all justifying the various practices involved in the implementation of the apartheid regime. That was how these "imaginary myths" were taught to young South Africans (White, Black, Indian and Mulatto) from primary school to the university, at home and at all levels of South African life. Eventually, such continuous ideological hammering turned "myths" into undeniable truths. Among those myths, let us mention the one purporting that "Whites and blacks arrived in South Africa at the same time." The majority of White South Africans were persuaded of the simultaneous migration of Whites and Blacks. For Cornevin, it is fraud:

> Twenty years ago, it was scientifically proved that the Blacks came first. Recent carbon 14 dating shows that Bantu-speaking peoples, ancestors of the South African Blacks, settled in the Northern Transvaal in the third century, i.e. 1,400 years before the Whites established themselves (p. 78).

The second "myth" that Cornevin exposes reinforces the first: "that blacks were migrants until they met the whites" (p. 82). As stated in a Standard-8 history textbook, in Cornevin's *Apartheid*:

> The Sotho people came from the Great Lake area in Central Africa. It is accepted that their migration to the South also took about 2,000 years. *They occupied* the central parts of southern Africa south of the Zambezi and north of the Orange River in three groups, between the years 1300 and 1400. Some authorities are of the opinion that they only reached their present territories in the year 1600 (p. 84).

This was a myth since we know, as Cornevin says: "Several accounts by shipwrecked survivors establish the presence of Nguni-speaking peoples in the north of the modern Transkei in the middle of the sixteen century, 100 years before the whites arrived at the Cape" (p. 86). It is clear that these two myths aimed at falsifying the historical reality by making people believe that South Africa was an uninhabited area. Thus, the White and Black populations have equal rights on the land since, historically, they were both present in South Africa. This effort to make of South Africa a virgin land at the very moment of British imperialist expansion can only be explained if one knows that it allowed whites to elude the fundamental issue of African land expropriations.

To these myths, I must add two more that are particularly important since they concern the territorial fragmentation, i.e. the "native reserves," known as Bantustans or homelands. The first "myth" can be formulated as follows: "that the homelands correspond to the areas historically occupied by each black nation. This was a myth in the sense that, according to Jacques Leguèbe (1978), "those areas historically occupied by Blacks represent 13% of the total area of South Africa, while in fact it is the totality of the land which was occupied by blacks before the whites" (p. 73). This myth also supposes that Blacks have entirely kept their traditional tribal areas where they met the Whites for the first time and have, thus, never been expropriated, which is contrary to historical data gathered by Cornevin. The second myth masks the first one by affirming that the fragmentation of the land into Bantustans is the direct result of tribal wars and conflicts of succession and not of an elaborate policy of dividing African populations for the purposes I mentioned earlier.

The ideological problem clearly appears as soon as it is a question of distorting reality and justifying the oppression and exploitation of Blacks. The historical domain becomes very important in any ideological justification. In this sense, Western imperialism has always falsified the history of colonized people by simply denying them one. That is how in South Africa, at all social levels, there were "myths," whose function was to give coherence to the whole social system. Ideology, thus, played the role of "cement." The ideological element was in all the spheres of society and assured their unity. This unitary function explained the omnipresence of ideology and the necessity of a continuous ideological intoxication of the masses for the purpose of justifying the segregationist practices of exploitation and oppression. Consequently, the myth of "superiority" becomes clear as it reinforces the Whites' complex of superiority and justifies their opulence and the wretchedness of most South African Blacks.

b. Religious Ideology

From a Marxian point of view, religious expressions are also ideological. Religion, as noted by Marx, has two characteristics: protestation and falsification of that protestation. On the one hand, religion is protestation of the proletariat against bourgeois materialist pretensions; on the other, religion is the bourgeoisie's last resort to mislead the proletariat, where materialism and politics have failed. He says: "*Religious* suffering is at the same time an *expression* of real suffering and a *protest* against real suffering. Religion is the sigh of the oppressed creature [. . .]" (p. 54). For Marx (1978), one must first explain the contradiction of terrestrial alienation; in other words, show the terrestrial reasons of religion. Religion has that power to raise the masses' enthusiasm and even love. That is why the state has to deal with religion and morale and that is why we witness the proliferation of religious activists from all denominations, and who seem to be more efficient in crowd control. Marx (1993) also observes that members of the ruling class tend to utilize religious ideas in politically and culturally conservative ways to rationalize and legitimate the inequalities of their societies.

In terms of racism and oppression, and throughout history, the Church has always blessed the cruelty perpetrated against Blacks in general.[19] Ironically, the KKK in America claims to be of Christian faith. In terms of colonization, the initial conquest of Black countries was made in the name of the three Gs (God, Gold and Glory). In South Africa, the imbrication of the apartheid ideology and the Calvinist religion was obvious, the latter explaining the former. As Cornevin says:

> To fully understand the "religious dimension" of the South African State, one needs to go back to the eighteenth century Trekboers[20] and the Voortekkers[21] of the Great Trek (1835–1843)[22] who, equipped with the Bible as their sole and unique cultural instrument, compared themselves to the Hebrews' "chosen people". "Egypt" was the Dutch administration for the Trekboers and the British administration for the Voortekkers; "The Promised Land" was the well-irrigated region, east of the Fish River for the Trekboers; and the immense and low populated veldt of the Orange and Transvaal Free States or the green hills of the Natal, for the Voortekkers. The "Philistines" were the Xhosa (p. 33).

Leguèbe noted that according to the 1970 census, 93.8% of the White population was Christian. If the majority of them supported the apartheid regime, the next step is to find the complicity between the Church and apartheid. The Dutch Reformed Church[23] has always been a defender of apartheid. In fact, it was impossible to separate the Church and State in South Africa. Cornevin affirms:

> None of the Churches in South Africa is subsidized. Despite this financial independence, it is impossible to speak of the "separation of Church and State" as regard the three Dutch Reformed Churches, least of all the NGK[24] . . . Since 1857, the NGK decided not to accept any more "pagan converts" into the White parish communities. By 1881, separate mission churches, called "daughter" churches had been set up for the Blacks and Indians (pp. 36–37).

Religious apartheid, thus, preceded political apartheid. Added to that is the fact that the Nationalist Party, promoter of apartheid, defined itself as "national Christian." The imbrication apartheid-religion (Calvinist) was "original." From the beginning, religion has been a basis for apartheid. In its name, the "divine origin of White superiority" and its Christian mission were developed as many justifications for apartheid.

The conclusion to draw from an analysis of these myths is that despite their "naïve" formulation, their quasi-"irrationality," they insert themselves into the logic of the racist system at its very ideological foundations. Historical and religious myths are important in any ideological justification, and South Africa under apartheid illustrates the use of ideology to maintain racism, distort reality, conceal and justify the oppression of Blacks. That is how, in the Republic of South Africa – and in any country obsessed with race and racism – there are myths at all social levels. Yet, both Blacks and Whites in the process of the ideological and political mystification they underwent could develop a racial consciousness of their conditions of existence.

Some people pretended and others did believe that the South African problem was a matter of racial conflict or racism. The reality is that the fundamental capitalist socio-economic structure of South Africa needed to brutally exploit the resources of the country and in order to do so safely, had to cover itself with the cape of race to hide that very exploitation. The effect is that scholars and activists confused the target with its shadow, allowing, thus, enough time for the South African government to initiate the reforms we are witnessing.

c. Law and Racism

Racism is also codified in laws. It takes the form of strict regulations or an incursion of the law into every aspect of social life. Moreover, the legal arsenal is extremely complex and that complexity is part of a repressive strategy. The law in South Africa was extremely detailed and therefore, impossible for the Black masses to understand or respect, thus, exposing them to constant police harassment. The whole South African society was regulated to the point that one can talk about a legal fortress or a police state. In South Africa – as well as in Stalin's Russia and Hitler's Germany – under the cover of state security, the power of the police was boundless. But while Cornevin's report reveals how the law is woven into the fabric of political power, she also gives us an idea of the volume of these laws.[25] She writes: "The number of repressive laws goes beyond imagination. Forty-nine racial laws were passed between 1909 and 1948; fifty-three between 1948 and 1960; ninety between 1960 and 1971" (p. 202). It is this legal arsenal that allows the White minority to control almost entirely the activities of the Black population. Therefore, racial segregation goes hand in hand with a legal arsenal.

Now, if in other capitalist countries, the law is proclaimed to be universal, in South Africa it openly serves the particular. The generalized use of legal force reveals racism's true nature as an integral part of the socio-political system. Here again, South Africa was special: if in other countries, a de facto inequality exists among members of the various groups, such an inequality is not officially advocated. But in South Africa, many political figures such as Dr. Malan, Dr. Verwoerd and former Prime Minister Vorster publicly affirmed that the objective of the apartheid regime was to maintain White supremacy in South Africa.[26] In fact, this situation was perceived by Jacques Derrida (1986) who described it as following:

> THE LAST, finally, since this last-born of many racisms [. . .], at least the only one still parading itself in a political constitution. It remains the only one on the scene that dares to say its name and to present itself for what it is: a legal defiance taken on by homo politicus, a juridical racism and a state racism. Such is the ultimate imposture of a so-called state of law which doesn't hesitate to base itself on a would-be original hierarchy – of natural right or divine right, the two are never mutually exclusive (p. 331).

On the other hand, in democratic countries that entertain racism, there is a legal arsenal to protect citizen's rights. However, none of these laws seem to be relevant when it comes to defend or protect Black people. The Rodney King[27] case may have triggered some sanctions against some of the police officers that clubbed him to the ground, but from widely publicized cases such as Abner Louima[28] or Amadou Diallo's[28] to Blacks' daily and individual racist experience, the democratic arsenal of laws, by not being enforced when it comes to Blacks, plays the same role as the one in South Africa under apartheid. Today, there seems to be a considerable continuity in racist policy and legislation South Africa and apartheid's draconian enforcement apparatus now focuses on immigration. According to Jonathan Crush and David A. McDonald (2001), "Apartheid-era immigration laws remain in force in South Africa [today], and many of the same apartheid-era images and stereotypes have simply been displaced onto African immigrants and refugees."

CONCLUSION

The intelligibility of racism can only stem from an analysis of the social structure on which racist prejudices rest. The analysis of the racist problematic reveals that it is really the capitalist system that secretes racism and, in various cases, favored its manifestations in the forms of Nazism in Hitler's Germany, colonialism in Africa, segregation in America and apartheid in South Africa. In this sense, all the theories describing racism today are pertinent in explaining the subtleties hidden in each social group. However, a theory that emphasizes race issues and ignores or forgets not only the material conditions, but also the constraints they impose on people, is just another ideology masking the super-exploitation of Blacks. Therefore what was called apartheid was not motivated by race. If ever so, it was only in appearance.

However, apartheid seems to contradict our understanding of ideology. In South Africa, ideology became cynical. The ideological system of apartheid openly advocated inequality and domination of Blacks, where ideology usually does its utmost to mask them. Therefore, ideology adjusts to the circumstances. Apartheid openly proclaimed what used to be "taboo" in order to create a false consciousness of the South African reality and this in the eyes of both Blacks and Whites. We can now affirm that racism cannot be understood by the simple evocation of moral principles. The formation and development of such ferocious racisms are based on economic laws, which are unveiled by historical materialism. That is why the Marxian analysis of ideology is the most appropriate tool for the study of racist ideologies.

If my analysis shows that ideology has a relative independence, it also shows it is inseparable from the real, i.e. social totality. It allows us thus, to understand that the particular "history of an ideology" coincides with "the effective history" of the concrete individuals of the social totality where that particular ideology has shown itself. Therefore, an analysis of the constitution and function of an ideology takes into account the economy and the social formation in which an ideology operates. This aspect is essential to explain the ideological system of any type of racism. It reveals the reality of an exploitation and domination behind all the racial discourses. Racism pervades every aspect of social life. Under such circumstances, it becomes a *card* to be played by the perpetrators or the victims as in Haiti. Therefore the analysis of the structures on which racism rests is a *sine qua non*. In Patrice de Comarmond and Claude Duchet's words:

> Le racisme est plus qu'une attitude. Il est aussi la situation sociale qui induit cette attitude. Le combat antiraciste est donc un combat pour un changement des structures sociales, c'est à dire un combat politique (p. 108).

> (Racism is more than an attitude. It is also the social situation, which induces such an attitude. The anti-racist struggle is thus a struggle to change the social structures, i.e. a political struggle).

NOTES

1. For West, Marxism poses a problem to African American realities for it reduces all issues to class struggle and economics. Therefore, he proposes what he calls a "neo-Gramscian" position, which allows him to seriously consider the multileveled oppression of African peoples, usually dismissed or relegated as secondary by monolithic orthodox Marxism. See "Marxist Theory and the Specificity of Afro-American Oppression" In: Cary Nelson and Lawrence Grossberg, 1988.

2. Dove uses an Afrocentric perspective to prove that Karl Marx was Eurocentric and his theories accomplice of White supremacy and oppression of Africans (Dove, 1995).

3. For Alain For Alain Tourraine, dominant classes attempt to manage a society's cultural meanings as well as its surplus productions (Fox, 1985).

4. Clark Kerr, a prominent ideologist, has already calculated that, the complex process of production, distribution and consumption of knowledge already gets 29% of the yearly national product in the United States; and that in the second half of this century, culture will be the driving force in the development of the economy, a role played by the automobile in the first half of this century and by railroads in the second half of the previous century (Debord, 1983).

5. "In bourgeois society, myth takes hold of everything, all aspects of the law of morality, of aesthetics, of diplomacy, of household equipment, of literature, of entertainment" (Barthes, 1989).

6. Marx gives a broad definition of ideology as the totality of ideas and values – or "representations" – common to a society or current in a given social group. In: Dumont, 1983.

7. "Ideology is the basis of the thought of class society in the conflict-laden course of history. Ideological facts were never simple chimera, but rather a deformed

consciousness of reality, and in this form, they have been real factors which set in motion deforming acts; all the more so when the materialization, in the form of spectacle, of the ideology, brought about by the concrete success of automized economic production in practice, confounds social reality with an ideology which has tailored all reality in terms of its model" (Debord, 1983).

8. "If in all ideology [humans] and their circumstances appear upside-down as in a camera obscura, this phenomenon arises just as much from their historical life process as the inversion of objects on the retina does from their physical life-process." In: Marx and Engels, 1983 (p. 25).

9. Senghor was a poet, essayist, scholar and statesman. He is considered the theorist of Négritude. He offers the most popular definition of Négritude as a cultural, racial and humanist concept; it is the sum total of Black cultural values (1959).

10. From my colleague Sante Matteo's review of the piece on Haiti.

11. Intellectuals such as Jean-Pierre Mars, J. Dorsinvil, and Arthur Holly propelled the ethnological movement that emphasized biological and cultural differences between Blacks and Whites (Dupuy, 1985).

12. A marriage between races is a marriage between cultures. Therefore, métissage is a symbiosis of values, hence the superiority of the métis or mulatto (Senghor, 1964).

13. Go to <http://allafrica.com/partners/bbc/african perspective.ram> There is a trend among some Black scholars to shift the blame of the system of slavery onto Africans. The truth is that psychologically Europe and White America have been carrying the guilt of having committed the most atrocious crime in the history of humankind: the enslavement of Africans and their "uprootedness." As a result, no efforts have been spared to displace it onto the other, the victims themselves. This ideology of blaming the other is very conscious of the fact that, by desperately denigrating Africa, or seeking forms or elements of slavery supposedly perpetrated by modern Africans, it will have negative and psychological effects on Blacks in the Diaspora and tends to create confusion and further isolate them from Africa, their motherland. This othering, as Edward Said would call it, is a sign of an internal trouble: Euro America is haunted by the specter of both slavery and its consequences. Millions of Blacks in the Diaspora! What to do with them? How to handle them? Because, after 400 years and an endless cycle of harassment, division, incarceration, and murder, they are still surviving, and more than ever, revealing their indispensability to modern society. To paraphrase Sander Gilman, I will say that it is clear that there is a need to locate the origin of slavery, since its source, always distant from Euro-America in the fantasyland of its fear, gives it assurance that it is not at fault.

14. For Fanonism, socialism is the theory for colonial and neo-colonial liberation and violence is the solution to revolution and freedom.

15. For Lenin, professional revolutionaries, armed by Marxist theory, will lead the proletariat, because they know what the true interests of the workers are (Hook, 1955).

16. The characteristic of African socialism is that it rejects both the Western capitalist and [ex]-Eastern socialist groups. Senghor defines what they kept of Western socialism; "we are not Marxist [. . .] in so far as Marxism is presented as esthetic metaphysics, a total and totalitarian view of the world, a Weltanschauung . . . We are socialist. We shall start from [Marx and Engels] works as from those of the utopian socialists [. . .] but we shall retain only the method and ideas [. . .]." In Markovitz, 1969. For a detailed debate on the various definitions of African socialism (Nkrumah, Nyerere, Touré & Boya) see Ayi K. Armah, 1967.

17. For Liberation movements, Marxism and violence would liberate Africa from colonialism. They played the role of avant-garde and their strategies were to militarily free the masses from colonialism or the local bourgeoisie and assure a political and economic independence. Lusophone Africa better illustrated this improved Fanonism where Amilcar Cabral (Guinea-Bissau) and Samora Machel (Mozambique) were the leaders and theorists of African Marxism-Leninism, geared to the rural masses that undertook the armed struggle against Portuguese colonial domination for fifteen years.

18. The product of neo-colonialism "is an economic impoverishment of newly independent Africa and its dependency on the former colonial rulers. In each region of the periphery exists a balkanization: the creation of several weak and unstable states that depend on former colonizers for economic aid" (Nkrumah, 1965).

19. The image of Africans as inferiors was reinforced further by arguments of several Christian missionaries, ministers, and others who explained that an African was better off a slave in a Christian society than free in an "African savagery." In his interview with *Essence* (December, 1987), Reverend Dr. Clarence E. Glover talks about what it means to be an African people in a land where Christianity has used the whip and justified slavery and segregation. For many African authors and Afrocentrists in the Black Diaspora, Western religion has been the best ally of colonialism or imperialism. See Ousmane Sembène's *Ceddo* (1976) or John Henrik Clarke's videocassette *A Great and Mighty Walk*. New York, NY: Black Dot Media, 1996.

20. Cattle breeders.

21. Members of the Great Trek.

22. The British abolished formal slavery in 1707; but the slave owners in South Africa were not willing to surrender their properties or to accept any limitations on their rights of ownership. Therefore, the combination of land hunger, dislike of British rule, and anger at the abolition of the system of slavery were the root cause of the Afrikaner exodus from the Cape Colony into the interior: it became known as the Great Trek (1835–1843) (Magubane, 1997).

23. The Dutch Reformed Churches is the collective name referring to Afrikaans (Descendents of the Dutch, German and French who settled in South Africa) churches.

24. Nederduitse Gereformeerde Kerk (NGK) is the oldest and most important of the reformed churches.

25. Among other sources, see "Dossiers et documents." *Le Monde Diplomatique*, Oct. 1979, for a list of the legal arsenal of repression.

26. They all are former South African Prime Ministers. Dr. Malan, for example, declared that he wanted to assure the security of the White race and the Christian Civilization, by a strict upholding of Apartheid principles and laws (Lugan, 1986).

27. In 1991, Rodney King was ordered out of his car and beaten by Los Angeles Police Department officers, with approximately fifty-six baton strokes: he was also kicked in the head and body and stunned with a teaser stun gun. The incident was caught on tape. The subsequent 1992 state court acquittal of four officers on assault with a deadly weapon led to rioting in the city.

28. Abner Louima is a Haitian immigrant who was arrested in 1997, and then beaten, brutalized, and sodomized with a toilet plunger by officers of the New York Police Department, Amadou Diallo, an African immigrant was shot and killed by four White New York Police Department officers who fired forty-one bullets at him. The officers were acquitted. They testified that they were looking for a rape suspect and thought that Diallo, who was clutching his wallet, was reaching for a gun.

REFERENCES

Althusser, L. (1969). *For Marx* (pp. 63, 83, 235). London: Verso.

Althusser, L. (1988). Ideology and Ideological State Apparatuses. *Lenin and Philosophy and Other Essays*. London: NLB, 1971.

Arendt, H. (1988). In: Mudimbe, *The Invention of Africa: Gnosis, Philosophy, and the Order of Knowledge* (p. 108). Bloomington, IN: IUP.

Aronowitz, S. (1974). Recent Development in Marxist theories of ideology. *Insurgent Sociology.* 13(4)(Summer), 5, 7, 8.

Asheron, A. (1973). Race et politique en Afrique du Sud. *United Nations* (pp. 6–7). IDEP.

Barrett, M. (1988). *Women's Oppression Today: The Marxist/Feminist Encounter* (rev. ed., p. 31). London: Verso.

Barthes, R. (1989). *Mythologies* (p. 148). New York, NY: Noonday.

Boswell et al. (1974). Recent development. *Insurgent Sociology.*

Brantlinger, P. (1986). Victorians and Africans: The Genealogy of the Myth of the Dark Continent. In: H. L. Gates (Ed.), *"Race," Writing, and Difference* (p. 217). Chicago, IL: U. of Chicago.

Crick, B. (1987). In: B. Magubane, *The Ties That Bind: African-American Consciousness of Africa* (p. 48). Trenton, NJ: AWP.

Cornevin, M. (1978). *Apartheid: Power and Historical Falsification* (pp. 78, 82, 84, 86, 116, 36, 37). Paris: UNESCO.

Cornevin, M. (1977). *L'Afrique du Sud en sursis* (p. 33). Paris: Hachette.

Crush, J., & McDonald, D. A. (2001). Evaluating South African Immigration Policy after Apartheid. *Africa Today, 48*(3), 7.

De Comarmond, P., & Duchet, C. (Eds) (1960). *Racisme et société* (p. 108). Paris: Maspero.

Debord, G. (1983). *The Society of the Spectacle*. Detroit, MI: Black & Red. Thesis #193, 212.

Derrida, J. (1986). Racism's Last Word. *"Race." Writing and Difference*, p. 331.

Dove, N. (1995). An African-Centered Critique of Marx's Logic. *The Western Journal of Black Studies, 19*(4).

Du Bois, W. E. B. (1997). In: B. Magubane, *The Making of a Racist State: British Imperialism and the Union of South Africa, 1870–1910* (p. 334). Trenton, NJ: AWP.

Du Bois, W. E. B. (1987). In: B. Magubane, *The Ties That Bind* (p. 16). Trenton, NJ: AWP.

Dumont, L. (1983). *From Mandeville to Marx: the Genesis and Triumph of Economic Ideology* (p. 17). Chicago, IL: UCP.

Dupuy, A. (1985). *Haiti in the World Economy: Class, Race and Underdevelopment Since 1700* (pp. 122–124). New York, NY: St. Martin's.

Durkheim, E. (1985). In: Fougeyrollas, *Les metamorphoses de la crise: racisme et revolutions au XXe siècle* (p. 38). Paris: Hachette.

Eagleton, T. (1991). *Ideology: An Introduction* (p. 1). London: Verso.

Fanon, F. (1967). *Toward the African Revolution (Political Essays)* (pp. 40–41). New York, NY: Grove Press.

Femia, J. V. (1981). *Gramsci's Political Thought, Hegemony, Consciousness, and the Revolutionary Process* (p. 136). Oxford: Clarendon Press.

Freiberg, J. W. (1974). Frantz Fanon: Left Hegelian. *Insurgent Sociologist, 4*(2)(Winter), 86–88.

Fougeyrollas, F. (1985). *Les métamorphoses de la crise: racisms et revolutions au XX e siècle* (pp. 74, 68). Paris: Hachette.

Fox, R. G. (1985). *Lions of the Punjab: Culture in the Making* (pp. 2, 3, 197, 205). Berkeley, CA: UC.

Gilman, S. (1985). *Disease and representation: Images of Illness from Madness to AIDS* (pp. 262–263). Ithaca, NY: Cornell U.

Goldberg, D. (1996). In: J. Solomos & L. Back, *Racism and Society* (p. 18). New York, NY: St. Martin's.

Habermas, J. (1987). In: D. Ingram. *Habermas and the Dialectics of Reason* (p. 6). Yale, NH: YU Press.

Harris, J. E. (1987). *Africans and Their History* (rev. ed., pp. 17, 19). New York, NY: Mentor Book.

Hegel, G. W. F. (1991). *The Philosophy of History* (pp. 91–93). Buffalo, NY: Prometheus.

Hook, S. (1955). *Marx and the Marxist: the Ambiguous Legacy* (p. 78). Princeton, NJ: D. Van Nostrand.

Hountondji, P. (1996). *African Philosophy: Myth and Reality* (2nd ed., pp. 23–24). Bloomington, IN: IUP.

Hume, D. (1898). Of National Character. *Essays: Moral, Political. and Literary. Vol. I* (p. 252). London: Longman.

Kant, I. (1996). Eurocentrism in Philosophy: The case of Immanuel Kant. *The Philosophical Forum: A Quarterly*, *27*(4), Summer, No. 339, 110–111.

Lugan, B. (1986). *Histoire de l'Afrique du Sud: de l'antiquité à nos jours* (pp. 205–206). Paris: Perrin.

Leguèbe, J. (1978). *Afrique du Sud contemporaine* (p. 73). Paris: PUF.

Magubane, B. (1987). *The Ties That Bind* (pp. 54, 28, 16). Trenton, NJ: AWP.

Mannheim, K. (1936). Ideology and Utopia. *Ideology and Utopia: An Introduction to the Sociology of Knowledge*. New York, NY: Harvest. Chapter 2.

Markovitz, I. L. (1969). *Léopold Sédar Senghor and the Politics of Négritude* (pp. 54–55). New York, NY: Athenum.

Marx, K., & Engels, F. (1983). German Ideology. *Selected Works, Vol. 1* (pp. 24–25). Moscow: Progress.

Marx, K., & Engels, F. (1983). *Selected Works*, Vol. 3. (p. 172).

Marx. K. (1987). In: B. Magubane p. 47

Marx. K. (1993). In: C. L. Pines, *Ideology and False Consciousness: Marx and His Historical Progenitors* (p. 67). Albany, NY: SUNY.

Morrison, T. (1993). *Playing in the Dark: Whiteness and the Literary Imagination* (p. 63). New York, NY: Vintage Books.

Nicolls, D. (1985). *Haiti in Caribbean Content: Ethnicity, Economy and Revolt* (pp. 23, 33, 126). New York, NY: St. Martin's.

Nkrumah, K. (1965). *Neo-colonialism: the Last Stage of Imperialism*. London: Heinemann.

Nkrumah, K. (1970). In:W. Cartey & M Kilson (Eds), Neocolonialism in Africa. *The Africa Reader* (pp. 217–218). New York, NY: Random.

Norval, A. J. (1994). In: E. Laclau, *The Making of Political Identities* (p. 118). London: Verso.

Paraf, P. (1972). *Le racisme dans le monde* (p. 7). Paris: Payot.

Poulantzas, N. (1982). *Political Power and Social Classes* (pp. 206–208). London: Verso.

Reid, M. A. (1997). *PostNégritude Visual and Literary Culture* (pp. 8–9). Albany, NY: SUNY.

Reich, W. (1985). Ideology as a Material Force. *The Mass Psychology of Fascism* (pp. 13, 79). New York, NY: Farrar.

Rogers, B. (1980). *D.I.V.I.D.E. and Rule: South Africa's Bantustans* (p. 7). London: IDF.

Said, E. W. (1979). *Orientalism* (p. 3). New York, NY: Vintage Books.

Senghor, L. S. (1959). Rapport sur la doctrine et la propagande du parti. *Rapport du Congrès* (p. 14). Typed fascicule.

Senghor, L. S. (1964). Le message de Goethe aux Nègres. *Liberté I: Négritude et humanisme* (p. 96). Paris: Seuil.

Solomos, J., & Back, L. (1996). *Racism and Society* (pp. 18). New York, NY: St Martin's.

West, C. (1988). Marxist Theory and the Specificity of Afro-American Oppression. In: C. Nelson & L. Grossberg (Eds), *Marxism and the Interpretation of Culture* (p. 18). Urbana, IL: U of Illinois.

Williams, R. (1985). In: R. G. Fox. *The Lions of the Punjab: Culture in the Making* (p. 205). Berkeley, CA.

PART III:
UTILIZING SURPLUS VALUE EMPIRICALLY

ESTIMATING GROSS DOMESTIC PRODUCT WITH SURPLUS VALUE

Victor Kasper, Jr.

ABSTRACT

This paper examines the relationship among Marxian determinants of surplus value and gross output. Two versions of a Marxian-based computer model that permit simulation and sensitivity analysis are discussed and an example provided by Marx in Chapter 17 is replicated. Estimates of aggregate surplus value and value are made and implications demonstrated for the distribution of value, use value and social labor. Total value produced or transferred is then compared to U.S. GDP. Interestingly, although not identical in concept, there is only a 15% difference. The model is then used to assess the difference. Implications for research and teaching are explored.

To sum up; the concepts which contain Marx's basic discoveries are: the concepts of value and use-value; of abstract labor and concrete labour; and of surplus-value.

That is what Marx tells us. And there is no apparent reason why we should not take him at his word (Althusser, 1968, p. 80).

I. INTRODUCTION[1]

Marx's value theory provides an alternative lens for examining the macro economy to traditional macroeconomic theory. Marx saw surplus value as a driving force for industrial capitalism.[2] It is the engine that powers the system.

Confronting 9-11, Ideologies of Race, and Eminent Economists,
Research in Political Economy, Volume 20, pages 121–183.

121

Labor power represents its fuel. The dynamics of social conflict, wages, aggregate property income, GDP, the price level, and potential industrial or financial crises are affected by the growth, stagnation or decline in surplus value. A Marxian-based computer model provides an alternative to traditional views, potential for counterfactual experiments, and the possibility for testing the consistency of Marxist theory and macro data. We describe here the development and testing of web-based interactive computer models of surplus value determination.

Surplus value and variable capital are reflected in total national output. Shaikh and Tonak have studied the relationships between Marxist theory and the national income and product accounts (Shaikh & Tonak, 1994). They interpreted the theoretical Marxian economic categories and related them to the National Income and Product Accounts (NIPA) and input-output data. One significant aspect of their work was a demonstration of how the NIPA and Input Output data could be used to estimate Marxian categories such as surplus value, variable capital, constant capital and the rate of surplus value. The approach we take is to develop a Marxian-based computer simulation model that estimates surplus value, variable capital and aggregate value produced given a minimum of key Marxian parameters that must be independently estimated. The model is used to estimate total Marxian value and this is compared to estimates of gross domestic product. It reverses the procedure taken by Shaikh and Tonak. They take detailed NIPA GNP estimates and input output data and use them to construct estimates of Marxian categories. Foley used an example in his book to relate several Marxian variables to gross output (Foley, pp. 122–123). For Foley this was a broad illustration of a point he was emphasizing, while this issue is the focus of study here.

The premises of conventional and some heterodox Macro theory (Neoclassical -Keynesian Synthesis, Post-Keynesian theory, New Keynesian theory, and New Classical Theory) and Marxian theory differ.[3] Traditional approaches try to explain the business cycle and growth. While the approach of Marx is concerned with instability and accumulation, it is broader and suggests fundamental long run unresolvable conflict.[4]

Model Development

In developing the model, we use both sensitivity analysis and simulation. We feel sensitivity analysis is consistent with an exposition technique that Marx used in Chapter 17 of *Capital*. Marx used sensitivity analysis to clarify key issues of theory. We use the technique as part of a computer model that can estimate surplus value under a variety of hypothetical conditions. The model incorporates the principles Marx discussed in Chapter 17. We test the model by replicating an example provided by Marx and then using two versions of the model to estimate total value produced in the U.S. The first version was designed to estimate surplus value and variable capital while the second version also has the ability to estimate constant capital. The output of the model includes estimates of surplus value, total value, the nominal average wage in the productive sector, the distribution of use value and social labor. We compare total Marxian value to gross domestic product.

The approach allows a comparison of aggregate output estimates based on different theories. Total Marxian value produced or transferred provides an alternative measure to the NIPA estimates of gross economic activity. A key assumption where the model is fundamentally different from the traditional approach is that surplus value and the rate of surplus value which are the source of property income are determined or created in the production process prior to circulation.

The more traditional market approach suggests that market prices affect revenues and ultimately total value added from the overall economy. In the traditional approach to GDP, aggregate revenues from final goods represent the opportunity costs of factors of production and depreciation on the national capital stock. The opportunity costs for the means of production are measures of value these resources have 'contributed' to output. Value in the traditional approach refers to exchange value. For Marx, the means of production can only enhance the contributions made by labor, the economic return paid to the owners of capital in the form of interest, rent and profits represents the appropriation by capitalists of surplus value. This is made possible by monopoly ownership of the means of production and a portion of the population that has nothing to sell but its labor. Alternatively, we assume that surplus value and value production are created in production by labor under specific social conditions of production.

The Examples of Marx

Marx titled Chapter 17, Changes in Magnitude in the Price of Labour Power and in Surplus Value (Marx, *Capital*, Vol. 1, pp. 519–530). He divided this chapter into four sections. The approach taken in each section could be called sensitivity analysis today. In each section he analyzed the impact of changes in key socioeconomic factors on the value and price of labor-power and surplus-value. These factors were not factors determined by the interaction of willing buyers and sellers in the marketplace but by historically developed social and political struggles. The factors determined value and surplus value which get reflected in the market.[5] For Marx the appearances of the market masked a variety of underlying social struggles reflected but not clearly exposed by the market.[6]

Marx first examines the impact of holding the length of the working day and the intensity of labor constant and then varies the productiveness of labor. The second section examines the impact of holding the working day and productiveness of labor constant and then varies the intensity of labor. In the third section, he varied the length of the working day and held the productiveness of labor and the intensity of labor constant. In the last section he varies all three. We contend that this sensitivity analysis can be useful for analyzing Marxian concepts and relating them to modern macroeconomic aggregates. We outline how this can be done and the expected implications.

The Basic Approach

We first replicate the sensitivity analysis that Marx presented in Chapter 17 using a computer model. Then, contemporary values for the key factors determining surplus value variables are estimated. We use government and market statistics and the work of Shaikh and Tonak as a source of data (Shaikh & Tonak, 1994). Using the principles discussed by Marx, we add additional parameters such as the subsistence bundle of use value, and socially necessary labor time embodied in gold to the analysis. To test the consistency of the model with Marx's example, we successfully replicated the results of Marx's Chapter 17 example. U.S. GDP is then compared to estimated Marxian total value. We find some consistency between the NIPA U.S. GDP estimate and the estimates of Marxian Total value.

The model we develop assumes for the purpose of illustration for this study that the intensity of labor are constant, while the length of the working day or the productiveness of labor is varied. However, several input parameters such as the intensity of labor and productiveness of labor can be altered by a web user. Aside from the three variables noted in Chapter 17, Marx implicitly included several additional factors in his analysis. One implicit factor was the reckoning name of gold (money as a measurement of value or ideal money or as a definition of gold) in terms of the local currency. Another assumption was that the subsistence bundle of use value required for the average worker was constant. This subsistence bundle included both physical and cultural needs and was determined for an epoch by cultural and historical forces.[7] A third variable also implicit was the number of socially necessary abstract labor (SNAL2 definition) hours required to produce gold.[8] We have also added the number of productive workers per unit of capital.[9] The number of workers as an input parameter facilitates the estimation of aggregate total value. With his analysis, Marx was able to show how the magnitude and rate of surplus value were determined and varied. The variables he identified were focal points influenced by a variety of productive forces and social relations.

Interestingly, none of the factors identified with the exception of the reckoning name of money are determined by a market process representing relative scarcities.[10] The market rather reflects the conditions determined by value and surplus value. The process of production of value and surplus value influence either directly or indirectly the supply and demand conditions that generate market prices. The two factors that serve to translate the surplus labor and necessary labor into surplus value, variable capital and value are the reckoning name of money and the socially necessary abstract labor (SNAL2) per unit of gold.[11] The reckoning name of money and the socially necessary labor per ounce of gold provide a measure of the value of money. To the extent that market forces cause the value gold to deviate from its value, the estimates of Marxian Total Value will be distorted. However, rather than the market influencing the magnitude of value through the reckoning name of money, it can distort the manifestation of value.

The potential to conduct sensitivity analysis was a feature, we felt should be built into the model. This could be used for both teaching and counterfactual analysis. A sensitivity analysis based on the length of the working day is the starting point for an application of the model. The length of the working day is increased in 1% increments. The first version of the computer model was designed to generate six tables. Initial input parameter estimates for demonstrating the first version of the model were based on rough estimates of input parameters to test the validity of the model and feasibility of further model development. The input parameters were later refined based on data obtained from government or market sources or from the work of Shaikh and Tonak. The more empirically based input parameters were used to test a second version of the model. Based on output of this model, we estimated total value and compared it to NIPA estimates of GDP reported by the Department of Commerce.

Marxian Fundamentals

The model is based on our interpretation of several Marxian principles, based on our reading. The basic fundamentals that we attempted to keep consistent with Marx were focused on labor power and socially necessary abstract labor. The principles dictated the variables that we selected as the initial input parameters. Several of these fundamentals, and why they led to the variables selected are discussed below.

For Marx a commodity was both a use value and a value. As a use value it was produced by concrete labor. As value it represented a portion of society's total labor (SNAL1). This labor represented the socially necessary abstract labor (SNAL1) hours required to produce the commodity. To access labor, capital must acquire labor power or capacity (L).[12] Labor power is the "aggregate of those mental and physical capabilities existing in a human being, which he [the worker] exercises whenever he produces a use-value of any description" (Marx, Vol. 1, p. 167). An important point to note here is that capital pays for L but receives the hours of labor in a working day per worker.

Expenditure of L represents the consumption of the life force of people in a process of production. Reproduction of labor power (L) requires access to a subsistence bundle of goods and services that will reproduce the aggregate worker. The subsistence bundle is a composite of commodities.[13] Each of these commodities represents specific use values. The mass of use value in the subsistence bundle is assumed to be measured as an absolute value.

The productive consumption of L yields labor in motion equal to the surplus hours in the working day that capital appropriates plus the hours required to reproduce that labor-power. The labor hours (HOL) require for reproducing labor-power (L) is embodied in the subsistence bundle. This subsistence bundle of commodities yields a flow of use value over a given working life to reproduce the worker as a worker. The production of these commodities requires a specific number of hours of living labor (HOLL – in the SNAL2 definition). The value of labor power is measured by the embodied HOLL (in the SNAL2 definition) in its subsistence bundle of commodities (representing a fixed amount of use value).

The value of the subsistence bundle will change with the value and mass of necessaries in the subsistence bundle (Marx, Vol. 1, p. 523). The mass of necessaries is the quantity of those subsistence goods required to provide the necessary use value for reproduction. The value of necessities is determined by the (SNAL2 definition) hours embodied in them. However, value is not expressed in HOL but in money terms. Money (Gold as measure of value or standard of price) provides one means of estimating both the value per HOL, the value per use value, and consequently the value of L. Given the SNAL2 hours of labor in an ounce of gold and the reckoning name of money (the price of gold), we can estimate the value of the use value in the subsistence bundle of a unit of labor capacity. This money measurement of the value of L is dependent upon the reckoning name of money (which under the assumptions of our model is the currency units per unit of gold) and the SNAL2 hours in an ounce of gold. Gold provides us with a measure of value that is used translating surplus labor and necessary labor into value terms.

Increases in the length of the working day will increase the amount of value and surplus value produced. Surplus value can only be produced if the average worker can produce more use value on average in a day than that required to reproduce his/her labor capacity over time.

The length of the working day (LOWD) and the number of productive workers are determinants of the maximum amount of total value that can be produced for any society.[14] The intensity of labor (IOL) is important for comparing labor expended between spheres of the economy, between different societies and in the same economy over time. One society can use up more labor capacity per hour because it uses labor more intensely. With a given LOWD, increasing the intensity of labor will increase both the value of L, surplus value and use value produced per day.[15] The initial assumption used in the development of the model was that the value of labor power consumed and the surplus value produced in any given hour of the working day increases in proportion to the increase in the intensity of labor relative to an hour of normal intensity. The products or use values produced for the more intensive hour should also be greater than that for an hour of ordinary intensity. In the first version of the model, the productiveness of labor has to be adjusted as an input factor by the web user to reflect the increased output of the more intensive hour. In the second version of the model, the model does this automatically.

II. THE DETERMINATE FACTORS

The seven input variables that determine the socioeconomic conditions are the productiveness of labor, the length of the working day, the intensity of labor, a measure of the absolute value of the average worker's subsistence bundle, the number of workers per capital, the reckoning name of money, and the SNAL2 hours per unit of gold.[16] These factors describe key aspects of the Marxian economic relations and play a more direct role in determining surplus labor, necessary labor, the rate of surplus value, the value of labor power, surplus value, the value of an average use value, the average wage in the productive sector, and the distribution of value and use value between workers and capital.

Below are brief definitions and discussions of the input parameters:

Productiveness of Labor
The productiveness of labor (POL) is a measure of new use value produced per hour of the working day.[17] This is assumed to be productiveness of labor in subsidence goods and services that yield a given quantity of use value.[18] The use value concept allows one to abstract from the large number of commodities that exist.[19] Marx refers to the impact of an increase the productiveness of labor as resulting in the situation ". . . whereby the same quantum of labour yields, in a given time, a greater or less quantum of product, dependent on the degree of development in the conditions of production" (Marx, Vol. 1, pp. 519–520).

Intensity of Labor

The intensity of labor (IOL) is a measure of how fast labor works. It assumes that the level of stress and nature of work has an impact on the ability of labor to reproduce itself. This increases the SNAL2 hours per unit of labor power. A value of one is taken as that of day of normal intensity. An intensity of labor greater than one indicates intensity greater than normal in which each hour of the more intense working day is represented by some multiple of hours of normal intensity. The labor used both for producing surplus product and for reproducing labor power are increased.

The intensity of labor measures the speed with at which labor power is expended. Greater stress and speed in the work process require a larger magnitude of commodities in the subsistence bundle and hence a greater magnitude of use value and SNAL2 to reproduce any given amount of labor power. For any given society there is assumed to be an average intensity of labor. For the analysis of a given society with a capitalist mode of production, the intensity of labor at a given point in time is not important. The intensity of labor becomes important for analyzing a society over time, comparing different economies, comparing different spheres of an economy at one point in time and for different capitals within a sphere. A society with an intensity of labor twice as large of another society may use twice as much labor power as the society with the lower intensity. This raises an issue of interpretation. The output of use value per hour is assumed by Marx in his example to increase in proportion to the intensity of labor so that the value per unit of product does not change. This means that one hour of labor of double intensity is equal to two hours of labor of normal intensity. Changes in the intensity of labor then alter the value of labor power, surplus value and the output of use value per hour. This assumes the LOWD has not changed. The model we developed here adjusts for intensity by increasing the value of the hours of labor of normal intensity required for surplus and necessary labor. In the first version of the model, the user must adjust for an expected increase in the use value produced per hour. In the second version of the model, the use value produced per hour automatically changes in direct proportion to the change in the intensity of labor. If the use value produced per hour increases in proportion to the intensity of labor, the variable capital and surplus value produced per day will increase in proportion to the intensity of labor. This is not necessarily the case, nevertheless, we assume this is the case for the second version of the model. Marx in discussing the impact of an increase in the intensity of labor, notes:

> ... It is clear that, if the value created by a day's labour increases from, say, 6 to 8 shillings, then the two parts into which this value is divided, viz., price of labour-power and surplus-value, may both of them increase simultaneously, and either equally or unequally. They

may both simultaneously increase from 3 shillings to 4. Here, the rise in the price of labour-power does not necessarily imply that the price has risen above the value of labour-power. On the contrary, the rise in price may be accompanied by a fall in value. This occurs whenever the rise in the price of labour-power does not compensate for its increased wear and tear (Marx, Vol. 1, p. 525).

It is assumed in this study that the increased intensity of labor increases the hours of labor per hour of the more intense working day by a multiple of the hours in a day of normal intensity. We assume the increase in the rate of productive consumption of labor power is proportional to the increase in the intensity of labor. In sum, in the first version of the model, output of use value per labor hour was not automatically increased as the intensity of labor is increased. Marx does imply that the required subsistence bundle (measured in SNAL2) is also proportional to the increase in the intensity of labor. He notes the following about the effect of an increase in intensity. ". . . Here, we have an increase in the number of products, unaccompanied by a fall in their individual prices as their number increases, so does the sum of their prices" (Marx, Vol. 1, p. 524). This is followed later by a statement that suggests that the price of labor-power may not always increase in proportion to the increased wear and tear on the laborer resulting from increased intensity. Greater value is created for any given hour of labor hour productively consumed.

The Length of the Working Day
The length of the working day (LOWD) represents the hours the average productive worker performs in a day[20] (productive labor is that which produces surplus value).[21] This is determined by historical and political conditions and will vary from one economy to another and in one economy over time. Given the other input parameters, the length of the working day will be a key determinant of the total value. More importantly, this is most useful for understanding value from the standpoint of total social capital. Marx indicates clearly that within certain limits the length of the working day is determined by political struggle. Note here that we are speaking of labor in the sense of aggregate worker and capital in the sense of total social capital. Marx notes:

> . . . Hence is it that in the history of capitalist production, the determination of what is a working-day, presents itself as the result of a struggle, a struggle between collective capital, i.e. the class of capitalists, and collective labour, i.e. the working-class (Marx, Vol. 1, p. 235).

Number of Productive Workers
The number of productive workers (NOW) represents the workers per capital or in a socioeconomic system. The number of workers per capital can be interpreted

in a number of ways depending upon the needs of the analyst. We will use this analysis to address macro aggregates and, therefore, it represents the number of productive workers in the economy. For estimates the number of productive workers, we made use of the proportion of productive workers to total employed workers. The information needed to estimate this was obtained from the work of Shaikh and Tonak (Shaikh & Tonak, 1994). Shaikh and Tonak estimate that the total employment in the U.S. in 1989 was 113,511,000 and that productive employment was 41,148,070 in the same year. The proportion of productive to total employment was estimated to be 36.25%. We use this proportion to arrive at an estimate of productive workers in the U.S. in 2000.

Social Necessary Labor Per Ounce of Gold

The socially necessary labor hours per ounce of gold (SLGD) represent the SNAL2 hours per ounce of gold. This variable is similar to what Foley calls the value of money (Foley, p. 15). However, we use Marx's second definition of the necessary labor that only includes the necessary labor associated with the variable capital used to produce gold.

The socially necessary labor per ounce of gold is one of two factors that are required to convert surplus labor and necessary labor into value terms. Marx avoids this issue in Chapter 17 by assuming that the worker produces a given mass of products and that the product has a unit price. He also assumes that value is equal to price but only as a working assumption. He implies often that this may not be the usual case.

To generate a model that is more useful and still consistent with Marxian theory, we need to convert labor hours (in the SNAL2 definition) per unit of L to value by finding a monetary expression of the value of a labor hour. One solution is suggested by Foley. If we know that the SNAL1 hours is represented by a given of money value that can be called the value of money, then the reciprocal of this ratio is what Foley calls the monetary expression of value. The resulting term measured in currency units per labor hour (in the SNAL1 definition) can be used to convert necessary labor, surplus labor and total labor time in into value terms. It must be noted that Foley uses the SNAL1 definition.

We decided on an alternative procedure. The procedure we used is based on gold and is controversial as Foley would agree, since current institutional arrangements do not use of gold as a monetary standard. We argue that though gold is not officially recognized as a monetary standard, it may be implicitly used as an index of value.[22] The market can still use gold as a measure of value even if national governments do not recognize it explicitly. We use the value of gold as reported by the London Bullion market to estimate the reckoning name of money. We use money here in its role as money of account (Marx, Vol. 1, p. 100).

We needed an estimate of the SNAL2 hours per ounce of gold. Since we are examining socially necessary abstract labor in Marx's second definition, the magnitude of this value cannot be directly observed. We would have to know the concrete hours of labor for producing gold, the level of skill per unit of labor used and the relative intensity of labor producing gold was relative to the social norm. This SNAL1 in an ounce of gold can be approximated by using the world market price of gold and the estimated average wage of productive labor. If we assume that the labor value of gold is equal the price of gold divided by the average wage in the productive sectors, we can arrive at a rough measure of the socially necessary labor per ounce of gold (in the SNAL1 definition). However, the necessary input the web user has to provide is in SNAL2 hours. An estimate of these hours must be made. For example, if we divided $275 per ounce for gold by an average wage in the productive sectors of $15.53, we have estimated the SNAL1 hours in an ounce of gold to be 17.7 hours. If we divide this by the length of the working day say 8.094, it yields 2.18 as the number of working days in an ounce of gold. If we multiply this by the number of SNAL2 hours per unit of L say 2.35, we have an estimate of 5.12 SNAL2 hours per ounce of gold. The length of the working day is an input parameter and the number of hours in a unit of labor power is determined independently of the SNAL2 hours per ounce of gold. We used this method in the study to infer a value for the socially necessary labor per ounce of gold. There is at least one theoretical qualification. To be consistent with Marx's theory, it would have to be assumed that the price of gold was equal to its value and the average daily wage (the price of labor power) in the productive sector was equal to the monetary expression of labor power per working day.

Reckoning Name of Money

The reckoning name of money (RNM) or the currency units per ounce of gold is assumed to be equal to the market price of gold per ounce. The reckoning name of money makes possible the use of currency as a unit of account. In an economy where gold might serve as informal backing for credit money (currency), we speculate that the introduction of excess paper credit or paper money relative to the world market supply of gold will act on the price level in this model by altering the reckoning name of money.[23]

The Use Value in a Subsistence Bundle of Commodities

The use value in a subsistence bundle of the average worker (SB) is a measure of the absolute level of the mass of use value in that bundle. Workers are assumed to have a required bundle of commodities for their reproduction. These commodities must provide a constant total use value to ensure reproduction. The bundle of commodities necessary to yield this constant use value can vary. The amount of use value in the subsistence bundle should be affected by the length of the working day and the intensity of labor. This model does not automatically make this adjustment.[24] In the first version of the model, the mass of use value was determined by the web-user's input value for the mass of use value in the subsistence bundle. This meant that as the number of working days increased so did the subsistence bundle of use value generated per year. We altered this assumption for the second version of the model. Increasing the number of working days per year beyond 214 in the second model will not alter the annual subsistence bundle and will result in an increasing rate of surplus value.

The measure of the subsistence bundle represents a bundle of commodities socially necessary to reproduce the worker over time.[25] Its value is equal to the labor time necessary to reproduce the worker over time. Marx assumes that the use value represented in this bundle was constant during an epoch. The subsistence bundle can be represented by a bundle of commodities or by a measure of use value from these commodities. A measure of use values is a simpler way of estimating this than using a bundle of commodities. It is also not affected by changes in relative prices. As relative prices change, the composition of commodities consumed by the worker will change but the worker can reproduce him/herself by substituting commodities in the bundle to obtain the mass of use value that is necessary to reproduce him/herself as workers. There is no certainty that a change in the composition of commodities consumed is going to result in the mass of use value that will yield that necessary for reproduction of the aggregate worker. For example, workers in response to relative price changes may change the composition of their purchased commodities and reproduce their labor only in the short-run. Such a system is not sustainable unless other aspects of the system change. Such an economic system will run itself down unless it can obtain labor from non-capitalist sectors of the economy. The significant point is that the purchased bundle of commodities may not always be the same thing as what Marx would call the subsistence bundle. Marx conceived of this concept under conditions where capitalist relations were the only relations that prevailed to illustrate how such a system would work. Under any given socioeconomic system atavisms of the past exist that are not completely consistent with industrial capitalism, the family, community networks, partially subsistence farmers, etc., small crafts operations, etc. Lack of workers in the long run will prevent the system from sustaining itself.[26]

A measure of the mass of use value in the subsistence bundle is not directly observable. However, given the LOWD and the IOL, there is a relationship between the rate of surplus value, the productiveness of labor and the use value in the subsistence bundle. The productiveness of labor and subsistence value of use value imply a given rate of surplus value. If we have estimates of the rate of surplus value, we can alter the ratio of the productiveness of labor relative to the use value per subsistence bundle to generate a specific rate of surplus value. This makes the rate of surplus value at least initially an input rather than an output of the model. However, it provides a means for estimating an empirically based ratio between the use value in the subsistence bundle and the productiveness of labor. The absolute value of these variables can take on any absolute value as long as the ratio between the two is consistent with our estimate of the rate of surplus value. It makes possible thought experiments where the ratio can be altered and we can evaluate the impact on the rate of surplus value. This procedure provides a benchmark ratio.

III. THE MODEL

The first version of the model has thirteen basic equations. The programming involves many more equations and manipulations but these are the basic equations.

$$NL = SB/(POL) \tag{1}$$

Equation (1) determines the socially necessary abstract labor per unit of productive labor capacity (L). Socially necessary abstract labor in Marx's second definition of the term – that is in the amount of labor required to reproduce the average worker *independent of the social structure of the economy*. It is measured in socially necessary labor time per unit of L per day. Socially necessary abstract labor is determined by dividing the quantity of use value in the daily subsistence bundle by the productiveness of labor in subsistence goods.

$$SL = LOWD - NL \tag{2}$$

Equation (2) determines the surplus labor appropriated by capital. Surplus labor is defined as the length of the working day minus necessary labor (in Marx's second definition of the term).

$$SBAI = SBUV*IOL \tag{3}$$

Equation (3) determines the quantity of use value in the subsistence bundle necessary for the average worker's reproduction adjusted for the intensity of work. It is a measure of the absolute level adjusted for intensity of labor.

$$NLAI = SBAI/(POL) \tag{4}$$

Equation (4) determines the SNAL2 hours (Marx's second definition). This is the necessary hours in the subsistence bundle adjusted for the intensity of labor. It is measured in hours of a working day of standard intensity. More intense labor will be measured in hours of a day of standard intensity. So if the intensity of the working day doubles, it implies that for every hour of the working day, two hours of a day of standard labor are used. The magnitude of NLAI is determined by the quantity of use value in the daily subsistence bundle per day of a unit of labor power (L) divided by the productiveness of labor (POL). The productiveness of labor is a measure of the quantity of new use value produced per hour of the working day by one worker.[27]

$$SLAI = (LOWD)(IOL) - NLAI \tag{5}$$

Equation (5) determines the surplus labor hours adjusted for intensity of labor and measured in hours of normal intensity. The intensity adjustment is relevant for analyzing different spheres of industry, capitals, workers, or different socio-economic systems. For the application of the model in this study, the intensity adjustment is not used. It will become important for projected future applications. The surplus labor hours adjusted for intensity are equal to the length of the working day (adjusted for intensity) minus the socially necessary labor hours in Marx's second definition of this term. The socially necessary labor is also adjusted for the intensity of labor.

$$RSV = 100*SLAI/NLAI \tag{6}$$

Equation (6) determines the rate of surplus value. The rate of surplus value is defined as surplus labor divided by necessary labor. It is to be noted that Marx first defines the rate of surplus value as surplus value divided by variable capital[28] (Marx, Vol. 1, p. 216). Later, he notes that:

The rate of surplus value is represented by the following formulae.

Surplus Value/Variable Capital (s/v) = Surplus Value/Value of labour-power = Surplus-labour/Necessary labour (Marx, Vol. 1, p. 531).

$$GDVLSB = NLAI * 1/SLGD \tag{7}$$

Equation (7) determines the gold value of the subsistence bundle measured in ounces of gold per subsistence bundle. It is equal to the SNAL2 hours in the subsistence bundle (adjusted for intensity) times the reciprocal of the labor value of an ounce of gold (SLGD). The labor value of an ounce gold (SLGD) is measured in SNAL2 hours.

$$VC = RNM * GDVLSB \tag{8}$$

Equation (8) is the relationship determining variable capital. Variable capital is equal to the value of labor capacity. Variable capital in the computer model is equal to the reckoning name for money times the gold value of the subsistence bundle. It allows money to be used as a measure of value. It allows the conversion of the gold value of the subsistence bundle into the currency units. The average daily price for gold in 2000 on the London Gold Market (as published on internet by the London Bullion Market Association) for the pm fix was \$274.63 an ounce (Data: taken from http://www.lbma.org.uk/statisticscover.html, July 26, 2002).

$$SNLHPD = SLGD/RNM \tag{9}$$

Equation (9) determines the socially necessary labor time in a currency unit. It is measured as the SNAL2 hours per dollar. In this paper, SNAL2 hours per dollar equals the socially necessary labor per ounce of gold (SNGD) divided by the reckoning name of money (RNM). The SNGD is the socially necessary labor in an ounce of gold by Marx's second definition of necessary labor.

$$VALUE = LOWD * (1/SNLHPD) * IOL \tag{10}$$

Equation (10) measures the value created in a working day per unit of labor capacity (L) measured in currency units (adjusted for intensity). It is equal to the length of the working day multiplied by the reciprocal of the socially necessary labor per currency unit (SNLHPD) adjusted for the intensity of labor (IOL).

$$SV = VALUE - VC \tag{11}$$

Equation (11) determines the surplus value produced in a working day measured in currency units. It is equal to the newly produced value per day (VALUE) per labor capacity (L) minus variable capital.

$$USEV = POL * LOWD \tag{12}$$

Equation (12) determines the quantity of use value produced by one worker per working day. It is equal to the productiveness of labor per hour times the length of the working day. This relation provides a theoretical means of estimating impacts on the real wage. It is assumed that use value is a measure of the real output of commodities produced. In the second version of the model equations are developed to consider the impact of the use value transferred from constant capital.

$$VPUV = VALUE/USEV \tag{13}$$

Equation (13) determines the currency price per unit of use value. It is determined by dividing the total value produced by the total use value produced. This relation can be used to develop a general price index which should be

capable of being used to simulate price level changes. In the second version
of the model, the value of a use value is equal to the total value produced or
transferred divided by the use value produced or transferred. Constant capital
is introduced in the second version of the model.

IV. THE EXAMPLES OF MARX

Marx provides four scenarios that he uses to illustrate how the productiveness
of labor, the length of the working day and the intensity of labor determine of
surplus value. Two of his examples are discussed here to illustrate the consistency of our interpretation of Marx's relations with his textual examples. Marx
makes several assumptions that are meant to hold for all of the examples in
Chapter 17. These include: (1) that the subsistence bundle is made up of the
necessaries of life and is constant; (2) that commodities are sold at their value;
(3) and that the price of labor power is equal to or greater than the value of
labor power.[29] Given these assumptions, Marx discusses the impact on the price
of labor power and surplus value of changes in the productiveness of labor, the
intensity of labor, and the length of the working day. Since it is assumed that
the value of commodities is equal to their prices, the price of labor power is
equal to the value of labor power.

We have summarized Marx's relations in a computer model and demonstrate
the model's potential for research and teaching below. Two of Marx's examples
are replicated illustrating the conceptual consistency of the model with Marx's
sensitivity analysis of Chapter 17.

One of Marx's examples illustrates how the length of the working-day can
influence surplus value and the price of labor-power when the productiveness
and intensity of labor are constant.[30] Marx in this example dispenses with the
need to estimate the socially necessary labor content of money and the reckoning
name of money by assigning values to surplus value and labor-power. In
addition, he excludes the subsistence bundle as a factor by assuming that it is
constant. In his example on page 526, he assumes that necessary labor is
6 hours and that the value of labor power is 3 shillings while surplus labor
represents 6 hours and surplus value is 3 shillings. This means that the value
of a day's production of 12 hours for one worker is 6 shillings. He then asks
what happens when the length of the working day (LOWD) is increased by
2 hours. If the price of labor power is constant, surplus value (s) and relative
surplus value (s/v) both increase. He does indicate, however, that when LOWD
is increased, the price of labor-power may fall below its value. This occurs
since the value of labor power may be increased as a result of increased wear
and tear that additional working time imposes on the worker. Here he relaxes

one of his assumptions by indicating the potential difference between the value of labor power and the price of labor power. If the increase in wear and tear on the worker from an extended working day is not compensated by an increase in the price of labor power, the price of labor power will fall below the value of labor power. This particular observation is important because it is textual evidence that Marx felt that these concepts are different and that these concepts are not identically determined. Marx indicates that in this circumstance both surplus value and the rate of surplus value can both potentially increase. Changes in the LOWD can result in changes in both surplus value and the value of labor power but not necessarily the price of labor power. Our model assumes that the value of labor power does not increase with an increase in the LOWD. For Marx, this is not necessarily the case. The increased LOWD will cause increased wear and tear on the worker. The increased wear and tear will mean that SNAL2 hours per unit of L will increase (i.e. there will be more necessaries of life in the subsistence bundle).[31] Future enhancements of the model will address this issue. Given the LOWD and the IOL, necessary labor in the model is determined by the relationship between the subsistence bundle of use value and the productiveness of labor in the production of subsistence goods.

The first version model that we develop has eight inputs. These include several factors that Marx does not consider. Although he deals with these factors elsewhere in his writings, the number of workers per capital, the use value in the worker's subsistence bundle, the reckoning name of money and the socially necessary labor hours per ounce of gold are not considered by Marx in the examples provided in Chapter 17.[32] To make the model more versatile, we have included these factors in the model. Replicating Marx's example with the model, we used the values indicated in Exhibit 1 to estimate surplus value and variable capital. The values for the reckoning name of money and the socially necessary labor (second definition of necessary labor) per ounce of gold were not used by Marx in his example. Marx made the assumptions that the total value produced per day was 6 shillings and the variable capital was 3 shillings and surplus value 3 shillings. To replicate this assumption for our model we had to estimate several factors. The reckoning name of money was assigned a value of 80 shillings per ounce and the socially necessary labor in an ounce of gold was equated to 160 SNAL2 hours. These values were based on examples that Marx used.[33] We assumed that only one worker is used and that the LOWD is incremented by 1% each period. The two key factors that determine the rate of surplus value, given the LOWD, are the productiveness of labor and the mass of use value in the subsistence bundle (assuming we keep the intensity of labor constant). The mass of use value in the daily subsistence bundle divided by the mass of use value produced in an hour by a unit of labor capacity yields

Exhibit 1.   Determinants of Surplus Value.

Length of working day	12 hours
Productiveness of labor	0.50 (use values produced per worker per hour)
Intensity of labor	1 normal intensity
Number of workers per capital as a measure for labor capacity (L)	1 worker
Quantity of use value in the worker's subsistence bundle	3.00 (measure of the use value in a worker's daily subsistence bundle)
Definition of gold	80 shillings per ounce
Socially necessary labor per ounce of gold	160 (SNAL [second definition] hours per ounce of gold)
Increment of to the length of the working day	1% (as measured by a percent of the working day)

the hours of SNAL2 hours per day per worker. This necessary labor subtracted from the LOWD yields the surplus labor. The surplus labor divided by the necessary labor yields the rate of surplus value. What is particularly important is the ratio between the subsistence bundle and the productiveness of labor (POL). For any given LOWD and intensity of labor, this ratio will imply a rate of surplus value. Marx's example implies a rate of surplus value of 100%. Any magnitudes for the subsistence bundle and the productiveness of labor that yields a ratio of 6 would be consistent with Marx's example (Where 6 hours of necessary labor in a 12 hour day yields a rate of surplus value of 100). We have used a value of 0.50 for the mass of use value produced per worker per hour and a mass of use value included in the worker's subsistence bundle of 3.00. These magnitudes directly reproduce Marx's assumptions and the analytical results of his example in Chapter 17. The data used in the model are obtained from other textual references in Marx's writings. The estimates of these input factors are used with the computer model to yield results consistent with his Chapter 17 example. Since Marx does not use the monetary factors that are included in the computer model, this trial run is only a partial validation of the approach used by the computer model to convert magnitude of labor values into money form. The approach is validated in the sense that it is consistent with Marx's theory in the manner that it treats money.

The output of the model examines the manifestation of surplus labor in the form of surplus value and use value that is implied by the input factors and Marx's economic relations incorporated in the model. The model also estimates the rate of surplus value and the hours of labor per use value. The output of the trial run of the computer model replicating Marx's examples are presented in Exhibits 2, 3, and 4. In Exhibit 2, we present the value produced per day per unit of labor capacity and its distribution between surplus value and variable capital. It must again be noted that Marx assumed a specific rate of surplus value. We have estimated the model by assuming a ratio of the subsistence bundle to the productiveness of labor that is consistent with the rate of surplus value Marx used. The results in Exhibit 2 are based on the assumptions used by Marx in his example. The trial run of the model is used to clarify the concepts, the consistency of the outcome to Marx's examples and the potential future use of the model. Marx argues that both the magnitude and rate of surplus value can increase as the LOWD increases. This will be the case if the value of labor power is assumed to be constant as the LOWD day increases. Exhibit 2 indicates that in the model's solution this is the case. The significance of the output is that it has demonstrated that the computer model can replicate Marx's results. The demonstration is significant because of the potential to replicate the variation on these calculations relatively quickly for a variety of scenarios, to check on the conceptual consistency of inputs, check the empirical consistency of outputs and because this model will serve as a component part for a more complex model to be developed later. The same results can be estimated for different values for all combinations of the eight inputs. The model can facilitate comparison of different empirical estimates of Marxian parameters, socioeconomic systems, different spheres of production, capitals and projections of change over time.

Exhibit 3 summarizes the distribution of labor time as the LOWD is increased with the subsistence bundle held constant. By assumption, necessary labor in Marx's second definition of the term is constant. As a result, increasing the LOWD increases surplus labor. For Marx, the market price of a unit of L, can vary from the value of labor power (L). This can occur if the value of labor power is unchanged while the length of the working day increases. Since increasing the LOWD will increase wear and tear on the laborer, the value of labor power productively consumed per day will increase. Marx assumed for his example that the value of labor power remained constant in the sense that the use value required for the subsistence bundle did not change. We believe he did this because he believed that the increase in labor capacity consumed would be less than proportional to the increase in LOWD. For increases in the LOWD over a given range this is probably true. He needed this assumption to demonstrate how increasing the LOWD might not only increase absolute surplus value but also relative surplus value. Increasing the wear and tear on the worker would increase the value of labor capacity or power consumed. If the price of

Exhibit 2. Composition of Total Value Produced per Worker per day and the Rate of Surplus Value.

LOWD increased by increments of 1%	Surplus Value plus Variable Capital per day per worker (shillings)	Surplus Value per day per worker (shillings)	Variable Capital per worker per day (shillings)	Rate of Surplus Value (%)
12.000	6.00	3.00	3.00	100
12.120	6.06	3.06	3.00	102
12.241	6.12	3.12	3.00	104
12.364	6.18	3.18	3.00	106
12.487	6.24	3.24	3.00	108

Exhibit 3. Labor Time, Surplus Labor and Necessary Labor.

LOWD increased by increments of 1%	Surplus Labour plus Necessary Labour per day per worker (hours)	Surplus Labour per day per worker (hours)	Necessary Labour per worker per day (hours)
12.000	12.00	6.00	6.00
12.120	12.06	6.06	6.00
12.241	12.12	6.12	6.00
12.364	12.18	6.18	6.00
12.487	12.24	6.24	6.00

labor power is constant and the value of labor power consumed increased, the price of labor power would fall below its value.[34] This occurs because more SNAL2 would be required per unit of labor power but the fixed nominal wage would no longer be able to purchase it.

Exhibit 4 illustrates the results of this trial run for production and distribution of use value. Use value represents a measure of real income.[35] Exhibit 4 depicts the manifestation of surplus labor as use value. Based on the model's assumptions, it depicts the distribution of real income (use value) between capital and labor. Under the conditions assumed, real income per worker remains constant as the LOWD increases but real income distributed to capital increases. Exhibit 4 also indicates the value per use value. The total value produced per worker per day divided by the use values produced per worker per day. This concept is potentially useful for development of a measure of the price level based on Marx's theory. The key determining factor for the value per use value is the POL.[36] The value of 1.00 was produced by altering proportionally the values of the subsistence bundle of use values (SBUV) relative to productiveness of labor (POL) while maintaining their ratio at 6. This procedure ensured that the rate of surplus value was consistent with Marx's example of 100%. The ratio between SBUV and POL can imply a given rate of surplus value (with a constant intensity of labor and LOWD). Altering the absolute value of the POL will alter the value that a unit of use value conveys. Thus, by altering the absolute values of the POL and SBUV proportionally, we can adjust the absolute value of the use value produced to equal to one. This provides us with a potential price index.[37] This procedure is important for providing benchmark estimates for POL and SBUV. Use value is not observable. The productiveness of labor measured in use value and the use value in the subsistence bundle cannot be

Exhibit 4. Production and Distribution of Use Value and Labor Value Per Use Value.

LOWD increased by increments of 10%	Use value produced per day per worker (units)	Use value going to Capital (units)	Use value for labor real day's wage (units)	Value per unit of Use value (shillings/use value)
12 000	6.00	3.00	3.00	1.00
12 120	6.06	3.06	3.00	1.00
12 241	6.12	3.12	3.00	1.00
12 364	6.18	3.18	3.00	1.00
12 487	6.24	3.24	3.00	1.00

observed. Estimates of the rate of surplus value are available. By altering the ratio of the units of use value in the subsistence bundle to the productiveness of labor, we can establish a specific rate of surplus value. The productiveness of labor can be adjusted to produce a ratio relative to SBUV that will generate a rate of surplus value that has been estimated. Then, absolute values of the POL and SBUV can be altered proportionally using the model to produce a value per use value equal to 1. This last step provides the basis of an index. The drawback of this method is that the rate of surplus value, at least, initially becomes an input into the model instead of an output. However, once the benchmark values for the productiveness of labor and/or the use value per subsistence bundles are established, counterfactual experiments conducted that evaluate changes in either the POL or SBUV on the rate of surplus value are possible. Another advantage of this method is that it allows us to estimate the productiveness of labor without knowing GDP beforehand. All we need with this procedure is the ratio of the SB to the POL.

In addition, the model will potentially provide a way to examine the impact of change on the price level. The distinguishing feature of this analysis would be its Marxian theoretical base.

The model solution in Exhibit 4 indicates that the increase in the LOWD has no impact on the price level. In other words, increasing the length of the working day increases both the value produced and use value produced proportionally.[38]

We use a second example of Marx from Chapter 17 to confirm the consistency of the model with Marx's economic relations represented in the computer model. This example is from the first section of Chapter 17 (Marx, Vol. 1, pp. 520–520). This particular example is used to illustrate the three laws determining the value of labor-power and surplus value. The third law states that surplus value will always change due to changes in the value of labor power but changes in the value of labor power cannot change as a result of a change in surplus value. Under the given conditions (constant LOWD and IOL), a change in the rate of surplus value and a change in the surplus value can only result from a change in the magnitude of the value of labor power. Since the productiveness of labor (POL) influences the value of labor power, changes in POL will change surplus value and the rate of surplus value.[39] In his example, Marx again assumes that the value of output per worker per day is 6 shillings and that the LOWD is 12 hours. He assumes that the value of labor power is equal to 3 shillings and that surplus value is also equal to 3 shillings.[40] Surplus labor is equal to 6 hours and necessary labor is equal to 6 hours. These are the same initial assumptions of the previous examples. The computer model replicates this example by using the same inputs as were used in the previous exhibits for the LOWD equal to 12 hours. Marx examines the impact on surplus value, the value of labor power, the rate of surplus value of changing the productiveness of labor. He indicates that the value of labor power is determined by the value of a quantity of "necessaries." He states "It is the value and not the mass of these necessaries that varies with the productiveness of labor" (Marx, Vol. 1, p. 523). This means that the unit value of a "necessary" measured in currency units is what the productiveness of labor influences. In the computer model this unit value is estimated by the value of a use value. In the first version of the model, the value of a unit of use value is determined by the product of the reckoning name of money (RNM), the reciprocal of the SNAL2 hours per ounce of gold (SNGD), and the reciprocal of the productiveness of labor.[41] Marx addresses the question of how the distribution of use value is affected when the productiveness of labor doubles. He shows that it is possible with an increased productiveness of labor, for the use value received by both workers and capitalists to increase. This means increased real income for both. This can take place in spite of the fact that the price of labor power and surplus value do not change. This illustration demonstrates his view that the price of labor power can remain unchanged even when the value of labor power declines. The value of labor power declines because the productiveness of labor in subsistence goods has increased and less labor is required to produce the subsistence bundle of commodities that represents a constant quantity of use value. In fact, if the price of labor power falls but falls proportionally less than the value of labor power, the real income of workers will still increase although not in proportion to the real income of capitalists.[42]

The computer model was used to replicate the assumptions and results of this example and are presented in Exhibits 5 through 7. Exhibit 5 indicates surplus value, the value of labor power, and the rate of surplus value under the assumption that the price of labor power falls to the value of labor power. This result assumes that there is no effective class struggle to prevent the price of labor power falling to the value of labor power. The value of labor power sets a limit for the fall in the price of labor power that would still be consistent with unchanged real income or the unchanged subsistence bundle for the worker. In his example Marx indicates that a doubling of the productiveness of labor results in a new value of labor power of 1 shilling 6d. This is equivalent to $1^1/_2$ shillings that is replicated by the computer model. The computer model indicates that the rate of surplus value increases to 300%, surplus value increases to 4.5 shillings, while the total value produced does not change. The results of the model are consistent with Marx's example.

Exhibit 6 indicates the distribution of labor time between the unpaid labor time appropriated by the capitalist and the necessary labor required for producing a unit of labor power. A unit of labor power (capacity) is represented

Exhibit 5. Composition of Total Value Produced Per Worker (Unit of Labor Capacity) Per Day and the rate of Surplus Value.

POL (use values per hour in the working day of productive workers in subsistence goods)	Surplus Value plus Variable Capital per day per unit of labor capacity (shillings)	Surplus Value per day per unit of labor capacity (shillings)	Variable Capital per unit of labor capacity per day (shillings)	Rate of Surplus Value (%)
0.50	6.00	3.00	3.00	100
1.00	6.00	4.50	1.50	300

Exhibit 6. Labor Time, Surplus Labor and Necessary Labor.

POL (use values per hour in the working day per productive worker)	Surplus Labor plus Necessary Labor per day per unit of labor capacity (hours)	Surplus Labor per day per unit of labor capacity (hours)	Necessary Labor per unit of labor capacity per day (hours)
0.50	12.00	6.00	6.00
1.00	12.00	9.00	3.00

by one worker per day under the assumption of normal intensity and unchanged social or family structure.

As a result of a rise in the productiveness of labor, surplus labor rises to 9 hours and necessary labor falls to 3.

Exhibit 7 indicates that the use value going to the capitalist increases to 9 while that going to the worker does not change (by assumption) as the productiveness of labor increases from 0.50 to 1.00 use values produced per hour of the working day.

The value per unit of use value falls by 50%. This would manifest itself as deflation if the value of money remained changed and credit money relative to commodity money was constant. As a result of the increase in productivity, we observe increased surplus value, an increased rate of surplus value, increased real income for capitalists, a constant real income of workers while total value produced has not changed. The value of labor power, however, has fallen but not the real income of labor as measured by the use value going to the worker.[43] Marx, in his example, notes that if the price of labor power does not fall to the value of labor power, the real income of workers might even increase simultaneously with surplus value and the rate of surplus value.[44] The point of this replication of Marx's example is not to review of Marx, but to validate the consistency of the model's result with the textual examples of Marx and to demonstrate the potential for using the model for counterfactual experiments and for teaching.

Given the interpretation of Marx incorporated in the Model, the Total Value produced or transferred of final goods and services is estimated and compared to Gross Domestic Product (GDP) in the U.S. in 2000.

V. ESTIMATES OF TOTAL VALUE AND GDP

A derivation of empirical estimates of Marxian categories from GNP data and IO tables has been conducted by Shaikh and Tonak (Shaikh & Tonak, 1994).

Exhibit 7. Production and Distribution of use value and value per use value.

POL (use values per hour of the working day per productive worker)	Use Value produced per labor capacity per day (units)	Use Value going to Capital (units of use value)	Use Value for labor (real day's wage) (units of use value)	Value per unit of use value (shillings/use value)
0.50	6.00	3.00	3.00	1.00
1.00	12.00	9.00	3.00	0.50

They discussed their interpretation of Marx's theory and then took national income and product account and Input output data and used it to estimate the Marxian categories of surplus value, value, productive labor and the rate of surplus value for the U.S. economy (Shaikh & Tonak, 1994, p. 95). Their objective was to develop an alternative means of measuring aggregate production from more conventional sources (Shaikh & Tonak, 1994, p. 1).

The approach taken in the current study involved development of a computer model for use in sensitivity analysis and simulation. The model incorporated relationships based on Marx's theory. Empirical estimates of input parameters used with the model resulted in estimates of U.S. Total Marxian Value of final goods and services. Also estimated was the average nominal wage rate for the productive sectors. The approach is also different from Shaikh and Tonak's approach in that it measured output just as it leaves the process of production not as it is interpolated from income or sales data. This estimate was compared to U.S. Gross Domestic Product (GDP) in 2000. In terms of the circuit of capital, it is assumed that we are measuring the value of commodity capital in the aggregate that has left the process of production during the entire year. This would be equivalent to the aggregate C' in Marxian circuit of capital. This C' includes the value of newly added surplus labor. The value of the year's output is greater than the value of inputs that existed at the start of the year that entered into the process of production.

Exhibit 8 represents our first attempt to estimate the values of surplus value and variable capital necessary to estimate aggregate value using the first version of the model. Exhibit 8 summarizes the input values that were used for the first estimate. The estimates are made on a daily basis. The value of ten for the length of the working day was arbitrarily selected. The value of one for intensity was selected to provide a benchmark.

The values for the use value per subsistence bundle and the productivity of use value measured in use value per day cannot be directly observed. Given the value of all other input variables, the ratio of the subsistence bundle to the productivity of labor implies a specific rate of surplus value. By altering this ratio, given the values for other input parameters, a specific rate of surplus value could be achieved. We originally assumed a rate of surplus value of 203% based on the estimate for 1979 for the U.S. by Shaikh and Tonak (Shaikh & Tonak, 1994, p. 333). The ratio of the subsistence bundle to the productiveness of labor of 3.29 implies a 203% rate of surplus value given the other input parameters. The absolute value per use value is affected by the productiveness of labor. It was determined that a value of 0.45 for the productiveness of labor would result in a value of one for the value produced per use value. We felt a value of one for the value per use value would provide a basis for the

Exhibit 8. Determinants of Surplus Value and Rate of Surplus Value.

1. Length of working day	10 hours
2. Productiveness of labor	0.45 (use values produced per worker per hour)
3. Intensity of labor	1 normal intensity
4. Number of workers per capital	49 workers
5. Use value in the worker's subsistence bundle	1.48 (measure of the use value in a worker's daily subsistence bundle)
6. Reckoning name of money	$450/ounce of gold
7. Socially necessary abstract labor hours per ounce of gold	10 SNAL2 hours
8. Increment of to the length of the working day	1% (as measured by a percent of the original length of the working day)

development of a price index. To obtain a measure for the use value in the subsistence bundle, we searched for the value that would generate a ratio of the subsistence bundle to the productiveness of labor that implied a rate of surplus value of 203%. The value for the subsistence bundle that produced this result was 1.48. This procedure provided benchmark values for the productiveness of labor and for the subsistence bundle assuming that all other input parameters were already estimated. In estimating the benchmark, the rate of surplus value and the value per use value become input variables, at least for determining the benchmarks. A better procedure would be to estimate the values of the subsistence bundle and the productiveness of labor independently of the rate of surplus value and the value per use value.

The number 49 represents 49 million workers or units of labor capacity. The preliminary estimate of the number of productive workers was based on the size of the employed workers in the U.S. in 2000 and a ratio of productive to employed workers taken from the work of Shaikh and Tonak.[45] They estimated that U.S. total employed productive workers and reported the total U.S. employed workers in 1989. The ratio between the two was 36.25. We assumed that the ratio was still about the same. Given that the average employment in the U.S., we estimated the number of productive workers to be about 49,000,000.

The reckoning name of money was arbitrarily fixed at $450 per ounce for the initial test of the model. We assumed the existence of commodity money. There are conceptual controversies here. Marx assumed the use of commodity money such as gold. He noted that governments set a reckoning name for money or mint price. He indicated though that governments could not set the value of money. We interpret this to mean that the value of money manifested by the market price of money would be an estimate of money that could be used as a standard of price and measure of value since we assume value and price are equal. We have called this the reckoning name of money. Marx also indicated that the domestic currency rested upon international currency. We interpret that to mean that the international price of gold could be an estimate of reckoning name of money. An additional issue here is convertibility. Marx felt that any currency if it were inconvertible to gold but denominated in gold would still have its basis as gold. Money in the U.S. is neither convertible to gold officially nor officially denominated in it. We make the assumption that paper money can be convertible to gold on the international market and, therefore, may still act as a form of universal money. In addition, as with many of Marx's concepts they are not directly observable.[46] Price or exchange value is a manifestation of value. Marx, to simplify his exposition, often noted that he assumed that prices were equal to values. However, under some circumstances, prices would not be equal to values. Nevertheless, we assume that the price of gold is equal to its value.

The socially necessary abstract labor hours per unit of gold is the substance and measure of the value of gold. This is not directly observable. Even if the concrete labor requirements were accessible, they would have to be convertible into SNAL1 or SNAL2 hours. The degree of skill and intensity of labor in gold production relative to the normal SNAL1 hours would have to be estimated. Initially, we used value of 10. This implies that 10 hours of living labor (SNAL2) were used to produce an ounce of gold. The use of SNAL2 is appropriate for use since both POL and SB are measured on the basis of SNAL2 requirements. The model increases the value of the working day in 1% increments. The sensitivity of the output variables such as value, variable capital, surplus value can then be observed.

Exhibit 9 is a presentation of the results of using the inputs presented in Exhibit 8. It indicates that about $22,050 per day of surplus value and variable capital were produced per day for 49 units of labor capacity per day. If we estimate that the number of working days per year as 290 and assume that 49 represents 49 million productive workers, we have an estimate of surplus value and variable capital for the U.S. in 2000 of $6,394,450. This is an estimate of value added, it excludes, however, constant capital. For Marx, the value of the means of production transferred during the year to output would be part of constant capital. Advanced constant capital is represented by depreciation on instruments of labor (buildings and machinery), raw materials (expended inventories of inputs such as steel) and auxiliary materials (coal, oil etc.). Any necessary labor that

Exhibit 9. Composition of Total Value Produced for 49 Units of Labor Capacity Per Day and the Rate of Surplus Value.

LOWD increased by increments of 1%	Surplus Value plus Variable Capital per day for all productive labor capacity ($/dollars)	Surplus Value per day for all productive labor capacity per day ($/dollars)	Variable Capital per day for all productive labor capacity per day ($/day)	Rate of Surplus Value (%)
10.000	22050	14798	7252	204
10.100	22271	14798	7252	207
10.201	22493	14798	7252	210
10.303	22718	14798	7252	213
10.406	22945	14798	7252	216

was embodied in constant capital of raw materials, auxiliary materials and semi-finished goods used from inventories or passing through inventories for producing final goods during the year is incorporated in the estimates of total Marxian final value. The use of the second definition of socially necessary abstract labor ensures that there is no double counting for intermediate commodities. We are estimating only the sum of prices of final output.

The magnitude of constant capital will reflect the wear and tear on fixed capital and circulating capital.[47] The Department of Commerce provides an estimate of consumption of fixed capital which represents the depreciation component of the advanced constant capital. The gross expended inventories of raw and auxiliary materials are a component of the advanced constant circulating capital that are used from exiting stock or inventories during the year should be considered as entering the value of the final product. The raw and auxiliary materials are excluded from our estimate of constant capital in this first trial run. The Department of Commerce estimate of the capital consumption allowance in 2000 was $1, 228.9 billion.[48] The estimate of surplus value and variable capital plus depreciation was used as a rough estimate of Total Marxian Value and GDP for the U.S. and was equal to $7,623.35 billion. The $7,623.35 billion was equal to the $6,394.45 billion of surplus value and variable capital plus the estimate of constant capital of $1,228.9 billion. The estimate of the GDP for the U.S. by the Department of Commerce for 2000 was $9,824.6 billion. Thus, the first estimate based on rough estimates for the input variables produced an estimate that was $2,202.25 billion short of the Department of Commerce GDP estimate. It was 22% lower than the Department of Commerce reported GDP estimate.

Refined Input Estimates

We refined our assumptions and expanded the model to incorporate constant capital more systematically. We called this model the second version. The initial assumptions used to test the model were reviewed and modified to conform more closely with market data, government data or data from Shaikh and Tonak's work. The values for the price of gold and the length of the working day used in the trial run of the first version of the model were too large. We added two more variables: (1) the partial organic composition of capital, and (2) the number of working days per year.

Exhibit 10 summarizes the values for the input parameters used for the trial run of the second version of the model. We felt the value for the length of the working day should reflect that for productive workers. We used information from the Bureau of Labor Statistics website to make an estimate (Bureau of Labor Statistics Website, Establishment Data, Historical hours and earnings.

Exhibit 10. Determinants of Surplus Value Model Version 2 Trial Run.

1.	Length of working day	8.094 hours/day
2.	Productiveness of labor (units of use value produced per hour of the working day)	0.45
3.	Intensity of labor	1 normal intensity
4.	Units of labor capacity	49 workers
5.	Units of use value in subsistence bundle per unit of labor capacity	1.059
6.	The reckoning name of money	$275 (ounce of gold)
7.	SNAL2 per ounce of gold	5.15 (socially necessary labor per ounce of gold)
8.	Partial Organic composition of capital (C/V)	2.89
9.	Number of working days in the year.	214 days
10.	increment of to the length of the working day	1% default value (as measured by a percent of the original length of the working day)
11.	Increment to the productiveness of labor	0% default value (as measured by a percent of the original productiveness of labor)
12.	Increment to the intensity of labor	0% default value (as measured by a percent of the original intensity of labor)

Available from <ftp://ftp.bls.gov/pub/suppl/empsit.ceseeb2.txt> [6 August 2002]). We selected data on hours of work per week for four productive sectors and determined a weighted average for the four sectors (Weighted by the proportion of employees). The sectors included mining, manufacturing, transportation and utilities and construction. The weekly average hours were then divided by a five-day week and resulted in an estimate of 8.094 hours per week for the U.S. for the year 2000.

The number 0.45 used as a measure of the productiveness of labor is the same value used in the first trial run.[49] The constraints on the value selected for POL were the specific values used for other input parameters of the model and the ratio of the units of use value in the subsistence bundle relative to the productiveness of labor. To provide initial empirical grounding for benchmark estimates for the value of the POL and the SB, it was decided to use values for the subsistence bundle relative to the productiveness of labor that would generate a ratio consistent with a rate of surplus value of 244%. This 244% was the estimate by Shaikh and Tonak for 1989 (Shaikh & Tonak, 1994. p. 333). Thus, the POL could take on any value initially as long as a specific ratio with the subsistence bundle was maintained.

Based on our selection of the productiveness of labor and the rate of surplus value estimated by Shaikh and Tonak, the units of use value in the subsistence bundle of labor capacity was estimated to be 1.059. The drawback of this method is that the absolute value of productiveness of labor and of the units of use value in the subsistence bundle are somewhat arbitrary and the rate of surplus value becomes an implicit input into the model. An advantage, once the initial value for these factors is determined, is that the values can be altered to examine the impact of change in either one on the rate of surplus value. The initial values are constrained by data that have some empirical grounding. Potentially, this method can provide a method to examine the consistency of different rates of surplus value from different sources to other Marxian variables and empirical observations of expected outputs. For example, Moseley has estimated the rate of value for several periods for the U.S. In 1987, a study indicated that the rate of surplus value was 1.98 in 1985 (Moseley, 1987, p. 394). Moseley also compares his estimates to that of Weisskoph (Moseley, 1985, p. 62). Kalmans estimated the rate of surplus value of Japan at 2.159 for 1980 (Kalmans, 1996, p. 15). The model can thus be used to examine if different estimated values of surplus value appear to be more or less consistent with the set of Marxian relations represented by the computer model and the approximations of GDP that this model generates.

The intensity of labor was set at one. This variable will become important in later applications and development of the model. It will allow comparisons between economies or spheres of industry with different intensities of labor or in examining the influence over time in one economy as the intensity of labor is varied. Moseley made use of several proxies to measure the change in the intensity of labor over the period between 1948 and 1979 (Moseley, circa. 1980s). These factors included cost of job loss, the intensity of supervision and earnings inequality. Research using such proxies with the model developed here would be able to project the impact of intensity change on the economy as a whole.

The number of workers was estimated at 49. This is measured in millions and represents the number of productive workers in the U.S. The estimation of this parameter was provided in the discussion of the first version of the model.

The two factors that translate the surplus labor and necessary labor into value form are the reckoning name for money and the SNAL2 hours in an ounce of gold. We used commodity money (gold) as a working hypothesis for the model. It was assumed that gold would provide a reasonable measure of international value and it is conceptually consistent with Marx.

The reckoning value of money was estimated to be $275 per ounce of gold.[50] As indicated earlier, a problem with determining the SNAL2 hours per ounce of gold is that it is not observable. Taking the market price of gold and dividing it by an estimate of the value of variable capital in the productive sector, we can estimate of the SNAL1 hours per ounce of gold. SNAL1 includes surplus labor, necessary labor and labor embodied in constant capital. SNAL2 includes only living labor use to reproduce labor power. We estimated the hourly wage in the productive sector to be $15.53 in the U.S. in the year 2000 from government sources.[51] Our computer model estimates the variable capital (hourly wage) as an output. The SNAL2 hours per ounce of gold can be varied as an input in the model to alter the projected average hourly wage in the productive sectors. This was done to achieve a wage per hour of $15.53 per hour which was consistent with government data. The SNAL2 that achieved this was 5.15 hours. This value turned out to be consistent with the partial organic composition of capital and the rate of surplus value, indicating the theoretical consistency of the model.[52] A higher price of gold would not be consistent with model results that produced a wage of $15.53 given the values of the other input parameters. The empirical consistency of the price of gold and the nominal hourly earnings in the productive sectors was consistent with the model's results. If the wage were higher than $15.53, the socially necessary labor would have to be lower than 5.15 per ounce to be consistent with the model. There is an inverse relationship between the two. The value of $275 per ounce taken from the London Bullion market as an input parameter generates a value of $15.53 per hour for the wage if the SNAL2 hours per ounce of gold is 5.15 hours. A significant additional point to note, however, is that there are not only two variables that are required to produce consistent theoretical results in input and output parameters being consistent with empirically estimated inputs and outputs. Consistency is reflected by the need for several social and productive conditions to exist simultaneously in order for the results to be empirically consistent with benchmark information obtained from government and scholarly sources.[53]

Thus, we have estimated the SNAL2 hours per ounce of gold and the reckoning name of money based on secondary market and government sources as inputs into a trial run of the second version of the model.

The partial organic composition of capital was a new input parameter added to the second version of the model. We call it the partial organic composition of capital because it does not include all the elements of constant capital that conceptually should be included in the composition of capital. In the Marxian composition of capital (C/V), the constant part of capital should include fixed capital, the depreciation of fixed capital that enters the valorization process, raw materials and auxiliary materials.[54] We included only advanced constant capital; that is depreciation, raw materials and auxiliary materials. We estimated the value the partial organic composition of capital (C/V) at 2.89 based on the work of Shaikh and Tonak for the U.S. for 1989.[55] It was use in the trial run of the second version of the model as an input parameter.

The number of working days per year was based on data from the Bureau of labor statistics.[56] The Bureau of labor statistics provides data on the hours of work per week for several productive sectors. We calculated the length of the working day by taking the average weekly hours of four productive sectors and then dividing by 5 for a five-day week. The estimation of the number of working days is not straightforward. The department of commerce does not report working days. Rones, Ilg and Gardner estimated the annual hours of work for men (1905 hours) and women (1526 hours) for the U.S. in 1993 (Rones, Ilg & Gardner, 1997, p. 11; U.S. Department of Labor, 1997). We then determined a weighted average of annual hours based on the proportion of total employment represented by each group for 2000.[57]

The increment to the length of the working day was maintained at 1%.

The Results

The current model generates eight output Exhibits. The purpose of the presentation of this material is to demonstrate the potential for conducting counterfactual experiments and for teaching. The values of the key Marxian input variables were estimated. These values were used in this second version of the computer model based on the Marxist economic theory to estimate Total Marxian value of final goods and services as a rough proxy for U.S. GDP in 2000.[58] The output was then compared with GDP estimates reported by the Department of Commerce on their web site. A summary of the output is presented in Exhibits 11 through 18. Differences between conceptually generated Total Values and NIPA estimates of GDP, raise questions about the theoretical specification of the model, the interpretation of results, the conceptual differences between value and GDP or estimates of the input parameters used in the model.[59]

Exhibit 11 summarizes the production of new value for all 49 units of labor power. The 49 units of labor power are representative of the estimated 49 million employed productive workers in the U.S. in 2000 (Productive of surplus value). The new value produced per day by 49 workers was estimated to be $21,178. The estimate of $21,178 estimated new value produced per day by 49

Exhibit 11. Output Summary: Composition of Total New Value Produced Per Capital (49 Workers Per Day) (Dollars) Model Estimates for the U.S. for 2000.

Length of the working day	New Value created S+V ($ per day)	Surplus Value ($ per day)	Variable Capital ($ per day)	Rate of Surplus Value (%)
8.094	21,178	15,020	6,158	244
8.175	21,390	15,232	6,158	247
8.257	21,604	15,446	6,158	251
8.339	21,820	15,662	6,158	254
8.423	22,038	15,880	6,158	258

Multiply each number by 1,000,000 to arrive at national estimates.

workers. It represents an estimate of $21.18 billion produced per day by 49 million workers each working day in 2000. The rate of surplus value was as expected, equal to 244%. This value had been implied by the selection of the values for the subsistence bundle and the use value produced per hour given the values of the other input variables. In this instance, the rate of surplus value was not an output variable. The rate of surplus value had been estimated by Shaikh and Tonak and was used as a basis for selecting the ratio between the SB and POL. This procedure was used to provide a benchmark estimates for initial input values for POL and the SB. The rate of surplus value here just confirms that the model is generating a value for the rate of surplus value that is consistent with both theory and the work of Shaikh and Tonak. The variable capital of $6,158 can be interpreted as the daily wage bill of a firm (capital) that employs 49 workers (units of labor power) or $5.16 billion for the country employing 49 million productive workers. Increasing the length of the working day, indicates as expected that the rate of surplus value increases. The theoretical rate of surplus value would not be expected to increase as much, since to some extent the wear and tear on workers would increase and therefore necessary labor (SNAL2) would increase.

Exhibit 12 summarizes the distribution of total newly produced per worker (unit of labor power). between labor and capital. The new value created per worker per day was estimated to be $432. The variable capital per day per worker was $126 and the surplus value per day per worker was $306. Variable capital per worker per day is an approximation of the daily wage for socially necessary abstract labor. The magnitudes of these values are consistent with reasonable market values for this period.

For Marx, commodities had several aspects. They conveyed value, had a material form in a product, and represented embodied labor. Exhibit 13 summarizes the distribution of labor between surplus labor and necessary labor per day per worker. The ratio between surplus value and variable capital is implied by the rate of surplus value which was implicitly an input in this trial run of the model. The significance of Exhibit 13 is the demonstration of the capability of the model to estimate the rate of surplus value for changes in a number of variables. The model provides a means of rapidly assessing the sensitivity of surplus value to a number of important factors such as the length of the working day, the number of working days per year, and the subsistence bundle. Given empirical proxies for these variables can be developed, the model will yield estimates of surplus value, an estimate of an average wage and a potential price index. The number 2.353 represents the number of socially necessary abstract labor hours needed to produce the subsistence bundle for a worker per day. The subsistence bundle of use value in the model is determined by multiplying

Exhibit 12. Output Summary: Distribution of Total Newly Produced Value Per Capital (1 Worker Per Day) (Dollars) Model Estimates for the U.S. for 2000.

Length of the working day	New Value created S+V ($ per day)	Surplus Value ($ per day)	Variable Capital ($ per day)	Rate of Surplus Value (%)
8.094	432	307	126	244
8.175	437	311	126	247
8.257	441	315	126	251
8.339	445	320	126	254
8.423	450	324	126	258

Exhibit 13. Output Summary: Distribution of Socially Necessary Abstract Labor (SNAL1) Per Unit of Labor Capacity Per Day for Various Lengths of the Working Day.

Length of the working day	New Value created S+V (hours day)	Surplus Value (hours per day)	Variable Capital (hours per day)
8.094	8.094	5.741	2.353
8.175	8.175	5.882	2.353
8.257	8.257	5.903	2.353
8.339	8.339	5.986	2.353
8.423	8.423	6.069	2.353

the subsistence bundle of use value per day which is an input into the model 214 days. The number of working days per year was estimated at 214. The number, 214, is a factor incorporated into the program and cannot be altered by the web user. It is used as a basis for determining the required use value per year. The actual number of working days used is an input into the model. Thus, the rate of surplus value will respond to a number of input variables including the length of the working day, the number of working days per year or other input parameters. Our interpretation of Marx is that in a fully developed industrial capitalist system, workers that are worked fewer working days per year than necessary to produce their subsistence bundle will not reproduce themselves as workers. This feature of the model would be useful to analyze the trend toward part time and temporary work. If one were analyzing the subsistence bundle over a year, there would be a minimum level of use value that would be required to sustain the average worker. This annual amount would have to be prorated over each working day in the year. To determine the use value in the subsistence bundle, an assumption about the standard year is made. If a web user of the model indicates that the subsistence bundle is 1.059 for a standard year of 214 working days, then increasing the input value of the number of working days will decrease the subsistence bundle received per day. This also increases the rate of surplus value. Reducing the number of working days will reduce the rate of surplus value.

The number 214 was obtained based on a study of annual labor hours (Rones, Ilg & Gardner, 1997). The Department of Commerce provides data on weekly hours by major industrial sector. The annual hours are not reported in the statistics routinely provided. The study indicated the annual hours worked for both men and women. We used a weighted average for the two. We divided the weighted annual average hours worked by the previously estimated length of the working day to arrive at an estimate of 214.

Another Marxian aspect of commodities is that they are represented by products. These products convey use value. In our interpretation of Marx, it is the constancy of a certain yearly use value regardless of the mix and mass of these subsistence commodities that is required for the reproduction of the aggregate worker. Labor must be expended to produce these commodities. Some output represents use value transferred by workers from the means of production. Use value transferred for Marx is directly proportional to the ratio between the mass of the means of production and labor power. This means that if values reflect the organic composition of capital, use value transferred will be proportional to the ratio of constant capital advanced to variable capital. This is consistent with Marx's statement that the mass of means of production (in a use value sense) must, other things remaining the same, be directly proportional to labor capacity. This means that if 52 units of use value carry the value of all labor power per day, then a partial organic composition of capital of 2.89 will mean that a level of use value equal to $2.89 \times 52 = 150.3$ will equal the use value transferred from constant capital by all labor per day. A worker may work 8.094 hours a day but the necessary labor time is, under the assumptions of the model, equal to 2.34 hours. It is this 2.34 hours that affect the amount of use value transferred from constant capital. At the aggregate social level, the use value transferred by labor is recaptured (assuming the system is sustainable) by capital and reinvested. The units of use value can be used to develop an index of real income. There are theoretical conditions that exist based on the Marxian model where decreasing exchange value of variable capital can actually be associated with increasing real income.

Use value is both created during the day and transferred from constant capital. Exhibit 14 indicates that use value that conveys the various component of the value of output. The use value transferred and created by all 49 workers per day has a value of 328. The use value received by workers is 52 while the use value conveying the value transferred from constant capital and carried by surplus labor and advanced constant capital is 277. Capital in a system that is sustaining itself will receive at least the proportion of total use value produced that represents the value of surplus labor and the that which carries the value of constant capital (277 in Exhibit 14). The last column of Exhibit 14 represents the value per use value. This is the total value produced by all 49 million productive workers in 214 working days divided by the total use value produced. This factor can theoretically be developed into a Marxian index of the overall price level. This factor can be affected by a number of input factors including change in the reckoning

Exhibit 14. Output Summary: Production and Distribution of the Use Value and Value Per Use Value for all Labor Per Day. Use Value is an Approximation of Real Income.

Length of the working day	Use Value Produced and Transferred by all labor (per day)	Use Value Received by capital (per day)	Use Value Received by Labor (per day)	Use value Transferred from Constant Capital (per day)	Value per use value ($ per use value – value includes labor embodied in c+v+s)
8 094	328	277	52	150	119
8 175	330	278	52	150	119
8 257	332	280	52	150	119
8 339	334	282	52	150	119
8 423	336	284	52	150	119

name of money and the productiveness of labor. A rising productiveness of labor can result in a falling value per use value and deflation ceteris paribus. The total use value representing the commodities that convey the value transferred by all labor per day from constant capital is 150.

The daily value of labor power is equal to the necessary labor in the subsistence bundle times the value per hour of necessary labor. Necessary labor here means Marx's second definition of the term. Increases in the productiveness of labor reduce the necessary labor in the subsistence bundle and hence the value of labor power. Dividing the daily value of labor power by the length of the working day provides an estimate of the hourly wage. Exhibit 15 indicates the nominal wage per hour if variable capital per day (the daily nominal money wage) is held constant. Increasing the length of the working day will mean that the hourly wage will decline as the length of the working day increased. The worker's daily wage would gravitate to the value of labor power divided by the length of the working day. Marx indicated that the wage was paid was the value of labor power, however, this represented only a fraction of value produced by the labor provided on the time embodied in his/her labor capacity. The first column of Exhibit 15 illustrates this issue. The $15.53 per hour represents the average hourly wage in the productive sectors. This value is consistent with the hourly earnings in four productive sectors, the rate of surplus value estimated by Shaikh and Tonak and the reckoning name for money measured by the market price of gold. The Marxian relations relate these factors in a way that are consistent with empirical observation. The sensitivity analysis indicates that ceteris paribus, as the length of the working day increases, the hourly wage declines.

The second column of Exhibit 15 will be useful for demonstrating the impact of changes in the productiveness of labor on the required nominal wage. If the productiveness of labor increases and the nominal wage does not change, workers will find they can purchase the same subsistence bundle with a lower nominal wage. The current Exhibit holds the productiveness of labor constant so this effect is not demonstrated.

The third column of Exhibit 15 is a measure of the real wage per hour. This column is only meaningful if the productiveness of labor is changing. Increasing productiveness of labor means that if the daily variable capital is held constant, the use value affordable will increase. Exhibit 15 just indicates the impact of an increase in the working day on the affordable use value per hour. The third column will only be different from the fourth column of this Exhibit if the productiveness of labor is changing. The third column will decline less than the fourth column if the productiveness of labor is assumed to increase.

The fourth column shows the use value per hour required to maintain the subsistence level if the subsistence bundle of commodities (use value) per day

Exhibit 15. Output Summary: Analysis of the Nominal Wage Per Hour and Use Value Per Hour Under Different Assumption about the Daily Wage as the Length of the Working Day is Increased.

Length of the working day	Value of Variable capital per day held fixed: Implied Nominal wage per hour	Subsistence bundle of use value per day held fixed: Implied Nominal wage per hour required	Daily variable capital held fixed: Use values affordable per hour	Subsistence bundle of use value per day held fixed: Use value needed per hour for subsistence
8.094	15.526	15.526	0.131	0.131
8.175	15.372	15.372	0.130	0.130
8.257	15.220	15.220	0.128	0.128
8.339	15.069	15.069	0.127	0.127
8.423	14.920	14.920	0.126	0.126

is held constant as Marx assumed it would generally be. The use value afford-able per hour declines as the length of the working day increases, however, the daily use value obtained will remain the same. This column is useful as a bench-mark against which to compare column three when the productiveness of labor changes. Increases in the productiveness of labor will show up as a measure of use value in the real wage received (column three) that rises above the use value required for subsistence (column four). Declines in productiveness of labor will show up as a measure of use value in the real wage that falls below the required real wage. In this case, the wage is no longer sustainable unless workers replicate themselves with less use value than before. In other words, they have to accept a lower real wage and still reproduce.

Exhibit 16 transforms Exhibit 15 from an hourly to a daily basis. Columns three and four have changed position. The significant point about this exhibit is the magnitude of the daily wage. The model provides this as an output. This provides a means of determining whether the model's output is producing empirically the meaningful results. In this case, the daily wage for the average worker was $125.66 per day.

Exhibit 17 provides a summary of the magnitude of total value of final goods and services produced or transferred in the economy and its distribution among surplus value, variable capital and constant capital. The model estimated that the total value produced or transferred for the U.S. for 2000 was $8.3 trillion. This included surplus value of $3.2 trillion, variable capital of $1.3 trillion and constant capital of $3.8 trillion. Under the conditions implied by the values of the input parameters and the model relations, the variable capital and constant remain unchanged as the length of the working day increases while the surplus value and total value increase. The constant capital transferred would also increase if the productiveness of labor in producing subsistence goods increased more than that the productiveness of labor in the production of the means of production. The model's assumptions currently preclude this. Such a situation would also alter the partial organic composition of capital. The model currently takes the partial organic composition of capital as an input parameter provided by the web user of the model.

How does the estimate of total Marxian Value of final goods and services compare with the estimates of GDP by the Department of Commerce? Exhibit 18 provides a comparison.[60] The estimate GDP for the U.S. in 2000 reported by the Department of Commerce was $9,824.6 billion. The computer model generated an estimate of Total Marxian Value produced or transferred of final goods and services was $8,340.6 billion. The difference between the two is $1,484 billion indicating that Marxian total value was 15% lower than the department of commerce estimates of GDP or that GDP estimates were 18%

Exhibit 16. Output Summary: Analysis of the Nominal Wages and Use Value Per Day Per Worker Under Different Assumptions about the Daily Wage and Subsistence Bundle as the Length of the Working Day is Increased.

Length of the working day	Daily Variable capital – held fixed ($/day)	Daily Nominal wage required for fixed subsistence bundle ($/day)	Use value required per day per worker	Use Value affordable per day per worker if variable capital is held fixed (This will vary if the value per use value changes)
8.094	125.663	125.663	1.059	1.059
8.175	125.663	125.663	1.059	1.059
8.257	125.663	125.663	1.059	1.059
8.339	125.663	125.663	1.059	1.059
8.423	125.663	125.663	1.059	1.059

Exhibit 17. Output Summary: Analysis of the Total Value Generated Per Year, Surplus Value, Variable Capital and Constant Capital for the Whole Economy.

Length of the working day	Total value produced or Transferred ($ millions)	Surplus Value Produced ($ millions)	Variable capital ($ millions)	Constant Capital Transferred ($ millions)
8.094	8,340,626.4	3,314,383.2	1,327,706.7	3,808,172.5
8.175	8,385,583.3	3,259,704.1	1,327,706.7	3,808,172.5
8.257	8,431,357.4	3,305,478.2	1,327,706.7	3,808,172.5
8.339	8,477,589.2	3,351,710.1	1,327,706.7	3,808,172.5
8.423	8.852483.4	3,398,404.2	1,327,706.7	3,808,172.5

Estimated Gross Domestic Product.

VICTOR KASPER, JR.

Exhibit 18. Output Summary: Estimated U.S. GDP 2000, Total Marxian Value Produced or Transferred, Total New Value Produced (S+V) and Total Constant Capital.

The Department of Commerce Estimate for GDP for the U.S. for the year 2000 was $9824.6 billion.

Length of the working day	Year	Estimated GDP for U.S. or Total Value generated per year ($ millions)	Total surplus value and variable capital produced per year ($ Millions)	Constant Capital Transferred per year ($ millions)
8.094	2000	8,340,626.4	4,532,089.9	3,808,172.5
8.175	2001	8,385,583.3	4,532,089.9	3,808,172.5
8.257	2002	8,431,357.4	4,532,089.9	3,808,172.5
8.339	2003	8,477,589.2	4,532,089.9	3,808,172.5
8.423	2004	8,852483.4	4,532,089.9	3,808,172.5

greater than Marxian total value. Thus, estimates based on the Marxian computer simulation model and values of input parameters based on secondary sources indicated a difference of between 15 and 20% between Marxian total value and the GDP estimates.[61] The total newly produced value in 2000 was estimated at $4,532.1 billion while the earnings of productive workers were estimated to be $3,808.2 billion. Total value includes constant capital. Part of this constant capital includes raw material and auxiliary materials. The value of labor embodied in the constant capital of raw materials, auxiliary materials and semi-finished goods should be included in the Marxian Total Value of final goods and services. The counterfactual experiment indicated that as the length of the working day increased, the total value produced would also increase.

VI. SUMMARY AND CONCLUSIONS

The paper summarizes the development of a computer model designed to reflect a model of the aggregate output based on Marxist theory. The model is developed to facilitate sensitivity analysis of the potential impact of change in key variables on the production of value, surplus value, the rate of surplus value, the nominal wage and real income, and as part of a continuing project developing a more elaborate simulation model. The basic relationships and equations of the model were discussed. The first version of the model excluded constant capital. The use of the first version of the model is discussed to show how the model can be used to estimate surplus value and the rate of surplus value. The first version of the model has seven input factors and a factor for the rate of change in the length of the working day. The inspiration of the model was Chapter 17. The input factors are the length of the working day, the intensity of labor, the productiveness of labor in subsistence goods, the reckoning name of money, a measure of the use value in a worker's subsistence bundle of commodities, the necessary labor in an ounce of gold and the number of productive workers in a firm or economy. The output generated includes surplus value produced, variable capital used, the rate of surplus value, the hourly nominal wage, the daily nominal wage, and the distribution of value produced, use value and labor hours between capital and labor. Rough estimates for the input factors were made and used with the first version of the model to estimate the surplus value and variable capital. The first version of the model included no estimate of constant capital. The Department of Commerce estimate of consumption of fixed capital was used as an estimate of constant capital. Conceptually this would exclude the value of raw materials and auxiliary materials. The estimate of Total Value of final good and services from the trial run of the first version of the model was $7,623 billion. This was

$2,201.2 billion lower than the reported Department of Commerce estimate of GDP. However, there are conceptual reasons why the two values should not be the same. Additional research indicated that some values of input parameters in the trial run with the first version of the model were not consistent with market or government sources. As an example, the value of gold used as an input was $450 per ounce where it should have been $275 an ounce. The lack of a theoretically consistent value for constant capital in the first version was also considered a problem.

A second version of the model was developed. It included two more variables. The additional input parameters included: The number of working days per year and the partial organic composition of capital. In addition two more dynamic factors were included. These were: (1) the rate of change in the productiveness of labor; and (2) the rate of change in the intensity of labor. The second version of the model provides an estimate of constant capital and GDP. Based on a refinement of the input variables, the second version of the model was used to estimate Total Marxian Value of final goods and services produced or transferred in the U.S. in 2000. It produced an estimate of $8,340.3 billion. This was an improvement over the estimate based on the first version of the model. The estimate of total value was 15% lower than the GDP estimate reported by the Department of Commerce. The results suggest that a computer simulated model based on Marxian economic relations can produce results that are rough approximations of the U.S. Department of Commerce reported estimates of GDP.

There are several potential areas where the model can be expanded and improved. The incorporation of constant capital in the model needs to be improved. Currently, the model assumes that the productiveness of labor in the means of production is the same as for the means of subsistence. The model also assumes that the socially necessary labor hours to produce a unit of the means of subsistence changes proportionally to that of for the means of production. The value per use value can be developed into a Marxian-based index of the price level. Additional growth factors for the measure of the subsistence bundle, the size of the productive work force and/or the reckoning name of money are issues that must be incorporated or improved. To be a model of accumulation, assumptions would have to be made about the proportion of surplus value that is reinvested and the relationship between improved productiveness of labor and the increment to the mass of the means of production. These would have to be made input factors. Monetary policy within the Marxian model would have an impact on inflation by altering the ratio of credit money relative to the value of gold. Alternatives to the reliance on commodity gold money need to be considered. The model can be currently used to estimate the growth rate of the economy for changes in the productiveness of labor, the intensity of labor and the length of the working day. More growth factors should developed, however, an accumulation component to the model should be developed if this research path is pursued. With such an improved model, impacts of changes in all variables on investment could be made and the number of employed productive workers could be made endogenous after the first year. Such an expanded model could also produce estimates of unemployment. The conceptual differences between GDP and Marxian total value should be clarified in future work. We speculate that if differences exist but are constant, the model can still be used to estimate values for GDP.

The discrepancy between the Department of Commerce estimate of GDP and the estimate of the model suggest several areas of enquiry related to the missing $1.5 trillion. The difference is related to either: (1) to the conceptual differences between GDP and total value; and/or (2) to the specific estimates of several input parameters. Input parameters that might be a source of difference include the number of productive workers, the number of working days per year, the length of the working day, the labor content of imports, the partial organic composition of capital, the productiveness of labor, the socially necessary labor per ounce of gold and the reckoning name for money.

Several thought experiments can both explore the use of the model and the source of difference between Total Marxian Value produced or transferred and GDP estimates. If we assumed that there was no difference, conceptually, between GDP and Marxian Total Value (TV) produced or transferred, we could evaluate differences in them using the model with counterfactual experiments to determine potential magnitudes of change in the estimated input parameters that would eliminate the difference. For example, the model would suggest that, ceteris paribus, if the number of productive workers were increased to 57.7 million from 49 million, the difference between GDP and TV would be eliminated. This is 8.7 million workers and would suggest that perhaps the proportion of productive workers relative to employed workers increased since 1989.

The number of working days per year of 214 was based on data from the Department of Commerce for 2000 in a study reported in the Monthly Labor Review of 1993 data. The model indicates that if the number of working days per year were increased to 284 or by 70 days, ceteris paribus, the difference in estimates would be eliminated. This would inconsistent with the report on annual hours in the Monthly Labor Review paper (Rones, Ilg & Gardner, p. 11). It would also imply that productive workers were working about 5.5 days per week assuming no holidays or vacations. If the length of the working day were increased to 10.8 hours or by about 2.7 hours, ceteris paribus, the TV and GDP estimates would be about the same. One question that this would raise would be: Were the working hours per day in the productive sectors underestimated by the Department of Commerce? In these thought experiments we were assuming that the Marxian relations are valid, that the model is a reasonable depiction of them, and that they could be used to estimate GDP.

An alternative thought experiment could seek the differences between estimates of GDP and TV in the foreign sector. The GDP estimate reported by the Department of Commerce (DOC) has net exports as one of its components. Since net exports for 2000 was negative $365.5 billion, the DOC estimate is by definition adjusted downward for this. U.S. Gross exports for 2000 were $1,101.1 billion and gross imports were $1,455.6 billion (Department of Commerce, BEA Website, BEA News Release, Table 1.b. Current dollar GDP revised estimates. Available from <http://www.bea.doc.gov/bea/newsrel/gdpnewsrelease.htm> [8:30 a.m. 31 July 2002]). If the content labor capacity of imports were higher than the labor capacity content of similar import substitutes, then the Department of Commerce estimates would have overestimated GDP if used as a proxy for estimating Marxian Total value since we actually imported more labor capacity based on U.S. measures of labor capacity. The ratio GDP to productive workers would have suggested that about 8.7 million units of yearly labor capacity measured in U.S. labor capacity units were incorporated in the use value of imports than showed up in the value imported. In other words, the U.S. would have been able to import goods whose labor capacity content measured in U.S. terms was much higher than represented by the value of Gross Imports. This speculation suggests that it would have been necessary to reduce the Department of Commerce estimate of GDP by more than the actual value of imports if it were to be compared to the computer model estimates of total value.

Another potential thought experiment would be to examine the partial organic composition of capital. If this value was larger, more value would be transferred from constant capital. If the partial organic composition of capital were increased from 2.89 to 4.02, the gap between total value and GDP would be eliminated. The 2.89 estimate was based on data from 1989 and the partial organic composition of capital would be expected to increase over time. Whether an increase of this magnitude is realistic is an open question.

Currently, the model as developed will not result in a user initiated change in the productiveness of labor to have an impact of the total value created or transferred. This is theoretically consistent with Marx as far as total value produced is concerned. Increasing the productiveness of labor in subsistence goods will increase surplus value produced for a given working day by reducing variable capital. This is not true for constant capital. If the productiveness of labor in subsistence goods increases relative to the productiveness of labor in the means of production, more value of constant capital will be transferred to the final product for a given value of variable capital. This will also alter the partial organic composition of capital. At present, the model assumes that when the productiveness of labor is increased in subsistence goods, the productiveness of labor in the means of subsistence increases in a like manner. This means that the productiveness of labor will always transfer the same proportional value of constant capital. The partial organic composition of capital is also an exogenous factor. An improved version of the model would allow the productiveness of labor in the means of subsistence to be changed independently of the productiveness of labor in subsistence goods. It would also allow the partial organic composition of capital to become at least partially endogenous. An increase in the productiveness of labor in subsistence goods relative to the productiveness of labor in the means of production would be expected to increase the partial organic composition of capital.

Raising the reckoning name of money would raise the computer estimate of Total value. If the reckoning name of money were $324 per ounce, the gap between GDP and Total Value would be eliminated, ceteris paribus. The issue here is that the average international price of gold that serves as an estimate of the reckoning price of money was on average $275 in the year 2000. This thought experiment would have indicated that increasing the price of gold as an input would have made it inconsistent with market estimates.

A decrease in the socially necessary labor per ounce of gold could also be a source of increasing the magnitude of total value. If gold contains less social labor, the labor value of all commodities measured in gold-based prices will rise. If the socially necessary labor per ounce of gold were decreased from 5.15 to 4.37 hours per ounce, the difference between GDP and TV would disappear. However, this would imply a weighted average wage of $18.30 per hour in the productive sectors. This would no longer be compatible with the $15.53 per hour earnings we estimated based on BLS estimates.

To make these thought experiments more meaningful, research would have to clarify outstanding issues about the conceptual relationship between GDP and TV of final goods and services and the stability of the relationship. Given this relationship, we would be able to use the thought experiments discussed above to evaluate consistency of the input variables of the model.

Other research applications of the model would be the tests of consistency of Marxian variables made by different research projects, Post-modern discussion of the last instance and overdetermination, and gender issues related to family structure and labor power.

Examples of how to apply the model for evaluating empirical consistency was provided by the discussion above. Others have estimated the rate of surplus value. Key Marxian variables estimated from a variety of studies could be tested for consistency with other Marxian concepts. Both the model and these variables could be evaluated based on the consistency of the model's input and output with data obtained from secondary sources.

There is controversy among Post-Modern Marxists about the last instance. This model could provide a point of departure for a discussion of both the last instance and the concept of overdetermination. We would argue that regardless of the intereffectivity of various class and non-class processes that there exist conditions of existence for industrial capitalism described by a Marxist theoretical framework. Wage labor is required for the existence of capital and for the generation of surplus value. The needs of workers and society are shaped by non economic or non class processes, however, specific relationships between these processes must exist for industrial-based capitalism to exit. There may be variations of how basic economic relations emerge or persist but if capitalism based on the production of surplus value, then wage labor and a set of property relations regarding the means of production must exist. The model developed here provides focal points for discussing or evaluating the conditions of existence for the generation of value and surplus value. Issues such as what makes something a use value in a particular society or what types of forces produce a particular organic composition of capital can be addressed. The answers will, to some extent, involve non-economic processes. However, these factors regardless of the specific form or historical path from which they emerge, must generate a specific set of relations in order for capitalism to function.

The issue of family structure as it affects and is affected the conditions of production could be partially analyzed with the model. Focal points would be the use value required in the subsistence bundle, the productiveness of labor and the length of the working day as they affect and are affected by family structure and roles. Two working partners might require a larger subsistence bundle and have a higher productiveness of labor. Trying to produce more labor power from a family unit may require an larger support infrastructure. These are research topics that can be addressed with the model.

Environmental issues could also be assessed. Greater pollution increases the subsistence bundle (increased health costs) and increases the magnitude of constant capital (by increasing the labor require to produce raw materials) The model identifies a number of sites of impact that could be evaluated for its effect on value, surplus value and the nominal wage.

Finally, the model needs to take into consideration and be modified to address the issue of interaction among the various input factors. The intensity of labor will interact with the length of the working day and the productivity of labor. Workers working longer hours may not be able to work more intensely. Marx considered interaction of these factors in Chapter 17. The organic composition of capital may be affected by the productiveness of labor on aggregate social scale. Also of importance will be the development of an accumulation model which will require assumptions about the proportion of surplus value invested and the relationship of this investment to the productiveness of labor.

NOTES

1. The simulation model discussed in this paper appears on the following web site (http://facstaff.buffalostate.edu/kasperv). The username to be used to enter the web site is sam and the password is part. Both the username and password should be in lower case. Once in the website go the drop down menu in the left frame and select latest surplus value model. Then click the go to selected page button. Once there, click the underlined link for the surplus value. This website is internet explorer 6 compatible but may not be for all versions of netscape.

2. Marx in discussing the productivity of labor comments on the importance of surplus value to the capitalist system:

> Firstly: It appears to be a contradiction that production directed towards exchange value, and dominated by it, endeavours to reduce the value of the individual product to a minimum. But the value of the product as such is a matter of indifference to capitalist production. Its goal is the production of the greatest possible amount of surplus value (Marx & Engels, *Collected Works*, Vol. 34, p. 110).

3. Marx in the preface to the first German edition of *Capital,* Vol. 1, notes that ". . . the ultimate aim of this work, to lay bare the economic law of motion of modern society . . ." (Marx, Vol. 1, 1967, p. 10). See Laurence Harris for his assessment of questions raised by Marx (Bottomore, p. 66).

Traditional macroeconomics is concerned with growth and stability. As such it is concerned with the size of the aggregate output and its medium term stability. See Dornbusch, Fischer and Startz for a discussion of the project of traditional macro-economics (Dornbusch, Fischer & Startz, 1998. p. 3).

4. These will be topics of a future paper.

5. The neoclassical approach has underlying essentials reflected by the market. These are factor endowments and their distribution, tastes and preferences and technology. These factors generate scarcity and relative prices. There is no acknowledgment of the class relations and conflict in the neoclassical analytical framework. The neoclassical approach takes methodological individualism as a starting point. The Marxian approach starts at a level of total social capital (volume I) and works successively to more concrete forms of expression of this social conceptualization of society. This study starts with a focus on the determination of total value and surplus value. In subsequent research we will develop Marxian based models that reflect spheres and capitals operating within a larger socioeconomic framework.

Wolff and Resnick articulate a position similar to the one taken here (Wolff & Resnick, p. 46).

Bator in developing his exposition of the analytics of welfare maximization for the neoclassical system identifies key assumptions. Initial supplies of resources (his initial assumption for resources was Austrian but does not alter the importance of the essentials of the neoclassical model), technology represented by production functions, and tastes and preferences represented by ordinal preference functions and a social welfare function (Bator, pp. 22–23).

6. The outcome of these social struggles are the length of the working day, the intensity of labor and the productiveness of labor. Chapter X of Volume 1 of *Capital*, pp. 231–321 dwells of the working day for 90 pages. Marx notes that the productiveness of labor and intensity of labor are associated with use of machinery in modern industry (Marx, *Capital*, Vol. 1, pp. 371–507).

7. Marx describes the means of subsistence of the worker as including more than physical necessities. He noted the importance of a moral and historical component of subsistence. He also noted the relative fixity of the bundle any given specific time period or in any country (Marx, Vol. 1, p. 171). Reproduction and educational costs were also assumed to be included (Marx, Vol. 1, p. 172). On the relative fixity of the subsistence bundle see also p. 519 of Vol. 1.

8. This factor will be useful later in evaluating changes in the abstract labor content of ideal money on the absolute magnitude of value and surplus value. Gold as ideal money is a representative of abstract labor. Some textual support for this factor in Marx can be found in Vol. 1 of *Capital* (Marx, Vol. 1, p. 98).

Socially necessary abstract labor is defined here in Marx's second definition of its meaning.

9. Marx uses two formulae for determining the mass of surplus value (Marx, Vol. 2, p. 304). One of them equates the mass of surplus value to the degree of exploitation times the average value of labor power times the number of laborers employed. The procedure used in this study for the estimate of aggregate surplus value is consistent with the relationships suggested by Marx.

10. The phrase is the reckoning name of money is a term found in of volume one of capital (Marx, Vol. 1, pp. 100–101). Marx refers to government setting the reckoning name of money or mint price. For example, the British government would under the gold standard set the pound to be £3 17 s. 10½ d. This was a reckoning name of money. Marx in this context is referring to paper money backed by gold. Our interpretation is that when he refers to paper money, he refers to it as either takes for gold (paper money backed 100% by gold) or credit money. Credit money could include paper money not formally backed 100% by gold or commercial credit. We interpret credit money as similar to the current currency system. Modern currency is nothing more than government debt (Currency) and/or checking accounts (bank debt). We use commodity money as a standard of price or measure of value. We assume that price to is equal to value. This is a working assumption.

11. For a discussion of this see Marx (Marx, Vol. 1, pp. 39, 44) and (Mohun, in Bottomore, pp. 1–2).

12. The distinction between L and hours of living labor (HOLL) must always be kept in mind in this analysis. (See Marx, Vol. 1, p. 193.)

Marx uses the label L for labor power in Volume of Two in capital when he notes: "If we call labour-power L . . ." (Marx, Vol. 2, p. 24).

13. This composite of commodities could vary over time and between countries. Marx, however, indicates "Nevertheless, in a given country, at a given period, the average quantity of the mens of subsistence necessary for the labourer is practically known" (Marx, Vol. 1, p. 171).

14. Each laborer represents a unit of L.

15. The intensity of labor means that more HOL of standard intensity are expended per hour in the working day. Greater intensity also results in more products or use value

produced for each hour of the working day. In other words an hour of a more intensive day produces more use values than one of ordinary intensity.

16. Marx referred to the reckoning name of money or the mint price as the price that the government gave to the unit of currency backed by gold (Marx, Vol. 1, p. 101).

17. Productiveness of labor refers to use value produced per hour. This should not be confused with productive labor. One aspect of productive labor is that it produces surplus value. To be a productive labor a laborer will have to have a level of productiveness that generates a total value of products or services in excess of variable capital and must also be involved in the process of production.

18. Future enhancements of the model will include productiveness of labor in other types of goods such as means of production and gold.

19. Use value is specific to each commodity. It cannot be summed over different representative commodities. We   make the initial assumption that the subsistence bundle can be represented as a value of overall use value derived from these commodities. The higher this value, the higher of absolute use value obtained. The value of commodities, however, is measured by their labor value and the production of commodities represent the production of goods and services. Use value here can be viewed a measure of real income.

20. The LOWD can affect the value of labor capacity (L). We assume in the model that the LOWD can be altered without affecting the value of L. However, the model can take this into account. If one increases LOWD, the value of the use value in the subsistence bundle can also be increased. Future enhancements of the model will address this issue. For a discussion of Marx on this issue see the following: Marx and Engels, Vol. 34, p. 68.

21. For a more in depth discussion of the nature of productive labor see Shaikh and Tonak (Shaikh & Tonak, p. 32); (Marx, Vol. 1, pp. 181, 509; Hunt, 1979; O'Connor, 1975; Laibman, Ch. 4). There are variety of controversies about the interpretation of productive labor. Gough provides a comprehensive review of this issue (Gough, 1972, 1973).

22. In contrast to Foley, Germer suggests that within Marxist theory gold may still have a role to play (Germer, 1998, p. 9).

23. De Brunhoff notes that Marx demonstrates the possibility of excess state issues of excess paper money relative to gold will result in rising prices (De Brunhoff, p. 36).

24. Future improvements to the model will incorporate these types of adjustments.

25. For details on Marx's position on what was included in the subsistence bundle of the worker see page 171 of Volume 1 of *Capital.*

26. Another aspect of the difference between the subsistence bundle and the purchased bundle is that changes in relative prices may cause workers to substitute commodities for offspring. Ideology, religion and deprivation of education in might serve as a social mechanism in influencing workers to accept a lower subsistence bundle.

27. The unit of labor power is held constant in the model. It is determined in the model by one worker per working day. It is a measure of labor capacity. Increases in the number of workers per day will increase the number of units of labor power consumed. This is a working assumption. For Marx other issues would also affect the unit of labor power. Marx refers to the value of labor power as being determined by the value the "necessaries of life habitually required by the average labourer" (Marx, Vol. 1, p. 519).

28. Our interpretation is that surplus labor divided by necessary labor provides the conceptually determinant ratio of the rate of surplus value. The other two formula are

only correct in so far as the variable capital paid by the capitalist coincides with the value of labor power.

29. For Marx the value of labor power is directly determined by the value of commodities in the subsistence bundle and to the quantities of those commodities. The quantity was considered to be relatively constant (Marx, Vol. 1, p. 519).

30. Marx's discussion of this appears in the third section of Chapter 17 of *Capital* Vol. 1. The section is titled, "Productiveness and Intensity of Labour Constant, Length of the Working-Day Variable" (Marx, Vol. 1, pp. 536–527).

31. For Marx's position on the relationship between an increase in the working day and impact of the value of labor power from increased wear and tear see p. 527 of Vol. 1 (Marx, Vol. 1, p. 527).

32. The socially necessary labor is measured in terms of Marx's second definition of the concept. This socially necessary labor includes the labor embodied by variable capital in gold.

33. The socially necessary labor of gold is based on Marx's second definition of the term. He clarifies the use of gold as a measure of value in "Contribution to the Critique of Political Economy (Marx & Engels, Vol. 29, p. 306). Marx provides a textual basis to estimate these numbers for the period in which he was writing. He notes that ". . . an ounce of gold, called £3 17s $^1/_2$ d. as the British standard of account, served as the legal standard of price." (Marx and Engels, Vol. 29. p. 312). In one of his examples he estimates the price of gold (Marx, Vol. 1, p. 101). Based on this we take the definition of gold in Britain in the 1840s to be £4 per ounce or 80 shillings (@20 shillings per £). For the details of the relationship of the price of gold to SNAL1 and SNAL2 contact the author.

34. In the future development of this model, we will make the price of labor power endogenous.

35. Marx also uses the term use value to refer to the real wage (Marx & Engels, Vol. 34, p. 65).

36. An interesting observation here is that when labor power is not equal to the price of labor power, the relative power of classes can potentially determine a new value of labor power. This will be limited by the change in the POL that generated the initial difference between the value and the price of labor power.

37. On the level of total social capital, Marx indicates that value produced must be equal to the sum of prices (Marx, Vol. 3, p. 173). If in the aggregate the sum of prices of production regulate prices, then the sum of aggregate prices approximates aggregate value produced. Therefore, value produced per use value can be used as an index of prices by setting it equal to 100.

38. In addition, it must be noted that labor, if the price of labor temporarily rises above the value of labor power, will have temporary access to an "article for individual consumption in general." We have found one reference in Marx for discussing such a circumstance. In critiquing Rodbertus and in the context of a discussion on the issue of a price of a commodity not always having to be equal to its value (Marx & Engels, Vol. 29, p. 260).

39. An interesting observation here is that when the value of labour power is not equal to the price of labor power, the surplus value is determined by the price of labor power not the value of labor power.

40. The value of labor power is manifested by value of the SNAL2 hours that the subsistence bundle of commodities embodies.

41. Marx uses the term use value in this example. Marx in the this example notes "The only result would be that each of them [surplus value and the price of labor power] would represent twice as many use values as before; these use-values being twice as cheap as before" (Marx, Vol. 1, p. 523).

42. For Marx the degree to which the price of labor power might fall would be limited by the new value of labor power. To what degree the price of labor power fell toward this limit would depend "on the relative weight, which the pressure of capital on the one side, and the resistance of the labourer on the other, throws into the scale" (Marx, Vol. 1, p. 523). We believe he is referring to class struggle as being the deciding factor.

43. This constant real income represents the income necessary to buy the subsistence bundle of commodities that yield an unchanged level of use value.

44. Marx notes:

If, however, the price of labour-power had fallen, not to 1s. 6d., the lowest possible point consistent with its new value, but to 2s. 10d. Or 2s. 6d., still this lower price would represent an increased mass of necessaries. In this way it is possible with an increased productiveness of labour, for the price of labour-power to keep on falling and yet this fall to be accompanied by a constant growth in the mass of the labourer's means of subsistence (Marx, Vol. 1, p. 523).

45. The proportion of productive workers estimated by Shaikh and Tonak was used as the initial value for this factor (Shaikh & Tonak, 1994). For details of its calculation consult the author. Data for total employed workers were obtained from the Department of Commerce BLS website (U.S. Department of Labor, Bureau of Labor Statistics website. Available from <http://www.bls.gov/schedule/archives/empsit_nr.htm> [29 July 2002]).

46. Althusser in discussing Marx's critique of Smith, where Marx remarks that Smith was preoccupied with the quantity "the magnitude of value" and paid little attention to the value form. Althusser notes:

On this point modern economists, despite the differences in their conception are on the side of the classics in attacking Marx for producing in his theory concepts which are 'non-operational', i.e. which exclude the measurement of their object: e.g. surplus-value. But this attack back-fires on its authors, since Marx accepts and uses measurement for the 'developed forms; of surplus-value (profit, rent and interest). If surplus-value is not measurable, that is precisely because it is the concept of its forms, which are measurable (Althusser, 1968, p. 161).

47. Shaikh and Tonak define constant capital as: "Constant capital is defined as the sum of depreciation and materials used in the productive sectors $(C^* = Mp = + Dp)$" (Shaikh & Tonak, 1994, p. 175). However, only Dp is included in their definition of Marxian Gross Value Added.

48. Estimates of the consumption of fixed capital and the GDP for the U.S. for 2000 can be obtained from the Department of Commerce site (U.S. Department of Commerce, BEA website, BEA news release. Available from <http://www.bea.doc.gov/bea/newsrel/gdpnewsrelease.htm> [31 July 2002]).

49. The 0.45 value for the productiveness of labor only represents newly formed use value. With the expanded model labor also transfers use value from constant capital so that the use value produced and transferred will be larger than this number. For example, in our model, we assumed that the partial organic composition of capital was 2.89 and that the rate

of surplus value 2.44. The resulting productiveness of labor in both transferring and producing new use value per hour would be $(1 + 2.44 + 2.89) \times (0.45/(1 + 2.44) = 0.828$ use values produced and transferred per hour per unit of labor capacity. The rate of surplus value is determined by the model.

50. We assume in our model that people still perceive their currency as convertible to gold in the international market and that gold is still recognized as an implicit international money form. The $275 per ounce estimate is the average daily PM price fix for the year 2000 posted by the London Bullion Market Association (London Bullion Market Association Website, London Market Statistics, Gold Fixes. London Gold Fixes, PM fixes based on dollars. Available from <http://www.lbma.org.uk/2000dailygold.htm> [6 August 2002]).

Marx implies that gold produced domestically was equivalent to buying gold from abroad (Marx, *Capital*, Vol. 2, p. 78).

51. This is the average hourly earnings of four productive sectors for the U.S. for 2000. The sectors include mining, construction, manufacturing, and utilities and transportation. The sectors were weighted by the employment in each sector (Bureau of Labor Statistics Website, Establishment Data, Historical hours and earnings. Available from <ftp://ftp.bls.gov/pub/suppl/empsit.ceseeb2.txt> [6 August 2002]).

52. For the details of the calculations and interpretation of this consistency contact the author. Also note that Shaikh and Tonak refer to what we call the partial organic composition of capital as the value composition of capital (Shaikh & Tonak, 1994, p. 124, Fig. 5.15).

53. The author also developed secondary set of calculations to demonstrate the theoretical and empirical consistency the models results to the estimates of the nominal wage in the productive sectors, the SNAL2 per ounce of gold and the international price of gold. Contact the author for details.

54. Shaikh and Tonak note that inventories of materials (raw and auxiliary) should be included in the stock of fixed capital (Our note – The stock of fixed capital is that part of constant capital that enters the production process without entering the valorization process) (Shaikh & Tonak, 1994, p. 122, Footnote 16).

55. We refer to this as the partial organic composition of capital because the C or constant capital that we include in this estimate only includes that portion of constant capital that has its value transferred to the output in the course of the year. This constant capital includes only materials consumed productively and depreciation on the instruments of labor. It excludes the value of the constant fixed capital that remains in the production process at the end of the year – that is not completely exhausted either in its material or value form at the end of the year. The Marxian concept the full sense of the organic composition of capital would include in its calculation the constant capital included in both the expended constant capital that took place and the value of the capital stock left at the end of the year including inventories of raw materials and auxiliary materials in process. The expended capital would include depreciation, raw materials and auxiliary materials. For a more complete discussion and example of this see Marx (Marx, Vol. 3, pp. 155–156). Shaikh and Tonak's estimate of the flow of advanced constant capital is on page 289 while their estimate of variable capital is on page 327 (Shaikh & Tonak, 1994).

56. It must be remembered that since the use value in the subsistence bundle is fixed on the basis of an working year of 214 days, increasing either the length of the working

day or the number of working days per year will increase the rate of surplus value. A more realistic model that we will consider later would increase to some degree the use value required for subsistence as hours per day or days per year are increased. Commuting and health costs would be expected to increase.

57. The weights were based on the proportion of each sex employed in non-agricultural industries 20 year old or older. The weights were 53.5% for men and 46.5% for women. The average annual hours came to 1728. This was divided by 8.094 or the average length of the working day to arrive at 214 working days (Department of Commerce, Bureau of labor Statistics, Available from <http://data.bls.gov/servlet/ SurveyOutputServlet> [7 August 2002]).

58. Total Marxian value produced or transferred is not in concept totally comparable to GDP. Shaikh and Tonak have discussed the conceptual issues for comparing GNP to Marxian Total value and Gross Factor Product. See pages 72–75 in their book cited previously. Their estimate of Marxian Total value is above and their estimate of Marxian Gross Value added is below NIPA GNP estimates. Our estimation procedure is based on simulation and not identical with Shaikh and Tonak's procedures who were working closing with NIPA and IO accounts for their data. A major issue in the comparison is the treatment of Marxian constant capital as an intermediate input. Intermediate sales should not appear in GDP. Constant capital used from inventories during the year and depreciation of fixed capital should appear in Marxian Total Value. Depreciation should appear in GDP but only changes in inventories appear in GDP. Our estimates of Marxian Value of final goods and services roughly be an alternative measure of aggregate economic activity as it measured by GDP.

59. The use of the model in this manner has precedents. An example would be the use of theory by astronomers in inferring the existence of planetary bodies that cannot be seen by using to theory to evaluate perturbations of stars. Another example would be the theoretical controversy caused by the Leontief paradox that led to research to resolve it. As noted, Shaikh and Tonak indicated that there are conceptual differences between Marxian Total value and GDP.

60. As indicated previously there are conceptual differences between Marxian Total Value and GDP. They will not be expected to be equal. The differences that we perceive are not totally identical with those identified by Shaikh and Tonak.

61. Shaikh and Tonak reported their Total Product estimate (that was equal to their estimate of Marxian total value) was 1.5 times larger than the conventional measure of GNP. However, their Gross factor product also based on Marx's theory was 15% smaller than GNP (Shaikh & Tonak, 1994, p. 221). They were mapping data from conventional estimates to Marxian categories while we were simulating values based on Marxian Theory. The procedures used are different and another study will address these differences.

ACKNOWLEDGMENTS

I am grateful for comments and criticisms on ideas used in this paper from Paresh Chattopadhyay, Duncan Foley, Doug Koritz, and Paul Zarembka. However, my friends and colleagues are not responsible for the views represented in this paper.

REFERENCES

Althusser, L., & Balibar, E. (1968). *Reading Capital*. Paris, France: Francois Maspero.

Althusser, L. (1965). *For Marx*. London, U.K.: Verso.

Balinky, A. (1970). *Marx's Economics*. Lexington, MA: D. C. Heath & Company.

Bator, F. M. (1957). The Simple Analytics of Welfare Maximization. *American Economic Review*. 22–59.

Bottomore, T. (1991). *A Dictionary of Marxist Thought* (2nd ed.). Cambridge, MA: Blackwell Publishers.

Bureau of Labor Statistics Website, Establishment Data, Historical hours and earnings. Available from <ftp://ftp.bls.gov/pub/suppl/empsit.ceseeb2.txt > [6 August 2002].

Bureau of labor Statistics Website, Available from <http://data.bls.gov/servlet/SurveyOutputServlet> [7 August 2002].

De Brunhoff, S. (1976). *Marx on Money*. New York: Unizen Books, Inc.

Dornbusch, R., Fischer, S., & Startz, R. (1998). *Macroeconomics* (7th ed.). Boston MA: Irwin McGraw-Hill.

Foley, D. K. (1986). *Understanding Capital Marx's Economic Theory*. Cambridge, MA: Harvard University Press.

Germer, C. M. (2000). Some Conceptual Elements for a Marxist Analysis of the International Monetary System. Paper prepared for presentation oat the Mini-Conference on Value Theory, At the Eastern Economics Association Annual Conference.

Germer, C. M. (1998). The Concept of the 'gold standard' and the misunderstanding of political economy. Working papers of the 1998 Mini Conference of the International Working Group on Value Theory held at the Eastern Economics Association Annual Conference.

Gough, I. (1972). Marx's Theory of Productive and Unproductive Labour. *New Left Review*, 76(Nov.–Dec.), 47–72.

Gough, I. (1973). On Productive and Unproductive Labour – A Reply. *Bulletin of the Conference of Socialist Economists*, (Winter), 68–73.

Hunt, E. K. (1979). The Categories of Productive and Unproductive Labor in Marxist Economic Theory. *Science and Society*, *3*, Fall, 303–324.

Hunt, E. K., & Sherman, H. (1990). *Economics An Introduction to Traditional and Radical Views* (6th ed.). New York, NY: Harper and Row Publishers Inc.

Kalmans, R. (1996). Some Empirical Considerations for the Question of Transformation. Paper presented at the Eastern Economics Associated Conference March 1996, pp. 1–41.

Laibman, D. (1992). Value *Technical Change and Crisis Explorations in Marxist Economic Theory*. Armonk, NY: M. E. Sharpe.

London Bullion Market Association Website (2002). London Market Statistics, Gold Fixes. London Gold Fixes, PM fixes based on dollars. Available from <http://www.lbma.org.uk/2000dailygold.htm> [6 August 2002].

Marx, K. (Engels, F., Ed.) (1967). *Capital*, Unabridged Vols 1, 2 and 3. New York: International Publishers.

Marx, K., & Engels, F. (1986). *Collected Works, Vol. 28, Marx: 1857–1861*. New York: International Publishers.

Marx, K., & Engels, F. (1987). *Collected Works, Vol. 29, Marx: 1857–1861*. New York: International Publishers.

Marx, K., & Engels, F. (1988). *Collected Works, Vol. 30, Marx: 1861–1863*. New York: International Publishers.

Marx, K., & Engels, F. (1989). *Collected Works, Vol. 31, Marx: 1861–1863*. New York: International Publishers.

Marx, K., & Engels, F. (1994). *Collected Works, Vol. 34, Marx: 1861–1863*. New York: International Publishers.

Mings, T., & Marlin, M. (2000). *The Study of Economics Principles, Concepts and Application* (6th ed.). Gilford, CT: Dushkin/McGraw-Hill.

Moseley, F. (1994). Capital in General and Marx's Logical Method: A Response to Heinrich's Critique. Unpublished paper, South Hadley, MA: Mount Holyoke College.

Moseley, F. (1987). Notes and Comments – The profit Share and the rate of surplus value in the U.S. Economy, 1975–1985. *Cambridge Journal of Economics, 11*, 393–398.

Moseley, F. (1987). The Rate of Surplus Value in the Postwar U.S. Economy: A Critique of Weisskoph's Estimates. *Cambridge Journal of Economics, 9*, 57–79.

Moseley, F. (circa 1980s). Estimating the Intensity of Labor. MA: Mt. Holyoke College. Unpublished mimeo.

O'Connor, J. (1975). Productive and Unproductive Labor. *Politics and Society*, 297–336.

Resnick, S. A., & Wolff, R. (1987). *Knowledge and Class – A Marxian Critique of Political Economy*. Chicago, IL: The University of Chicago Press.

Rones, P. L., Ilg, R. E., & Gardner, J. M. (1970). Trends in Hours of Work Since the Mid-1970s. *Monthly Labor Review*, (April).

Shaikh, A. M., & Tonak, A. E. (1994). *Measuring the Wealth of Nations The Political Economy of National Accounts*. Cambridge, U.K.: Cambridge University Press.

U.S. Department of Commerce (2002). BEA website, BEA news release. Available from <http://www.bea.doc.gov/bea/newsrel/gdpnewsrelease.htm> [31 July 2002].

U.S. Department of Commerce (2002). BEA Website, BEA News Release, Table 1.b. Current dollar GDP revised estimates. Available from <http://www.bea.doc.gov/bea/newsrel/gdpnewsrelease.htm> [8:30 a.m. 31 July 2002]

U.S. Department of Labor (2002). Bureau of Labor Statistics website. Available from <http://www.bls.gov/schedule/archives/empsit_nr.htm> [29 July 2002].

U.S. Department of Labor (1997). Bureau of Labor Statistics. February. Workers Are On the Job More Hours Over the Course of the Year. Issues in Labor Statistics.

Wolff, R. D., & Resnick, S. A. (1987). *Economics: Marxian vs. Neoclassical*. Baltimore, MD: John Hopkins.

PART IV:
CRITIQUES OF KEYNES' *GENERAL THEORY*, OF RICARDO'S TRADE THEORY, AND OF THE MARKET

COLLECTIVE AND INDIVIDUAL RATIONALITY: MAYNARD KEYNES' METHODOLOGICAL STANDPOINT AND POLICY PRESCRIPTION

Andy Denis

ABSTRACT

Some advocates of laissez-faire, including Smith and Hayek, have proposed various 'invisible hand' mechanisms to ensure that self-seeking behaviour at the micro-level leads spontaneously to desirable social outcomes at the macro-level. Keynes shares their holistic approach, but rejects their invisible hand mechanisms. He analyses the pathology of capitalism as rooted in a multi-player prisoners' dilemma. Keynes assigns a critical role to his own class, the 'educated bourgeoisie' in the reform process required to resolve that dilemma. The paper highlights the distinction and intimate connection between micro-level individualism, and the macro-level planning required to preserve it, in Keynes' policy standpoint.

I. INTRODUCTION

In previous papers (Denis, 1996a, b, 1997, 1999a, b, 2000, 2002a, b), and in my Ph.D. thesis (Denis, 2001), I have tried to show two things: Firstly, that in a world of partially overlapping and partially conflicting interests there is good reason to doubt that self-seeking behaviour at the micro-level will spontaneously

Confronting 9-11, Ideologies of Race, and Eminent Economists,
Research in Political Economy, Volume 20, pages 187–215.
ISBN: 0-7623-0984-9

lead to desirable social outcomes at the macro-level. And, secondly, that some sophisticated economic writers who would like us to rely on the spontaneous interaction of self-seeking agents, writers advocating a *laissez-faire* policy prescription, have proposed various 'invisible hand' mechanisms which can, in their view, be relied upon to 'educe good from ill'. Smith, I argued, defended the 'simple system of natural liberty' as giving the greatest scope to the unfolding of God's will and the working out of 'natural', providential processes free of interference by 'artificial' state intervention – the expression not of divine order but of fallible human reason. Hayek, adopting a similar policy stance, based it in an evolutionary process in which those institutional forms best adapted to reconciling individual interests would, he believed, spontaneously be selected for in the inter-group struggle for survival.

The purpose of the present paper is to cast a light on this issue from another direction by displaying an example of the policy consequences of adopting an alternative methodological stance. The argument of the paper is that: (a) staying within the holistic methodological framework of Smith and Hayek, but (b) rejecting their invisible hand mechanisms, leads (c) to the rejection of their reductionist *laissez-faire* policy stance as well.

The structure of the paper is as follows. In Section II, I show Keynes' view of the historical role of capitalism and his analysis of its pathology, rooted in what we would now refer to as the prisoners' dilemma. Section III draws attention to the fundamental significance of his methodological standpoint. This lays the basis for a consideration of his policy prescription in the following two sections. Section IV looks at two very important aspects to the question, spelling out Keynes' call for planning, and explaining exactly what he meant by this. Before doing so however – and this is the other key aspect to the question – the section examines Keynes' *class* standpoint, showing the critical role he expected his own class, the 'educated *bourgeoisie*', to play in the reform process he mapped out. Section V adds a further layer to the consideration of Keynes' policy prescription, drawing out the distinction, but also the intimate connection, between, on the one hand, micro-level individualism (the 'Manchester System'), and, on the other, the macro-level collective action ('planning') required to preserve it. Finally, Section VI concludes by considering Keynes in relation to the themes of the research of which this paper is part – Smith and Hayek, holism, reductionism and the invisible hand.

II. KEYNES' HISTORICAL PERSPECTIVE

Whereas, for Smith and Hayek capitalist individualism is the terminus of an *ontogenetic* process, for Keynes it is something transitional, something with a historical and conditional validity. Keynes' historical perspective is thus consistent with a *phylogenetic* evolutionary stance. *Laissez-faire* in Keynes' conception performed a vital historical role, carrying us from an Era of Scarcity to an Era of Abundance. It was precisely because it had substantially fulfilled that role that it had become counter-productive. The point is controversial. Joan Robinson claimed that Keynes 'saw the capitalist system as ... a phase in historical development' (Robinson, 1964, p. 71); Geoffrey Pilling, on the other hand, criticising both Keynes and Robinson, writes that 'It is just this historical conception of capitalism which is absent in Keynes' (Pilling, 1986, p. 35, n. 1). The purpose of this section is to show that Robinson was right, and Pilling wrong,[1] on this point: to establish Keynes' conception of the historical role of capitalism – though not, I should emphasise, necessarily to defend it.

In order to establish Keynes' view of the historical and historically limited role of *laissez-faire*, we must say something about his conception of the historical context, that is, about his periodisation of history. I have attempted to reconstruct Keynes' view here by rereading 'Am I a Liberal?' (Keynes, 1925b) in the light of his later works, in particular 'Economic Possibilities for our Grandchildren' (Keynes, 1930c), and Book VI of the *General Theory*, 'Short Notes Suggested by the General Theory' (Keynes, 1973a, pp. 313–384).

The first great era in Keynes' scheme takes in prehistoric, ancient and medieval times. In the 'Era of Scarcity' (Keynes, 1972a, p. 304) production is overwhelmingly production for the sake of consumption, indeed subsistence purposes: 'The economic problem, the struggle for subsistence, always has been hitherto the primary, most pressing problem of the human race – not only of the human race, but of the whole of the biological kingdom from the beginning of life in its most primitive forms' (Keynes, 1972a, pp. 326–327). During the Era of Scarcity, there is an overwhelming obstacle to the accumulation of capital in the form of uncertainty driving the marginal efficiency of capital (*MEC*) below the rate of interest (*i*):

> The destruction of the inducement to invest by an excessive liquidity-preference was the outstanding evil, the prime impediment to the growth of wealth, in the ancient and medieval worlds. And naturally so, since certain of the risks and hazards of economic life diminish the marginal efficiency of capital while others serve to increase the preference for liquidity. In a world, therefore, which no one reckoned to be safe, it was almost inevitable that the rate of interest ... would rise too high to permit of an adequate inducement to invest (Keynes, 1973a, p. 351).

At – so to speak – the other end of history from the era of scarcity, in the near future, lies 'our destination of economic bliss' (Keynes, 1972a, p. 331), 'economic paradise' (Keynes, 1972a, p. 268), 'the age of leisure and abundance' (Keynes, 1972a, p. 328). 'The economic problem may be solved, or be at least within sight of solution, within a hundred years ... the economic problem ... is not the permanent problem of the human race' (Keynes, 1972a, p. 326). The essence of the era of abundance is that 'needs are satisfied in the sense that we prefer to devote our further energies to non-economic purposes' (Keynes, 1972a, p. 326). Thus, we may note in passing, production here, too, is for the sake of consumption in the broadest sense: 'for the first time since his creation man will be faced with his real, his permanent problem – how to use his freedom from pressing economic cares. ... to live wisely and agreeably and well' (Keynes, 1972a, p. 328).

The following year, in the Preface (dated 1931) to *Essays in Persuasion* (Keynes, 1972a), a collection of essays spanning a dozen years, this approaching liberation from economic care has become his 'central thesis throughout': 'the day is not far off when the economic problem will take the back seat where it belongs, and that the arena of the heart and head will be occupied ... by our real problems – the problems of life and human relations, of creation and behaviour and religion' (Keynes, 1972a, p. xviii). This messianic strand, though expressed in more sober language, still plays a central, and, indeed, even more urgent, role in the *General Theory*. The age of abundance now appears as the 'quasi-stationary community' (Keynes, 1973a, p. 220), and is to be attained, not in our grandchildren's time, but 'within a single generation' (Keynes, 1973a, p. 220), 'say within twenty-five years or less' (Keynes, 1973a, p. 324).

The modern period, the third historical division or 'economic order' (Keynes, 1972a, p. 304) in Keynes' schema, is the age of capitalism. This period does not have the fundamental, self-sufficient character of the other two epochs, but is simply the period of transition from the one to the other. As such it is not an end in itself but a means to an end lying beyond itself, namely our entry into the 'economic paradise'. Hence our judgement of capitalism must refer, not to how pleasant or otherwise it may be, but to its efficacy in achieving that end:

> Many people, who are really objecting to capitalism as a way of life, argue as though they were objecting to it on the ground of its inefficiency in attaining its own objects ... For my part I think that capitalism, wisely managed, can probably be made more efficient for attaining economic ends than any alternative system yet in sight, but that in itself it is in many ways extremely objectionable (Keynes, 1972a, p. 294).

Capitalism achieves this end, in Keynes' view, by means of the accumulation of capital, and, for Keynes, the rate of capital accumulation is the measure of the rate of our approach to the economic paradise. To denote the motives to this accumulation of capital, Keynes spoke of 'compound interest' (Keynes, 1972a, p. 324) and 'purposiveness' (Keynes, 1972a, p. 329). By this latter peculiar expression, 'purposiveness', he merely means money-making as an end in itself, saving, ostensibly for future consumption, but actually for the sake of accumulating claims on future production; saving not in order to enjoy the deferred consumption later, but in order to secure a stream of unearned income. Keynes analyses 'purposiveness' psychologically as an attempt to gain immortality by projecting one's actions into an indefinite future by means of an infinite regress:

> purposiveness means that we are more concerned with the remote future results of our actions than with their own quality ... the purposive man is always trying to secure a spurious and delusive immortality for his acts by pushing his interest in them forward in time (Keynes, 1972a, p. 330).

Just as Marx, in the Communist Manifesto, for example, was outspoken in his praise for the achievements of capitalism (Marx & Engels, 1976, p. 489), Keynes, too, paid tribute to those achievements: 'In the nineteenth century this epoch culminated gloriously in the victories of *laissez-faire* and historic Liberalism.' (Keynes, 1972a, p. 304) The accumulation of capital depended upon the freedoms of *laissez-faire* – in particular, private properly in the means of production and unrestricted scope for the operation of market forces:

> The system worked, throughout Europe, with an extraordinary success and facilitated the growth of wealth on an unprecedented scale. To save and invest became at once the duty and the delight of a class. The savings were seldom drawn on, and, accumulating at compound interest, made possible the material triumphs which we now all take for granted. The morals, the politics, the literature, and the religion of the age joined in a grand conspiracy for the promotion of saving (Keynes, 1972a, p. 62).

In one of his essays on Liberalism, where he applied to his own views the term 'New Liberalism' (Keynes, 1972a, p. 305), he remarked that 'old-fashioned individualism and laissez-faire ... contributed to the success of the nineteenth-century ... I should have belonged to this party [sc the Liberal Party] if I had been born a hundred years earlier' (Keynes, 1972a, pp. 300–301).

While recognising the historical necessity and legitimacy of the *laissez-faire* system, and appreciating the benefits of its 'material triumphs', Keynes never-theless deprecated the subversion of morals he believed it involved: 'we have exalted some of the most distasteful of human qualities into the position of highest virtues.' (Keynes, 1972a, p. 329) Keynes is here protesting against the fact that capitalism requires, and *laissez-faire* permits, the transformation of the economy from production for the sake of consumption to production for the sake of profit, for the sake of the accumulation of wealth. Saving for the sake of future consumption Keynes can put up with; saving in order 'to exploit the scarcity value of capital' (Keynes, 1973a, p. 376) is morally reprehensible.

That mankind has had to depend on this sort of egoistic materialism in order to raise itself from scarcity to abundance had had, according to Keynes, widespread deleterious consequences. Defining capitalism as 'egotistic atomism', he complains that: 'modern capitalism is absolutely irreligious, without internal union, without much public spirit, often . . . a mere congeries of possessors and pursuers' (Keynes, 1972a, p. 267). 'I think that Capitalism . . . in itself is in many ways extremely objectionable' (Keynes, 1972a, p. 294).

> [T]he moral problem of our age is concerned with the love of money, with the habitual appeal to the money motive in nine-tenths of the activities of life, with the universal striving after individual economic security as the prime object of endeavour, with the social approbation of money as the measure of constructive success, and with the social appeal to the hoarding instinct as the foundation of the necessary provision for the family and for the future (Keynes, 1972a, pp. 268–269).

The ultimate problem with Capitalism, however, was when it became ineffective as a means to the end which justified it: 'Capitalism . . . is not intelligent, it is not just, it is not virtuous – and it doesn't deliver the goods' (Keynes, 1982, p. 239). Nevertheless, despite these criticisms of capitalism, Keynes was anxious not to throw out the baby with the bathwater:

> It is common to hear people say that the epoch of enormous economic progress which characterised the nineteenth century is over . . . I believe this is a wildly mistaken interpretation of what is happening to us. We are suffering, not from the rheumatics of old age, but from the growing pains of over-rapid changes, from the painfulness of readjustment between one economic period and another (Keynes, 1972a, p. 321).

The fundamental, underlying problem in this period is that production is not directly production for the sake of consumption, as it is in the two great eras of scarcity and abundance, instead we have production for the sake of profit, of accumulation, for the sake, that is, of production itself. A comparison of the category 'consumption' as it appears in 'Economic Possibilities for our Grandchildren' (Keynes, 1930c) with that in Keynes, 1973a shows it in two diametrically opposed rôles. Consumption today is consumption for production: it does not matter what it is consumption *of* so long as it contributes to aggregate demand and hence keeps the accumulation of capital going. In the future, in the 'economic paradise', production is a mere means, and consumption the end: in that context consumption means 'learning to live wisely and agreeably and well' (Keynes, 1972a, p. 328), solving 'the problems of life and human relations, of creation and behaviour and religion' (Keynes, 1972a, p. xviii). The critical importance of this view of consumption, and its methodological implications, will be taken up in the next section.

The problems of this period of 'capitalistic individualism' are for Keynes precisely those arising from its transitional nature. The MEC is falling precisely because it has fulfilled its purpose. Its purpose was to promote the accumulation of capital and, in general, the wealth of society: the falling *MEC* (and marginal propensity to consume, *MPC*) are the inevitable result of that accumulation. Indeed, for Keynes, the definition of the 'economic paradise' is that the *MEC* has fallen to zero. There is nothing pathological about this – on the contrary, it is to be expected and desired.

The trouble arises from the institutional context within which the transition was taking place, namely that of *laissez-faire*. Under *laissez-faire*, Keynes believed, and believed he had demonstrated, the *MEC* falls faster, and further, than the rate of interest (*i*). This is due to a peculiarity of money that it can act as a store of value for the individual but not for the community – what is true for each individual taken separately is not true for all the individuals taken together. '[T]here is no such thing as liquidity of investment for the community as a whole' (Keynes, 1973a, p. 155). If the community tries to convert part of its aggregate income into a hoard of money, total income simply declines to the point where the community no longer tries to do so.

Keynes' argument is that the natural tendency for the *MEC* to decline with increasing abundance of capital should be matched by an offsetting tendency for *MPC* to decline with increasing income. *i* should therefore decline *pari passu*: the opportunity cost of investment – that is, the foregone or postponed consumption – should fall to zero, since that portion of income is saved anyway. Given an adequate institutional framework this is what will happen. The *MEC* can then decline to zero without falling below *i* and hence without investment being brought to a standstill. Once the *MEC* has fallen to zero, capital goods are essentially free and we have entered the economic paradise.

However, the institutional framework is *not* adequate: the *laissez-faire* system introduces an intolerable level of uncertainty. If every agent were in some way linked up to every other so that they could act in concert, each would realise that it is in the interest of all to make sure that their saving and investment correspond. No-one could have any interest in a beggar-thy-neighbour policy of hoarding money. But *laissez-faire* means, precisely, that this coordination is lacking. *Laissez-faire* divides everyone from everyone else: it's every man for himself. Every agent must now be in ignorance as to what his fellows are going to do. Instead of assessing real economic conditions each agent must now devote himself to guessing what all the *other* agents think of those conditions, or, rather, to guessing what each other agent guesses every other agent guesses . . . A rational saver may know that it would be best for all if he (and everyone else) were to restrain himself from hoarding money; he may even assume that everyone else knows this in theory, but he cannot be certain that everyone will have the necessary restraint not to save money 'just in case'. Any such suspicion means that he would be well advised to increase the liquidity of his assets a little. But if he, as a rational agent, finds that necessary, then so presumably do other agents. Every increase in the demand for money as an asset, a store of value (or liquidity preference, as Keynes calls such demand), is a reduction in aggregate demand (*AD*). A reduction in *AD* means a fall in the *MEC*. The agent must now believe, correctly, that a severe economic recession is on the way, and would be foolish not to build up as large a pool of liquid wealth as possible, thereby driving up i yet further. Even if the agent is fully conscious that he is contributing to the crisis, exacerbating it, there is absolutely nothing that he, as an isolated individual, can do about it.[2]

> Many of the greatest economic evils of our time are the fruits of risk, uncertainty, and ignorance ... these ... factors are ... the cause of un-employment ... Yet the cure lies outside the operations of individuals; *it may even be to the interest of individuals to aggravate the disease*. I believe that the cure for these things ... would involve Society in exercising directive intelligence ... over ... private business (Keynes, 1972a, pp. 291–292; my emphasis).

The essence of the prisoners' dilemma (Denis, 1996a, 2001 Ch. 2) is that the prisoners are compelled to pursue their partially overlapping and partially conflicting interests rationally but without collaboration. It shows how rationality at the individual (micro) level necessarily leads to irrationality at the collective (macro) level under these conditions. The essence of Keynesian opposition to *laissez-faire* is that by artificially dividing economic agents from each other it compels them, in individual self defense, to act in a manner detrimental to themselves as a group. Keynesian agents thus find themselves in what we in retrospect can see as a prisoners' dilemma. Not, indeed, a one-shot game, but an indefinitely repeated one. Players in an indefinitely repeated game may under certain circumstances – a sufficiently large probability of further rounds of the game together with a sufficiently low rate of discount of future payoffs – find their way to a cooperative outcome. However, while this is the case for two-player games, the achievement of such desirable outcomes rapidly becomes extremely difficult as the number of players rises above two. With any significant number of players, it becomes impossible to discriminate between cooperators and defectors, leading to the collapse of reciprocity: defection is once more the dominant strategy. And in the Keynesian case we have a multi-player game with the number of players being the number of wealth owners who need to determine the proportions of money and other assets to hold in their portfolios.

Keynes says something remarkable, in this connection, in his 'Notes on the Trade Cycle' (Keynes, 1973a, Ch. 22, pp. 313–332). The crisis, he says, is due to an 'error of pessimism' in which:

the investments, which would in fact yield 2% in conditions of full employment, are expected to yield less than nothing; and the resulting collapse of new investment then leads to a state of unemployment in which the investments, which would have yielded 2% in conditions of full employment, in fact yield less than nothing (Keynes, 1973a, p. 322).

Clearly this is not an 'error' on the part of the *individual* investors: they expected yields to fall by more than two percentage points and that is exactly what happened; their expectations were quite rational. The 'error' is on the part of the investors *as a whole*: it was sheer insanity for them to be pessimistic as it was precisely that pessimism which led to the collapse in new investments, the consequent unemployment and hence the collapse in yields. The institutional framework of *laissez-faire* dictates individual decision-making on an issue which is fundamentally not an individual matter.

Laissez-faire divides economic agents from each other and leads to uncertainty; uncertainty leads to increased liquidity preference; raised liquidity preference leads to recession; and recession leads to unemployment: 'A monetary economy . . . is essentially one in which changing views about the future are capable of influencing the quantity of employment' (Keynes, 1973a, p. xxii). 'Unemployment develops . . . because people want . . . money' (Keynes, 1973a, p. 235). Because of this irreducible uncertainty associated with the *laissez-faire* system, Keynes believed that capitalism would settle down to a normal condition of under-employment equilibrium: 'Unemployment . . . apart from brief intervals of excitement is associated – and in my opinion, inevitably associated – with present day capitalistic individualism' (Keynes, 1973a, p. 381). 'We oscillate . . . round an intermediate position appreciably below full employment' (Keynes, 1973a, p. 254).

This outcome has two particularly deleterious consequences, other than the obvious one that unemployment and a fall in aggregate income is in no-one's interest. Firstly, the regular fall in the *MEC* towards zero, and what that is an index of, namely, the accumulation of capital up to the desired level of intensity, is broken off. For as long as *MEC* is below *i*, this process cannot continue. Hence our entry into the 'New Jerusalem', as Lambert (1963, p. 358) puts it, is postponed for as long as we remain in this rut of under-employment.

Secondly, and this is critical for Keynes, unemployment may lead to damaging, revolutionary changes, either in the direction of fascism or of communism: 'it is certain that the world will not much longer tolerate [this] unemployment' (Keynes, 1973a, p. 381). 'If [income deflation] occurs, our present regime of capitalistic individualism will assuredly be replaced by a far-reaching socialism' (Keynes, 1971, p. 346). On another occasion, he took comfort from a general willingness to drop the philosophy of *laissez-faire* for similar reasons to his own – fear that the existing institutions would otherwise be jeopardised. He could discern, he claimed, 'a general conviction that the stability of our institutions absolutely requires a resolute attempt to apply what perhaps we know to preventing the recurrence of another steep descent' (Keynes, in Hutchison, 1977, p. 65).

Keynes thus wants reform in order to forestall revolution. Only change can keep things the same. The next section examines in more detail Keynes' methodological holism which laid the basis for his policy prescription, and subsequent sections examine what Keynes believed had to change, what he wanted to remain the same, and how it should be done.

III. KEYNES AND HOLISM

In the previous section, I argued that, for Keynes, the underlying problem with capitalism was that production was not for the sake of consumption, but for the sake of production itself. To elucidate the relation between production and consumption in Keynes, we need to consider a number of passages from the *General Theory* and early drafts. In a draft chapter of the *General Theory* (Keynes, 1979), Keynes adopted Marx's formulae for simple commodity circulation and capitalist circulation, $C - M - C'$ and $M - C - M'$. The first formula says that a commodity, C, is exchanged for money, M, and the latter used to purchase another commodity, C'. The difference between C and C' is qualitative: they are different commodities. The second says that a quantity of money, M is invested in commodities, C, and the latter sold for a quantity of money, M', greater than the original quantity ($M' = M + \Delta M$, $\Delta M > 0$).[3] The mistake of the classical economists,[4] Keynes says, was to assume that money has the role only of means of exchange, as it does in simple commodity circulation, rather than store of value, as in the circulation of capital. In simple commodity production, production is still for consumption: the original commodity is produced in order to sell it and with the proceeds purchase the commodity desired for consumption. In capitalist production, the purpose of production is to augment the value of the capitalist's wealth, and consumption is reduced to a means to this end. In the one case, money is a convenience allowing the commodity owner to translate his commodity, produced only for the market, into the one he wants to consume. In the other, money is money capital, money is the goal and criterion of production.

> Karl Marx . . . pointed out that the nature of production in the actual world is not, as economists seem often to suppose, a case of C – M – C', ie of exchanging commodity for money in order to obtain another commodity. That may be the standpoint of the private consumer. But it is not the attitude of *business*, which is a case of M – C – M', ie of parting with money for commodity in order to obtain more money (Keynes, 1979, p. 81).

While the formula for the circulation of capital expresses the 'standpoint of business', and the structure of incentives under capitalism, in Keynes' view this involves contradictions: although we might behave as though production were carried out for its own sake, this cannot literally be true: 'capital is not a self-subsistent entity existing apart from consumption' (Keynes, 1973a, p. 106); 'the expectation of consumption is the only *raison d'être* of employment' (Keynes, 1973a, p. 211); 'consumption – to repeat the obvious – is the sole end and object of all economic activity' (Keynes, 1973a, p. 104). The point Keynes is insisting on here is that production has to be validated by consumption to *count* as production: output must be sold to convert it back into money, and, indeed, more money than was started with. The subordination of consumption to production implicit in classical *laissez-faire* capitalism sets up a continually re-emerging barrier to accumulation in the form of under-consumption and failures of aggregate demand.

Keynes' approach here illustrates the methodological significance of his critique of classical economists, from Ricardo to Pigou. For the individual household, 'the standpoint of the private consumer', we have $C - M - C'$: consumption is the immediate goal of economic activity. So does this mean that $C - M - C'$ is valid for society as a whole? That is what 'economists seem often to suppose'. But that is reductionist: it is saying that what is true of the parts is therefore true of the whole. '[T]he nature of production in the actual world' is the opposite: $M - C - M'$: economic activity is directed towards the accumulation of claims on future production.

This rejection of reductionism is evidenced over and over again in Keynes' writings. In the famous passage from the 'Preface' to the French edition of the *General Theory*, cited in Section VI of the present paper, Keynes criticises the classical economists for erroneously 'extending to the system as a whole conclusions which have been correctly arrived at in respect of a part taken in isolation' (Keynes, 1973a, p. xxxii).

The same line of criticism is apparent in Chapter 2 of the *General Theory*. Here Keynes criticises Ricardo for focusing on microeconomic problems concerning relative prices and the allocation of resources between different uses, and his denial of the desirability, indeed possibility, of macroeconomic analysis of the level of economic activity as a whole. Keynes cites Ricardo's letter to Malthus of 9 October 1820:

> Political economy you think is an enquiry into the nature and causes of wealth – I think it should be called an enquiry into the laws which determine the division of the produce of industry amongst the classes who concur in its formation. No law can be laid down respecting quantity, but a tolerably correct one can be laid down respecting proportions. Every day I am more satisfied that the former enquiry is vain and delusive, and the latter only the true objects of the science (cited in Keynes, 1973a, p. 4).

Later in the same chapter he criticises the classical school for its reductionist approach to the wage bargain. Keynes sets out his famous 'two postulates of classical economics: that 'The wage is equal to the marginal product of labour', and that 'the utility of the wage when a given volume of labour is employed is equal to the marginal disutility of that amount of employment'. The first says that firms are optimising in the labour market, the second that households are. Keynes conceded the first but denied that the second held as a rule. Classical economists who assumed it to be true forgot, he claimed, firstly, that the relationship between real and money wages was different for the individual industry and the whole economy:

> In the case of a change peculiar to a particular industry one would expect the change in real wages to be in the same direction as the change in money wages. But in the case of changes in the general level of wages . . . the changes in real wages associated with a change in money wages . . . is almost always in the opposite direction (Keynes, 1973a, p. 10).

Keynes is clearly reiterating the point that the whole cannot be understood as the sum of its parts: the relationship between real and money wages is transformed as we change levels. Here, an increase in money wages in an isolated industry would also be an increase in real wages, as the aggregate price level is unaffected; when we come to industry as a whole, a change in output will, in Keynes' opinion, be associated with a rise in the price level, and a smaller rise in the level of wages: real wages will fall.

Secondly, according to Keynes – and this is really the same point made another way – the classical economists forgot that the principle, that unemployed workers can always underbid the employed and so bring supply and demand into equilibrium in the labour market, is 'intended . . . to apply to the whole body of labour and do[es] not merely mean that a single individual can get employment by accepting a cut in money-wages which his fellows refuse' (Keynes, 1973a, p. 11). The point is, that if one worker 'considered in isolation' were to accept a cut in wages, this would be relative to a given price level, which would remain unchanged by his actions – and so his, or her, real wage would decline in the same proportion as the money wage. The actions of a single worker, in an economy of any significant size, have a vanishingly small impact on the general price level. For the actions of the workers as a whole this is no longer true: an attempt to reduce the general level of money wages, via their impact on firms' marginal costs, would lead to reductions in the general price level of about the same magnitude, leaving real wages where they were (Keynes, 1973a, p. 12). Again, it is clear that Keynes is making a point about the relationship between phenomena at the system and substrate levels, and criticising the classical economists for failing to see it. At the substrate level, the general price level is a parameter, at the system level it is a variable.

Numerous further examples from Keynes could be cited. At the risk of labouring the point, just two more instances will be considered here, both from the *General Theory*. In Chapter 19, on 'Changes in Money Wages', Keynes once again takes the 'classical economists' to task, in a passage of such clarity as to render exegesis redundant, for impermissibly transferring unexceptionable micro statements to the macro context:

> In any given industry we have ... the demand schedule for labour in the industry relating the quantity of employment to different levels of wages ... This conception is then trans-ferred without substantial modification to industry as a whole; and it is supposed by a parity of reasoning, that we have a demand schedule for labour in industry as a whole relating quantities of employment to different levels of wages ... [S]urely [this] is fallacious. For the demand schedules for particular industries can only be constructed on some fixed assumption as to the nature of the demand and supply schedules of other industries and as to the amount of the aggregate effective demand. It is invalid, therefore, to transfer the argument to industry as a whole ... But if the classical theory is not allowed to extend by analogy its conclusions in respect of a particular industry to industry as a whole, it is wholly unable to answer the question what effect on employment a reduction in money wages will have (Keynes, 1973a, pp. 258–260).

Finally, and for exactly the same reasons, we may note that in the chapter of the *General Theory* on 'The Theory of Prices' (Keynes, 1973a, Ch. 21, 292–309), Keynes rejects the classical dichotomy 'between the theory of value and distribution on the one hand and the theory of money on the other hand' (Keynes, 1973a, p. 293).

> The right dichotomy is, I suggest, between the theory of the individual industry or firm and of the rewards and the distribution between different uses of a *given* quantity of resources on the one hand, and the theory of output and employment *as a whole* on the other hand (Keynes, 1973a, p. 293).

Keynes is again clearly articulating a holist conception here. The classical dichotomy distinguishes between a real supply side and a purely nominal demand side – a standpoint which, as he points out, implies that at the macro level 'the elasticity of supply must have become zero and demand proportional to the quantity of money' (Keynes, 1973a, p. 292). This classical standpoint tacitly – and illicitly – assumes that what is '*given*' at the micro level, namely the quantity of resources which is employed in the economy as a whole, must also be given at the macro-level, the level to which monetary theory applies. This leaves money with no real effects (the real and monetary sectors are dichotomous): from our standpoint as observers it is a mere veil over the real workings of the economy. In opposition to this classical dichotomy, Keynes proposes his own micro-macro dichotomy: a micro sphere of analysis in which conclusions can be 'correctly arrived at in respect of a part ... taken in isolation'

(Keynes, 1973a, p. xxxii), and a macro sphere to be analysed as a whole, as a system, and in which money attains critical importance for real outcomes.

IV. KEYNES' POLICY PRESCRIPTION

The overview, in the previous two sections, of Keynes' dynamic and historical view of the pathologies of capitalism, and of his clear sighted articulation of the micro and macro levels in economics, lays the basis for an understanding of his policy prescription. Only one further point is required. In utter contrast to Smith's invisible hand of god, and Hayek's evolutionary theory of group selection, Keynes never for a moment assumes that we live in a world endowed with providential, pro-human qualities. His standpoint is entirely consistent with that of A. E. Houseman's 'heartless, witless Nature' (cited, Dawkins, 1995, p. 155). If good is to be found in the world, it must be the result of our own activity. In such a world, a policy of *laissez-faire* is a non-starter.

So what was Keynes' policy prescription – and, moreover, who was to execute it? A careful reading of Keynes makes it quite clear what he was prepared to sacrifice, and what he was determined at all costs to retain – what it was about 'our institutions' and 'the kind of system in which we actually live' (Keynes, 1973a, p. 247) which he thought worth keeping. What Keynes was concerned to defend was the liberties, the privileges, the prestige, the security, the standard of living, and in short the whole mode of life of the class of which he was a member: 'If I am going to pursue sectional interests at all, I shall pursue my own. When it comes to the class struggle as such . . . the *Class* war will find me on the side of the educated *bourgeoisie*' (Keynes, 1972a, p. 297). Far from expressing any narrow, sectarian point of view, however, Keynes was able to take this stance because of the *universality* he ascribed to his class. As we shall see, the 'educated bourgeoisie' was a universal class in the sense that, by following its own interests, it would lead the whole population to the destination of economic 'bliss'.

The 'educated bourgeoisie' comprised for Keynes all those sections of society that his own activities made him part of – business management and public administration, and the worlds of academia and the arts. It excluded the actual owners of the means of production, the rentier capitalists, and it excluded the 'ordinary' people who 'sell themselves for the means of life' (Keynes, 1972a, p. 328). Keynes invented a rather grotesque *raison d'être* for this stratum, which runs as follows. The big problem with the approach of the 'economic paradise' is that *ordinary* people will not know what to do with themselves:

> I think with dread of the adjustment of the habits and instincts of the ordinary man, bred
> into him for countless generations, which he may be asked to discard within a few decades
> ... must we not expect a general 'nervous breakdown'? (Keynes, 1972a, p. 327) There is
> no country and no people, I think, who can look forward to the age of leisure and abundance
> without a dread ... It is a fearful problem for the ordinary person, with no special talents,
> to occupy himself ... (Keynes, 1972a, p. 328).

Fortunately, however, there are strata of the population who are not 'ordinary',
who do have 'special talents'. (These 'talents', however, turn out to be of the
monetary variety.)

> It will be those people, who can keep alive, and cultivate into fuller perfection, the art of
> life itself, and do not sell themselves for the means of life, who will be able to enjoy the
> abundance when it comes ... the wealthy classes in any quarter of the world ... are, so
> to speak, our advance guard – those who are spying out the promised land for the rest
> of us and pitching their tent there ... those who have an independent income but no
> associations or duties or ties (Keynes, 1972a, p. 328).

Keynes immediately takes the opportunity of castigating the *idle* rich, the
rentiers: 'most of them have failed disastrously ... to solve the problem which
has been set them' (Keynes, 1972a, p. 328). Keynes is attacking them for failing
to live up to the role he ascribes to the rich – the development of a good life
of culture and consumption, rather than 'purposiveness' and hoarding – and
thereby undermining the *raison d'être* of the class system. Keynes' attitude
towards the rentier class is ruthless. If they will not spend their money, take it
off them. He regarded the inheritance of fortunes as a specially pernicious,
feudal institution, and favoured high death duties to counter its effect on the
MPC (Keynes, 1972a, p. 299; Keynes, 1973a, pp. 95, 372–373; Keynes, in
Hutchison, 1977, p. 72). Meanwhile, to the rest of us he addresses an appeal
for another chance: 'I feel sure that with a little more experience we shall use
the new-found bounty of nature quite differently from the way in which the
rich use it today, and will map out for ourselves a plan of life quite otherwise
than theirs' (Keynes, 1972a, p. 328).

Keynes' belief in the importance of class distinctions comes out clearly when
he states his differences from communism:

> How can I adopt a creed which, preferring the mud to the fish, exalts the boorish proletariat
> above the *bourgeois* and the intelligentsia who, with whatever faults, are the quality in life
> and surely carry the seeds of all human advancement ... It is hard for an educated, decent,
> intelligent son of Western Europe to find his ideals here ... It exalts the common man and
> makes him everything (Keynes, 1972a, pp. 258–259).

We should be quite clear, here, what Keynes means by the *bourgeoisie*. Just
as he borrowed the designation 'classical economists' from Marx and then

proceeded to use it in a completely different – almost opposite – sense,[5] his use of the term bourgeois has little or no overlap with Marx's conception of the capitalist class. The 'educated bourgeoisie', the 'bourgeoisie and intelligentsia', in Keynes do not include the owners of the means of production, the capitalists *per se* (whether holders of debt or equity). When he explicitly sides with the bourgeoisie, by no means is Keynes erecting an apology for the rentier. The latter he regards as a parasitic excrescence on the productive apparatus of society, and one which is in the course of quiet liquidation by the spontaneous development of the economy itself:

> The rentier aspect of capitalism [is] a transitional phase which will disappear when it has done its work . . . the euthanasia of the rentier, of the functionless investor, will be nothing sudden, merely a gradual but prolonged continuance of what we have seen recently in Great Britain, and will need no revolution (Keynes, 1973a, p. 376).

This particular terminology adopted by Keynes means that when he speaks of 'private initiative and responsibility', 'the traditional advantages of individualism', 'personal liberty', and so on, as desirable attributes of capitalism which will be retained in the new society (Keynes, 1973a, Ch. 24 passim), he is not referring to private property in the means of production. Indeed, the question of private or public ownership of the means of production was a non-issue as far as Keynes was concerned:

> It is not the ownership of the instruments of production which it is important for the state to assume. (Keynes, 1973a, p. 378) There is no so-called important political question so really unimportant, so irrelevant to the reorganisation of the economic life of Great Britain, as the Nationalisation of the Railways (Keynes, 1972a, p. 290).

Nationalisation was a non-issue for Keynes because the 'educated bourgeoisie' was in fact taking, or had already taken, control of the bulk of industrial – and, indeed, non-industrial – institutions. This theme in Keynes – the separation of ownership and control, leading to the hegemony of the managers in industry and state – has since become a major tradition in its own right. The theme originally had two aspects, distinguishing between holders of debt and equity. In 1923 Keynes described what he calls 'the Investment System', in these terms:

> Under this phase of capitalism, as developed during the nineteenth century, arrangements were devised for separating the management of property from its ownership . . . Contracts to receive fixed sums of money at future dates must have existed as long as money has been lent and borrowed . . . But during the nineteenth century they developed a new and increased importance, and had, by the beginning of the twentieth, divided the propertied classes into two groups – the 'business men' and the 'investors' – with partly divergent interests . . . business men might be investors also, and investors might hold ordinary shares; but the division was nevertheless real (Keynes, 1972a, pp. 61–62).

The second phase, so to speak, occurs when the rentiers, or 'investors', buy up the shares, too, and leave the managers without any ownership stake in the enterprise.

> A point arrives in the growth of a big institution . . . at which the owners of the capital, ie the shareholders, are almost entirely dissociated from the management, with the result that the direct personal interest of the latter in the making of great profit becomes quite secondary (Keynes, 1972a, p. 289).

Keynes calls this 'the tendency of big business to socialise itself' (Keynes, 1972a, p. 289), and describes it as 'a natural line of evolution. The battle of Socialism against unlimited private profit is being won in detail hour by hour' (Keynes, 1972a, p. 290). A salient example cited by Keynes in this context, and – significantly – prior to its Nationalisation, is that of the Bank of England: 'there is no class of persons in the kingdom of whom the Governor of the Bank of England thinks. less when he decides on his policy than of his shareholders. Their rights, in excess of their conventional dividend have already sunk to the neighbourhood of zero' (Keynes, 1972a, p. 290).

This conception of what has since been sensationalised as a 'managerial revolution' is crucial to the understanding of Keynes' policy prescription. Keynes' aim is an adequate policy framework for '[t]he transition from economic anarchy to a regime which deliberately aims at controlling and directing economic forces' (Keynes, 1972a, p. 305). He wants 'a somewhat comprehensive socialisation of investment' (Keynes, 1973a, p. 378); he wants 'planning' (Keynes, in Hutchison, 1977, pp. 72, 77); he wants, as he told Hayek, 'more planning' (Keynes, 1980, p. 387). He was enthusiastic about the proposals for a national plan contained in the Mosley Manifesto (Keynes, 1930b). 'The central debate in politics, he [sc Keynes] wrote, was between planning and laissez-faire' (Skidelsky, 1975, p. 241).

But what sort of planning does Keynes want? Planning by whom? For whom? We have already seen his contempt for 'the ordinary man with no special talents', and for 'the mud . . . the boorish proletariat' who 'sell themselves for the means of life'. He is even less sympathetic towards those at the opposite pole of the social spectrum. Keynes clearly believed that the 'beastly', 'avaricious' Jews were over-represented, to put it no more strongly than that, among the rentier capitalists. He writes in 'A Short View of Russia' (Keynes, 1925a) that 'the mood of oppression . . . in Russia . . . is the fruit of some beastliness in the Russian and Jewish natures . . .' (Keynes, 1972a, p. 270), and in the same article remarks that the Russian Revolution has failed to make the Jews any less avaricious (Keynes, 1972a, p. 259). In a highly sinister passage, Keynes daydreams about the fate of Jewish financiers in the economic paradise to come:

The love of money as a possession ... will be recognised for what it is, a somewhat
disgusting morbidity, one of those semi-criminal, semi-pathological propensities which one
hands over with a shudder to the specialists in mental disease ... Perhaps it is not an
accident that the race which did most to bring the promise of immortality into the heart
and essence of our religions has also done most for the principle of compound interest and
particularly loves this most purposive of institutions (Keynes, 1972a, pp. 329–330).[6]

Keynes' vision of planning, therefore, is one in which the main role is taken
by the 'educated bourgeoisie', excluding the 'common people' on the one side,
and the (mainly Jewish) rentiers on the other. While expressing no particular
desire to dispense with parliamentary democracy, he clearly regards it as simply
irrelevant: 'in the future the Government will have to take on many duties which
it has avoided in the past. For these purposes Ministers and Parliament will be
unserviceable' (Keynes, 1972a, pp. 301–302).

So, in answer to the question of what it is that Keynes wants to preserve in
'existing economic forms', what he means when he refers to the preservation
of 'individual initiative' and its 'successful functioning' (Keynes, 1973a,
p. 380), I have argued that Keynes is anxious, above all, to preserve the status
and privileges of his own class, the 'educated bourgeoisie', the 'advanced guard
... spying out the promised land'. It is *their* 'individual initiative' which he
wishes to defend. 'Private self interest', expressed through consumer preferences
on the market, and the exercise of 'enterprise and skill in the estimation of
prospective yields' (Keynes, 1973a, p. 221) on the part of the entrepreneur,
'will determine what in particular is produced, in what proportions the factors
of production are combined to produce it, and how the value of the final product
will be distributed between them' (Keynes, 1973a, p. 379). Just as when Smith
and Hayek speak of the rights of 'the individual' they refer to the individual
owner of wealth, the individual as vehicle for capital, and in every other context
the individual is the servant of 'society' (Denis, 1999b, 2001 Ch. 5), so for
Keynes the 'individual' who is truly efficacious, who enjoys freedom, opportunity and activity, is the 'educated *bourgeois*', the gentleman of independent
means and public spirit.

It seems fair to summarise Keynes' vision of planning as a network of
'semi-autonomous bodies' – quangos and quagos linked together and to the
national bank by a board of public investment:

Progress lies in the growth and the recognition of semi-autonomous bodies within the state
... bodies which in the ordinary course of events are mainly autonomous within their
prescribed limitations, but are subject in the last resort to the sovereignty of the democracy
expressed through Parliament (Keynes, 1972a, pp. 288–289).

Now, even the private enterprise firms of the *laissez-faire* period were 'in
the last resort' subject to parliamentary sovereignty. To say this of the

'semi-autonomous bodies' is to say very little. In practice, what we have is a new *laissez-faire*, differing from the old in being collective rather than individualistic. The managerial class, which has quietly triumphed in both the formally private and the formally public sectors, is to be allowed to get on with it, free – in the ordinary course of events – of effective parliamentary supervision, regulation or restraint.

Keynes' articles in *The Times* in January and March, 1937, provide perhaps the most explicit statement of how these 'semi-autonomous bodies' are to be linked, as well as a useful ostensive definition of 'semi-autonomous body':

> Now is the time to appoint a board of public investment ... to make sure that detailed plans are prepared. The railway companies, the port and river authorities, the water, gas and electricity undertakings, the building contractors, the local authorities, above all, perhaps, the London County Council and the other great corporations with congested population, should be asked to investigate what projects could be usefully undertaken if capital were available at certain rates of interest – $3^1/_2$%, 3%, $2^1/_2$%, 2%. The question of the general advisability of the schemes and their order of preference should be examined next. What is required at once are acts of constructive imagination by our administrators, engineers, and architects, to be followed by financial criticism, sifting and more detailed designing (Keynes, in Hutchison, 1977, p. 72).

This is one half of the strategy. The other half is to ascertain from the mass of information obtained in this, and every other conceivable way, what rate of interest would be compatible with a flow of new projects just sufficient to absorb what the nation chooses to save:

> The rate of interest must be reduced to the figure that the new projects can afford. In special cases subsidies may be justified. But in general it is the long-term rate of interest which should come down to the figure which the marginal project can earn ... We have the power to achieve this. If we know what rate of interest is required to make profitable a flow of new projects at the proper pace, we have the power to make this rate prevail in the market (Keynes, in Hutchison, 1977, p. 73).

There are three points worth noting here, as to why Keynes is so confident about the rate of interest, when, after all, he had only recently proclaimed himself 'somewhat sceptical of the success of a merely monetary policy directed towards influencing the rate of interest' (Keynes, 1973a, p. 164).

The first point is that the Bank of England had already been cited by Keynes as a progressive example of 'semi-autonomous body', and of course the Treasury consists entirely of administrators and economists. The two institutions could therefore be depended upon, once Keynesian ideas had made themselves felt, to take the side of the 'educated bourgeoisie' against the rentiers, on the one side, and against interference by the electorate via parliament, on the other.

The second point is that due to the institutionally powerful position in the market of the Treasury and central bank, 'it lies within their power . . . to make the long-term rate of interest what they choose within reason' (Keynes, in Hutchison, 1977, p. 73). The channeling of savings through the national bank, too, would give the state additional leverage against the rentier class and under-mine the ability of the latter to dictate absolutely the rate of interest on borrowed capital (Keynes, in Hutchison, 1977, p. 73, Keynes, 1973a, p. 376).

Thirdly, the plan has been drawn up by the business community themselves, and in a collective rather than individualistic way. Everyone knows what the rest of the economy is doing and no-one has any incentive to increase his liquid reserves. Consequently, there is nothing to force i up above MEC at full-employment. Uncertainty has been eliminated at the outset by removing the artificial isolation of economic agents imposed by the anachronistic *laissez-faire* approach to policy. The payoffs to holding money and bonds have been changed so that the prisoners' dilemma has been removed.

V. DID KEYNES REJECT LAISSEZ-FAIRE?

So, did Keynes rejected *laissez-faire*? In the past three answers have been given – *yes*, *no*, and *yes and no* – all of them false. The first has tended to be associated with more left-wing interpreters of Keynes, such as Joan Robinson, and the second both with more conservative interpreters, and with left-wing anti-Keynesians, such as Geoffrey Pilling. The third alternative, that Keynes was inconsistent in his attitude to *laissez-faire*, has been a very common one, and in the 1930s cartoons used to appear in the press of Keynes as a double-jointed man supporting, for example, both free-trade and protection.

These approaches fail to do Keynes justice. It is true that Keynes did not make the final break with classical economic theory until around 1933, and he himself aptly summarised his life to this point as 'a long struggle of escape' (Keynes, 1973a, p. xxiii). In spite of this, his general social and political philosophy was consistent throughout his productive life and, I would argue, the changes in his economic theory were designed specifically to supply a theo-retical underpinning for his political attitudes: 'The field of social philosophy is the field in which Keynes remained consistent throughout his career' (Lambert, 1963, p. 344).

> While the *General Theory* marks a sharp break in economic theory, the 'social philosophy' implications he drew from the work [in Ch. 24] are consistent with his earlier views. In fact the *General Theory* can be viewed as giving an economic theoretic rationalisation for views that Keynes' ethics and intuition had led him to (Minsky, 1975, p. 145).

While they can thus agree that Keynes was consistent, commentators are anything but agreed on what it was that Keynes was (supposedly consistently) saying: 'Keynes [is] essentially an economic liberal arguing for specific non-liberal measures solely in periods of unemployment' (Corry, 1978, p. 26). 'When the whole question of seeing that potential savings are not run to waste in unemployment . . . is added to the *agenda* [of government], it seem as if there is precious little *non-agenda* left' (Robinson, 1964, p. 81).

The reason why these views are mistaken is that they take the supposed Keynesian rejection of *laissez-faire* (whether they assert or deny that rejection) to be a rejection *a limine*. It is not. An implication of the present paper is that it is a *critique* – a concrete negation with a concrete result. Keynes' view of *laissez-faire* is not absolute but conditional and historical. His call for state intervention to equilibrate saving and investment is, in his own view, by no means timelessly or universally valid.

The difference between himself on the one hand, and, on the other, the old-fashioned Liberals as well as the classical school whose theories underlay the *laissez-faire* approach, was that Keynes 'explained the phenomena, which the old Liberal school attributed to the unchanging and universal character of natural law, in terms of positive and therefore changeable laws and of the particular conditions obtaining at a given time and a given place' (Lambert, 1963, p. 345).

Lambert here is commenting on Keynes' first book, *Indian Currency and Finance* (1913), written when Keynes was still, in terms of economic theory, entirely within the neoclassical school. The point is that even where, as in his work prior to World War I, Keynes obtained results formally consonant with the neo-classical and liberal traditions, such as the correctness of the *laissez-faire* approach to the economic policy framework in the nineteenth century, these results were obtained on the basis of a different, more concrete and more historical methodology. It was this methodology which enabled him to develop a *vision* of what was wrong with *laissez-faire*, when his contemporaries could only see that *something* was wrong (Pigou, for example, in the 1930s), and hence enabled him to develop a theoretical account of the economic problems of his time.

* * *

Whilst, therefore, the enlargement of the functions of government involved in the task of adjusting to one another the propensity to consume and the inducement to invest, would seem to a nineteenth-century publicist or to a contemporary American financier to be a terrific encroachment on individualism, I defend it, on the contrary, both as the only practicable means of avoiding the destruction of existing economic forms in their entirety and as the condition of the successful functioning of individual initiative (Keynes, 1973a, p. 380).

This passage, from the final chapter of the *General Theory*, is a concise statement of Keynes' rejection of *laissez-faire*. Yet taken out of context, it could be extremely misleading. The 'enlargement of the functions of government' does, it is true, include an expansion in the role of the existing state. This is concerned principally with the adjustment of the propensity to consume by manipulation of the rates of income tax and death duty, and by deciding how sharply progressive should be the former, channeling savings through a national savings bank, and a programme of emergency public works in severe recessions.

But this is not the main point for Keynes. His goal is not simply an 'enlargement of the functions' but a change in the *nature* of the state. What he wants is an extra- or non-parliamentary state consisting of a central bank and a national planning board linking together the enterprises (in the broadest sense) of the country into a single organization. This organization would, through discussion, draw out a consensus of the whole of the 'educated bourgeoisie'; there would be no call for compulsion. The cancellation of the artificial separation and atomization of the 'entrepreneurs' (that is, the managerial class), by the principles of *laissez-faire*, would eliminate the uncertainty which gives rise both to damaging fluctuations in economic activity and to the under-employment equilibrium around which the economy oscillates.

This, then, is how a theory can be simultaneously 'revolutionary' (Keynes, 1935) and 'moderately conservative' (Keynes, 1973a, p. 377) in its implications. The (revolutionary) introduction of central controls and planning to achieve full employment at the macro level is to provide the necessary environment in which the (conservative) micro-level 'Manchester system' comes into its own' (Keynes, 1973a, pp. 378–379). Keynes wants to combine micro-level individualism with the macro-level planning required to preserve it. To put it another way, individual self-seeking behaviour at the micro level will generate desirable social outcomes at the macro level when the institutional framework ensures that the payoffs to individual actions are such as to avoid prisoners dilemmas.

The transition from the Era of Scarcity to the capitalist epoch required central controls on production and distribution to reduce uncertainty and the rate of interest, and raise the marginal efficiency of capital. This was the age of mercantilism and absolutism. Now, in the period of transition from capitalism to the 'economic paradise', similar problems call for similar solutions: a latter-day mercantilist policy (Keynes, 1973a, Ch. 23), 'promoted by an authority unlikely to be superseded' (Keynes, 1973a, p. 203).

VI. CONCLUSION: KEYNES AND PROVIDENTIALISM

In a holist view of the world, the individual agents composing an economic system are, and are *primarily*, components of a social totality: their life process is determined by their mutual relations, the totality of which is the economic system. Under capitalism, however, the individual agents are divorced from each other and their relations are refracted through their sole link with society: the money nexus. This gives them the appearance of independent, asocial, biological totalities, and hence gives the real social totality the appearance of a mere *congeries*.

It is in a sense immaterial where the economist commences his study of society, whether he 'starts' from the part and deduces therefrom the nature of the whole, or *vice versa*. Friedman, for example, correctly observes that both he and Keynes work 'from the top down', while many monetarists and Keynesians work in the opposite direction (Friedman, 1976, p. 316). That makes no difference: what matters is not where you 'start' but where you end up: do you understand the economy as a totality – with Keynes, Marx, Hayek, and Smith – or as a congeries – with Friedman, Lucas, and the neoclassical school.

Reductionism is implicit in the 'classical' methodology that Keynes criticised, as well as the methodology of those neoclassical writers, such as Friedman, who re-assert the claims of pre-Keynesian economics post-Keynes. The agent is a rational, utility-maximising being; since society is merely a mass of like individuals, the results of the analysis of his behaviour can be applied directly to society as a whole. Thereby the latter is shown to be a rational, welfare-maximising aggregate of many individuals. Protracted, general, involuntary unemployment is not possible: no rational individual would under-utilize scarce resources, so humanity in the aggregate must necessarily be just as rational. On the other hand, the *appearance* of unemployment can be explained away as *false* appearance concealing the intrinsic rationality of the system: irrationality on the level of the system cannot be the fault of the system but only of the individuals comprising it – so apparent unemployment must in fact be voluntary, caused, for example, by wage rigidity or other micro-irrationality.

Keynes, summarising his whole approach in a passage to which I have already drawn attention, goes straight to the heart of this question:

> I have called my theory a *general* theory. I mean by this that I am chiefly concerned with the economic system as a whole ... And I argue that important mistakes have been made by extending to the system as a whole conclusions which have been correctly arrived at in respect of a part taken in isolation (Keynes, 1973a, p. xxxii).

Keynes is saying that the principal *differentia* of his method from that of the 'classical economists' is that the system as a whole cannot be considered as a mere congeries of individuals 'taken in isolation'. This is so because those individuals *are not isolated* from each other: what one does affects others. An individual's decision to save or to invest or to hold money, for instance, has consequences for other individuals who are not party to the relevant transaction and hence unable to affect its outcome.

In this clash between the private form and public consequences of the decisions to consume, and to save, to hold money and to invest, we see again the combination of independence in form and interdependence in content of those decisions, which lies at the heart of the prisoners dilemma (Denis, 1996a, 2001 Ch. 2). Keynes sees this clash between private action and public consequence as remediable only by the removal of the anachronistic private form of decision-making. Hence Keynes' opposition to *laissez-faire* and his demands for social control of the propensity to consume, for the 'comprehensive socialisation of investment', and for 'communal saving through the agency of the state' (Keynes, 1973a, pp. 376, 378).

Keynes' holism lies essentially in this: were the community as a whole, or some state agency representing it, to control saving and investment, there would need never be any discrepancy between the two. The desirability of the marginal unit of investment would be equal to the sacrifice involved in the marginal unit of saving, and with the accumulation of wealth, both would decline to zero.

The problem is the presence of an anachronistic institutional framework – *laissez-faire* – which fragments the decision-making process without mitigating the social consequences of the decisions made. The *community* can only do *two* things with its income: consume it or invest it. The individual acting on the basis of self-interest, however, has third alternative: he can hoard part of his income as money. Indeed, if he foresees any slackening of aggregate demand, he would be unwise not to, even if he realises the damage he will inflict on the economy thereby: 'Every act of saving involves a 'forced' inevitable transfer of wealth to him who saves, though he in his turn may suffer from the saving of others.' (Keynes, 1973a, p. 212) Hence hoarding, which is the cause of the economic disease, is the rational response of individuals to the fear of that disease: 'It may even be to the interest of individuals to aggravate the disease.' (Keynes, 1972a, p. 318). Though in practice the matter might be highly complex, the solution is in principle simple: that individuals should act no longer as individuals but as a collectivity, in so far as *quantitative* investment decisions are concerned.

* * *

The assumption standing behind pre- and post-Keynesian mainstream economics is that the unintended consequences of individual actions are *essentially* benign.

This providential assumption pervades the writings of Smith and Hayek, Friedman and Lucas. Keynes devoted his theoretical life to the demonstration that unintended consequences, just because they *are* unintended, are uncontrolled and liable to be thoroughly malign:

> The world is *not* so governed from above that private and social interests always coincide ... It is *not* a correct deduction form the principles of economics that enlightened self-interest always operates in the public interest." (Keynes, 1972a, pp. 287–288) "There is no design but our own ... the invisible hand is merely our own bleeding feet moving through pain and loss to an uncertain ... destination (Keynes, 1981, p. 474).

Keynes' rejection, in these passages, of providentialism and the invisible hand bring us full circle. The episodes in the history of economic thought considered in Denis (2001) have shown that the combination in decision-making of independence in form and interdependence in content is an issue which continually re-emerges in political economy. At every stage there is a clash between the scientific and the vulgar, the desire to understand and explain, on the one hand, and fear of the consequences of doing so, on the other. Providentialism plays a key role here.

In Denis (2001) I focused on two sophisticated attempts to underpin a reductionist *laissez-faire* policy prescription with a holistic methodology. Smith and Hayek, though separated by two centuries, have proposed very similar invisible hand mechanisms to mediate between the holistic nature of the world and the reductionist character of their desired policy framework. Consideration of Keynes has shone a light on their attempts: his account gives us an outstanding example of the fate of *laissez-faire* political economy if a holistic approach is not supplemented with the *deus ex machina* of an invisible hand.

The precise content of Keynes' escape from the twin *laissez-faire* strategies of reductionism, on the one hand, and holism plus an invisible hand, on the other, is perhaps of less interest than its existence. Keynes had a particular view of the class of which he was part – he saw it as a universal class in a Hegelian sense, leading humanity from darkness into light. He was also, in my reading, a virulent racist with very strong, deeply ambiguous feelings about Jews.[7] I believe that all of this shaped and coloured his reading of writers such as Ricardo and Marx, his positive analysis, and his policy prescription. So from the perspective of this paper, the details are less important than the fact that he showed that there was an escape route: the economy is to be studied as a system and not as a congeries, and our default is to act, not to do nothing. Against the atomism of the 'classical' economists he argues for a clear, holistic, systems view, and against the providentialism of the invisible hand theorists he simply and clear-sightedly denies that any such providential mechanism exists, and shows in detail the implications, positive and normative, of that denial.

So for Keynes, the invisible hand ensuring that desirable social consequences flow from self-seeking individual behaviour is a myth: but the job it was supposed to do, the reconciliation of partially conflicting and partially over-lapping interests, still needs to be done. This reconciliation is to be achieved in Keynes' view by the universal class, the educated bourgeoisie, and, in partic-ular, by the extra-parliamentary state which it will build, based around a board of national planning linking all the enterprises of the country to the central bank. For Keynes it is precisely the educated bourgeoisie which will take the place of the invisible hand.

NOTES

1. It has been argued (Geoffrey Kay, personal communication) that both Robinson and Pilling were right, here, since they meant different things by 'historical'. However, Pilling clearly believed he was talking about the same thing as Robinson and that she was wrong: 'One cannot . . . accept Joan Robinson's confident assertion about Keynes' – ie the assertion that Keynes viewed capitalism as a phase in historical development (Pilling, 1986, p. 57). On this latter point Pilling was clearly wrong and Robinson right. However, one might wish to go further and argue that there was a sense in which Pilling was right about Keynes being unhistorical because he, Keynes, had a notion of capital which was in some sense timeless. But this goes beyond the question of whether Keynes had a historical view of capitalism, and slides over into another question, namely whether he had what one believes to have been the *correct* historical view of capitalism. That is not an issue I am addressing here.

2. In the context of a discussion of different forms of the prisoners' dilemma Douglas Hofstadter has introduced a concept of 'reverberant doubt' which describes exactly what Keynes is concerned with here: 'Isn't this an amazing and disturbing slide from certain restraint . . . It is a cascade, a stampede, in which the tiniest flicker of doubt has become amplified into the gravest avalanche of doubt. That is what I mean by 'reverberant doubt' and one of the annoying things about it is that the brighter you are, the more quickly and clearly you see what there is to fear' (Hofstadter, 1985, p. 753).

3. In Marx, the second formula is true of merchant capital, which buys cheap in one market and sells the same commodities dear in another market; in capitalist production proper the original money capital is invested in means of production – constant and variable capital (c, v) – which are then consumed in the process of production, generating new commodities which are subsequently sold for more than the value of the means of production: $M - C: MP (c, v) \ldots P \ldots C' - M'$ (Marx, 1974, p. 25).

4. Throughout this paper, the term 'classical' follows Keynes' usage, not Marx's. See next note.

5. For Marx, 'classical' political economy referred to scientific economics – i.e. economics which, he felt, tried to explain, rather than to explain away, the nature of capitalistic production – from Petty in the late 17th century on, and culminating in Smith and Ricardo. Subsequent mainstream economists Marx designated 'vulgar', and considered to be only interested in explaining away the undesirable features of capitalism

Marx, however, explicitly noted Ricardo's acceptance of Say's Law as an apologetic and vulgar element 'unworthy' of his otherwise classical and scientific approach. For Keynes, on the contrary, 'classical' economists are precisely those mainstream economists, since Ricardo, who, like Ricardo himself, adopt Say's Law: he names JS Mill, Marshall, Edgeworth and Pigou as examples (**GT**: 3). Hence, for Keynes, the labour theory of value of Smith and Ricardo is 'pre-classical' (**GT**: 213).

6. It should, I think and hope, be clear that presenting my interpretation of economists' writings implies no endorsement of their stance, but so that there should be no possibility of misinterpreting my motives in reporting Keynes' views here, I completely dissociate myself from his racist remarks and standpoint regarding supposedly 'avaricious' Jews and 'boorish' proletarians alike.

7. This was mixed up in his mind with sexual questions – passages in his essays on Einstein and Dr Melchior being particularly remarkable expressions of this potent mixture of racial and sexual issues. It would be inappropriate, however, to develop this theme further here.

ACKNOWLEDGMENTS

This paper has been presented at the London Guildhall University Department of Economics research seminar and the fourth annual conference of the Association for Heterodox Economics, Dublin, July 2002, and I should like to thank seminar participants, and Mary Denis, William Dixon, and Geoffrey Kay, for their support and helpful comments.

REFERENCES

Dawkins, R. (1995). *River out of Eden – A Darwinian View of Life*. London: Phoenix/Orion.

Denis, A. (1996a). Collective and Individual Rationality in Economics: the Prisoners' Dilemma. City University Department of Economics and Applied Econometrics Research Unit, Discussion Paper Series, 53, London.

Denis, A. (1996b). Collective and Individual Rationality in Economics: Arrow's Impossibility Theorem. City University Department of Economics and Applied Econometrics Research Unit, Discussion Paper Series, 54, London.

Denis, A. (1997). Collective and Individual Rationality in Economics: The Invisible Hand of God in Adam Smith. City University Department of Economics and Applied Econometrics Research Unit, Discussion Paper Series, 62, London.

Denis, A. (1999a). Was Adam Smith an Individualist? *History of the Human Sciences, 12*(3)(August), 71–86.

Denis, A. (1999b). Friedrich Hayek: a Panglossian evolutionary theorist. City University School of Social and Human Sciences Interdisciplinary Seminar Discussion Paper, London.

Denis, A. (2000). Epistemology, observed particulars and providentialist assumptions: the *Fact* in the history of political economy. *Studies in the History and Philosophy of Science, 31*(2), 353–361.

Denis, A. M. P. (2001). Collective and Individual Rationality: Some Episodes in the History of Economic Thought. Ph.D. Thesis, City University, London.

Denis, A. (forthcoming, 2002a). Methodology and policy prescription in economic thought: a response to Mario Bunge. *The Journal of Socio-Economics*.

Denis, A. (2002b). Was Hayek a Panglossian evolutionary theorist? A reply to Whitman. *Constitutional Political Economy, 13*(3)(September), 275–285.

Hofstadter, D. R. (1985). *Metamagical Themas*. Harmondsworth: Penguin.

Hutchison, T. W. (1977). *Keynes vs the Keynesians . . .?* London: Institute of Economic Affairs.

Keynes, J. M. (1923). The Social Consequences of Changes in the Value of Money. Reprinted in: *Collected Writings* (Vol IX, pp. 59–75).

Keynes, J. M. (1926). The End of *Laissez-faire*. Reprinted in: *Collected Writings* (Vol IX, pp. 272–294).

Keynes, J. M. (1925a). A Short View of Russia. Reprinted in: *Collected Writings* (Vol IX, pp. 253–271).

Keynes, J. M. (1925b). Am I a Liberal? Reprinted in: *Collected Writings* (Vol. IX, pp. 295–306).

Keynes, J. M. (1930b). Sir Oswald Mosely's Manifesto. *Nation and Athenæum*, 13 December. Reprinted in: *Collected Writings* (Vol. XX, pp. 473–476).

Keynes, J. M. (1930c). Economic Possibilities for our Grandchildren. Reprinted in: *Collected Writings* (Vol. IX, pp. 321–332).

Keynes, J. M. (1933). National Self-Sufficiency. *Yale Review*, and *New Statesman and Nation*, 8 and 15 July. Reprinted in: *Collected Writings* (Vol. XXI, pp. 233–246).

Keynes, J. M. (1935). Letter to GB Shaw. Reprinted in: *Collected Writings* (Vol. XIII, pp. 492–493).

Keynes, J. M. (1937a). How to Avoid a Slump. *The Times*, January. Reprinted in: Hutchison (1977).

Keynes, J. M. (1937b). Borrowing for Defence. *The Times*, March. Reprinted in Hutchison (1977).

Keynes, J. M. (1944). Letter to FA von Hayek reviewing the latter's *Road to Serfdom*. Reprinted in: *Collected Writings* (Vol. XXVII, pp. 385–388).

Keynes, J. M. (1971–1979). *The Collected Writings of John Maynard Keynes* (A. Robinson, E. Johnson & D. Moggridge, Eds). London: Macmillan, for the Royal Economic Society:

Vol. VI (1971) [1e: 1930]. *A Treatise on Money*, Vol. II

Vol. VII (1973a) [1e: 1936]. *The General Theory of Employment, Interest and Money*.

Vol. IX (1972a) [1e: 1931]. *Essays in Persuasion*.

Vol. XIII (Ed. D. Moggridge) (1973b). *The General Theory and After. Part I. Preparation*.

Vol. XX (Ed. D. Moggridge) (1981). *Activities 1929–1931. Rethinking Employment and Unemployment Policies*.

Vol. XXI (Ed. D. Moggridge) (1982). *Activities 1931–1939. World Crises and Policies in Britain and America*.

Vol. XXVII (Ed. D. Moggridge) (1980). *Activities 1940–1946. Shaping the Post-War World. Employment and Commodities*.

Vol. XXIX (Ed. D. Moggridge) (1979). *The General Theory And After: A Supplement*.

Lambert, P. (1963). The social philosophy of J. M. Keynes. In: J. Cunningham Wood (Ed.), 1983, *John Maynard Keynes: Critical Assessments*. London: Routledge.

Marx, K. (1974). *Capital. A Critique of Political Economy*, Vol. II, *The Process of Circulation of Capital*. London: Lawrence & Wishart.

Marx, K., & Engels, F. (1848). *Manifesto of the Communist Party*. In: K. Marx & F. Engels, 1976, pp. 477–519.

Marx, K., & Engels, F. (1976). *Collected Works*, Vol. 6, *Marx and Engels: 1845–1848*. London (for the Institute of Marxism–Leninism, Moscow): Lawrence & Wishart.

Minsky, H. P. (1975). *John Maynard Keynes*. London: Macmillan.

Pilling, G. (1986). *The Crisis of Keynesian Economics: A Marxist View*. London & Sydney: Croom Helm,

Robinson, J. (1964). *Economic Philosophy*. Harmondsworth: Penguin/Pelican.

Skidelsky, R. (1975). *Oswald Mosley*. London: Macmillan.

ON THE ART OF INNUENDO: J. M. KEYNES' PLAGIARISM OF SILVIO GESELL'S MONETARY ECONOMICS

Guido G. Preparata

ABSTRACT

Keynes' allegedly revolutionary theory of money was in truth inspired, if not borrowed, from the early intuitions of a German social reformer by the name of Silvio Gesell, a forgotten figure traditionally classed amongst the anarchist dissenters of the early XXth century. This paper explores this connection and thereby attempts to re-establish some balance in the book of intellectual paternity, by laying emphasis on the original monetary themes of Gesell, and on the Keynesian recasting of those self-same themes into the 1936 classic, The General Theory. It is here argued that Keynes appropriated Gesell's insights into the nature of money and interest, and stripped them of their radical implications, so as to fashion an explanation of the crisis that would pose no threat to the foundations of the capitalist order.

Confronting 9-11, Ideologies of Race, and Eminent Economists,
Research in Political Economy, Volume 20, pages 217–253.
Copyright © 2002 by Elsevier Science Ltd.
All rights of reproduction in any form reserved.
ISBN: 0-7623-0984-9

INTRODUCTION

Plagiarism, *n*. the appropriation or imitation of the language, ideas, and thoughts of another author, and representation of them, as one's original work (*The Random House Dictionary of the English Language*).

After more than a decade of incessant operation at the highest levels of the British society, John Maynard Keynes appeared to have come across a theoretical formula that quenched his heuristic aspirations with regard to monetary phenomenology. Indeed, his new treatise, which was printed in 1936, was forthwith labeled a "general theory."

The book, given the reputation of its author, was immediately hailed a masterpiece. Quaintly, after Keynes' opus had been widely lauded, began the interminable debate over *what*, in fact, had been written therein. In the midst of this adventure in the realm of economic thought, a fringe of scholars, which has had a fair record of recruitment among the newer generations, has made it its duty to ferret out of the tangle of the more or less illustrious inspirers of the *General Theory* the exiguous figure of a German crank named Silvio Gesell.

Truly, on account of the scant number of contributions on this subject, and of the sober tone of the exposition, common to all such references, this German connection, for all practical purposes, would have carried no weight and would have thus been lost to memory by fault of its imputed trifling significance, had there not prevailed among the contributors a unanimous apprehension of the profound impress of Gesellian traces into the whole make-up of the *General Theory*'s monetary foundations. Then, once the link between the two was secured by scholarship,[1] and given thicker relevance than what Keynes himself had been willing to concede in a concluding section of his book, the juxtaposition of Gesell's and Keynes' ideas would soon fall prey to the play of uncomfortable analogies – uncomfortable, that is, considered the diverse stations the two men had occupied in their lifetime. Thus, Gesell – an ex-businessman turned anarchist guru[2] and reformer, who participated in the second Republic of the Soviets in Munich, April 1919, as Finance Minister—, vis-à-vis Lord Keynes, a high product of the late Victorian epoch – the son of a Cambridge don, and later a don himself, a zealous negotiator for the British Treasury at the end of WWI, a protégé of Alfred Marshall (this last a frequent guest at the Keyneses), and later in life, a High Steward, as well as, amongst the multitude of honorific titles he assumed, Chairman of the National Insurance Company, and Director of the Bank of England.

Why would a leading member of the British intelligentsia, nay, a paragon of gentlemanly breeding such as Keynes, draw upon the economic reveries of an anarchist prince? In our modern era, what could have been the *use* for the financial constituency – which found in Lord Keynes a most up-to-date-mouthpiece – to incorporate, in a surreptitious fashion (as will be canvassed in the paper), the monetary cures of a protagonist, albeit ephemeral and atypical, of Germany's post-WWI debacle? *Quo animo*?

The discussion presented herein will revolve round a synthesis of Gesell's most important contributions to the theory of money, namely the theory of interest and the monetary theses of his *Natural Economic Order (die Natürliche Wirtschaftsordnung)*. There follows an appraisal of Keynes' monetary economics in the *General Theory*, in the light of its relation to the work of Gesell. The analysis is conducted along lines of comparison with a view to isolating from the monetary constructions of the *General Theory* the Gesellian source, and accounting for the motive of its adoption and manipulation by Keynes.

Many authors' contributions to monetary economics have been incorporated in the *General Theory*, but none other than Gesell's *Theory of Interest* has set in motion the so-called "Keynesian revolution"; this it did so markedly as to suggest that such input went far beyond the mere agency of "inspiration": Keynes stole the idea, but – and here is the rub –, he cast the purloined intuition in a form that allowed him to account for the financial collapse of the 'thirties, without attacking the network of privilege erected on the monopolistic manufacture of the means of payment, that is, *banking*. He robbed the intuition, deliberately confused the premises of the argument, and employed its basic mechanisms to explicate the financial mismatch to which the world economy had fallen prey. Thus, he achieved three goals at once: (1) shielded oligarchy, and offered the banking brotherhood an honorable compromise that would forever acquit it of institutional foul play ('the price of money, interest, is a fact of life: the best that can be wished is to have it reduced'); (2) provided a much needed academic brochure for monopoly capitalism (concentrated industries and socialized investment), Nazi Germany being a formidable instance of the transformation; (3) disfigured an alien monetary scheme (Gesell's), which had identified the source of economic disintegration, with a view to appropriating the justness of the intuition in times of capitalist overhaul.

For, indeed, the Keynesian legacy consists, in essence, of but two loose propositions:

(1) Deficit spending allows the system to tide over the slump.
(2) There exists an **interest barrier** that prevents the expansion of investment, growth and production.

Now, the first proposition is a truism as old as economics itself; it is the second proposition that bespeaks of plagiarism. To this at present we turn.

I. AGING THE CURRENCY:
THE IDEAS OF SILVIO GESELL ON MONEY

Ich bin sozusagen die fleischgewordene Lehre
vom Zins.[3]

Silvio Gesell, *Verteidigungsrede*

A. *The Bite*

To Silvio Gesell, the economic discourse may properly begin only by questioning the origin and nature of *interest*.

Goods, he argues, perish, rust and rot. Time consumes both humans and
merchandise mercilessly. Everything perishes. But one thing does not, and this
is gold. *Interest,* says Gesell, *is the toll price we pay for the usage of gold.*

Silvio Gesell defined gold – and the paper money emanating from it – as
"the archetype of death." As he put it: "In the substance of money we seek
negative, not positive properties. The minimum of material properties is what
all men demand of the material part of money" (Gesell, 1920, p. 52). Gold, for
instance, owes its eternalness to the fact that it "neither rusts nor rots, neither
grows nor decays, neither scratches, nor burns, nor cuts. Gold is without life,
it is the archetype of death" (Gesell, 1920, p. 52). Since it is such a unique
medium of exchange, men have vied to possess as much of it as they possibly
could. Would one rather have goods, which will progressively lose value, or
gold, which never does, and thus have the option to purchase whatever is desired?

Two opposing forces have always wrestled: on the one side, we find the
supply of goods – which immediately translates into the demand for money –
and on the other, the demand for goods – which is represented by the supply
of money. Yet, the type of configuration the market locks in when these two
forces encounter one another is not easily entitled to claim much resemblance
to the customary equilibrium scenarios evoked by the neoclassical disciples of
British Liberalism. Instead, the relationship that comes about between the
holders of money and the producers of goods and services is of a peculiar sort.

The demand for money – that is, the supply of goods[4] – consists of an
aggregate of goods, material, tangible, perishable; the supply of money, instead,
is not even "grazed" by the erosion of time: the former is like a swollen river
which, by its very nature, continually floods the market looking for buyers; the
latter can afford to wait, imperturbable, for more advantageous conditions.
The goods comprised in the supply deteriorate every day, and consequently,
fresher merchandise will be sold at a higher price; for the supply of goods,
postponing the exchange is lethal. Money, however, by reason of its negative

properties, not being prodded by "impulses" inherent in the substances that compose the goods, has no fear of procrastinating the transaction with its counterpart. And such an advantage has rendered money, since its birth, the umpire of market exchanges.

> The merchant is of course in need of commercial profit, and he can only satisfy this need through the purchase of commodities. The impulse stimulating the merchant's purchases of commodities is not, however, physical necessity, but the wish to obtain the commodities as cheap as possible ... The consumer, under the pressure of personal wants, cannot wait ...; neither can the producer wait ... But the possessor of money ..., the holder of the universal, essential medium of exchange, can wait and thereby embarrass both producer and consumer by holding back the medium of exchange (money) ... The products of our labor cause considerable expense for storage and care-taking, and even this expense can only retard, but cannot prevent their gradual decay. The possessor of money, by the very nature of the money-material (precious metal or paper) is exempt from such loss. In commerce, therefore, the capitalist (possessor of money) can always afford to wait, whereas the possessors of merchandise are always hurried. So if the negotiations about the price break down, the resulting loss invariably falls upon the possessors of goods, that is, ultimately, upon the worker (in the widest sense). This circumstance is made use of by the capitalist to exert pressure upon the possessor of goods (worker), and to force him to sell his product below the true price (Gesell, 1920, pp. 226, 137).

Therefore, he who holds money has no difficulty in asking for a tribute, a reward for his unavoidable services. The premium that is claimed in exchange for the medium of payment – the *conditio sine qua non* for the survival of trade – is indeed interest: *basic interest (Urzins)*, as Gesell calls it.

Historically, merchants were the purveyors of gold; in the epoch of Natural Liberties, bankers – the direct descendants of the *mercatores* – relayed their predecessors' activity: bank paper – sealed by the colluded "State" – and, for the most part, virtual ciphers perform the like duty vicariously. They are the *private* providers of the means of payment, and for their service they ask for a fee: *interest*. For millennia, the average price of money, according to Gesell, has hovered around 5% (6%, according to others) per year. However, although basic interest appears during the exchange, the role of the merchant, indeed, reduces to that of a mere "taxman-middleman," since basic interest, which has to be squeezed out of the margin earned, must be handed over, unfailingly, to the provider of money. And who shall grant the money? As we move back to the origin of the chain of promises, we again meet *the banker*.

It is thought that interest, like calves, reflects nature's fertility. Interest is introduced as that bonus that is legitimately asked by the money-lender to the borrower by virtue of the natural fertile increase to which all things natural are subject. Such common reasoning wishes to intimate that the particular percentage that is charged to the borrower – the $x\%$ – is a **mirroring image of the** *physical* **increase** triggered by that additional, loaned, money. The reasoning is thus: "if you'll increase production by 10% with my money, there is nothing wrong in my asking, say, 5% for it " (that would leave a net 5% profit for the entrepreneur).

The reasoning is fallacious.

On the simplest plane of consideration, two scenarios need be considered: either *the banker refuses to put more money in the system* after the physical increase has taken place – in which case he will exact interest by commanding a greater portion of a representative bundle of goods, whose price has decreased owing to that gain in efficiency brought about by the loan (a so-called productive investment: there are more goods around than previously); or, *if the price level is not to decrease* (fixed or rising prices), he shall have to inject an additional quantity of money so that he can carve out his quota of interest, which action, indeed, the banker will agree to effect only by charging another dose of interest for this second injection, which is nothing but another *loan*.[5]

The first is a story of deflation. In the banking of yore, this cumbrous operation was frequent, and was suffered acrimoniously by the common man who then obtained newly minted coins (corresponding to a higher gold- or silver content), but at a much higher price apiece (in terms of goods offered in exchange). Credit dynamics in the modern machine-age, instead, came to adhere closely to the second scenario, wherein bankers manipulated credit in such a way as to inflate the price level and recoup interest in the price differentials thus created; in such an artificial monetary margin, combines of investment bankers, through business, compete against one another by means of techno-logical innovations and aggressive marketing. The price rises steadily, at the cost of sizeable injections of credit money and concomitant interest charges, and adversarial consortia bank on efficiency advantages that will enable them to keep abreast of, if not crush, the competition. The resulting tension on the market owes its pull from two angular sources, the first being the immediate clash among manufacturers, the second originating within the combine itself – that is, between the producer and the banker, who is not willing to unlace the mouth of his purse, if he is not paid *interest*.

Indeed, as a routine, the money-lender asks for a *minimal*, fixed, rate of interest, *irrespective* of the actual conditions on the market.

This *fixed* charge is but one of several components within that enigmatic percentage the world at large takes for granted. It hides among risk premiums of various strains (insurance fees), depreciation charges, and a *hausse* premium (an addition that is incorporated in the interest in view of expected price surges) (Gesell, 1920, p. 275 and ff.), all of which sum up to the incumbent $x\%$ spoken of as 'the current rate'; the fixed charge hides among licit economic allowances, but *it* is of an altogether foreign, non-economic breed.

The fixed component is *usury* proper – something in the nature of a pure tribute, an exaction. The Hebrew word for interest is *nesheck*, "which literally means a 'bite' " (Bonder, 1996, p. 125). The fixed component – concealed like noble metal encrusted in ore – serves as the *anchor* of monetary construction; the *Urzins* inscribes itself as the primal constraint of the Gesellian model portraying the economy.

> Money-interest is the product of an independent capital, namely money, and is comparable with the tolls exacted in the Middle Ages by robber barons, and until lately by the State, for the use of roads ... *Interest on money is not influenced by interest on so-called real capital (houses, factories, etc.) though the converse ... is true.* Basic interest has up to the present escaped observation because it was concealed behind its offspring, ordinary interest upon loan-money ... The interest paid by the merchant for loan-money is not the beginning, but the end of the whole transaction. The merchant uses money to exact basic interest from the wares, and as the money does not belong to him, he delivers the basic interest to the his capitalist. He acts here simply as cashier for the capitalist ... Basic interest is exacted during exchange, not during production. (Gesell, 1920, pp. 236, 265, and 264, emphasis added).

Basic interest is bandied as a *percentage* of some given amount; it is bitten off *something* – something that economists would define as the *just price* (Gesell, as shown above, named it the *true* price). A price, i.e. that: (1) affords the sustenance and covers the expenditures of the producer, and (2) enables him to replicate another unit (or batch) of the same good in the following period (Steiner, 1993, p. 83). If we warrant the existence of such a price, then that x % that is torn off it with the bite is "basic interest" proper – the hard core of usury: the price for the usage of the means of payment.

B. The Obstacle to Physical Investment: Basic versus Real Interest

The unalterable condition for money to circulate is that prices should not fall.
If they do, the margin above the cost of production is virtually eliminated and therefore there is no slack from which interest may be recouped. When prices plummet, the possessors of money withdraw it from circulation for it does not yield interest anymore. At that point a crisis begins. Gesell contends that the division of labor is not systematically balanced by an adequate stock of money, and this discrepancy – many goods versus scarce money – acts only to depress further the price of commodities. It is precisely because prices fall, that money hides to be hoarded. The supply of money decreases, the demand for money increases;

so does the supply of goods, which pile up in warehouses. Negative expectations compound the pressure and the process of contraction winds downward in a spiraling path with self-reinforcing impetus: fearing that prices might further decrease, no merchant dares to purchase anything; goods are "unsellable" because they are cheap and threaten to become even cheaper. The crisis begins. An increase in prices has symmetrical repercussions: the holder of money knows that what he has bought today can be sold tomorrow at a higher price; thus he buys as much as he can, relying heavily on credit leverage. Banks will encourage speculation as long as they feel they are in a bull market. Even in this case, the dynamics is of a self-reinforcing kind, yet with an inflationary bias: "prices rise because they have risen" (Gesell, 1920, p. 103).

> ... How do the makers of goods act when they cannot sell their products for money? Does the cabinet-maker sleep in his coffins, does the farmer eat all his potatoes? Nothing of the kind; they try to effect the sale by reducing their prices, they all try to attract money by lowering their demands. If capitalists and savers have withdrawn money from circulation and will only return it if promised interest, they obviously find the ground well prepared for the levy of interest in the readiness of the possessors of goods to surrender part of their produce for the use of money. ... Interest is the condition we lay down ... The cause of the crisis lay in the fact that capitalists refused to invest their money unless they obtained interest, and that when the supply of houses, industrial plant, and other instruments of production passed a certain limit, the rate [of remuneration of such activities] fell below the minimum yield necessary to pay the interest on the money invested in them ... As soon as this point was reached employers were no longer able to pay the interest demanded of them, and capitalist had no motive to lend their money gratis. They preferred to wait for the crisis which could be counted on to "ease" the situation and restore the normal rate of interest ... Thousands of years of experience have taught the owners of money that their money will fetch 3, 4 or 5%, according to the investment, and to obtain this rate of interest they need only wait. So they would have waited (Gesell, 1920, pp. 187, 196, 198).

It would then appear that the theoretical intricacies that have customarily obscured the conception of the notion of "interest" should be ascribed chiefly to two phenomena. The first is the characterization of interest as a *natural* element of the putative inexorable laws of economics. The second is the confusion between interest on money – that is, basic interest – and *interest on capital*. These two variables, argues Gesell, must be distinguished.

Basic interest is a monetary phenomenon: it is the price for the use of the medium of exchange. Owing to the power of exacting a tribute, money may properly be regarded as a kind of capital. Interest on capital is a by-product of basic interest.

> But if no money is given for the construction of houses unless they can exact the same interest that money itself exacts for the wares, building is suspended and the consequent scarcity of houses raises rent; just as the scarcity of factories reduces wages (Gesell, 1920, p. 240).

Houses, machinery, and plants are capital. However, unlike money, these goods do not exact interest during the exchange, so that it may be handed over to the banks, the "manufacturing center for the means of payment," as Schumpeter called them (Schumpeter, 1983, p. 73). Instead, interest upon capital arises in the course of the production process and is collected by the owners of capital goods.

"This power does not, however, lie in the characteristics of such things, but in the fact that money here, precisely as with the [perishable] wares, prepares the market conditions necessary for the collection of interest" (Gesell, 1920, p. 240). Houses, machinery and factories are real goods, but owing to the fact that money, at the origin, claims a reward for the services it provides, industrial capital – which has to be financed with money – will have to be allocated in such a way as to exact a similar tribute.

Usury, a purely monetary phenomenon, propagates its logic to the means of production. Since the foundation of usury is, according to Gesell, the capacity to "embarrass" the counterpart – that is, to enmesh the will of the transacting party –, in the economic realm, this condition translates into *an artificially limited supply with respect to demand.* In other words, in order to collect interest, it is necessary to effect a willful curtailment of the goods and services that cater to the community's needs. *Money, machinery, factories, houses, and so on, yield interest because they are scarce.* More specifically, basic interest is the equilibrium value interest upon capital converges to.[6]

Moving on to its ultimate implications, the Gesellian reasoning affords a final confluence of the monetary muddle into the grievances of labor economics, and the crux of remuneration.

> The employer does not buy work, or working hours, or power of work, for he does not sell the power of work. What he buys and sells is the product of labor, and the price he pays is determined, not by the cost of breeding, training and feeding a worker and his offspring (the physical appearance of the workers is only too good a proof that the employer cares little for all this), but simply by the price the consumer pays for the product. From this price the employer deducts the interest on his factory, the cost of raw material, including interest, and wages for his own work. The interest always corresponds to basic interest: the employer's wage, like all wages, follows the laws of competition: and the employer treats the raw material he intends his workmen to manufacture as every shop-keeper treats his merchandise. The employer lends the workmen machinery and raw material and deducts from the workers' produce the interest with which the raw material and machinery are burdened. The remainder, so-called wages, is in reality the price of the product delivered by the workmen. Factories are simply, therefore, pawn-shops (Gesell, 1920, pp. 258–259).

In this portrayal, the factory itself is capable of generating interest, insofar as the total number of factories is scarce (and wage-labor is abundant). Machinery is scarce and so are raw materials. And moving backward along the chain of production, we are bound to reencounter money and the concomitant basic interest.

C. Dying Currency

The prescription follows: the ideal monetary system – one freed from all kept money-owners, who derive an income for supplying what ought to be the "most public" of all goods – is a system tenanted by *free-money*. Free-money is perishable money: if money were given an *age* by *stamping* it, and thus make it lose value day after day (or, e.g. on a monthly basis – the time interval for affixing the stamps on the scrip is a matter of convenience and arbitrary choice) like any other good yielded by nature, it would be irremediably forced to circulate.

No one would be thus inclined to hoard it; there would be available funds for all sorts of enterprises. One would reckon a paper bill for each good, and not too few bills for a glut of commodities (deflation), or too many notes for only a few commodities (inflation). The rate of interest would taper off and finally become zero. This proposal is brought forth as the completed synchronization of goods and money: the purpose being that of making money as perishable as the products of industry broadly defined.

For petty transactions, the public would use a definite sum of paper scrip, which would lose value as time passes. The stamps would be on sale at government offices, and the revenues forthcoming therefrom would be tantamount to an effective taxation of the community.

The amount saved by households will be entrusted to the care of credit institutes, which will be compelled no less than their clients to keep it in motion: state-sanctioned depreciation will enjoin the institutes to loan such savings to entrepreneurs. By dint of such compulsion, trades are bound to flourish, accompanied, as they would be, by bouts of renewed inventiveness within the realms of organizational and technical improvement.

> When I have saved a sum of money I now do exactly what I did formerly – I take it to the savings bank which enters the amount in my savings book. In this respect nothing has changed. It was said that the sum of money entered in the savings book would be subject to the same amount of depreciation as Free-Money, but that is nonsense. The savings bank owes so many dollars, American Standard, but not the notes which I handed in. And the standard dollar stands above the notes. If I lend somebody a sack of potatoes for a year, he will not give me back the same sack of potatoes, which have meanwhile rotted, but a sack of new potatoes. It is the same with the savings bank. I lent it 100 dollars, and it agrees to give me back 100 dollars. The savings bank is in a position to do so, since it lends the money on the same terms, while the tradesmen and farmers who obtain money

at the savings bank for their enterprises do not keep the money at home. They buy goods for use with it, and in this way the depreciation loss is distributed among all the persons through whose hands the money has passed in the course of a year . . . Now, in the economic life of the individual, to save means to do much work, to produce and sell much, and to buy little . . . But what must happen if everyone brings 100 dollars worth of produce to market, and only buys for 90 dollars, that is, if everyone wishes to save 10 dollars? . . . Free-money applies the Christian maxim: whatsoever ye would that men should do to you, do you even so to them. It says: if you wish to sell your produce, buy the produce your neighbor wishes to sell . . . Otherwise savers mutually deprive one another of the possibility of carrying out their purpose (Gesell, 1920, pp. 166–167, 169–170).

A rate of interest equal to zero implies a corresponding investment so intense as to keep depreciation at bay – an endeavor the saver would have had to fight on his own, had there not been the opportunity to delegate such a task to an enterprising counterpart by the means of organized lending and investment. Paraphrasing the gist of Gesell's "Robinson Crusoe" dialogue (Gesell, 1920, pp. 217 and ff.), a null (or even negative, depending on the current rate of depreciation) rate of interest may thus be deemed a convenient arrangement by the owner of several (perishable) resources, who could scarcely manage on his own to conserve such goods, be they foods, barns, or buildings, from the persistent wear and tear of time. He is then willing to confide to a third party (the investor) a portion of the goods laid in (saved) in exchange for a promise on the part of the newly appointed care-taker to return that same amount, say, a year thenceforth. The zero-interest contract (loan) is a bargain for both parties, for the saver sees his possessions reconstituted by the end of the year, and the investor (or entrepreneur) derives sustenance (and an eventual surplus) from the employment of another's property.

Gesell's blueprint for centralized monetary management in the new system is confined to the sketching of the fundamental tasks falling to an *ad hoc* institution, the National Currency Office (*Reichswärungsamt*), which

does not carry on banking business of any kind. It does not buy or sell bills of exchange; it does not classify business firms as first, second, or third rate. It entertains no connections with private persons. The national Currency Office issues money when the country needs it, and withdraws money when money is in excess . . . After Free-money has been put in circulation and metal money withdrawn, the sole function of the National Currency Office is to observe the ratio at which money and the goods are exchanged and by increase or decrease of the monetary circulation, to stabilize the general level of prices (Gesell, 1920, pp. 139, 141).

The depreciation rate, i.e. the percent charge to be deducted (at n regular intervals for an amount of $(X/n)\%$, if $X\%$ is the rate of depreciation) from the freshly issue note of the National Currency Office would reflect the technological features of the peculiar system. Gesell contemplated possible rates ranging from

5 to 12% per annum. As a measure of the liquidity needs of circulation, a competent division of the Office should be appointed to devising a statistical ratio that accounts for the overall rate of depreciation, over a comprehensive estimate of capital appreciation triggered by productive investment. A temporary dearth of currency would be overcome with tax remission, whereas an excessive spurt of liquidity would evaporate of its own accord thanks to the built-in perishability of the means of payment (Gesell, 1920, pp. 144 and ff.).

In brief, Gesell's storybook on pecuniary vicissitudes is comprised of three main yarns: first, the acknowledgment of a usurious tribute that is asked for the purveyance of the means of payment, as the embodiment of the worldly insufferableness of transience (resistance to death); this usurious exaction takes the form of a percent deduction, whose lower bound (the threshold) is to be set in the environs of 2 or 3%. Second is the strict causal nexus from such a *monetary* rate of interest to all other *real* rates, that is, rates of return upon capital: the former determines the latter, and not vice-versa. This conditioning of basic interest "embarrasses" entrepreneurship to a point where it will have to effect the creation of rent-generating monopolies that mimic the interest-bearing faculty of gold, with a view to securing profit and remunerating the interest-yielding money that is financing the investments: a setting of artificial scarcity makes the levy of an agio (a "plus" above what consumers reckon as the *true*, or just, price) a matter of resigned apprehension. This anchoring of production to the drift of financial exigencies obtrudes itself as an impediment to the progress of the industrial arts. Third is the remedial advocacy of stamped money as a means to defeat the purpose of hoarding, and thereby break this fettering of physical expansion.

II. A "GENERAL THEORY" OF MONEY
THE STRIVINGS OF JOHN MAYNARD KEYNES

[Keynes' *General Theory*] is a work of profound obscurity, badly written and prematurely published. All economists claimed to have read it. Only a few have.

(J. K. Galbraith, 1975, p. 218).

Nothing in Keynes' previous life or work really quite prepares us for the *General Theory* [. . .]. There is reason to believe that Keynes himself did not understand his own analysis [. . .]. When finally mastered, [the] analysis is found to be obvious and at the same time new. In short it is the work of genius.

(P. A. Samuelson, 1964, pp. 316, 323).

The *General Theory* is one of the greatest puzzles in the history of ideas [. . .]. [Keynes' letters to his friends and collaborators are] disappointingly incommunicative about his deeper vision of the basic ideas that composed it and how he made his inspired connections among them. His intuition asserting its claim here, they remain illuminations, a series of epiphanies vouchsafed only to the seer.

(David Felix, 1995, pp. 107, 131).

One of the perplexing riddles in the history of social science is how a man of the intellect of Keynes could have labored for years on what he considered to be a revelation without becoming aware of its multifarious antecedents, and how such a large segment of the English-speaking community of economists could have accepted his analysis and policy conclusions as such.

(George Garvy, 1975, p. 391).

[Keynes] had a wonderful memory for arguments, but no memory for their authors. If next day you returned to the same problem, you were as likely to find him parading your arguments of yesterday – if they were good arguments – as his own [. . .]. He remembered vividly the ideas which he absorbed into his own thinking. But he did not remember with great certainty whence he got them [. . .]. Indeed, I find it strange that Keynes, the great stylist, should be remembered principally by the least well written of his books.

(E. A. G. Robinson, 1964, pp. 86, 88).

A. Prodromes

> *Viola.* Disguise, I see, thou art a wickedness
> Wherein the pregnant enemy does much.
> Shakespeare, *Twelfth Night, (II,ii)*

"Writing to George Bernard Shaw on New Year's Day, 1935, [Keynes] said: To understand my state of mind, you have to know that I believe myself to be writing a book on economic theory which will largely revolutionize – not, I suppose, at once but in the course of the next ten years – the way the world thinks about economic problems" (Galbraith, 1975, p. 216).

The 'revolutionary' treatise was published in 1936 in England under the title, *The General Theory of Employment, Interest and Money*. Afterwards, Keynes' premonition came to pass: no sooner had the book been printed than, much like Smith's *Wealth of Nations*, it became an "instant classic": that is, a work commissioned and immediately endorsed by the intelligentsia.[7]

It was not until 1930, when Keynes was forty-seven, that a thorough taxonomy of the protean expressions of money was attempted with the publication of his *Treatise on Money*. Protocolar paeans from several academic quarters notwithstanding, the book so came to be rated a generalized miss as to bring its author to repudiate it without a trace of vindictive after-thought.

Two months after the *Treatise* was published [10/31/30], Keynes wrote to an economist-correspondent, "My own feeling is that now at last I have things clear in my own head, and I am itching to do it all over again" (Felix, 1995, p. 81).

The shortcomings. For one, the *Treatise*'s model – which consisted of a re-edition of the quantity theory of money, complemented by several additions of parameters included by way of realistic variety – assumed, on the eve of the Great Depression, constant output based on full employment. Eventually, the Scottish barrister, Hugh Macmillan – chairman of that notorious committee, in which sat Keynes himself, and assembled also to give a fair hearing to the cries and *doléances* of heretics and rank-and-filers of the depressed economy – sentenced: "I cannot believe that finality has been reached even in an exposition by you" (Felix, 1995, p. 94).

Presumably, to be counted amongst those pieces of analysis that prevented Keynes from reaching finality, was Knut Wicksell's distinction between *market* and *natural* rate of interest.

Following a spiritual crisis, before he moved on to become the founder of the Swedish school of macrodynamics, Wicksell had recanted religious belief and fashioned himself thereafter a neo-Malthusian atheist who wanted to improve the lot of mankind by rational means (Niehans, 1990, p. 248). It is by means of sympathy that things are done; and thus it was, even if stealthily, that Keynes was drawn to the Swede.

> On a trip to London, financed by the Swedish Central Bank, [Wicksell] met young John Maynard Keynes, who seems to have treated him condescendingly, not realizing what he could have learned from him (Niehans, 1990, p. 249).

> While Wicksell flourished a long generation before Keynes, the *Treatise* discussed the great Swede as if he and Keynes were contemporaries, with Wicksell perhaps a half-step behind (Felix, 1995, p. 68).

> Wicksell visualized a closed economy with inconvertible bank notes, in which banks set a lending rate and supply all money demanded at that rate ... Under these conditions, the banks can set the market rate of interest, i, at any level they wish. However, it is Wicksell's main point that there is only one rate, called the normal rate, r, that keeps prices stable. This normal rate is tightly related to the real returns on capital goods, which Wicksell calls the natural rate. The two are not identical, though, because one applies to bank loans and the other to real capital goods, which have different risks. According to Wicksell's hypothesis the course of prices is governed by the difference $i–r$ (Niehans, 1990, p. 255).

This view is the obverse of Gesell's: here the causal link runs *from* the rate upon capital – the original yield of the barter economy – *to* the superimposed monetary rate set by banks, as a result of the substitution of fiduciary money and credit for the sheep and cowry shells. Wicksell therefore made price oscillations dependent upon the mismatch between rates, which is likely to be observed when economic agents, such as banks, as they fund new initiatives, have no option but to grope in setting their rate, around a nondescript natural rate – which the theory postulates, presumably as an average growth index of the physical economy.

> As long as the market [monetary] rate stands below the normal rate, prices will continue to rise, and vice-versa, until the difference is eliminated. Once it is eliminated prices will remain at their highest (or lowest) level. The present price level thus appears as the legacy of past interest policies. The crucial point is that with respect to the banks' lending rate, the economy is unstable. However, a constant market rate would not, in general, suffice to keep prices stable, because the natural rate is subject to constant fluctuations due to, for example, inventions, discoveries or changes in expectations. This helps explain why market rates that are high relative to their trend are often associated with rising prices; the real returns on capital [i.e. natural rate] may be higher still (Niehans, 1990, p. 257).

This theory of interest Keynes had made, in a slightly varied guise, his own ("I defined what purported to be a unique rate of interest, which I called the natural rate of interest – namely the rate of interest which . . . preserved equality between the rate of saving and the rate of investment" (Keynes, 1950, pp. 242–243)) – the pivot of his *Treatise*. He soon was to forsake it for a better alternative (". . . It was a mistake to speak of the natural rate of interest or to suggest that the above definition would yield a unique value for the rate of interest irrespective of the rate of employment. I had not then understood that, in certain conditions, the system could be in equilibrium with less than full employment" (Keynes, 1950, ibid.)), which he had a mind to couple with a solution to the issue of underconsumption and effective demand.[8]

For Keynes, then, the dismissal of Wicksell's "natural rate" was reserved as a back-up to the frontal attack launched from the overture of the *General Theory*, against one of the undisputed axioms of orthodoxy – the so-called "law of outlets" (*loi des débouchés*), or Say's Law. As known, "Say's Law . . . held that, from the proceeds of every sale of goods, there was paid out to someone somewhere in wages, salaries, interest, rent or profit . . . the wherewithal to buy that item. As with one item, so with all. This being so, there could not be a shortage of purchasing power in the economy . . . If people saved more than was invested, the surplus of savings would bring down interest rates. Investment would thus be stimulated and saving (at least in theory) discouraged" (Galbraith, 1975, p. 218). "The intended meaning of Say's law can be paraphrased by the negative proposition that money is not being hoarded, at least not in the aggregate and in significant amounts . . . If for one person, because he accumulates cash balances, demands falls short of supply, another person may use up cash balances, so that in the aggregate, demand still matches supply . . . The significance of this proposition, if true, was twofold. First, it implied that aggregate production could never be excessive in the sense that it could not be sold at a cost. No matter how abundant the factors of production, they could always be productively employed . . . Overproduction in some products might easily occur, but it must necessarily have a counterpart in the underproduction of others. The historical significance of this reasoning was that general overproduction ceased to be a respectable explanation of depression" (Niehans, 1990, pp. 112–113).

Keynes re-appropriated the Malthusian argument favoring the creation of unproductive labor to be paid out of revenue and combined it with the preconized avoidance of any form of sterile accumulation. Malthusian echoes are clearly discernible in the following passage:

> I distinctly maintain that an attempt to accumulate very rapidly which necessarily implies a considerable diminution of unproductive consumption, by greatly impairing the usual motives to production must prematurely check the progress of wealth (Keynes, 1933, p. 129).

Already in his *Treatise on Money*, he had stated the known equivalence between saving and investment in his parable of the "banana plantations."

> Let us suppose a community owing banana plantations and labouring to cultivate and collect bananas and nothing else; and consuming bananas and nothing else. Let us suppose, further, that there has been an equilibrium between saving and investment in the sense that the money-income of the community, not spent on the consumption of bananas but saved, is equal to the cost of production of new investment in the further development of plantations . . . Into this Eden there enters a Thrift Campaign, urging the members of the public to abate their improvident practices of devoting nearly all their current incomes to buying bananas for daily food. But at the time there is no corresponding increase in the development of new plantations (Keynes, 1950, p. 176, Vol. II).

Because the portion of bananas that was devoted to investment is not recycled in production, it rots and the price decreases. Producers react. What follows is the customary chronicle of incipient unemployment, *not* accompanied in this instance by an over-abundance of capital goods, which would have been the expected result of rapid capital accumulation prompted by the Thrift Campaign (and feared by Malthus). Keynes outflanks Malthus's primary concern, and includes the variant that savings, if not hoarded, are swallowed by *impairing* forms of investment. This is Johannsen's *Neglected Point*: so long as the community "continues to save in excess of new investment," the conditions will not cease to deteriorate; productive investment is sacrificed to a *speculative purchase of deeds and evidences of debt tendered by the bankrupt portion of the economy* (that is, the impairing form of investment, which is to be distinguished from productive investment, and hoarding) (Johannsen, 1971, pp. 84 and ff.). In other words, the capitalists' money, instead of funding new and expansionary ventures, is channeled towards the acquisition of titles of ownership issued in the past, representing goods and claims to wealth already in existence. In extreme circumstances, this may configure a buying-out of an insolvent economy by those possessing sufficient capital to do so.

Again, the frame of the problem is Malthusian, but the pivot of the discourse is the *Neglected Point*, with which Keynes was acquainted, and which he borrowed (Faye, 1980, p. 670). In the *General Theory*, this classic ground of economic controversy was enriched by Keynes' intent to challenge the hypothesized automatic adjustment of the interest rate in the equilibration process between saving and investment.

> ... It is notable that even in his path-breaking masterwork, *The General Theory* [...], Keynes adhered to the entirety of neoclassicism, micro and macro – deviating with respect to only *one* assumption: that savings are a function of the rate of interest. If that is *not* so – if, as Keynes argued, savings are instead a function of the level of income – Say's law collapses, as does a major pillar of *laissez-faire* capitalism (Dowd, 2000, pp. 127–128).

B. Borrowing from Gesell, on the Sly

Because the rate of interest was the key variable of monetary economics, a refutation of the dominant theories could only have been sharpened on the edge of alternative conceptions of money. Keynes set out to rid his plan of unwarranted assumptions, such as Wicksell's "natural rate of interest" – purportedly, as reported above, a hypothetical rate of return of the factors of production in a non-monetary (barter) economy (i.e. a measure of the economy's *real*, or physical, powers of reproduction) –, and account for the returns upon capital, by coining the appellation *marginal efficiency of capital*.

> When a man buys an investment or capital-asset, he purchases the right to the series of prospective returns, which he expects to obtain from selling its output, after deducting the running expenses of obtaining that output, during the life of the asset. This series of annuities $Q1$, $Q2$, ..., Qn it is convenient to call the *prospective yield* of the investment. Over against the prospective yield of the investment we have the *supply price* of the capital-asset, meaning by this ... the price which would just induce a manufacturer newly to produce an additional unit of such assets, i.e. what is sometimes called its *replacement cost* ... I define the marginal efficiency of capital as being equal to that rate of discount which would make the present value of the series of annuities given by the returns expected from the capital-asset during its life just equal to its supply price (Keynes, 1973, p. 135).

The marginal efficiency of capital equates the stream of future (expected) returns from the equipment (i.e. it dams the stream into one single measurable figure) to the total cost of financing the venture.[9] This rate establishes the relationship between the cost and prospective gains of an investment, and thus serves as an ordering index of potential projects: the higher the marginal efficiency, the more promising the investment. "Marginal efficiency of capital" is but another name for the "internal rate of return" of a capital investment. Gesell called it *interest upon capital*, and, as illustrated in the previous section, proceeded to contrast this figure with *basic interest* – i.e. the banking rate, the price for imperishable money. So long as the former (interest upon capital) is greater than the latter (basic interest – the overhead charges of banking), manufacturers have an incentive to invest and produce. Were the market to succumb to a saturation of capital equipment, and thereby experience a violent depression of the returns upon capital, basic interest would loom as a paralyzing obstacle to further expansion and production. Incidentally, it may be noted that Michał Kalecki, employing the Marxian construct of capital over-accumulation, had observed this basic mechanism in similar terms. However, there appears to be no evidence that Kalecki was acquainted with the work of Gesell, nor that Keynes drew upon Kalecki as well.[10]

The Gesellian theme (basic interest vs. the rate upon capital) recurs in the *General Theory* numerous times; after each allusion, Keynes proceeds to redefine the concept of the interest rate, and of its source, money. In Chapter 14 ("The Classical Theory of the Rate of Interest") he writes:

> The significant conclusion is that the output of new investment will be pushed to the point at which the marginal efficiency of capital become equal to the rate of interest; and what the schedule of the marginal efficiency of capital tells us, is, not what the rate of interest is, but the point to which the output of new investment will be pushed, given the rate of interest (Keynes, 1973, p. 184).

Interest is no longer contemplated as that abstract variable equilibrating savings and investment, but is attributed a position of macroeconomic responsibility in deciding the fate of investment opportunity. Keynes anticipates the forthcoming inquietude of the orthodox reader and intersperses the path to a final definition of the interest rate with what, at a first glance, appear as diversionary observations on the nature thereof.

Psychology, Conventions and Scarcity
First, he looks at the matter from the investor's viewpoint, and by playing on the trade-off – arising from an increase in the interest rate – between capital account losses (through the decline of bond prices) and gains in interest revenue, Keynes hints, on the strength of these speculator-like similes, at the "highly psychological" connotation of the interest phenomenon (Keynes, 1973, p. 202).

This is Keynes' preliminary explanation of the interest rate's "stickiness from below," and the one that all macroeconomics textbooks would have eventually adopted.This first supposition holds that what prevents the rate of interest from sinking below the threshold to levels as low as 1% or less ("which leaves more to fear than to hope") (Keynes, 1973, p. 202) is the high risk entailed by the holding on to bonds at low levels of the interest rate, for the lower is the interest rate, the more damaging is the capital loss, and the more insignificant is the gain in interest revenue for a given percent *increase* in the rate on a fixed-income security.[11]

To prevent the security's value to drop to low levels, investors, once the *short-term rate passes a certain threshold*, start to accumulate liquid balances rather than loan them and thus provoke a further fall of the rate.

> The lender would be inclined to lend when he expected the interest rate to fall because his loan as capitalized in a long-term bond would be worth more, while withholding his funds upon the opposite expectation (Felix, 1995, p. 165).

But when

> [b]ond prices are so high . . ., no one expects them to rise still higher. Consequently everyone prefers to 'hoard' idle cash and monetary policy is put out of commission (Blaug, 1985, p. 661).

This appears to be a macro-economic justification of hoarding (of idle cash), whose mark of disrepute, however, can hardly be cleansed on account of its being practiced as a standard financial routine 'by the many' – the fact remains: the money is withdrawn, and the economy thereby paralyzed, for the return on the investment (the price offered to "investors" to part with their money) is considered "not good enough."

Yet ethical preoccupation, it too, is here "put of commission," for this psychological routine prescinds from the moral imperative. As Keynes learnt at Cambridge from philosopher G. E. Moore – a great inspiration to him – "Ethics is quite unable to give us a list of duties . . . The utmost that Practical Ethics can hope to discover is which, among a few alternatives possible under certain circumstances, will, on the whole, produce the best results" (Moore, 1988, pp. 149, 151). For the psychology of the *individual* investor, hoarding, "under certain circumstances," is thus deemed to "produce the best results."

Second, a few paragraphs below, Keynes points to the conflictive tendencies stemming from a high rate: it is beneficial to international investing (for it attracts foreign capital), but detrimental to domestic employment (for it dispirits young enterprises). This second trade-off, Keynes argues, is evidence of interest's "highly conventional, rather than psychological" figure of the phenomenon.

In Chapter 16 ("Sundry Observations on the Nature of Capital), Keynes writes:

> The only reason why an asset offers a prospect of yielding during its life services having an aggregate value greater than its initial supply price is because it is *scarce*; and it is kept scarce because of the competition of the rate of interest on money (Keynes, 1973, p. 213).

Which passage is nothing but a disguise of Gesell's observation that physical capital is to be made scarce in order to remunerate the money that went into financing it. A perishable means of payment, supported by massive capital production and consumption would have driven pecuniary yields to a zero, and brought endless abundance. Keynes assents, and further challenges what he thought were the obsolete tenets of orthodoxy:

> Capital has to be kept scarce enough in the long-period to have a marginal efficiency which is at least equal to the rate of interest for a period equal to the life of the capital, as determined by psychological and institutional conditions. What would this involve for a society which finds itself so well equipped with capital that its marginal efficiency is zero and would be negative with any additional investment; yet possessing a monetary system, such that money will 'keep' and involve negligible costs of storage and safe custody, with the result that in practice interest cannot be negative; and, in conditions of full employment, disposed to save? (Keynes, 1973, p. 217).

"Money that will 'keep'" – that is, that will not perish – in a regime of *laissez-faire* will watch, unconcerned, the return upon capital sink below basic interest. Stagnation ensues, and the system freezes.

Keynes concedes: the conclusion is disturbing. Yet in the space of three pages, he writes for three times of the uncouth impediment created by the "psychological and institutional" factors behind the rate of interest on money. Not once, so far, does he broach the question of perishability, however.

The institutional factor: the reader suddenly acknowledges the appearance of a *lower bound* – a threshold – for the rate of interest.

> In particular the costs of bringing borrowers and lenders together and uncertainty as to the future of the rate of interest ... set a lower limit, which in present circumstances may perhaps be as high as 2 or $2^{1}/_{2}\%$ on long term (Keynes, 1973, p. 219).

By the sixteenth chapter, Keynes must have sensed that he was endeavoring to picture the dynamics of interest from too many angles – it was time to serve a proper definition. Yet he persists for the length of a few more pages to inveigh against wasteful expenditure.

> If – for whatever reason – the rate of interest cannot fall as fast as the marginal efficiency of capital would fall at a rate of accumulation corresponding to [desired] conditions of full employment, then even a diversion of the desire to hold wealth towards assets, which will in fact yield no economic fruit whatever, will increase economic well-being. In so far as millionaires find their satisfaction in building mighty mansions to contain their bodies when alive and pyramids to shelter them after death ... the day when abundance of capital will interfere with abundance of output may be postponed. 'To dig holes in the ground', paid out of savings, will increase, not only employment, but the real national dividend of useful goods and services. It is not reasonable, however, that a sensible community should be content to remain dependent on such fortuitous and often wasteful mitigations [. . .] (Keynes, 1973, p. 220).

The measure prescribed by Keynes to overcome the barrier of basic interest is State intervention. The State will bring about the equalization of interest upon capital and monetary interest at a level compatible with full employment. Eventually, under the aegis of government control, the marginal efficiency of capital will be reduced to zero, and rentiers, annihilated

Keynes' General Theory of Interest
Then, Keynes turns the page to Chapter 17 ("The Essential Properties of Interest and Money"). There, he will deliver the long awaited definition of interest. He does it in three installments:

(1) Positing money as a commodity.
(2) Revealing the virtues of this special commodity.
(3) Contriving the so-called "liquidity preference curve" to account for the determination of its yield.

First installment:

> It seems, then, that the rate of interest on money plays a peculiar part in setting a limit to the level of employment ... The money-rate of interest – we may remind the reader – is nothing more than the percentage excess of a sum contracted for forward delivery, e.g. a year hence, over what we may call the 'spot' or cash price of the sum thus contracted for forward delivery. It would seem, therefore, that for every kind of capital-asset there must be an analogue of the rate of interest on money (Keynes, 1973, p. 222).

Interest, which for the length of sixteen chapters, had seemed to mirror Gesell's "archetype of death" is here finally revealed to be, instead, a *merchandise*; it is assimilated to all the other, scarce, commodities, each with its own "natural yield." This is the first step.

In the second installment, Keynes has to justify the putative pre-eminence, in macroeconomic terms, of this particular (money-)commodity. He does it by positing three fundamental attributes possessed in differing degrees by capital assets (Keynes, 1973, pp. 225–226): (1) The *yield* – that is, a net return upon the asset's generative powers; (2) *carrying costs* (related to the wastage affecting perishable equipment and commodities); (3) the facility wherewith the capital asset can be transformed into immediate liquid means, called, the *liquidity premium*. Thus, "the return expected from the ownership of the asset" is the sum of these three components (Return = Yield-Carrying Costs + Liquidity Premium) – where, of course, wastage is included as a negative charge.

Keynes admonishes the reader that it is now a matter of judicious distinction not to liken traditional money (gold and bank notes) to conventional staples, for it is barren and bears no fruit – no yield, in the "natural" acceptation of the term. Thus, the yield is nil, but so is the carrying cost (wastage); as to the liquidity premium – compared with all other capital assets –, it is likely to be high – indeed, money is liquidity by definition. There lies the core of money's powers of resistance.

After much taxonomic effort, Gesell's basic interest (*Urzins*) is reintroduced inconspicuously in the theoretical texture of the *General Theory*, yet not as Gesell defined it, namely, as the usurious tribute exacted for the mere handling of money, but as an impersonal premium arisen out of pragmatic necessity, and thereby hardened by *tradition* (wholesome and immutable, by default).

> In attributing . . . a peculiar significance to the money-rate of interest, we have been tacitly assuming that the kind of money to which we are accustomed has some *special characteristics* which lead to its own-rate of interest in terms of itself as standard being more reluctant to fall as the stock of assets in general increases than own-rates of interest of any other assets in terms of themselves (Keynes, 1973, p. 229, emphasis added).

Now, the reader of *The General Theory*, who, most likely, has never heard of Gesell, may want to know why the rate of interest declines most slowly, when all the other definable "own-rates" (e.g. the rates of return for all sorts of commodities, and various types of ventures that are postulated at the beginning of the 17th chapter) may easily plummet and become negative under the pressure of unbridled investment. In other words, why can't the rate of interest *on money* be ever **negative**? Keynes finds himself at a delicate juncture, for in his biased replica of Gesell's theory of interest, he is at this point sailing close to the unconditional arraignment of imperishable metals, which is a spot he wishes to elude. But by having reduced money to an ordinary commodity and depicted its rate as but one of a myriad envisionable yields, Keynes now has the leeway to discuss with detachment the source of the occasional rigidity encountered in the marketplace, which, as he learnt from Gesell, is, of course, *gold*. Notice the subtlety: unlike Gesell, Keynes does not suggest that gold usurped the symbolic nature of money, reified its function, and thereby demanded a toll for its usage; he affirms, instead, that amongst many commodities money is one, which chanced to be gold by way of traditional practice, and that the physical properties of the metal may at times be expected to obstruct the free flow of trade.

To explicate gold's viscous reaction to industrial transformation, Keynes reproduces two of the traditional observations on the subject: first, he maintains that gold possesses an extremely contained *elasticity of supply* – i.e. owing to the rarity of the precious metal, increases in the prices of gold on the market are capable of stimulating only less than proportional increases in the production of it; second, gold supposedly has a *null elasticity of substitution*, which means that as the price of gold – intended as a means of payment – rises, no alternative forms of payment are introduced to substitute the costlier metal; the same quantity will be demanded, irrespective of price fluctuations (within allowable bounds). In other words, the traders cannot find a more suitable money than "money" itself (i.e. gold-money).

At last, comes the so-called "Keynesian trap."

> We come to what is the most fundamental consideration in this context, namely, the characteristics of money which satisfy liquidity-preference. For, in certain circumstances such as will often occur, these will cause the rate of interest to be insensitive, particularly below a certain figure, even to a substantial increase in the quantity of money in proportion to other forms of wealth. In other words, beyond a certain point money's yield from liquidity does not fall in response to an increase in its quantity to anything approaching the extent to which the yield from other types of assets falls when their quantity is comparably increased. In this connection the low (or negligible) carrying costs of money play an essential part (Keynes, 1973, p. 233).

From the unresponsiveness of gold-digging to price surges, the argument has shifted to the negligible carrying costs of money.

In the Keynesian scheme, the demand for money is divided into two main components[12]: a demand for transaction purposes (i.e. day to day purchases), which is a positive function of income; and a speculative demand for money which is a negative function of the rate of interest: as the rate of interest soars, the investor has an incentive to renounce immediate liquidity and "solidify" his money balances (whatever is left over, after all necessary transactions have been deducted) into longer-lived investments. This second demand function is the concise microeconomic tool employed by Keynes to summarize the habits of the community in managing a hypothetical "collective portfolio." Keynes conceives this so-called *liquidity preference* (the third installment of his comprehensive description of the nature of interest) as a putative expression of the aggregate saving and investing behavior of a diverse mass of savers: it allegedly indicates the masses' desire to hold wealth in liquid form (cash vs. other types of less liquid investments). The interest rate is then determined as the intersection of this last demand and a *fixed* supply of money provided by the central bank (from which one needs to subtract the quota of liquidity devoted to transactive purposes). In the words of Keynes, and contra Say: "The rate of interest is not the 'price' which brings into equilibrium the demand for resources to invest with the readiness to abstain from present consumption. It is the 'price' which equilibrates the desire to hold wealth in the form of cash with the available quantity of cash" (Keynes, 1973, p. 167).

In the quoted passage above, the reader should deduce that, once the threshold (a rate of 2 or $2^1/_2\%$) is reached, persistent State-mandated injections of paper in the economy might not be capable of forcing down the rate of interest. The monetary policies of the authorities would then be "trapped." The reason? Negligible carrying costs, answers Keynes. If accumulate he must, now that the threshold has been crossed, the saver would rather have gold, than, say, lettuce, which would not last the day. Keynes goes on to argue that

> The readiness of the public to increase their stock of money in response to a comparatively small stimulus is due to the advantage of liquidity having no offset to contend with in the shape of carrying-costs mounting steeply with the lapse of time. In the case of a commodity other than money a modest stock of it may offer some convenience to users of the commodity. But even though a larger stock might have some attractions as representing a store of wealth of stable value, this would be offset by its carrying-costs in the shape of storage, wastage, etc. (Keynes, 1973, p. 233).

In essence, Keynes is once more reiterating the Gesellian intuition, according to which, the possessor of wealth, not trusting in any foreseeable upswing, as a *routine*, transforms his substance in liquid balances (gold, bank notes or bank accounts), so as to protect the nominal figure of his principal. The difference between the original Gesellian exposition and the Keynesian reworking thereof is that the latter presents the process of *hoarding* more as a matter of rational economic choice than as an automatism dictated by the veritable nature of traditional money (something that is legally acknowledged never to die). Instead of affirming, as Gesell does, that everything is fated to decay, with the sole, and incongruous, exception of money, Keynes suggests that all things have their "own-rate of return," as well as their "carrying-costs"; and so it happens that some of these wares are more suitable than others for storing, and thereby have been historically selected to perform such an important duty. But, to Keynes, noble metals have no own-rate, yet they do command a "liquidity premium," which is still a form of return, and so, being the most resistant to erosion, they, though sterile, have been traditionally elected as optimal stores of value.

There follows the constraining influence of the money rate upon the rate of return of physical goods, which is identical to that of Gesell.

Undoubtedly, in fashioning the liquidity preference curve, Keynes drew to a certain extent upon the Cambridge heritage, which harbored particular strains of thought that had survived the century long Currency Controversy in England. One such strain was the Banking School (Tooke, Fullarton, Wilson), which taught that "it does not lie in the power of the banks-of-issue to increase or diminish their note circulation . . . The quantity of notes in circulation is settled by the demand within the community for media of payment . . . Expansions and contractions of the quantity of notes in circulation are said to be never the cause, always only the effect, of fluctuations of business life" (Von Mises, 1980, pp. 339–340). Indeed, the imputed passive role of banking does bear upon the question of the alleged inefficacy of monetary policy in time of crisis, for it follows therefrom that "every attempt to extend the issue of notes beyond the limits set by the general conditions of production and prices is immediately frustrated by the reflux of the surplus notes, because they are not needed for making payments" (Von Mises, 1980. ibid.). "The 'excess issue' would flow back to the bank through repayment of loans or conversion into specie" (Blaug, 1985, p. 202). This appears to be the seed of Keynes' compassing of hoards in relation to his liquidity preference curve: here the routines of bank depositors dictate the overall drift of business. Yet Tooke's so-called contra-quantity theory[13], which focuses on expenditure flows, rather than on the stock of money, as the source of economic changes, can under no circumstance claim primacy over Gesell's theory of interest for shaping the monetary economics of the *General Theory*, because the pivotal element, the reason behind the impediment to investment (Gesell's basic interest), is entirely missing from this Cambridge connection. In truth, the popular notion of the "trap" appears to be drawn almost word for word from the following revealing passage of Gesell's *Natural Economic Order*, in which he counters the advocacy of unrestricted public money-issuance in times of crisis:

> The State prints money and advances it [even at a rate of 0%] to the employers if the money of capitalists is held back ... Those who have money have the right of immediately purchasing wares ... If you have no personal need of wares you can buy bills of exchange, promissory notes, mortgage-needs and so forth from persons who are in need of wares and have no money ... The surplus production of the savers is not bought with their money, but with new money. For the moment this is unimportant; with the help of the new money, the building of houses, factories and ships proceeds without interruption. [Employers receive a low return on their enterprises, but so is the interest charged by the state for the new money.] Many still find it advantageous to lend their savings at the lower rate of interest, but others will return to the old custom of keeping their savings at home and renouncing interest ... The State replaces this amount by the issue of new money ... The crisis is averted ... But the fresh fall in the rate of interest will still further check the flow of savings into the savings-bank ... Soon even the larger class of savers will begin to find it scarcely profitable to bring money to the savings-banks ... A mighty stream of paper money, of demand due day to day, will be lost to sight. The more the rate of interest falls. Finally, before the market is satiated with real capital, when interest has fallen to about 1%, no one will bring his savings to the savings banks ... Billions of dollars are lent on mortgage. But if mortgages bring in no interest they will be foreclosed and the money hoarded. The State must replace these billions by new issues (Gesell, 1920, p. 116).

It thus appears that Chapter 17 of *The General Theory* was so constructed as to eliminate the manifestly condemnatory flavor of the notion of *basic interest (Urzins)*, the exaction of which, for Gesell, is by definition an unjustified and exploitative act.

But at this juncture, Keynes finds himself forced to make some kind of concession to the German, still not hazarding, however, to mention clearly his name in the main body of his treatise.

> Those reformers, who look for a remedy by creating artificial carrying-costs for money through the device of requiring legal-tender currency to be periodically stamped at a prescribed cost in order to retain its quality as money, or in analogous ways, **have been on the right track**; and the practical value of their proposals deserves consideration (Keynes, 1973, p. 234, emphasis added).

Even so, the problem remained: even if gold (and its management by the financial oligarchy) is not to be attributed any sinister connotation – as the Gesellians would have wished –, because it is inelastic, it is still, by nature, apt to cause unemployment and trade paralysis: if the metallic monetary base cannot grow as fast as economic activity, the system would inevitably suffer a breakdown.

C. The Remedy: The Socialization of Investment

> Unemployment develops, that is to say, because people want the moon; men cannot be employed when the object of desire (i.e. money) is something which cannot be readily choked off. There is no remedy but to persuade the public that green cheese is practically the same thing and to have a green cheese factory (i.e. a central bank) under public control. It is interesting to notice that the characteristic which has been traditionally supposed to render gold especially suitable for use as the standard of value, namely, its inelasticity of supply, turns out to be precisely the characteristic which is at the bottom of the trouble (Keynes, 1973, pp. 235–236).

At last, Keynes joins in with that motley crowd of agitators, so vocal during the interwar period, uniting *völkisch* sun-worshippers, radicals of the extreme left and right, Utopian socialists and anarchists, left-winged Nazis, and disconsolate bourgeois, all serried, in spite of their marked diversities, by a cementing dissatisfaction with the working of the Gold Standard. So how does Keynes himself wish to reform this rigid world?

> The remedy for the boom is not a higher rate of interest but a lower rate of interest! For that may enable the so-called boom to last. The right remedy for the trade cycle is not to be found in abolishing booms and thus keeping us permanently in a semi-slump; but in abolishing slumps and thus keeping us permanently in a quasi-boom ... In conditions of laissez-faire the avoidance of wide fluctuations in employment may, therefore, prove impossible without a far-reaching change in the psychology of investment markets such as there is no reason to expect. I conclude that the duty of ordering the current volume of investment cannot safely be left in private hands ... I should readily concede that the wisest course is to advance on both fronts at once. Whilst aiming at a socially controlled rate of investment with a view to a progressive decline in the marginal efficiency of capital, I should support at the same time all sorts of policies for increasing the propensity to consume (Keynes, 1973, pp. 320, 322, 325).

Socially controlled investment in public hands, a lower rate of interest to be achieved by means of an expansive monetary policy, and Malthusian unproductive consumption: on the face of it, Keynes' succinct remedy is no

less a green cheese craving than the nineteen-thirties heretics' daydream of
financial revolt, for not much in the way of institutional detail is being provided
in his analysis. Keynes deflects his attention from the questions touching the
proper arrangements conducive to such a monetary expansion; a study of
the procedures affecting the note-issuing institute, a re-definition of gold's de-
monetization, an investigation of absentee owners': a. command over resources,
b. investing habits, and c. manifold repercussions under varying scenarios of
public policy, and the type of stimulants to consumption envisaged by remedial
action, unfortunately, have not been incorporated in the *General Theory*. And
for good reason: *The General Theory* was never drafted with a view to dissecting
the intricacies of ownership and the banking mechanisms that actually caused
the breakdown; it never was a book of *observation*, i.e. of theory: Keynes'
"classic" was a rewrite of liberal pragmatism, whose task was to add to the
refurbished corpus of business principles a few, pregnant, apothegms that left
the door open on ways to succor the capitalist machine in times of disarray.

By the end of the book, there remained to dissipate the strong Gesellian
after-taste of this long monetary discourse. Keynes discharged the duty in
that remote 23rd chapter, in which the so-called "underworld" of economic
heterodoxy is paraded somewhat hastily.

Keynes pays homage to his intellectual forefathers: Malthus, Mandeville,
Hobson, and other sources of inspiration, such as Gesell (mentioned at last)
and, in fine, Douglas. Of Gesell, he confesses his initial diffidence and recollects
those hectic times when Gesellites literally "bombarded" him with publications
of the *Freiland-Freigeld-Bund,* which he had failed to appreciate fully, repelled
as he was by certain "palpable defects" of the arguments.

> As is often the case with imperfectly analyzed intuitions, their significance only became
> apparent after I had reached my own conclusions in my own way ... Since few of the
> readers of this book are likely to be well acquainted with the significance of Gesell, I will
> give to him what would be otherwise a disproportionate space (Keynes, 1973, p. 353).

In the "disproportionate" course of five pages, Keynes sketches a biography of
the German reformer, and then proceeds to review Gesell's "flashes of deep
insight"; the ostensible similarities between the newly printed theories of Keynes
and the summarized ideas of Gesell are condensed into a brief description,
which is suddenly truncated by Keynes' criticism that the German had failed
to provide a fully characterized determination of the rate of interest. According
to Keynes, Gesell had ignored psychological factors and a suitable money
demand function (Keynes' "liquidity preference"), which, coupled with a supply
function (of money, by the note-issuing institute) would explain why, in fact,
the "own-rate" of money is *positive*. The rate of interest should thus be the

intersection point of a "micro-macro" demand curve (a synthesis of the public's pecuniary behavior) and a somewhat stable money supply that is governed to a certain extent by the central bank in accordance with the exigencies of business.

Gesell is criticized for not completing his analysis with a mechanism that accounts for the oscillations of the interest rate – expressed as a function of the public's imputed financial routines. This would be, indeed, the theoretical purpose of the "liquidity preference"(Keynes, 1973, p. 356).

> The rate of interest will be determined immediately by the liquidity preferences of those who are marginal between holding money and purchasing an interest-bearing security. The rate of interest will always be high enough to overcome the liquidity preference of all those who want cash somewhat less intensely than those who actually hold the *limited* supply available. An increase in the desire to shift wealth from securities into money is what causes a rise in the price that must be paid to marginal holders to induce them not to hoard. Only those most insistent on having cash will be able to get it. The doubts and fears of others will be lulled by interest payments (Dillard, 1958, p. 182).

Again, this illustrates how the notion of interest-determination has been resolved within the Keynesian framework: the model opts for the "psychological" explanation, which views the price of money as the result of the interaction between a money-providing authority and a broadly defined group of agents, who at any point in time may decide they are willing to shift cash balance to locked (durable) investments, and vice-versa. What motivates such abrupt, or tempered movements from one type of money (mere purchase money, cash) to another (loan money, invested wealth) is not discussed.

> . . . Keynes often appeared to be on more than one side of some questions. With a casualness that imposed hard work on his interpreters, he often spoke of the "public" or the "individual" in relation to liquidity preferences (Felix, 1995, p. 164).

In truth, it is only with stammering conviction that *The General Theory's* monetary theses have been upheld by Keynes' followers, the difficulty stemming from that impatient aggregation of "micro" decisions into a streamlined demand curve, such as the liquidity preference. The latter, in fact, is being proposed as an analytical tool depicting "psychological" motivation and capable of achieving a synthesis of collective behavior in the setting of the interest rate, by dispensing with an account of the nature of the several routines forming the aggregate. Within academia, of the pillars of Keynesian thought, the liquidity preference was the first to crumble (Galbraith, 1975, p. 220).

> There is a relationship but not an identity between Keynes' concept of liquidity preference for the speculative motive and the common sense notion of hoarding. Unemployment and depression are sometimes attributed to hoarding although the exact meaning of this term is usually not clear (Dillard, 1958, p. 181).

[Keynes] said absolutely nothing about how the wealth-holder actually transferred his money (for a price that was by definition too high) to the entrepreneur-borrower. We do not see how the three liquidity motives affect this putative rentier to part with his funds, nor do we see how he imposes his judgment upon the entrepreneur to achieve the lending-borrowing transaction. We are not shown *how* the interest rate is determined (Felix, 1995, pp. 167–168).

As for the perishability of money, Keynes said no more than that those advocating it "were on the right track." This happened in the midst of the seventeenth chapter of his *General Theory*. The argument is no sooner broached than it is dropped, and covered by the successive argument of gold's inelasticity of production as a reminder that central banking is too old and reverend an institution to be challenged on the basis of the isolated accusations of a few impassioned eccentrics; that banking operates with gold; and that since there was little of that noble metal (i.e. it is scarce), the best that could be wished for was a providential lowering of its price (that is, the interest rate).

Keynes would return one last time to Gesell's stamped money proposal in Chapter 23 to close the door on the perilous subject. He again concedes that "the idea is sound," and goes on to venture a personal estimate as to what should be the cost of the stamp. He believes "it should be roughly equal to the excess of the money-rate of interest (apart from the stamps) over the marginal efficiency of capital [expected average rate of physical capital] corresponding to a rate of new investment compatible with full investment. The actual charge suggested by Gesell was 1 per mil. per week, equivalent to 5.2% per annum. This would be too high in existing conditions, but the correct figure, which would have to be changed from time to time, could only be reached by trial and error" (Keynes, 1973, p. 357).

But Gesell, argues Keynes, has seemingly failed to consider that the so-called liquidity premium, that "plus" the public is willing to pay to petrify wealth into means not eroded by time, attaches not just to money – which, indeed, possesses the highest premium of all available storage forms – but to a whole range of products, such as "bank-money, debts-at-call, foreign money, jewelry, and precious metals in general," which could easily give shelter to legions of frightened savers within hypothetically unstable communities that should decide to embark upon the experiments of a perishable currency.

However, it may be stressed here that Keynes' qualification does not do justice to Gesell's reform, for the latter had foreseen how the failed adoption of stamped scrip on the part of a world-community, however one may go about defining such a "community" in terms of resource and organizational relationships, would spell doom for the introduction of dying money from the outset: it can only work if a cooperative union of nations endorses it.[14]

This concluding critique, wherewith, strategically, Chapter 23 does not end, seems it almost for fear of granting Gesell the extra-benefit of a meditative pause, covers the length of two paragraphs. Its brevity has bequeathed to the entire Gesellian parenthesis a strong air of marginal subservience to the overall make-up of the *General Theory*: in the new Keynesian configuration, Gesell is but an appendix, a curiosum.

Thus masterly robbed and shunted aside, Gesell stands on the periphery of the Liberal bible, hapless, and prone to the remarks of sneering Keynesian compilers, who have regularly taken the liberty of dismissing his dreams as "clever-crazy prescriptions for an inflationary bonfire" (Felix, 1995, p. 193).

III. SUMMARY AND CONCLUSION

Keynes, after a more attentive re-evaluation of those Gesellian pamphlets he had been bombarded with in the nineteen-twenties, convinces himself of the validity of the dominant intuition, and thus proceeds to reform British orthodoxy at the time of the Great Depression by producing a bowdlerized edition of Gesell's ideas. Gesell's theory of interest consists in essence of two propositions: (1) imperishable commodities, unfairly employed as means of payment, command a tribute: interest; (2) this basic interest dictates the level of the yield upon capital), and a prescription (to avoid hoarding and paralysis, let the currency age and die). Keynes will discard the prescription (too radical) and appropriate the theoretical propositions by re-fashioning them in ways that would broadly account for the crisis and legitimize an overhaul of the system conducted 'behind closed doors', so to speak (by the pecuniary custodians themselves). Indeed, "one of Keynes' main aims (as an enlightened conservative) was to save capitalism" (Dowd, 2000, p. 131), and that is why "modern macroeconomics was founded on capitalist agony" (De Angelis, 1997, p. 14). The time was thus ripe to weave into the fabric of academic belief the hitherto disbelieved notion of *crisis*: this was a strategic move designed to conserve the idiom and ways of capital by acknowledging the plight of the common man, and thereby seeking avenues of compromise, material and intellectual, between absentee owners and labor, which, however, were not, at all times, to scathe the perquisites of business tenure.

To achieve this, Keynes casts aside Say's Law and its compatible monetary appendage, Wicksell's theory of interest, both discredited by the new turn of events, and adopts in their stead a revisited version of Malthus's underconsumptionist thesis seasoned with Johannsen's insight, and Gesell's theory of interest. Gesell's "interest upon capital" he names "marginal efficiency of capital," Keynes retains the univocal determining causal link *from* the monetary rate *to* the real (capital) rate, but waters down the notion of basic interest by holding on to the conception of money as a *commodity*, and by making money the *primus inter pares* in a range of means of payment, which are ranked according to their degree of perishability and of convenience in use. He thus attributes to traditional money (gold) the highest "premium for liquidity," to whose indirect, and unavoidable, effect he ascribes the formation of Gesell's threshold, and excludes the issue of perishability from the argument. Instead, this peculiar percentage (i.e. the rate of interest) asked by money-owners is defined as that fee that recompenses money for being the most liquid asset – the most practical, thus scarce, and justly rewardable for the service offered. Keynes reaffirms the institutional necessity of employing a scarce resource (gold and its accounting more or less virtual derivatives) as an inalterable fact of economic life.

In his hands, money relapses into its condition of commodity – as the best-suited commodity for effecting commercial exchange –, whereas basic interest's threshold is justified by the additional (and politically preferable) argument that investors have much to fear from a low level of the rate of interest, for an expected rise in it would shrink the capitalized value of debts.

No usury, but scarcity; no problematic (for the economy as a whole) wish to hoard, but a psychological preoccupation to preserve one's mite from the intemperance of time; the canons of bank lending are saved. And what is more, they are salvaged in the face of mounting unemployment. Money is gold, and gold is scarce, *tertium non datur*, hence the high liquidity premium and the 2% (or thereabouts) uncrossable threshold.

Keynes must have thought that Gesell was right when the latter declared that basic interest foists artificial curtailment of production upon the physical component of the economy; if interest sank to zero one should expect a burgeoning of capital investment: this Gesellian piece of economic prophesying was drawn verbatim (excepting the appellation of the real rate) into the *General Theory* and made an insistent slogan thereof.

The main difference lay in the prescriptive measures envisioned by the two authors: Gesell made the de-monetization of gold the *sine qua non* of the reformed system. No more than the stamps' revenue and an essential drafting of the rules would have fallen to the State's share in a regime of dying money, where, as Gesell's disquieting eugenistic proclivities led him to hope, by virtue of a re-instituted wholesome competition among manufacturers, poverty, ugliness and infirmities would have been driven out of existence.[15]

On the other hand, for Keynes, who did not renounce gold and never went as far as advocating its de-monetization (his directorship at the Bank of England, and ultimate allegiance to the money cartel in charge of World Affairs, is borne out by his proposal at Bretton Woods to float *Bancor*, a special drawing right initially anchored to gold) the solution to the crisis would have consisted in a benevolent entreat of the constituted financial oligarchy, better still if encompassed within a fascist coalition, to lower the bank rate so as to allow the rate upon capital to decrease and thus spur production. Short of proclaiming the Gesellian reform of dying currency, the best that could be achieved within the regime of the Vested Interests, of which Keynes was an able publicist, was a regimentation of the factors of production and a unilateral decrease of the price of money (the Gesellian threshold of basic interest) promulgated by the central bank to spur capital expansion.

The *General Theory* is a significant book, not for what it intimates, but for what it represents. It is the rushed and necessarily allusive response – given the compromissary nature of the treatise – of the leading faction of the British oligarchy to the foundering of the old "World Market Economics," managed by the usufructuary gentlemen of the Gold Standard. In the face of inexorable price decline and sweeping bankruptcy, rallying movements around communal values are a common occurrence, whose subtler purpose is to re-circulate the hoarded savings responsible for the collapse.

> The common will, embodied in the policy of the State, ought to be directed to increasing and supplementing the inducement to invest (Keynes, 1973, p. 377).

Once the causes of instability are comprehended, it is a matter of linear reasoning to predict the emergence of a movement that shall endeavor to re-establish order, by availing itself of varying degrees of violence. Thorstein Veblen had predicted the development at the end of the Great War:

> It may be remarked that vigilant and impartial surveillance of this system [business enterprise] by an external authority interested only in aggregate results, rather than in the differential gains of the interested individuals, might hopefully be counted on to correct some of the shortcomings which the system shows when running loose under the guidance of its multifarious incentives (Veblen, 1919, p. 159).

There is little doubt that the *General Theory* was inspired by the German Recovery of the nineteen-thirties under *Reichsbankspräsident* Hjalmar Schacht; the team of banking oligarchs that cooperated with the Nazi regime effected precisely this routine: it banned any radical platform of monetary reform and harnessed the commercial banking sector to a centralized policy of cheap credit engineered on the banks' behalf by the *Reichsbank* (the central bank) to finance public, and, up until 1935, to a minimal degree, martial infrastructure. As noted by many (for instance, Galbraith, 1987, pp. 222–223; Garvy, 1975), Keynes invented nothing, the Germans had preceded him by a long stretch: indeed, it is here contended that he used Gesell's insight to construe the Hitlerite recovery and made of his *General Theory* a palimpsest, whose new engraved lines encouraged the democratic West, by way of innuendo, to take after the method employed by Schacht under Hitler.

NOTES

1. See for instance Darity (1995), Dillard (1958), and Seccareccia (1988).
2. Pacifist anarchists generally claim Gesell as one of their own. Gesell's connection to Gustav Landauer places him in that camp, even though the monetary reformer never defined himself as an "anarchist" *tout court*. Instead, he occasionally referred to his movement as a form of Neo-Physiocracy; the label is suggestive of a keen harking back to tradition – to those times in which men were engaged with a radical investigation of the economic patterns of growth and social distribution. It has been justly argued, however, that this particular caption (Physiocracy) may be misleading, for the political frequentations of Gesell (all firmly encompassed within the socialist, syndicalist and anarchist fringes), and especially the 11–point program of the *Physiokratische Kampfbund* (the Physiocratic Fighting Alliance), which he personally drafted in 1924, leave no doubt as to Gesell's true colors. Point 1 demands the "removal of the State, wherever its activities may be replaced by private initiative (*"Für den Abbau des Staates dort, wo er durch Privatinitiative ersetzt werden kann . . ."*); point 2 calls for the abolition of public charity and welfare (*Wider . . . staatlicher Wolhtaten, staatlicher Fürsorge . . .*). The removal of state interference in family matters, schooling, the arts and sciences (points 3,4 and 5 respectively); the opposition to war, the class-economy, and any state-mandated duty (points 6 and 7), are the defining strokes of what is considered a quintessential manifesto of anarchism. Indeed, *"Für di Lebensfreude des einzelnen Menschen. Wider die 'Lebensfreude' des Staates"* ("For the fulfillment of individuals. Against the 'fulfillment' of the State") is the final insubordinate cry of this revealing document. (Bartsch, 1989).
3. "I am, so to speak, the incarnated theory of interest" [Gesell, 1992, p. 39].
4. For Gesell these expressions are interchangeable: whoever **demands** money is an agent **offering** products therefor; whereas, whoever **offers** money **demands** goods.
5. An example will best serve this point: if the banker A loans to B a sum of $100, to be repaid after a number of years, n, with the addition of interest, X, A can retrieve $100+X$ (we exclude foreign markets) only by **loaning** the missing quota, X, to the economy, thus burdening the system with ever growing strata of overhead charges (interest payments) in his favor. Alternatively, consider the deflationary case – that in which the banker *de facto shrinks* the money supply: before the loan, $100 fetch, say, 100 units of a representative bundle of goods. After the loan – which by assumption was devoted to the expansion of production – that same amount buys 200 units (that is to say, the price level decreases by 100% by virtue of technical advance); this implies that the "new" dollar, to be put into circulation in the second cycle with a view of purchasing the doubled amount of produce, will be worth twice as much as the "old" one. In the metal exchanges of times past, the passage from the old to the new parity signified that the unit of account (the dollar) would correspond to an increased amount of fine silver (or gold). In a period of decreasing prices, and outstanding debt contracted in the old dollar, the newly minted issues are hoarded, as the system progressively freezes into palsy and unemployment soars. A paroxysm of this type of crunch was recorded at the time of the great Castilian deflation of 1680, when the grooms of the

royal stables, for lack of cash wherewith to procure forage, were forced to butcher the steeds of the King (Vilar, 1974, p. 294).

6. For instance, if many houses were to be built so as to force interest (that is, rent) below basic interest, money will cease to be loaned until, for a series of circumstances (such as a great population increase), a house-rationing level that will warrant the exaction of basic interest is reestablished. Conversely, if the demand for housing far exceeds the available supply, interest upon capital (rent) would gradually rise above basic interest. The opportunity to exploit the return differential would prompt money to forage real estate investments. The financing will continue until the two rates are brought into equality.

7. Whether the "classic" was forthwith read by a multitude of academics and professionals is beside the point: Smith's *Wealth of Nations* and Keynes' *General Theory* were **never** "devoured" by the 'great Public'. Nor were they ever meant to be. The question was whether the commissioned classic could form a rallying point in the corridors of the propaganda network, of which academia is one of the main pillars. These tomes were far too intricate to be digested even by a learned audience. The review was thus confined to those clans of higher learning versed in the technique of expert caviling and dogmatic elucubration. The debates stemming from such distinguished opuses served the purpose of provisioning the pool of rhetoric in times of political shift (conservation vs. revolution). Their chief aim was that of indoctrination; seldom did they affect the thrust of real policy: the 'instant classics' were drafted to provide slogans and facile formulas; never were they intended to 'change the world'. There seems to be agreement amongst scholars on this point: namely, that political expediency drives the elite's *promotional* endorsement of a particular book, and is thus ultimately responsible for making it a 'classic' (see M. Perelman, 2000, p. 176, and R. H Campbell and A. S. Skinner, 1976, pp. 41–42, to read of the concerns expressed by David Hume, a leading exponent of British intelligentsia, as to whether the *Wealth of Nations* could fit the mold of a 'popular' work).

8. In matters of rates of interest, Keynes is willing to afford neo-classical dogma an honorable dismissal: he concedes that one may speak of a *natural* rate of interest (i.e. a rate that equates savings and investments) *only* in connection with a static economy featuring full employment of resources. This special natural rate is to be called the *neutral* rate. It is and shall remain a supreme and useless abstraction. Keynes thus allows the neutral rate to figure as the boundary case of his re-formulated theory of interest. But he will not make any use whatsoever of this newly coined tool in the treatise. It lingers there as evidence of lip service to all those erroneous precepts he had abided by in the past, and as a decorous farewell to the "old school" (Keynes, 1973, p. 243).

9. The marginal efficiency of capital, m, is obtained by solving to the following customary formula:

$$\text{Replacement Cost} = \frac{Q_1}{(1 + m)} + \frac{Q_2}{(1 + m)^2} + \ldots + \frac{Q_n}{(1 + m)^n}.$$

10. Joan Robinson wrote in an introduction to a collection of essays by Kalecki: "The *General Theory of Employment and Money* was published in January 1936. Meanwhile, without contact either way, Michał Kalecki had found the same solutions" (J. Robinson, 1966, p. ix). Kalecki explores the juxtaposition of basic interest to the rate upon capital in the following terms: "To be sure, banks can increase the demand for credit by lowering the rate of interest. Its reduction encourages investments, since it

increases the profitability of future enterprises by a reduction in charges for interest payments. The rise in investment activity is financed from bank credits, and by lowering the rate of interest banks can thereby grant more credits than before. Indeed, this is the typical method of intervention of the banking system aimed at improving business conditions. However, to a large extent this influence is illusory. The rate of interest is not a decisive factor in undertaking investments. More important is the expected gross profitability of the enterprise, estimated on the basis of profitability of existing enterprises. During crisis, when this profitability falls considerably below its average level, with very slack employment of existing plants, a reduction in the rate of interest has only a weak influence on the desire to invest, and in any case, takes a long time to produce perceptible effects" (M. Kalecki 1990, p. 151). As in Gesell, the crisis is here accounted for in terms of a misalignment of two rates: the rate upon capital (Kalecki names it 'gross profitability') and basic interest (the ordinary rate of interest). Kalecki doesn't acknowledge the imperishable nature of money in this instance, and thus lays emphasis on the rate upon capital as the determining rate of the dynamics, whereas Gesell insists much on the 'threshold' of basic interest. Otherwise, the mechanism illustrated is analogous.

11. Keynes' illustration: "Every fall in [the rate of interest] reduces the current earnings from illiquidity, which are available as a sort of insurance premium to offset the risk of loss on capital account, by an amount equal to the difference between the *squares* of the old rate of interest and the new. For example, if the rate of interest on a long-term debt is 4%, it is preferable to sacrifice liquidity unless on a balance of probabilities it is feared that the long-term of interest may rise faster than by 4% of itself per annum, i.e. by an amount greater than 0.16% per annum. If, however, the rate of interest is already as low as 2%, the running yield will only offset a rise in it of as little as 0.04% per annum. This, indeed, is perhaps the chief obstacle to a fall in the rate of interest to a very low level. Unless reasons are believed to exist why future experience will be very different from past experience, a long-term rate of interest of (say) 2% leaves more to fear than to hope, and offers, at the same time, a running yield which is only sufficient to offset a very small measure of fear" (Keynes, 1973, p. 202).

By "running yield" Keynes implies the (fixed) income of the security; he then derives his equilibrium rate as that *higher* (risen) rate for which the loss in capital value of the bond attending a rise in the interest rate is exactly compensated by the security's income (interest revenue), namely, the running yield. Thus, any rate higher than this "equilibrium" rate will entail a capital loss *greater* than the running yield. Formally, if A is the price of the bond, r is the interest rate and Q is the running yield, one can write the following relationship for a fixed-income security: $Ar = Q$. If r increases to become r', the previous identity becomes $A'r' = Q$, where $A' < A$, and $r < r'$. To find the equilibrium rate, one has to solve the following equation: $(A - A') = Q$, which yields the following expression for r':

$$r' = \frac{r}{1-r} \cong r + r^2 + O(r^3)$$

Dillard provides a simplified example of the Keyensian argument: "When the rate [of a fixed-income security] is 5%, a bond paying $50 per year is purchased at $1000. Three years later the rate of interest on this type of security rises to 6% as a result of which the price of bond falls to $833 (at 6% will purchase an income of $50 a year). The capital loss is $167, but during the three-year period, interest income amounting to $150 has been collected. Hence the net loss is negligible. In contrast, when the rate of interest is 2%, a bond paying $20 can be purchased for $1000. Three years later the rate of interest rises to 3%, as a result of which the price of the bond falls to $667 (at 3% $667 will purchase an income of $20 a year). The capital loss of $333 is offset only to the extent of $60 in interest income received in the three-year period. Thus the loss arising in the interest rate from 2 to 3% is much greater than from 5 to 6%, first, because the loss in capital value is greater, and, second, because the interest income is less at the lower level" (Dillard, 1958, pp. 179–180).

12. With the auxiliary prompting of the so-called "precautionary" motive, which is an extension of the transactions' requisite: that is, cash laid in for security purposes in the face of uncertainty (Keynes, 1973, p. 170).

13. Another rubric under which the ideas of the Banking School are classed.

14. Here is a collection of excerpts of Gesell's blueprint for an international currency union anchored to Free-money: "The great importance of external trade makes it desirable that there should be an international agreement to stabilize the international exchanges ... International paper-money issued in one denomination under the supervision of the countries concerned, and for this purpose only, would circulate freely ... and regulate import and export, thus keeping the exchange in equilibrium ... Gold will lose the "right of free coinage", and the coins will be deprived of their quality as legal tender [...] For payments abroad use can be made as heretofore of bills of exchange offered for sale by merchants who have shipped goods abroad ... Countries desiring to join the International Valuta Association [our proposal for an international union] adopt the "Iva" unit of currency standard ... The monetary systems of the Iva countries remain national but are based on unified principles ... A special form of international paper-currency is issued which is imported and exported without hindrance by all the countries of the Association and is recognized by them as legal tender at par with the national currency ....This international paper-money is issued at a center – the Iva Office in Bern – to the countries of the Association and under their supervision. The Iva notes are issued free of cost ... For the amount of the Iva notes issued to each country the Iva Office receives a bill of exchange ... To dissolve the Association, these bills of exchange could be paid to the Iva Office which could then destroy the Iva notes so recalled" (Gesell, 1920, pp. 137–138, 211–212).

15. For a comprehensive survey of Gesell's ideas, see G. G. Preparata and John Elliott (2002).

REFERENCES

Bartsch, G. (1989). *Silvio Gesell, die Phyiokraten und die Anarchisten*. http://userpage.fu-berlin.de/~roehrig/schmitt/text1.htm

Blaug, M. (1985). *Economic Theory in Retrospect*. Cambridge: The Cambridge University Press.

Bonder, N. (1996). *The Kabbalah of Money, Insights on Livelihood, Business, and all Forms of Economic Behavior*. Boston: Shambhala.

Campbell, R. H., & Skinner, A. S. (1976). General Introduction. In: A. Smith, *An Inquiry into the Nature and Causes of the Wealth of Nations*. Indianapolis: Liberty Press.

Darity, W. Jr. (1995). Keynes' Political Philosophy: the Gesell Connection. *Eastern Economic Journal, 21*(1)(Winter).

De Angelis, M. (1997). Class Struggle and Economics: the Case of Keynesianism. *Class, Economic Theory and State Practice. Research in Political Economy*, Vol. 16.

Dillard, D. (1958). *The Economics of John Maynard Keynes, the Theory of a Monetary Economy.* London: Crosby Lockwood & Son Ltd.

Dowd, D. (2000). *Capitalism and Its Economics: A Critical History.* London: Pluto Press.

Faye, J. P. (1980). *Langages Totalitaires.* Paris: Hermann.

Felix, D. (1995). *Biography of an Idea. John Maynard Keynes and The General Theory.* New Brunswick: Transaction Publishers.

Galbraith, J. K. (1975). *Money. Whence it Came, Where it Went.* Boston: Houghton Mifflin Company.

Galbraith, J. K. (1987). *A History of Economics, the Past and the Present.* London: Hanish Hamilton.

Garvy, G. (1975). Keynes and Economic Activists in pre-Hitler Germany. *Journal of Political Economy*, 2(83).

Gesell, S. (1920). *The New Economic Order.* San Antonio: Free Economy Publishing Co.

Gesell, S. (1992). *Gesammelte Werke.* Lütjenburg: Fachverlag für Sozialökonomie, Band 12 [1921].

Johannsen, N. J. (1971). *A Neglected Point in Connection with Crises.* New York: Augustus M. Kelley Publishers [1908].

Kalecki, M. (1990). The Business Cycle and Inflation. In: J. Oisatynski (Ed.), the *Collected Works of Michał Kalecki, Volume I, Capitalism: Business Cycles and Full Employment.* Oxford: Clarendon Press [1932].

Keynes, J. M. (1933). *Essays in Persuasion.* London: Macmillan.

Keynes, J. M. (1950). *A Treatise on Money.* London: Macmillan and Co. [1930].

Keynes, J. M. (1973). *The General Theory of Employment, Interest and Money.* London: Macmillan and Co. [1936].

Moore, E. H. (1988). *Principia Ethica.* New York: Prometheus Books [1902].

Niehans, J. (1990). *A History of Economic Theory, Classic Contributions, 1720–1980.* Baltimore: The Johns Hopkins University Press.

Perelman, M. (2000). *The Invention of Capitalism, Classical Political Economy and the Secret History of Primitive Accumulation.* Durham: Duke University Press.

Preparata, G. G., & Elliott, J. E. (2002). Free-Economics: The Vision of Reformer Silvio Gesell. *International Journal of Social Economics* (Festschrift in Honor of John C. O'Brien. Forthcoming).

Robinson, E. A. G. (Austin) (1964). John Maynard Keynes, 1883–1946. In: R. Lekachman (Ed.), *Keynes' General Theory, Reports of Three Decades.* London: St. Martin Press [1946].

Robinson, J. (1966). Introduction. In: M. Kalecki, *Studies in the Theory of the Business Cycle, 1933–1939.* New York: Augustus M. Kelley.

Samuelson, P. A. (1964). The General Theory. In: R. Lekachman (Ed.), *Keynes' General Theory, Reports of Three Decades.* London: St. Martin Press [1946].

Schumpeter, J. A. (1983). *The Theory of Economic Development.* New Brunswick, NJ: Transaction Books [1934].

Seccareccia, M. (1988). Le système monétaire et loi d'entropie: la notion gesellienne de préférence pour la liquidité. *Economies et Sociétés*, 9, 57–71.

Steiner, R. (1993). *Economics, The World as One Economy.* Bristol: New Economy Publications [1922].

Veblen, T. (1919). *An Inquiry into the Nature of Peace and the Terms of its Perpetuation.* New York: B. W. Huebsch.

Vilar, P. (1974). *Or et monnaie dans l'histoire 1450–1920.* Paris: Flammarion.

Von Mises, L. (1980). *The Theory of Money and Credit.* Indianapolis: Liberty Fund [1934].

A POLITICAL ECONOMY CRITIQUE OF THE RICARDIAN COMPARATIVE ADVANTAGE THEORY

Turan Subasat

ABSTRACT

Comparative advantage theory remains one of the most controversial theories in economics. Given its increasing importance, it is rather peculiar that Marxist writers have not paid much attention to international trade theory. This paper assesses the work of two classical Marxist political economists – Shaikh and Hudson – on international trade theory and contributes to this very limited literature by providing an alternative approach. The findings of this paper are consistent with the classical Marxist perspectives, in that, exploitation takes place in the production process but not in exchange. This, however, does not mean that countries do not lose from free trade and specialization based on comparative advantage.

I. INTRODUCTION

Comparative advantage theory remains one of the most controversial theories in economics. According to Paul Krugman (1998, p. 35), 'Ricardo's idea is truly, madly, deeply difficult. But it is also utterly true, immensely sophisticated

Confronting 9-11, Ideologies of Race, and Eminent Economists,
Research in Political Economy, Volume 20, pages 255–292.
Copyright © 2002 by Elsevier Science Ltd.
All rights of reproduction in any form reserved.
ISBN: 0-7623-0984-9

– and extremely relevant to the modern world.' Although Krugman clearly exaggerates the degree of difficulty and sophistication of Ricardo's theory, there can be very little doubt about its relevance to the modern world. International trade has been expanding much faster than production since the Second World War and countries have become more open particularly since the 1980s. There is now almost unanimous belief in the benefits of free trade and specialization based on comparative advantage.

Given its increasing importance, it is rather peculiar that Marxist writers have not paid much attention to international trade theory. Guglielmo Carchedi (1986) rightly observes that the theory of international trade is one of the least developed in Marxist economics, which is particularly unfortunate in this era when capitalism is going through some fundamental structural change. This indifference could partly be explained by the fact that Marx has never written explicitly on international trade and Marxists perhaps feel uncomfortable writing in this unfamiliar field. It is difficult (but not unfeasible) to develop a theoretical framework that involves class perspectives within the context of international trade. As international trade inevitably involves the relationship between states, any work on international trade runs the risk of falling into the boundaries of mainstream economics. In fact, the lack of class angle has been a major drawback in this literature and this article is not an exception. Class perspectives, in our view, are relevant to international trade. However, whether and how such ideas can be incorporated into trade theory remains to be researched and beyond the limited objectives of this article.[1]

Despite all the theoretical difficulties involved, the Marxist political economy view will have to pay more attention to international trade if it will ever become a major player in the academic economic thought again. As Ian Steedman (2002) argues, closed economies do not exist and a theory that does not integrate trade into its core arguments will be less than realistic.

The aim of this paper is to assess the work of two classical Marxist political economists – Shaikh and Hudson – on international trade theory and contribute to this very limited literature by providing an alternative approach. It will be beyond the scope of this paper to consider non-Marxist and dependency political economy perspectives. A large part of the paper examines Anwar Shaikh (1980, 1995, 1999a, b) who has been writing on international trade since the early 1980s. Despite the important contributions he has made to this literature, his work largely remains unnoticed and does not get the consideration it deserves. Michael Hudson (1992) primarily focuses on the usual criticisms of the assumptions of the Ricardian Comparative Advantage Theory. Carchedi (1986, 1991), another prominent Marxist writer, also heavily criticizes Ricardo's theory by arguing that it has logical flaws. His criticism however is based on a simple misunderstanding of Ricardo and will not be analyzed in detail.This paper first emphasizes the ideological origins of Ricardo's theory of comparative advantage. After a brief exposition of the theory, its criticisms from the Marxist political economy view are elaborated. It will be argued that even though these critics reduce the relevance of the theory for justifying free trade, they have not been detrimental to its overall validity. This paper will conclude by discussing those weaknesses of the theory that invalidate it as a policy guide for international trade.

It is important to emphasize that the findings of this paper are consistent with the classical Marxist perspectives, in that, exploitation takes place in the production process but not in exchange.[2] This, however, does not mean that countries do not lose from free trade and specialization based on comparative advantage. Specialization in certain commodities may result in permanently low income resulting in endemic poverty and should be avoided. Our arguments suggest that protectionist policies could be a permanent feature of international trade policy of a country and could be justified not only in the short run but also in the long run. Moreover, because specialization and international trade do not benefit all countries evenly, international trade will always create international tensions and conflict and will never be a smooth process as predicted by the comparative advantage theory.

II. A BRIEF HISTORICAL REVIEW

The first problem out of which political economy developed was concerned with international trade. Before classical theory, it was believed that national wealth could be increased by maintaining a continuous trade surplus, thus increasing the national ownership of gold and silver. This theory, known as mercantilism, therefore excluded the possibility of free and equal exchange. Mercantilism was the popular ideology and the voice of the growing merchant class during the 17th and 18th centuries. Mercantilists could not even imagine that it was possible for one country to get richer without impoverishing another. Trade was like war. The victory of the one country meant the defeat of another (Emmanuel, 1975). The merchants were perceived to be the supreme creators of wealth and the risky nature of international competition required a strong and supportive state. In return, the strength of the state depended on the merchants.

The liberal doctrine was the ideology of the newly born industrial bourgeoisie at the end of the 18th century. The industrial bourgeoisie were against all restrictions, which acted in favor of the merchants and feudal landlords. They demanded economic and political freedom as the industrial sector required bigger markets, cheap inputs and free labor force.

Mercantilism was fundamentally undermined by the free trade theories put forward by the classical economists, the most important of whom were Adam Smith and David Ricardo. They rejected the idea that one nation could enrich itself by impoverishing another and instead argued that trade could only benefit one country if it also benefited another through fair exchange.[3]

Hudson (1992), however, notes that the 'laissez-faire doctrine was based on a more static analysis than the development-oriented analysis which characterized the preceding mercantilism and subsequent protectionism'. The Ricardians replaced the assumption of increasing returns by the mercantilists with that of diminishing returns, which led them to ignore the dynamic nature of development.

At the beginning of his *Wealth of Nations,* Smith argued that the major source of the difference in the wealth of nations was the extent of the division of labor within each society. He believed that the extent of the market could limit the development of the division of labor. Smith favored free trade because large markets were preconditions to create the potential for exploiting the growing division of labor, which was necessary for productivity increase.[4] Smith's argument was based on the theory of absolute advantage. It was dynamic in nature compared to Ricardo's static comparative advantage theory in which production costs were assumed to be constant. According to absolute advantage theory, commodities should be produced where the absolute cost of production is the lowest. This would allocate resources efficiently. The theory asserts that the advantage of free trade is derived from purchasing commodities cheaper from abroad rather than producing them more expensively at home. Thus, from this perspective, the international division of labor is the natural extension of the division of labor in domestic markets. This is the main reason why Smith was so enthusiastic about international trade. He saw international trade as a non-zero positive sum game and believed that by expanding the market, trade would create conditions for a deeper division of labor, productivity increase and continuous capital accumulation.

Like Smith, Ricardo also approved of capitalism, but unlike Smith, he was pessimistic about its future. Ricardo produced his theory of income distribution between factors of production in order to investigate whether capital accumulation could continue indefinitely. He used the labor theory of value to analyze the distribution of income among capitalists, landlords and workers. This analysis displayed his belief that capitalists were the only source of investment and capital accumulation, whereas landlords, a parasitic class, were the source of luxury consumption.[5] Therefore, the important question was whether or not capitalists received enough income to maintain accumulation.

Ricardo believed in a stationary state because of declining productivity in agriculture. Ricardo's application of the value theory to agriculture differed substantially from his treatment of manufacturing. He argued that as accumulation proceeds, capitalist farmers move from more productive land to less productive land, and the average productivity of land diminishes. This would result in increased rent on more productive land. As agricultural production moves to less and less productive land, the rent on the more productive land would keep increasing. Given a subsistence wage level (which could not be altered), the profit rate would decline as the rent share increased. As capitalist accumulation proceeds, landlords would increasingly take the benefits of production. Thus, capitalist accumulation would stop and the economy would reach a 'steady state'. This theory accounts for Ricardo's antagonism towards landlords.

Pressurized by landlords and laborers, the best that capitalists could hope for was a postponement of the decline in the rate of profit. Ricardo conceived of a number of ways in which this decline might be postponed. One was by the application of new technology to agriculture. But he thought of this as an unpredictable process and not amenable to policy action. The alternative method was to raise labor productivity by intensifying work. However, making laborers work harder was not compatible with the assumption of a subsistence wage.

Once the improvement of British agricultural productivity was ruled out, Ricardo realized that the only way to postpone the decline in the profit rate was to import cheap food. Free trade, particularly for food grains, was a major issue in British politics in the first half of the 19th century. The money price of wine in England had been steady for a period of about 150 years. At the end of the 18th century, it rose due to restrictions on corn trade. The price was high through the first decade of the 19th century, after which a series of good harvests caused a sharp decline in price. It was in reaction to this sharp fall that in 1815 restrictions on wine imports (the so-called Corn Laws) were tightened.[6]

Ricardo used his analysis to show that cheap imports of wage goods lowered the labor time embodied in the subsistence wage and thus could permit the rate of profit to be maintained. Furthermore, he suggested that both trading countries would gain from free trade, even if both commodities could be produced in one country with less labor than in the other country.

This background helps one to understand the ideological nature of Ricardo's comparative advantage theory. He produced this theory as a justification for the abolition of the Corn Laws, which he believed had benefited the landlord class and harmed the industrial bourgeoisie. Ricardo, like Smith, was the advocate of the industrial bourgeoisie against the domination of landlords. This underlying ideological affiliation led to the construction of his theory and resulted in a number of exaggerated assumptions. Diminishing returns on land, for example, cannot be easily supported when one considers the dramatic productivity increase on land, even during his own lifetime.

Malthus, a supporter of the landlord class, argued for retention of the Corn Laws which he thought would allow the landlords to invest in land, increase productivity and reduce food prices.[7] 'It is ironic that the theory of economic rent had first been put forth in 1777 by the Scottish agriculturalist James Anderson specifically in reference to increasing returns!' (Hudson, 1992, p. 113). Smith and Marx also based their theories on ever-increasing productivity levels.[8] Consequently, one may wonder whether Ricardo was unable to see the potential for productivity increase on land or whether he preferred ignoring it in order to build his theory.

III. RICARDO'S THEORY OF COMPARATIVE ADVANTAGE

Smith's absolute advantage theory looked persuasive but trade was impossible when one country produced all commodities cheaper than the other. Ricardo dealt with this problem by developing the theory of comparative advantage. This demonstrated that both countries could benefit from specialization in particular lines of production even where the costs of production for all of the producers were initially higher in one country than in the other. What was required was for relative prices to differ. Ricardo revolutionized the foreign trade doctrine through a famous example: he compared the effects of the introduction of trade in two commodities between England and Portugal, where each was producing both commodities and the costs of both commodities were higher in England than in Portugal. Ricardo argued that even though the absolute prices of both commodities were lower in Portugal, trade was possible since the relative prices were different. As can be seen from Table 1, wine is relatively cheaper in Portugal and cloth is relatively cheaper in England.

Ricardo's model is based on a number of simplifying assumptions. Hudson (1992, p. 120) summarizes these assumptions as follows: constant returns to scale; the traded goods are produced in both countries; no trade in common factor inputs; no underutilization of labor, capital or land, and in particular no import-displacement of domestic labor and capital; no emigration or capital outflow; no imbalance in international trade and payments; no impact of monetary inflation or deflation or of domestic and foreign debt on comparative costs; no conflict between private-sector interests and general (long-term) social utility.

Table 1.   Ricardian Comparative Advantage.

	Production per worker (productivity)		Price (£)[9] (inverse productivity)	
	Portugal	England	Portugal	England
Wine	1.25	0.83	0.80	1.20
Cloth	1.11	1.00	0.90	1.00
Wine to cloth ratio			0.89	1.20

To demonstrate the gains from trade, a simplified version of Ricardo's example will be used. Table 2 shows that the productivity level and, thus, the price of cloth are the same in England and Portugal.[10] Portugal, however, has an absolute advantage in wine production since productivity is higher and the price is lower. The relative prices indicate that wine is relatively cheap in Portugal and cloth is relatively cheap in England.

According to absolute advantage theory, there is no case for trade since the price of cloth is the same in both countries and wine is cheaper in Portugal. Given these prices, England would benefit from importing the cheaper wine from Portugal but this is not possible because England cannot export to Portugal. Ricardo argued against absolute advantage theory by demonstrating that if Portugal produces only wine, in which it has a comparative advantage, and England produces cloth, both countries would gain from trade, because total production would be higher. The relative price of cloth is cheaper in England and the relative price of wine is cheaper in Portugal.

Table 2.   Ricardian Comparative Advantage (Modified).

	Production per worker (productivity)		Price (£) (inverse productivity)		Total production[11]	
	Portugal	England	Portugal	England	Portugal	England
Wheat	1.8	0.6	0.55	1.66	180	60
Cloth	1.2	1.2	0.83	0.83	120	120
Wheat to cloth ratio			0.66	2.00		

A graphical illustration of the gains from trade for both countries is displayed in Fig. 1.[12] In the absence of trade, a nation's production possibility frontier is also its consumption frontier. Domestic consumption patterns and productivity levels will determine the production patterns. Before trading, Portugal may choose to produce and consume a combination of the commodities at point A, and England at point A'. With trade, Portugal specializes in wine and England in cloth. After trading, the consumption pattern is different from the production pattern. There will be only one price for both commodities in both countries and relative prices will be the same in both countries.[13] For Portugal, consumption increases from A to E, for England from A' to E'. The total quantity of the commodities (Ricardo's 'sum of enjoyments') is increased. The increased consumption is the result of increased production through specialization.

Given the simplicity of the model and its assumptions, Ricardo believed that:

> Under a system of perfectly free commerce, each country naturally devotes its capital and labour to such employment as are most beneficial to each. This pursuit of individual advantage is admirably connected with the universal good of the whole. [. . .] It is this principle, which determines that wine shall be made in France and Portugal, that corn shall be grown in America and Poland, and that hardware and other goods shall be manufactured in England (Ricardo, 1992, p. 81).

Even though various thinkers have developed this model, the basic principles have not changed. Ricardo's labor theory of value has been rejected, but his comparative advantage theory has become the cornerstone of neo-liberal trade theory. The idea that the free market's 'admirable' pursuit of individual advantage will produce the best results for each country became a quasi-religious belief. Influenced by this conviction, contemporary trade theories display corresponding problems and that is why it is worth analyzing this model in more detail.[14]

IV. CRITIQUES OF RICARDO'S THEORY

There are various critiques of Ricardo's theory, from the Marxist left to the neoclassical right. The neoclassical economists accommodate Ricardian comparative advantage theory, but reject its 'hopelessly naive assumptions, particularly its attachment to the labour theory of value and the single-factor assumption.' (Gomes, 1987, p. 162) They have instead developed a 'more sophisticated' model of trade based on factor endowment theory. In our view, far from being a step forward, the Heckscher-Ohlin model represents a leap backward in international trade theory. Neoclassical economists not only created confusion through the use of ambiguous concepts (e.g. capital and labor 'endowments'), but also muddled Ricardo's original theory through their confusion over how prices are formed.[15]

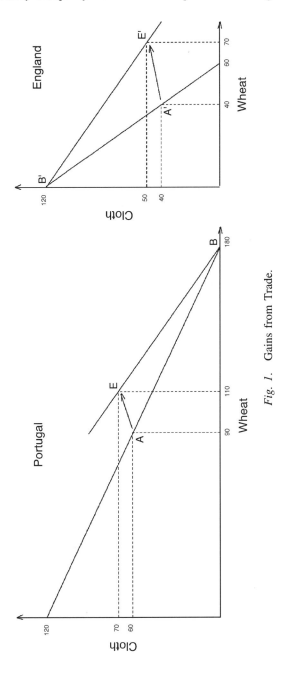

Fig. 1. Gains from Trade.

Structuralist economists, such as Singer (1984), agree with the basic tenets of Ricardian theory and accept that international trade based on comparative advantage would indeed benefit all participating countries. They argue, however, that these benefits are unequally distributed between developed and developing countries as a result of the peculiarities of the commodities exported by developing countries. They recommend temporary protectionist measures for the industrial sector, until competitiveness is achieved.

One of the strongest critiques of comparative advantage theory has come from the dependency theorists, particularly Emmanuel (1972 and 1975) who argued that developing countries are exploited at the level of exchange because trade is based on 'unequal exchange'. This unequal exchange, he argued, occurs as a result of the wage and price level differentials between developing and developed countries. Whereas the international mobility of commodities and capital equalizes the profit rate internationally, as a result of the immobility of labor, wage rates vary from one country to another according to historical conditions. Low wage levels allow developing countries to lower the prices of their export commodities. In developed countries, however, monopolistic labor and commodity markets keep export prices high. As a result of these different price levels, developed countries transfer some of the economic surplus from developing countries and reduce the latter's accumulation and economic growth rates. This article will not deal with Emmanuel's theory. Good critiques of his arguments can be found in Bettelheim (1972), Edwards (1985), Weeks (1991) and Carchedi (1991).

Carchedi (1986 and 1991) also criticizes the basic logic and internal consistency of the theory. He argues that Ricardo's theory 'is a non-starter' because it has logical flaws and because Ricardo compares 'uncomparables'. According to Carchedi:

> Ricardo's mistake resides in comparing productivities between branches. Portugal, it is said, is more productive in wine than in clothing. This is why it specializes in wine production. The opposite holds for England. But productivity differences can be compared only within branches. In this case they do reflect profitability differentials. Such a comparison is meaningless between branches. It is the comparison of the productivity of wine producers both in England and Portugal, which can be taken as an indication of profitability differentials (and thus of specialization), not the comparison between the relative productivity of wine and that of clothing in Portugal (Carchedi, 1991, p. 220).

And thus,

> [t]here is no reason to assume that wine production is more efficient and thus more profitable than cloth production because it takes 80 hours to produce one gallon of wine and 90 hours to produce one yard of clothing. There is thus no reason to assume that capital in Portugal will move out of cloth and into wine production. It is therefore meaningless to hold that

Portugal specializes in wine because Portuguese wine producers are 'more efficient' than Portuguese cloth producers (Carchedi, 1986, p. 436).

Carchedi's criticism, however, is based on a simple misunderstanding of Ricardo's theory. Ricardo did not compare uncomparables such as apples and pears but compared comparables like price differentials for apples and pears in different countries. Ricardo did not argue that Portugal specializes in wine because Portuguese wine producers are more efficient than Portuguese cloth producers. He argued that Portugal specializes in wine because Portuguese wine producers are 'relatively' more efficient than Portuguese cloth producers.

Carchedi admits that the principle of comparative advantage leads to saving universal labor time, but he argues that this will not lead to specialization because capitalists are only concerned with their profits and not with saving labor time. This argument is also obscure. It is obvious that capitalists only care about profit and are not concerned with saving labor time to produce commodities. The point however is that the free trade mechanism makes it unprofitable for Portuguese (England) cloth (wine) producers to stay in business since English (Portuguese) cloth (wine) producers become more competitive through the mechanisms of the theory.

One of the first systematic attempts to analyze Ricardo's theory from the view of radical political economy came from Anwar Shaikh (1980, 1987, 1999a, b). Apart from Shaikh and Carchedi, however, international trade is one area about which classical Marxists have been very silent. Marx himself planned to write a volume on trade, as part of his famous work *Capital*, but never actualized it before his death.[16] In this section, Shaikh's work on international trade and Ricardian theory will be analyzed in detail.

Most criticisms of Ricardo's theory are mainly leveled at the restrictive assumptions of the model. Many critics, such as Hudson (1992), stress the importance of the assumptions for the theory and argue that once they are suitably modified the theory loses its explanatory power. This is not necessarily true. As will be argued in detail in this section, these critics have not threatened the most fundamental tenets of the theory. Unrealistic assumptions do cause difficulties for the theory but modifying them does not invalidate the theory altogether.

There is very little doubt that Ricardo's theory has serious theoretical weaknesses and that it cannot be used to justify the benefits of free trade to all participants. However, not all the critiques and indeed theories that allegedly 'improve' the theory have always been fair to Ricardo. He deserves some credit for his contribution to international trade theory for his argument against the theory of absolute advantage. A country can indeed trade based on its comparative advantage. Whether this would benefit that country, or whether this trade is the best option open to the country are other matters. Given that the critiques of the theory are not always accurate, it will be argued that Ricardo's contribution should be recognized and credited. This section will first criticize the work of Shaikh and Hudson and then argue that the fundamental weakness of the theory lies in its static nature and its overly simplistic interpretation of labor value theory.[17]

A. The Mechanism of the Theory and Shaikh's Critique

Anwar Shaikh is perhaps the only person who has done considerable work on Ricardo's theory from a classical Marxist perspective. This section will summarize and evaluate his work. Shaikh wrote a number of articles and mostly focused on the weaknesses of the mechanism of the Ricardian model. One obvious problem that the model faces is providing an explanation for how an absolute disadvantage can be transformed into a comparative advantage. Given that one country has absolute advantage in both commodities, how is it possible that consumers in that country will be willing to buy goods from the other country? When there is free trade, it is obvious that consumers in both countries would have the incentive to buy both commodities from the first country.

Ricardo produced a mechanism based on the 'quantity theory of money' which asserts that when the barriers to free trade are removed, the prices will rise in the surplus country and fall in the deficit country until the deficit country becomes competitive in the commodity for which it has a comparative advantage. In his very first article on the subject in 1980 Shaikh argued that Ricardo's mechanism had serious theoretical problems and would not work. Free trade would not lead to specialization but to chronic trade deficit and would eventually collapse (Shaikh, 1980, p. 38).

Ricardo's argument asserts that, due to a trade deficit (surplus) there will be deflation (inflation) in England (Portugal) and these price changes will eventually bring comparative advantage to a competitive advantage by increasing (decreasing) England's (Portugal's) competitiveness in cloth. Average prices in England will fall since the money outflow will reduce the money supply (gold). Prices in Portugal will rise, since the money inflow will increase the money supply. The idea is simple. If the supply of any commodity is higher (lower) than its demand, the price of that commodity will be lower (higher) than its 'direct price' or the price of production until the supply adjusts itself to the demand conditions. The same thing is assumed to hold for the commodity money, gold. Any increase in the supply of gold would reduce its price lower than its direct price. At this point Marx's objection becomes relevant. As Shaikh (1980) puts it, the excess supply of gold is a very different thing from an excess supply of any other commodity since money can be hoarded or transformed into luxury articles without losing its value. In this sense, the commodity money does not have to be (and in fact cannot be) sold. Some quantity of gold is needed in circulation to facilitate the circulation of commodities. The gold that is not needed will be taken out of the circulation in order to be hoarded or transformed into luxury goods.

According to Marx's theory of money, Ricardo's inflation theory is erroneous, in that any increase in the money supply due to a trade deficit will not have any impact on the overall price level. This does not mean that any increase (decrease) in the money supply as a result of a trade surplus (deficit) will not have any impact on the economy. Marx argues that an increase in gold reserves will lower the rate of interest and increase demand in the economy. This is where Ricardo's full employment and constant technology assumptions become important. When there is extra demand in the economy and production cannot be increased, then prices must go up. But Marx argued that full employment is a "vulgar" fantasy (Shaikh, 1980, p. 33). When there is unemployment in the economy, extra demand can be met by increasing production. In such a case, quantities but not the prices adjust to the increased demand.

From this perspective, the English/Portuguese trading scenario would be as follows: When trading starts, Portugal exports both commodities to England. Cloth and wine production in England shrinks and expands in Portugal. The constant outflow of money from England reduces the money supply and increases the interest rate, which has a further negative effect on production. In Portugal, on the other hand, the expanded gold reserves increases demand and production, and decreases the interest rate. The excess gold, which cannot be absorbed in the circulation of the commodities will be hoarded or used to produce luxury articles. In this model, there is no in-built mechanism to bring about trade equilibrium. England's absolute disadvantage will cause a chronic trade deficit balanced by a persistent outflow of gold, until England runs out of gold reserves and the system eventually collapses.[18]

As an alternative to CAT, Shaikh believes in absolute advantage theory (AAT). He argues that in AAT, the 'correct' terms of trade are those regulated by relative real costs, and persistent trade imbalances are perfectly 'correct' outcomes of free trade. Thus, the appropriate policy prescription is to improve real competitiveness by reducing real costs. In what follows Shaikh's above arguments will be assessed.

In his first article Shaikh does not criticize the basic tenets of Ricardo's theory. Rather he directs his criticism at the inflation (deflation) mechanism of Ricardo, through which comparative advantages become competitive advantages. The logic of Shaikh's arguments suggests that if one rejects this mechanism, then one has to reject the whole theory. In his view, absolute advantage is the rule for trading, not comparative advantage. If a country does not have an absolute advantage in any commodity, then that country cannot trade since any attempt to trade will destroy its existing domestic sectors.

Shaikh's argument on Ricardo's mechanism and the quantity theory of money is an important contribution.[19] However, the drawback of Ricardo's mechanism does not invalidate the theory altogether. As will be argued, there is another mechanism whereby comparative advantages become competitive ones even if Ricardo's inflation (deflation) mechanism is not valid. Furthermore, we will argue that Shaikh's arguments on impact of devaluations on real exchange rate (RER) has important weaknesses and when commodity money is replaced with paper money, a country may face no difficulty in devaluing its currency until some of the commodities (those that are relatively cheaper) become competitive in international markets.

In the following analysis, an alternative mechanism that can work with Ricardo's assumptions will be shown. This mechanism does not need an inflation (deflation) price adjustment mechanism in order to work. Naturally, if there is such a mechanism, Shaikh's critique of comparative advantage theory fails. This mechanism, however, requires interventionist-protectionist policies to bring about the desirable outcomes of trade. In the following example, Ricardo's original static model is employed.

Before free trade, we assume that England has some gold reserves. When free trade begins, England will import both commodities (wine and cloth) and the domestic production of both commodities will decline. Until gold reserves are exhausted, prices in England will fall, not because of a reduction in the domestic money supply (an overall deflation as Ricardo would anticipate) but because of cheaper imports. On the other hand, there is no inflation in Portugal as a result of money inflow because in Portugal quantities adjust rather than prices.[20] As England cannot export anything, sooner or later England's gold reserves are exhausted. When the reserves are exhausted, the prices of both commodities will gradually rise towards their pre-trade levels, as imports of both commodities are restricted due to gold shortages.[21]

Thus, in this model, as opposed to the quantity theory of money, the first impact of a fall in reserves is not a fall in prices but an increase. When the prices for cloth and wine are high enough, the domestic production of both commodities can start in England again and the prices will stabilize at the pre-trade level. The only difference is that now England has no reserves to import cheaper Portuguese commodities. But as the price of wine increases more than the cloth (because the price gap is bigger for wine), it will be profitable for a merchant to sell English cloth to Portugal below its domestic price and to import cheaper Portuguese wine into England, where it can be sold at a higher price and still make profit.

To illustrate this point, we go back to our earlier example (see Table 1). A merchant starts with £100, buys 100 units of cloth in England, sells them in Portugal for £90 (charges £0.9 for per unit) and makes a loss. With that £90, s/he buys 112.5 units of wine and sells them in England for £135 and makes £35 profit.

In this scenario, trade would take place even though there is no inflation (deflation) mechanism involved. At the end of this process, when the profit opportunities for the merchants are exhausted, the prices of both commodities will be equalized in both countries. But what if the cloth producers in Portugal decide to fight back by reducing their prices? Obviously, to eliminate the competition, they can reduce their prices even more since they are more productive. This is not possible, however, in the long run. For the merchants, there is no limit for a price cut for cloth as long as they make up the difference from the profit they make when they sell wine in England. They make losses because of lower export prices for cloth but they make extra profit because of higher wine prices in England. Cloth producers in Portugal cannot compete with this.

As mentioned earlier and will be explained later in detail, when specialization takes place, England gains more than Portugal because only a small price undercut for Portugal's cloth producers is required to be competitive. The price fall for wine in England, however, is large. Thus, the relative price change in England is larger than Portugal and England gains more. This scenario implies that Portugal gains from tariffs. As long as the gap in the wine price is still profitable for the merchants, any increase in tariffs will force the traders to reduce cloth prices further to be able to compete in Portuguese markets and the net revenue from tariffs will be the net gain of Portugal. In fact, Portugal can increase tariffs even higher in order to transfer most benefits to itself. Thus, as a rule, an intervention in trade rather than a free market approach would benefit Portugal most.

On the other hand, for this mechanism to work,[22] England's reserves must first be completely exhausted. Otherwise, importing commodities into England will be more profitable. But if England starts with a substantial amount of gold reserves, until the time that all the reserves are exhausted, both sectors in England might be completely destroyed. There will be no sectors to compete even if the prices are high enough again. This scenario indicates the necessity of controlled trade for England. England must control the cheaper cloth imports, preferably by import restrictions, and Portugal must tax cloth imports, if there is to be some gain for Portugal from this trade.

It is important to note that this model does not require full employment in order to work. As long as relative prices are different, traders will find it profitable to exploit them and comparative advantages will become competitive advantages. In view of the above argument it is reasonable to conclude that there is no case for free trade but there is still a case for controlled trade.

The above mechanism also holds in a world economy where money is no longer commodity money but there exist national currencies. When free trade starts, the domestic prices of both commodities decline in England. The relative price of wine in England declines more because England has a comparative disadvantage in wine production. When foreign currency reserves decline, the prices of both commodities increase back to their pre-trade levels. Now, as the cheaper Portuguese goods cannot be imported as a result of foreign currency shortages,[23] the demand for and price of foreign currency will increase. It is still profitable to sell cloth to Portugal below its actual price in order to obtain the currency and buy the wine in Portugal to sell in England.

In his later articles Shaikh also objected to such an exchange rate devaluation mechanism. In two follow-up articles in 1995 and 1999, Shaikh developed his arguments further and made a case against the idea that when commodity money is replaced by paper money the currency devaluations may transform comparative advantages into competitive advantages. Indeed, Shaikh's arguments above are based on a critique of Ricardo's quantity theory of money. Even if Shaikh was right in his critique, it could be argued that in the case of paper money, devaluations may lower prices in the deficit country and allow competitiveness based on comparative advantage. He, however, claimed that exchange rate devaluations would have no influence on term of trade[24] and will not alleviate persistent structural trade disequilibrium. Moreover, higher interest rates resulting from capital outflows would attract capital inflows, which would finance trade deficit and cause long term trade disequilibrium.

In Ricardian two-country/two-good model, trade disequilibrium is rectified by relative price changes. A trade disequilibrium between participating countries is assumed to be corrected by relative price changes after specialization takes place. In other words, excess demand (supply) for a commodity would be eliminated by a rise (fall) in its price. This implies abandonment of the labor value theory since prices are now determined not by their production costs but by their relative demand and supply. Shaikh's arguments are based on the contention that relative prices of tradables are determined by their relative real costs but not demand and supply conditions. If prices are determined by their cost structure, necessary price changes to clear the market will not take place and free trade would lead to persistent trade disequilibrium. In other words, the 'correct' terms of trade,[25] will be determined by the relative cost structures of the commodities and any attempt to change it through exchange rate devaluations will be unsuccessful. Moreover, money outflow in the deficit country will reduce liquidity and raise interest rates, thus attracting capital inflows, which will finance the trade deficit and exacerbate the trade disequilibrium.

Shaikh's arguments in his earlier and later articles reveal some marked differences. His arguments in his earlier article are based on the contention that when free trade is allowed prices would not adjust and specialization would not take place as long as one country has absolute advantage in both commodities. In other words, having an absolute advantage in one of the commodities for each country is a precondition for a successful specialization and beneficial trade. In his later articles, however, he assumed that specialization would take place but free trade would lead to permanent disequilibrium. The implication of these two positions is considerable and there seems to be a logical inconsistency in his later articles.

In his two-country/two-good model Shaikh first argues that 'at the beginning of free trade, there will be two prices for each commodity, since each country produces each good. For a given good, the lower cost producer will become the regulating one, and will therefore be able to seize some part of the other's market through its own exports.' (Shaikh, 1999, p. 9) Then he assumes that one country (Portugal) ends up exporting one good (wine), and the other country (England) ends up exporting the other good (cloth).[26] He does not explain what he means by the "lower cost producer" in this context, and why/how Portugal ends up exporting wine, and England exporting cloth. This is important because, according to AAT (that Shaikh believes in), free trade would lead to persistent trade disequilibrium and eventually collapse before specialization takes place if one of the countries had absolute advantage in both commodities. When he says Portugal ends up exporting wine and England cloth, he either assumes that Portugal has absolute advantage in wine and England in cloth, in this case his further criticism of the CAT is invalid; or he assumes that countries are specialized according to CAT. That is, England may have absolute disadvantage in both commodities (i.e. necessary labor time to produce both commodities are higher in England) but it has comparative advantage in cloth. In this case he agrees with CAT, that is, specialization occurs according to CAT even when one country has absolute advantage in both commodities.

Secondly, in this article Shaikh seems to be addressing a very specific demand/supply problem in two-country/two-good model that could easily be resolved in a more than two-country/two-good model. In a close economy the production composition of the commodities is determined by the demand composition. In other words, the demand for cloth and wine determines how much cloth and wine will be produced in each county. Therefore, there can be no long-term over (under) supply of the commodities. When free trade begins and specialization takes place, however, the production composition will be different from the demand composition and this may cause demand and supply imbalances. Shaikh argues that once specialization is complete, there is no reason to expect that trade will be balanced. Portugal, for instance, may end up with importing more than exporting, a trade deficit. This means that Portugal (England) is producing more (less) wine (cloth) than the aggregate demand in both countries.

As verified earlier, the expectation of the Ricardian model is to have price adjustments to balance the demand and supply and bring the economies into equilibrium. In other words excess (deficient) demand for cloth (wine) would raise (reduce) its price and restore equilibrium. This means that the relative prices are determined by not cost structure but by demand. This is what Shaikh rightly objects to. In a two-country/two-good model, it would be a coincidence to have a balanced trade.[27]

This problem is not specific to specialization according to comparative advantage and the same problem can arise even when countries specialize according to their absolute advantage. Moreover, partial specialization is the solution to such disequilibrium. Since there is more (less) demand for cloth (wine) that England (Portugal) produces, the relative price would temporarily rise (fall) to a level at which the production of cloth would be profitable in Portugal. As a result, Portugal would produce both commodities and England would produce only cloth. In this case, as Portugal produces both commodities, the relative prices would be determined by production costs in Portugal. In other words, the relative prices (or the terms of trade) of both commodities would be equal to pre-trade level in Portugal. In a more than two-country/two-good model there would be no such mismatch in the long run. If demand for one commodity is less than its supply, its price would fall and some countries would be forced to leave the market. Eventually the price of that commodity would go back to its normal level (or a little lower if we assume that the least productive countries leave the market).

Thirdly, Shaikh uses the terms of trade as a measure of RER in a very specific theoretical context. In a two-country/two-good model, the terms of trade is the only measure of RER after specialization takes place. In the above example, once Portugal specializes in wine and England in cloth, the only measure of RER is the terms of trade. As the relative price of commodities is determined by their production costs, demand/supply imbalance cannot be eliminated by devaluations and the system will be locked in a permanent disequilibrium. Consequently, in this model devaluations are irrelevant and cannot produce a permanent solution to the problem.

Before complete specialization, however, the RER could be measured as the domestic and international relative price of exportable commodities. In other words, the relative price of wine in Portugal and England in international currency is the RER for Portugal.[28] Only after specialization is completed can the terms of trade be taken as RER. This has implications for the specialization process that Shaikh objects to in his first article. If the prices of wine and cloth in common currency were higher in England than Portugal when free trade is allowed, a devaluation would reduce their prices in common currency until cloth becomes competitive.[29] At this level of devaluation, price of wine will not be competitive and as a result wine producers will leave the market in England.

When specialization is complete, the terms of trade may be taken as the only measure of RER. But the nature of this RER is rather different. In this case the competition is not between wine/cloth producers in both countries but between wine producers in Portugal and cloth producers in England. In this very specific case Shaikh is right in arguing that the relative prices of wine and cloth would be determined by their relative costs of production but not by demand and supply. Demand and supply conditions would only determine how much of these commodities will be produced.[30] In this case exchange rate devaluations would change the terms of trade for a short while but not in the long run. If England devalues its currency in order to sell more cloths (which would increase the relative price of wine and reduce its demand), Portugal will have no difficulty in responding in the same manner.

In a more than two-country/two-good model, the terms of trade can be considered as a measure of RER only under "big country" assumption. A nominal devaluation in a big country (main or the only producer in the world) may affect the terms of trade. In the case of a small country, where prices of tradables are externally given, a devaluation would not have any impact on the terms of trade. The RER should be measured by comparing the prices of exportable commodity in domestic and international markets in a common currency.[31] In this case however, exchange rate devaluations are relevant yet again and would reduce the price of exportable commodity in international currency and make it competitive.

Shaikh's arguments on the negative impacts of higher interest rates and capital inflows resulting from a decline of liquidity which would finance and cause long term trade deficit is compelling. This, however, is not a direct challenge to the basic tenets of CAT. First, there is a need to separate financial liberalization from trade liberalization. It is a common surveillance that uncontrolled international financial movements are a source of trade disequilibrium. If countries did not have access to international finance or had regulated financial markets where foreign borrowing is restricted to curb destabilizing financial movements and liberalized their trade, they would specialize according to their comparative advantage without any trade disequilibrium. Countries would import as much as they could export.

In reality, of course, countries do borrow from the international markets and this may cause temporary or even permanent trade disequilibrium. When there is trade deficit, a country may wish to finance it via foreign borrowing. If deficit is temporary, this is sensible. Borrowing money to finance trade deficit for forever, however, is not an option for most countries. It may occur under special circumstances such as the case for the USA or many low-income countries that receive large amounts of aid.[32] Countries may borrow beyond their ability to pay and may have to borrow more to pay back their old debts. This is the case when developing countries were encouraged to borrow with low interest rates during the 1970s, resulting in the "debt trap" in the 1980s. When borrowing is not possible, devaluations would either increase exports or reduce imports and equalize trade. In fact by competitive devaluations, a country may become competitive in all tradable commodities that it can produce. Whether this will be a wise thing to do is another matter.

Second, the fact is that, under free trade, countries would specialize in line with their comparative advantage whether or not trade is balanced. Ricardo had two important propositions: (1) Trade amongst two countries is possible even if one county has no absolute advantage in terms of the cost of production; (2) Free trade would lead to equilibrium and any disequilibrium would be temporary. Shaikh's criticism is more relevant on the second proposition. Trade disequilibrium, however, may exist not because comparative advantage theory is wrong but because of anomalies in the financial sector.

What is wrong, then, with relying on exchange rate devaluations as competitive tools? Indeed, exchange rate devaluation does not always lead to the solution of trade disequilibria. First of all, as Shaikh states, there is the elasticity problem. If the price elasticity of exports is low and the price elasticity of imports is high, the devaluation can only worsen the situation. Secondly, a related issue is the fallacies of composition argument. If the overall demand elasticity of an exportable item is low, as in the case of agricultural and primary commodities, competitive devaluations among producer countries will only make the situation worse. Thirdly, even though the benefits of having a 'realistic exchange rate' are not a matter of debate, relying only on exchange rate devaluation is wrong. There might be many cases in which devaluations cannot help. For example, when there is a demand shock for exportable commodities, relying only on exchange rate devaluation can make matters worse. Fourthly, devaluations make importable commodities more expensive. As many developing countries depend on the importation of capital goods, this may limit their development. Controls on imports might be a better alternative to devaluations.

Fifthly, exchange rate devaluations are non-discriminatory and lead countries to specialize in commodities for which they have a comparative advantage and that may not serve well their long-run development. What countries need to do is to promote specific industries by reallocating some of the surplus from the competitive sectors. Thus, industrial policy, as well as a realistic exchange rate, is necessary to change the current cost structure.

In our view Shaikh's criticism of CAT has limited success and his narrow focus on trade disequilibrium is misplaced. His arguments are accurate only within the limits of the theoretical framework he works in. For him, comparative advantage means free trade and any diversion from free trade represents a diversion from CAT and signifies the accuracy of AAT. Trade policy, however, would not confront CAT unless it is designed to change existing relative cost structure.[33] In other words, if intervention is only designed to restore trade equilibrium without changing the underlying relative cost structure, it would only affirm specialization based on comparative advantage. In the same manner, a trade disequilibrium does not denote inaccuracy of CAT. Countries can have trade disequilibrium for many reasons. A relative demand fall for their export commodities for instance, may cause short or long-term disequilibrium.

International competitiveness can be achieved either by increasing the productivity of exportables or by devaluing the currency. Shaikh exclusively focuses on the former and ignores the importance of the latter. It is obvious that competitiveness based on productivity increase is more beneficial. Countries, however, do compete with devaluations. Many developing countries, for instance, rely more on competitive devaluations.[34] In what follows, we will show that, in a three-good model, exchange rate devaluations does matter for a country's competitiveness.

In a model where there are three goods, exportables, importables and home goods (or non-tradables) and international prices of the tradables are externally given (small country assumption) the aim of exchange rate devaluations is to change the prices of tradables relative to non-tradables. Indeed, when a currency is devalued, the relative prices of exportables and importables would both increase compared to home goods. Thus, the impact of devaluation is to encourage production of exportables as well as importables and to discourage the domestic consumption of both commodities. Obviously, by definition importables refer to commodities that have relatively high costs. Devaluations, thus, are designed to make exportable commodities internationally competitive first. As argued earlier, however, a country may become internationally competitive in all the tradable commodities that it produces by competitive devaluations. Whether this will be beneficial to its economy is another matter. Once the exportable commodities can profitably be exported and trade is balanced, there is no reason to continue with devaluation.

Let us substantiate these arguments with the following example. For the sake of simplicity, in a country (say Portugal), the pre-trade domestic prices of exportables (P_X), importables (P_M) and home goods (P_H) are assumed to be the same and determined by the cost of production:

$$P_X = P_M = P_H$$

Given this domestic price structure, by definition, the international prices of exportables (P_{XI}) must be higher than importables (P_{MI}).

$$P_{XI} > P_{MI}{}^{35}$$

Before free trade begins, Portugal has an absolute disadvantage in both tradable goods. This means that the domestic prices of tradables, expressed in a common international currency (say in the U.S. dollar – given the prevailing exchange rate ER), are higher than the international prices.

$$ER.P_X > P_{XI} \text{ and } ER.P_M > P_{MI}$$

When free trade starts, Portugal either must import both commodities and in that case there will be a persistent trade deficit until the exchange rate is devalued,[36] or the producers of both commodities must reduce their domestic prices $(P_{XI}$ and $P_{MI})$ and therefore suffer from profit losses. If the exchange rate stays constant:

$$ER.P_{XI} = P_{XI} \text{ and } ER.P_{MI} = P_{MI}$$

where

$$P_{XI} < P_X \text{ and } P_{MI} < P_M$$

As the international price of importables is lower than the international price of exportables, the price of importables would fall more than exportables:

$$P_{XI} > P_{MI}$$

This would increase the relative domestic price and profitability of home goods compared to tradables:

$$P_H > P_{XI} > P_{MI}$$

If the exchange rate is devalued (ER_1) until the price of exportables reaches its pre-trade level,

$$ER_1.P_X = P_{XI}$$

The pre-trade price level for importables, however, would be still uncompetitive,

$$ER_1.P_M > P_{MI} \text{ or } ER_1.P_{M2} = P_{MI}$$

Thus, the domestic price of importables (P_{M2}) would stay lower than the exportables and act as a disincentive for the domestic producers.

$$P_H = P_X > P_{M2} \text{ where } P_M > P_{M2} > P_{MI}$$

As a result of free trade, the producers of importables would become uncompetitive and gradually leave the market. It is important to note that, after specialization takes place, the domestic relative prices of home goods and exportables would be the same as pre-trade level. The relative price of importables, however, would decline compared to both exportables and home goods. This makes sense since a decline in the relative price of importables would discourage the domestic production of importables. The relative price of exportables and home goods would stay the same, and both would be produced domestically.[37] As a result this model does not imply an abandonment of the labor value theory.

The above implies that, as free trade takes place, the relative price of importables would change in comparison to exportables and home goods. The relative price of exportables to home goods would stay the same. The first impact of free trade is to change the relative price of tradables or the terms of trade. This is because the international relative prices of tradables determine the domestic relative prices. Once specialization takes place, however, the terms of trade are fixed and devaluations cannot change them.

Devaluations can only change the prices of tradables relative to home goods. For example, suppose there is inflation in the economy, which increases domestic prices. As the international prices of tradables are fixed and externally determined, the relative price of home goods will increase against tradables. The profitability for exportables will decline and exporters will become uncompetitive in international markets. This 'overvaluation' of the exchange rate is good for imports as the relative price of imports is now lower. The same is not true for exporters. The lower prices of tradables, although they increase imports by encouraging people to consume more importable goods, they also decrease exports by discouraging the producers of exportable goods. The result is an increasing trade deficit. Devaluation becomes necessary to change the prices of tradables relative to home goods. Once the currency is devalued, the relative price of tradables would increase and the external balance would be restored. The devaluation would increase the relative prices of both tradable goods and by doing so would decrease the demand for importables and encourage the production of exportables. Thus a devaluation influences importables in two ways. First, it decreases the consumption of importables by increasing their relative prices and secondly, if sufficient, it encourages the domestic production of importables. In other words, devaluation has two functions: it promotes exports and substitutes imports. These arguments, of course, go against the conventional views on import-substitution and export-promotion.

B. The Assumptions: Hudson's Critique

As mentioned earlier, the assumptions of the theory have attracted most of the criticism. Hudson (1992) has summarized these assumptions and criticized them in detail. This section will not explain all the debates surrounding the assumptions of the theory but it will highlight some of the problems of these criticisms. It will be argued that most critiques (although valid) do not nullify the theory. The theory indeed runs into difficulties as a result of some of its extreme assumptions. Nevertheless, the basic arguments of the theory, which aim to justify trade based on comparative cost, survive even when the assumptions are relaxed.

One important assumption in the model is constant returns to scale. As a simplifying assumption, constant returns to scale is helpful but it obviously distorts reality. In real life constant returns to scale are not often observed. To drop this assumption, however, in no way invalidates the theory. Neither increasing nor diminishing returns to scale would fundamentally alter Ricardo's arguments.

Partial specialization is the rule when there are diminishing returns to scale. Increasing returns to scale would in fact strengthen the case for trade based on comparative advantage. As the "new" growth theories argue, the total gain from specialization would be even greater. Increasing returns to scale, however, would violate the assumption of perfectly competitive markets and require short-term protectionist policies due to the fact that short- and long-term comparative advantages might be different. The modification attempts under monopolistic markets and the dynamic versions of the theory are extensive and will not be covered here. However, Hudson's argument that 'increasing returns have steadily widened the cost advantages enjoyed by industrial lead-nations vis-à-vis less developed countries' (Hudson, 1992, p. 122) is not particularly accurate. Hudson argues that

> [a]griculture and other primary production in the nineteenth century were characterised by moderately increasing returns while industrial productivity increased by leaps and bounds. [Thus] even if agricultural productivity did not increase, England's production-possibility curve in the Ricardian example would rise in cloth making. But Portugal, which chose to specialise in wine or other agricultural commodities under the dictates of free trade, would suffer an opportunity cost for not having industrialised (Hudson, 1992, p. 123).

The fact that productivity increases more in the industrial sector than in agriculture is not a matter of concern for the Ricardian model. In fact the theory implies that the terms of trade would improve for primary and agricultural commodity producers as a result of the different levels of productivity increase. The prices of industrial products would diminish as a result of high productivity increase whereas the relative prices of agricultural goods would increase. The prices of non-renewable resources would also increase as the supply of such commodities is limited by nature and their demand increases with economic development. As Hudson notes, it is particularly ironic that when Ricardo analyzed trade, he neglected diminishing returns on land, which was the backbone of the theory he used in arguing against the Corn Laws. As was revealed earlier, however, from the logic of this theory, diminishing returns on land would not act against the agricultural sector because Ricardo argued that an increasing share of total value-added would accrue to agricultural sector (landlords). This would reduce the share of profits of the industrial sector as agricultural production moved onto less productive lands. Thus, if anything, specialization in agriculture would only be more beneficial.

The argument by Hudson implies that if productivity had increased faster in the agricultural sector than in the industrial sector, agricultural producers would have been in a better position. This is not so. In fact if productivity increase in agriculture had been faster, it would have reduced the relative demand for these commodities even faster and the producers would have been in even greater difficulty. As will be argued later, the real problem with specializing in agricultural products is not that productivity increases slower than in the industrial sector but rather that the agriculture in general is a low skill, low value-added activity and there is a limited and relatively diminishing market demand for the agricultural commodities.

Another important assumption of the theory is that each country can produce the entire range of traded commodities. In Ricardo's example, for instance, England and Portugal can both produce wine and cloth. This is obviously an unrealistic assumption. Thus, Hudson argues that if in Ricardo's example England and Portugal can only produce one of the commodities, comparative advantage theory becomes obscure since '[n]o comparative-cost lines could be constructed if England could not produce wine, and Portugal could not produce cloth' (Hudson, 1992, p. 122). It may also be the case that England could only produce cloth whilst Portugal could produce both commodities. This argument against Ricardo's theory, however, is irrelevant. In the first case both countries have absolute advantage in a particular commodity and there is a case for free trade. The relative cost of producing an unproducible commodity in both countries could be seen as infinitely high. In the second case, England has a comparative advantage in cloth production, as the relative cost of producing wine is infinite.

Another often-criticized assumption of the theory is related to the idea that only consumption goods are traded. The theory excludes trade in common factor inputs. Thus, Hudson argues that this theory only applies to

> trade in consumption goods not to trade in production goods or raw materials. Ricardo's reasoning would be undercut by trade in capital goods, raw materials or any other production inputs capable either of altering international endowments and productivity. [...] For instance, exporting capital goods would violate his assumption of fixed factor productivity among nations (after all, the purpose of importing machinery is to improve production functions) (Hudson, 1992, p. 126).

This is an important critique of the neoclassical version of the comparative advantage theory. The Heckscher-Ohlin theory of comparative advantage predicts specialization based on factor endowments. If factors of production are internationally mobile, there can be no specialization based on factor endowments. This critique, however, also does not shake the fundamental logic of Ricardo's theory. Indeed, the post-trade relative cost structure in both countries might be rather different from the pre-trade relative cost structure. As a result of the importation of capital goods, for example, England (Portugal) may become relatively more productive in wine (cloth). In this case, England (Portugal) would specialize in wine (cloth) production even though its pre-trade comparative advantage was in cloth (wine). As long as relative costs are different, there is a case for specialization and trade based on comparative costs.

Probably the most criticized assumption of the theory is that of the full employment of all resources (labor and capital). There are two reasons for this criticism. First, comparative advantage theory is based on the concept of opportunity cost. Opportunity cost can be defined as the opportunities foregone in undertaking one activity measured in terms of the other possibilities that might have been pursued using the same expenditure of resources. Opportunity cost is based on the assumption of full employment of all resources. For example, the opportunity cost of producing wine for England (Portugal) is cloth (wine) production that has been foregone and which could be more beneficial. If all resources were not fully employed, however, the opportunity cost would be zero as idle resources could be employed in the production of both commodities. That is why, it could be argued that the emphasis should be on how to employ these idle resources rather than on efficiency considerations.

Secondly, the full employment assumption guarantees that there is no employment loss as a result of free trade and specialization. Labor and capital are assumed to be fully mobile between the sectors and can be shifted from one sector to the other without causing unemployment. It is obviously unrealistic to assume that the wine (cloth) producers in England (Portugal) would move from rural (urban) areas to urban (rural) areas, change their lifestyle and learn the necessary skills to produce cloth (wine). Neither is it realistic to assume that capital is homogenous and can be transferred from the production of wine (cloth) to the production of cloth (wine). Structural inflexibilities may cause long-term unemployment of factors and may eliminate the benefits of trade.

These critiques are indeed important and damage the free trade idea based on comparative advantage theory. They do not, however, completely invalidate the basic arguments of the theory. First, even though policies to employ un-employed resources might be more important than a gain from static-efficiency through specialization, there still exists a static opportunity cost when the resources are employed in producing the commodities of which a country has a comparative disadvantage. In the case of England (Portugal) for example, resources would bring higher returns if they were employed in cloth (wine) production than wine (cloth) production. Thus, when less than full employment is assumed, the static-efficiency argument is weakened but not completely refuted.

The immobility of the resources is also a valid critique of the free market arguments but not of specialization based on comparative advantage. It may indeed be very difficult to shift resources from the production of one commodity to another. However, this transition from more diversified to more specialized production might be a gradual process rather than a rapid one. A country may direct new resources into the production of commodities for which it has a comparative advantage. Thus, even though England (Portugal) cannot remove resources from wine (cloth) production immediately to cloth (wine) production, the production of wine (cloth) could gradually be discouraged and the production of cloth (wine) could be encouraged. The government of England (Portugal), for example, could initially protect the wine (cloth) producers from foreign competition but then gradually reduce this protection to discourage wine (cloth) production. Thus, it can direct new resources into the production of cloth (wine) rather than wine (cloth).

V. THE REAL PROBLEMS OF THE RICARDIAN MODEL

So far in this article it has been argued that, in its simplest static form, Ricardo's theory of comparative advantage holds out against the criticisms. When the extreme assumptions are modified, the implications of the theory change to a certain extent. The theory remains intact as a justification for international trade.

There are, however, three fundamental problems with the theory. The first one is its lack of clarity on how the benefits of trade are distributed among the participant countries. The second one is its static nature. And the last one is its simplistic interpretation of labor theory of value.

The first important problem in Ricardo's theory concerns with how the extra 'sum of enjoyments' that are created as a result of trade, are distributed between countries. The model simply assumes that both countries benefit from the specialization in specific commodities as total production increases. As long as both countries benefit, they will be willing to participate in international trade. Their willingness, however, will be determined by how much they gain from trading. If all or most of the benefits from trade are captured only by one country, the other may not be willing to participate in trade. To demonstrate these arguments, Fig. 1 is reorganized in an Edgeworth box.

In Fig. 2, both countries are plotted into the same figure. The area between the two solid lines represents the possible gains from specialization and trade. The broken line in the middle represents the relative prices of both commodities in both countries after trade. As trade takes place, both countries face the same prices for both commodities and move onto this line. The gain from trade for each country depends on where this broken line is placed between the solid lines, as it is determined by the changes in the relative prices of the tradable commodities. The larger the relative price change, the bigger the benefit will be. For example, England would benefit more if the broken line was closer to Portugal's pre-trade relative price line. The same is true for Portugal. In the figure, point 'E' represents a gain for both countries as they increase the consumption of both commodities. Obviously, the broken line could be anywhere between the solid lines and there are no clear-cut rules to predict where it will be. The determinant factor for the location of the broken line is the policy mix of the two countries.

It is possible that the broken line may be placed on any of the solid lines indicating that one country does not benefit from trade due to a lack of change in relative prices after trade. It is also possible that the broken line may lie not between the solid lines, indicating that one country will lose as a result of trade.

As mentioned before, the logic of the theory suggests that in the absence of any intervention England, as the less productive country, would obtain most of the benefits of trade. The broken line would be very close to (or on) Portugal's pre-trade solid line. Thus Portugal would not benefit much from trade. The reason for this is as follows.

From the above example it is obvious that a marginal price reduction[38] would be enough to make England's cloth competitive as the pre-trade price is same in both countries. This can be demonstrated in Table 3.[39]

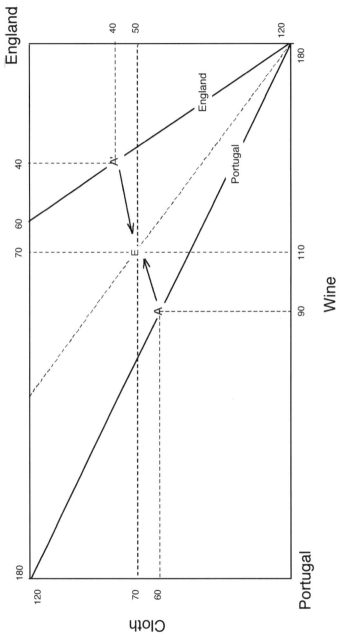

Fig. 2. Gains from Trade (Reorganized in an Edgeworth Box).

Table 3. Comparative Advantage and the Gains from Trade.

	Price (Before Trade)		Price (After Trade)	
	Portugal	England	Portugal	England
Wheat	0.55	1.66	0.55	0.55
Cloth	0.83	0.83	0.82	0.82
Wheat to cloth ratio	0.66	2.00	0.67	0.67

Initially the price of cloth is the same in both countries and wine is cheaper in Portugal. When England devalues its currency, cloth producers in England become more competitive and England specializes in cloth production. When specialization occurs, England produces only cloth and Portugal produces only wine. As a result of free trade, the prices of the commodities will converge and a single international price will be formed. The international price of wine will be the same as Portugal's pre-trade price and the international price of cloth will be marginally less than the pre-trade price in both countries. As the table shows, the relative price fall of wine in England[40] is much greater than the relative price fall of cloth in Portugal.[41] As a result, the broken line in Fig. 2 will move very close to the solid line of Portugal. Thus, if we ignore the marginal price change, Portugal will not benefit from trade. England will be the only beneficiary.

The above argument suggests that the benefits of trade for Portugal are determined by the extent of the price reduction, which is required to make England's cloth competitive. If a marginal fall is enough, Portugal will not benefit much from trade. In such circumstances, one option open to Portugal is to put a tax on its imports to force England to reduce its cloth price further. In fact by using import taxes, Portugal may force England to reduce its prices to the limit where England only marginally benefits from this trade. In this case the broken line in the figure would be very close to England's solid line. Of course, England may retaliate and also put an import tax on wine.

In this model free trade is more beneficial to a country that has an absolute disadvantage. The other country, therefore, has every incentive to use import taxes to increase its share from this trade. Here, import taxes are not adopted to protect domestic producers but to transfer the benefits of trade. The significance of the above arguments is that international trade is never a smooth process based on mutual benefits but is essentially an unstable process exhibiting fundamental conflicts between countries.

The second important problem of the theory is related to its static nature. Ricardo's theory is based on a short-term static-efficiency gains through specialization and 'implies that nations should live permanently in the short-run rather than maximizing their productive power over time. This reasoning leaves open to protectionists the reply that the theory of comparative cost does not help build a better bridge to the future but leaves less developed countries stranded in a chronic low-productivity present' (Hudson, 1992, p. 116). When there is free trade, developing countries may indeed specialize in commodities for which they have comparative advantage as the theory predicts. This is precisely why they should avoid adopting free trade policies that may not be to their advantage in the long run.

The problem of the static nature of the theory is well recognized in the literature. The recent 'dynamic' versions of comparative advantage also do not overcome the shortcomings of the theory. As we have discussed elsewhere in more detail, dynamic comparative advantage is misleading since comparative advantage is by its nature a static concept (Subasat, 2000). Comparative advantage refers to specialization based on static (short- or long-run) relative cost which conditions the options of policymakers. It is something that guides the policymakers in the production of a particular commodity. If competitiveness is created by the policymaker's conscious decisions, however, comparative advantage becomes an empty concept.

The third problem with the theory is related to its simplistic treatment of labor value theory. The theory, at the highest level of abstraction, assumes that commodities are exchanged according to their values.[42] In turn, the value of a commodity is determined by the necessary labor time employed to produce it. For example, if it takes two hours to produce one unit of wine and it takes one hour to produce one unit of cloth, then one unit of wine will be exchanged for two units of cloth. This is, however, an abstraction as two different types of labor power are considered as one for simplification purposes. It is simply assumed that one labor hour creates an equal amount of value in wine and in cloth production.

In reality, however, this is not true as the different types of labor power have different characteristics. Marx recognizes this and explains it in terms of 'complex' and 'simple' labour.[43] According to Marx, '[m]ore complex labour counts only as *intensified*, or rather *multiplied* simple labour, so that a smaller quantity of complex labour is considered equal to a larger quantity of simple labour' Marx (1990, p. 135). For example, the value created by spending one labor hour in computer engineering is not equal to the value created by spending one hour in shoe polishing. In reality there are high skill, high technology and high value-added jobs as well as low skill, low technology and low value-added jobs. Some jobs bring higher income than others, not because there is an unequal exchange between them, but simply because some types of labor power create higher value than others.

From this point of view, it is possible to argue that specialization will not benefit some countries and will not benefit some individuals. In societies, a division of labor is inevitable and it increases productivity by saving labor time. It is, however, not true that everybody benefits equally from this specialization. It is probably better to be the worst off doctor in business than the best earning street sweeper. From an individual's point of view, it is disadvantageous to specialize in street sweeping. In society, some members might be forced to specialize in certain professions. This is not necessarily true for countries. As a consequence of the division of labor, an individual may have no other option but to specialize in low skill jobs. For a country, however, specialization in low skill, low technology and low value-added commodities would imply being poor forever.

This is not exploitation through exchange (or unequal exchange) but simply wrong specialization. It is beneficial for individuals as well as countries to try to specialize in commodities that bring long-term benefits. Thus, there is a fundamental conflict in international markets, which is similar to the conflict in society. Not all participants in international trade will benefit equally from specialization in the same way as not everyone will benefit equally from specializing on low value-added jobs. It is the nature of jobs and commodities, which determines how one will benefit from specialization.

In reality, there are various reasons why income from different occupations may vary. The class structure and technological changes can be considered as the two most important reasons. The class struggle over the economic surplus is the basic focus of Marxist theory. On the other hand, new technologies may also create income inequality in the society by skilling and de-skilling the labor force. Increasing computerization, for example, creates, on the one hand, highly skilled and well-paid professionals, such as computer programmers, and on the other hand, it de-skills some professions such as the cashiers at the checkout who are poorly paid.

The above argument implies that it is simply wrong to specialize in low-skill, low technology and low-income commodities. It is also wrong to specialize in commodities for which there is no future demand. Individuals as well as the countries, which specialize in commodities that are not and will not be demanded will suffer as a result of this specialization. Consequently, what matters is not specialization itself but the commodities in which individuals and countries specialize.

VI. CONCLUSION

Stiglitz (1998, p. 15), the ex vice-president of the World Bank, accepts that '[t]rade liberalisation is neither necessary nor sufficient for creating a competitive and innovative economy' and he does 'not fully understand the process by which trade liberalisation leads to enhanced productivity', but he blindly sticks to the predictions of the standard comparative advantage theory and argues that import-substitution policies proved to be a highly ineffective strategy for development. By ignoring the compelling evidence against, he still insists that the East Asian countries are a powerful example of the benefits of free trade based on comparative advantage.

The assertion that unrestricted international trade is beneficial to all participating countries, however, is contested by the fact that free trade has always been favored by stronger economies.[44] Most countries developed behind protective barriers, and allowed free trade only after they succeeded in developing international competitiveness.[45] The world is disorderly and fractured, in which the observed reality is uneven development. As an Oxfam report argues, '[t]his approach ignores the fundamental reality of the market place: namely, that [countries] enter markets as unequal partners, and they leave them with rewards, which reflect those inequalities' Oxfam (1995).

The primary proposition of this paper is that, from the perspective of developing countries, international trade is neither inherently good nor bad. Trade has the power to create opportunities and it has the power to destroy livelihoods. Behind the elegant theories of free trade lies a basic fallacy. Free trade and specialization based on comparative advantage bring benefits to some but not all countries. The liberalization process does not produce a natural tendency towards mutual benefit. It creates further disequilibrium and conflict. This is because the nature of the capitalist production processes creates a tendency toward increasing centralization and concentration of production, which lead to uneven development and crises. As a result of this centralization and concentration, the 'existing advantages are reinforced and the resulting spatial distribution of economic activity is likely to exhibit strong divergence, leading to increasing inequalities within and between regions' (Kozul-Wright, 1995, p. 138). Consequently, the strong countries will increase their lead and a process of uneven development will result. 'Some countries will become advanced centres of modern industry with high wages, rapid capital investment and excellent public services; others will become backward raw material producers without the technical capacity to modernise on an autonomous basis' (Brett, 1985, p. 58). This explains how 'even' development under capitalism is impossible. The unplanned and anarchic nature of capitalism creates uneven development over time (boom and bust periods) and over space (developed and developing countries).

The above argument implies that no trade policy will serve all countries equally, be it free trade or protectionism. Free trade policies accelerate and reinforce uneven development on a larger scale. Alternative interventionist trade policies cannot solve all problems either. Uneven development is intrinsic to the capitalist development process, unless there is conscious management of the world economy. The implications of this argument for neoclassical as well as structuralist theories is overwhelming. The failure of many countries to solve their development problems and the persistent crises are the result of the natural functioning of the system, not the result of the incompetence of policymakers. The development process is a non-linear and complex process and no simple rules can be advised to developing countries. Explaining development in a particular country does not imply the possibility of generating development elsewhere.

This argument is a rather sad yet realistic view of the world. Nevertheless, uneven development does not imply an absolute barrier that keeps developing and developed countries apart. It does not mean that developing countries are trapped in underdevelopment and cannot break free from their subordination. They can indeed progress, and in some cases they may even join the ranks of the developed countries. Moreover, the above arguments do not confront the necessity of more pragmatic and sensible trade policies. Underdevelopment is not their destiny. There are alternatives to the free market orthodoxy. Development requires far more interference with the free market than what is recommended by neoclassical and many structuralist theories. Unless governments take radical steps to limit the functioning of the market mechanism, there is not much scope for a successful transformation of the world economy within a more progressive framework.

NOTES

1. In other words, this article will not attempt to develop a comprehensive Marxist theory of international trade that would involve class relations.

2. Exploitation through exchange is the core argument of the dependency view and criticized by the classical Marxists.

3. Thus, Smith wrote that, "if a nation could be separated from all the world, it would be of no consequence how much, or how little money circulated in it. The consumable goods which were circulated by means of this money would only be exchanged for a greater or a smaller number of pieces; but the real wealth or poverty of the country, they allow, would depend altogether upon the abundance or scarcity of those consumable goods" (Smith, 1991, p. 377).

4. This view is very close to what are nowadays called 'dynamic comparative advantage' arguments.

5. He assumed that workers were paid wages at a subsistence level.

6. For more detail, see Hudson (1992) and Edwards (1985).

7. Ironically, when Malthus argued against the 'Poor Laws' which increased the government's budget deficit and annoyed the higher classes, he preferred not to see the productivity increase on land.

8. So much so that Marx even completely excluded the agricultural sector from his analysis.

9. Commodity money (gold), expressed in pounds, i.e. 'in England around Ricardo's time, roughly 1/4 ounce of gold was known as a "pound" (£)' (Shaikh, 1980, p. 285).

10. In Ricardo's original example both commodities are cheaper in Portugal than England. Here, for the sake of the simplicity of the graphical demonstration one commodity is kept at the same price level.

11. When all workers, say 100, are employed.

12. This example is borrowed from Salvatore (1995).

13. The slope of the BE line is equal to the slope of the B'E' line.

14. For a critical review of the neo-classical comparative advantage theory see Subasat (forthcoming).

15. A detailed critique of the Heckscher-Ohlin model can be found in Subasat (forthcoming).

16. Some, however, argue that he changed his mind later. See for example Lapides (1998).

17. The static nature of the model is well recognized in the trade literature where there are attempts to create a more dynamic version of the theory. As we have argued elsewhere, however, 'dynamic comparative advantage' is a contradictory concept. Comparative advantage is, by its nature, static theory and cannot be dynamic. See Subasat (2000) for further details of the argument.

18. Alternatively, England may barrow from Portugal to finance its trade deficit. This, however, is a temporary measure, as England cannot finance its trade deficit in the long run by external borrowing and "would have to eventually pay back not only the original loan, but also the interest on it" (Shaikh, 1980, p. 39).

19. Sau (1982, p. 13) also agrees with Shaikh's argument on the QTM, but argues that '[Shaikh] overlooked the totality of Marx's views on foreign trade, which are far more complex and fundamental. To give a minor example, in Marx's analytical framework there is an adjustment mechanism which in today's jargon would appear close to the Keynesian foreign trade multiplier'.

20. Here we drop Ricardo's controversial assumption of full employment.

21. As argued earlier, England may barrow from Portugal to finance its trade deficit temporarily, which will eventually be paid back.

22. As opposed to Ricardo's mechanism where the inflation (deflation) mechanism starts working immediately after trade begins.

23. In this case, England represents the low-productivity developing country and its currency is not internationally accepted.

24. A measure of real exchange rate in two-country/two-good model.

25. The relative price of wine (cloth) to cloth (wine) for Portugal (England).

26. Shaikh uses countries A and B, and capital and consumption goods in his article.

27. Even if relative price changes could balance trade, this specialization may not be in the interest of Portugal that has to reduce the price of wine in order to increase demand. This may signify an absolute loss for Portugal and all benefits of trade will be transferred to England.

28. $RER = ER*P_{WP}/P_{WE}$, where ER is nominal exchange rate, P_{WP} is the price of wine in Portugal in domestic currency and P_{WE} is the price of wine in England in international currency.

29. This assumes that there is no foreign borrowing. If there were foreign borrowing to cover trade deficit, there would be no specialization.

30. That is the reason why we have earlier argued that one country may end up with producing both commodities, partial specialization.

31. $RER = ER*P_{WP}/P_{WI}$ where ER is nominal exchange rate, P_{WP} is the domestic price of wine in Portugal in domestic currency and P_{WI} is the international price of wine in international currency.

32. In his 1998 article Shaikh exclusively focuses on trade disequilibrium between the USA and Japan. He argues that this persistent disequilibrium is a reflection of their relative cost structure and such imbalance is a perfectly general phenomenon. It is beyond the aims of this article to evaluate this work in detail and we will only highlight the following anomaly. Even though Sheikh's focus on such disequilibrium is justified, it is a mistake to generalize it. In fact an observation of the OECD countries prove that; with an exception of a number of EU countries such as Greece, Portugal and Spain that receive financial resources from the rest of the EU; most have perfectly balanced trade.

33. Separating free trade policy from comparative advantage theory, Schydlowsky (1984, p. 447) goes too far and argues that there is no real contradiction between structuralism and comparative advantage theory. He states that CAT is well known in Latin America, but not by that name. Rather it is called industrialization policy that is associated with structuralism.

34. The fact that per capita GNP underestimates the level of economic development in developing countries is an evidence of this claim. When competitiveness is achieved as a result of productivity increase, the nominal exchange rate tends to appreciate. Devaluations, however, reduce average domestic prices in international currency units (i.e. U.S. dollar). This is a well-known fact and unless price differences as a result of exchange rate devaluations are taken into account, per capita GNP underestimates the level of economic development in developing countries. In order to have a more accurate measure of economic development, per capita GNP levels need to be adjusted with the price level.

35. Or more correctly: $(P_{XI}/P_X) > (P_{MI}/P_M)$.

36. Note that a fall in the nominal exchange rate (ER) implies a depreciation of the currency.

37. Theoretically, the exchange rate could be devalued (ER_2) until when the importables also become competitive. In this case, however, the exchange rate would be 'overvalued'. Producers of exportables would make extra profits (P_X would rise to P_{X2}). $ER_2.P_{X2} = P_{XI}$ and $ER_2.P_M = P_{MI}$ where $P_{X2} > P_X > P_{X1}$.

38. From 0.83 to 0.82 which could be achieved by an exchange rate devaluation.

39. The first part (pre-trade price level) of Table 4 is the same as in Table 2.

40. From 2.00 to 0.67.

41. The wine/cloth ratio increases from 0.66 to 0.67.

42. This is obviously a simplification. Commodities are not exchanged for their exact values and their market prices will be modified by different capital-labor ratios, scarcities, skills, monopolies, and tastes (Fine 1975, p. 22).

43. Or 'skilled labor power' and 'unskilled labor power'.

44. Brett (1985, p. 52). 'The weak have always taken a much less enthusiastic view, since they were always more likely to find that their markets would be taken away from them by the more efficient foreign producers unless the state intervened to erect protective barriers behind which they would shelter' Weiss (1997, p. 13).

45. It is not surprising that free trade theory emerged in the United Kingdom, the first industrialized country. In the 19th and early 20th centuries, continental Europe or the United States did not echo the demand for freer trade. On the contrary, they were firmly protectionist. It was not until the end of the Second World War, when the United States became the strongest trading country, that its government advocated free trade. The then-weakened United Kingdom, together with all other European countries, remained protectionist until the 1960s.

ACKNOWLEDGMENTS

The author would like to thank Anwar Shaikh and Alfredo Saad Filho for very useful email exchanges.

REFERENCES

Bettelheim, C. (1972). Theoretical Comments. In: A. Emmanuel, *Unequal Exchange: A Study of the Imperialism of Trade* (Appendix I, pp. 271–322). New York: Monthly Review Press.

Brett, E. A. (1985). *The World Economy Since the War: The Politics of Uneven Development.* London: Macmillan.

Carchedi, G. (1986). Comparative Advantages, Capital Accumulation and Socialism. *Economy and Society, 15*(4), 427–444.

Carchedi, G. (1991). *Frontiers of Political Economy.* London: Verso.

Edwards, C. (1985). *The Fragmented World: Competing Perspectives on Trade, Money and Crisis.* London: Methuen.

Emmanuel, A. (1972). *Unequal Exchange: A Study of the Imperialism of Trade.* London: NLB.

Emmanuel, A. (1975). *Unequal exchange revisited.* University of Sussex, Institute of Development Studies.

Fine, B. (1975). *Marx's Capital.* London: Macmillan.

Gomes, L. (1987). *Foreign Trade and the National Economy: Mercantilist and Classical Perspectives.* London: Macmillan.

Hudson, M. (1992). *Trade, Development and Foreign Debt,* Volume I. London: Pluto.

Hudson, M. (1992). *Trade, Development and Foreign Debt,* Volume II. London: Pluto.

Kozul-Wright, R. (1995). Transnational Corporations and the Nation State. In: J. Michie & J. G. Smith (Eds), *Managing the Global Economy.* Oxford: Oxford University Press.

Krugman, P. (1998). Ricardo's Difficult Idea: Why Intellectuals Don't Understand Comparative Advantage. In: G. Cook (Ed.), *The Economics and Politics of International Trade.* London: Routledge.

Lapides, K. (1998). *Marx's Wage Theory in Historical Perspective: Its Origins, Development, and Interpretation*. Westport, Conn.: Praeger.

Marx, K. (1990). *Capital*, Vol. I. London: Penguin.

Oxfam (1995). *The Oxfam Poverty Report*. Oxford: Oxfam.

Ricardo, D. (1992). *Principles of Political Economy and Taxation*. London: Everyman's Library.

Salvatore, D. (1995). *International Economics*. New Jersey: Prentice Hall.

Sau, R. (1982). *Trade, Capital and Underdevelopment: Towards a Marxist Theory*. Oxford: Oxford University Press.

Schydlowsky, D. M. (1984). A Policymaker's Guide to Comparative Advantage. *World Development, 12*(4), 439–449.

Shaikh, A. (1980). Foreign Trade and the Law of Value: Part II. *Science and Society, XLIV*.

Shaikh, A. (1995). Free Trade, Unemployment, and Economic Policy. In: J. Eatwell (Ed.), *Global Unemployment: Loss of Jobs in the '90s*. New York: M. E. Sharpe.

Shaikh, A. (1999a). Real Exchange rates and the International mobility of Capital. Working Paper No. 265, New School University.

Shaikh, A. (1999b). *Explaining the U.S. Trade deficit*. Testimony before the Trade Deficit review Commission, Washington, D.C.

Singer, H. W. (1984). The Terms of Trade Controversy and the Evolution of Soft Financing: Early Years in the UN. In: G. M. Meier & D. Seers (Eds), *Pioneers in Development*. New York: Oxford University Press for the World Bank.

Smith, A. (1991). *The Wealth of Nations*. London: David Campbell Publishers Ltd.

Steedman, I. (2002). *Marx After Sraffa and the Open Economy*. A paper presented at the 4th Annual Conference of the Association for Heterodox Economics, Dublin, July 9–10, 2002.

Stiglitz, J. (1998). *More Instruments and Broader Goals: Moving Toward the Post-Washington Consensus*. Helsinki: The 1998 WIDER Annual Lecture.

Subasat, T. (forthcoming). What does the Heckscher-Ohlin model contribute to international trade theory?: A critical assessment. *Review of Radical Political Economy*.

Subasat, T. (2000). *Export-led Development: A Theoretical and Empirical Investigation*. Ph.D., School of Oriental and African Studies, University of London.

UNDP (United Nations Development Programme) (1998). *Human Development Report, 1998*. Oxford: Oxford University Press.

Weeks, J. (1991). Unequal Exchange. In: T. Bottomore, L. Harris, V. G. Kiernan & R. Miliband (Eds), *A Dictionary of Marxist Thought*. Oxford: Blackwell.

Weiss, L. (1997). Globalization and the Myth of the Powerless State. *New Left Review, 225*, 3–27.

THE MARKET AS DISCIPLINARY ORDER: A COMPARATIVE ANALYSIS OF HAYEK AND BENTHAM[1]

Massimo De Angelis

ABSTRACT

This paper compares Hayek's market order (supposedly maximising individual freedom) and the social order arising out of Bentham's panopticon (an institution of confinement, surveillance and extraction of labor). Although at first the two institutions appear to belong to two quite different categories, the author identifies at least eight similarities between the two orders and argues that both are disciplinary mechanisms faced by individuals whose "freedom" is confined to a range of choices set by an agency outside them (the "planner"). This opens the way to understand the contemporary market order as a modality of power that rests on the panoptical principle of "seeing without being seen".

I. INTRODUCTION

The argument of this paper is that a socially pervasive market order such as the one we inhabit presents organizational and disciplinary characteristics that are similar to those of a prison, not just any prison, and not simply a prison, but an "inspection house", as understood by Jeremy Bentham who, in the late XVIII century, enthusiastically designed what he called "the panopticon" in

Confronting 9-11, Ideologies of Race, and Eminent Economists,
Research in Political Economy, Volume 20, pages 293–317.
Copyright © 2002 by Elsevier Science Ltd.
All rights of reproduction in any form reserved.
ISBN: 0-7623-0984-9

order to extract work from the inmates and deal with emerging problems of social control. The reader may find this comparison odd, if not paradoxical. After all, the market and the panopticon seem to inhabit two different universes. The former, following the narrative of its promoters, is the galaxy of freedom, the order of a *cosmos*, emerging as an unintended result of the interaction of choices freely made by individuals. The latter is the constellation of dungeons, the *taxis* designed by the freedom of the planner who holds with a grip the lives of the subjects of the plan and who has a project in mind and wants to put it to work. Friedrich Hayek, the paladin of market freedom and spontaneous order, seems so distant from Jeremy Bentham and his like, the rationalist constructionists with their designed orders[2].

Yet, in this paper I argue that there is a common theoretical plane between the market mechanism understood in Hayek's terms as a mechanism of co-ordination of individual plans, and Bentham's principle of panopticism, understood as a disciplinary device, secure management of a multitude, and extraction of labor. Clearly, this common theoretical plane cannot be found in what Hayek and Bentham supposed were the sources of their respective mechanisms (the market for Hayek and the panopticon for Bentham). Here they obviously differ. While Bentham's panopticon is designed, Hayek believes that the market order is the result of spontaneous evolution, and he does not acknowledge a substantial role for power, struggles and states in the emergence of property rights, for example through a variety of enclosures.[3] Hayek's understanding of the role of the market order and Bentham's understanding of the panopticon can be compared once we abstract from Hayek's metaphysical views on the spontaneous evolution of markets, and regard Hayek's market and Bentham's panopticism as two given mechanisms, their rationales rather than their believed genealogy.

But again, even abstracting from their perceived genealogical differences, a prison, even loosely defined as "inspection house", is different from a market. The fact that they may share something in common does not make them similar. A pine tree is certainly different from an oak tree, and this difference is not even overcome when one notices that they share the basic processes of photosynthesis, although the latter is the basis for their general classification as plants. So in a sense, in this comparison I am interested to find out the common ground between these *prima facie* so diverse social organizations. It is this common ground that, as in the case of different trees, would allow us to recognize them as two different *forms* of the same thing. The implication of this is important. If the market and the "inspection house" (the plan) are two forms of the same thing, and this thing, as I will show, is ultimately a disciplinary mechanisms in which the individual freedoms are limited to a choice within a given menu and prevented from defining the *context* of their interaction, then emancipatory political theory and practice must find a way beyond this dichotomy, to discover *forms* of social interaction that cannot be reduced to the disciplinary and organizational features of the market or the prison.

As far as I know, the common ground between the market order and the panopticon has never been highlighted by a comparative analysis. There is of course a good reason for this. The two authors belong to two different strands of liberal thinking. Bentham was regarded by Hayek as a rationalist constructivist who, together with Descartes, Hobbes and Rousseau, held the "erroneous conception" that societies can give themselves "laws" in accordance with some high principle of justice (Hayek, 1973, p. 95). For utilitarianism, optimization of pleasure provides the only rule by which to judge the institutions governing human behavior ("the greatest happiness for the greatest number"). For Hayek this rule would rely on the assumption of omniscience, an assumption the challenge of which is at the basis of all Hayek's major theoretical contribution.

In Bentham's panopticon however, unlike his general utilitarian philosophy, omniscience is *not* a pre-given assumption, nor a result of the social interaction organized by the panopticon. Instead, the need for the panopticon as a mechanism of inspection arises, so to say, out of the acknowledgement of the ignorance of the "central planners". Like the market, for Hayek, the panopticon for Bentham provides a mechanism to overcome this ignorance. Never in the order of the panopticon there is the presumption that power "knows it all", only that the inspected, the unwilling participant in this order, would *conceive* power as omniscient. On the other hand, power in this order acknowledges the "tacit" aspect of this "knowledge of the inspected," and the panopticon order is designed precisely to capitalize on this.

Prima facie, therefore, there are important similarities between Hayek's and Bentham's systems. The similarities that emerged in an initial superficial comparison are, I believe, confirmed when one analyses the two systems in detail.

In Section II, I will review the broad features of both Hayek's idea of market order and Bentham's *panopticism*. In Section III I discuss the overlap between the two systems, while in the conclusion I briefly discuss the implications of the common theoretical plane between these two apparently opposite systems. Here I suggest that the current global market order can be theorized in terms of a "fractal-panopticon", that is a series of overlapping and interrelated virtual "inspection houses" in which competition *and* the configuration of property rights combine to constitute a global disciplinary mechanism in the form of market freedom. Section IV concludes.

II. MARKET ORDER AND PANOPTICISM:
THE TWO PRINCIPLES STATED

Hayek's Spontaneous Order

Designed versus Spontaneous order

Hayek's general theory of spontaneous order points out that capitalism is the unintended outcome of the widespread observance of certain "non-designed", non-planned norms. Hayek identifies an important dualism between designed and spontaneous order, "a profound tension between the goals of designed institutions and the resulting spontaneity of an evolving order" (Sciabarra, 1995, p. 31).[4] This tension between two extreme ordering principles of individual activities *within* a systemic whole constitutes the horizon of intervention of Hayek's academic and political work.

To put the problem of order at the center and to point to its spontaneous emergence implies a conceptualization of the individual as *social* individual. This is not only because

> Living as members of society [we are] ... dependent for the satisfaction of most of our
> needs on various forms of co-operation with others (Hayek 1973, p. 36).

Adam Smith had already recognized this social dimension of production. But unlike Smith and the Robinsonisms of neoclassical economists, Hayek's whole is more than the sum of its parts, because it includes *relations* among them. In this order, "each element affects and is affected by the others, jointly constituting and being constituted by the whole" (Sciabarra, 1995, p. 31). Because of these relations, the whole is not apprehensible through a synoptic understanding. The structure of social order can only be grasped from a specific vantage point (Sciabarra, 1995, p. 31).

We should not be enchanted by Hayek's social individual. The latter is far from a transhistorical figure, it is a social individual of a particular kind, defined *ex post*, after a given configuration of property rights poses individuals as *private* individuals.

The problem of order emerges from this definition of individuals as private (in Marx's sense (1844), as alienated). By virtue of being fragmented private individuals, they have expectations and plans that do not match. The "matching of the intentions and expectations that determine the actions of different individuals is the form in which order manifests itself in social life" (Hayek, 1973, p. 36).

This matching of expectations of *private* individuals can, according to Hayek, be the result of two ordering principles, one of which "derives ... entirely from the belief that order can be created only by forces outside the system (or 'exogenously')" (Hayek, 1973, p. 36). This is the authoritarian ordering principle. In the other principle, an order is "set up from within (or 'endogenously') such as that which the general theory of the market endeavours to explain. A spontaneous order of this kind has in many respects properties different from those of a made order" (Hayek, 1973, p. 36).

The superior character of spontaneous order in relation to designed order resides in the use that this order makes of knowledge in society (Gray, 1998, p. 28). Because "knowledge . . . exists . . . solely as the dispersed bits of incomplete and frequently contradictory knowledge which all the separate individuals possess" (Hayek, 1945, p. 77), the

> economic problem of society is thus not merely a problem of how to allocate 'given' resources – if 'given' is taken to mean given to a single mind which deliberately solves the problem set by these 'data'. It is rather a problem of how to secure the best use of resources known to any of the members of society, for ends whose relative importance only these individuals know. Or, to put it briefly, it is a problem of the utilization of knowledge which is not given to anyone in its totality (Hayek, 1945, pp. 77–78).

The problem of social order is thus a problem of how social knowledge is created and distributed among private individuals, and what rules or patterns are created to connect and match their independent plans.[5] Knowledge thus not only takes up the form of individual plans, i.e. private purposes, but also that of *praxis,* of rules followed by private individuals in their interaction.[6]

Private individuals follows three kinds of rules, and these "chiefly negative (or prohibitory) rules of conduct . . . make possible the formation of social order." First, there are those "rules that are merely observed in fact but have never been stated in words." Second, "rules which we are able to apply, but do not know explicitly." The second type of rules, through they have been stated in words, still merely express approximately what has long before been generally observed in action." Finally, third, there are those "rules that have been deliberately introduced and therefore necessarily exist as words set out in sentences." The problem with all kind of constructionists is that they "would like to reject the first and second groups of rules, and to accept as valid only the third group" (Hayek, 1970, pp. 8–9).

The first and second groups of rules instead constitute tacit knowledge. It is precisely because of tacit knowledge that, according to Hayek, a central authority cannot solve the co-ordination problem. The latter would not only face the impossible task of collecting all the information from individual agents including the tacit components, but also it would also have to feed back to agents the information necessary to adjust individual plans to the central authority master plan. The only way to solve this problem is through a *mechanism* that uses *individual knowledge*, but at the same time in which each individual is *ignorant* of the overall outcome. The solution lies in the duality between individual *absolute knowledge* of (and engagement with) their private sphere and purposes (which include tacit components), and individual *absolute ignorance* of (and indifference to) the forms and outcome of their interaction. The model is a characteristic model of utter systemic opportunism; "I am only doing my job," says Hayek's individual, never pondering about the social meaning of that "job." That is, in what ways and how is that job articulated within the whole.

The Market

Let us now see the qualities of 'spontaneous order' understood as market order. The market system is, according to Hayek, the best example of this evolved set of institutions. It is an impersonal *mechanism* with a problem to solve, that of co-ordinating individual knowledge and plans. This problem is discernible only if we drop the unrealistic assumptions of neoclassical economics that can show the benefit of competition only in the presence of an unlimited number of suppliers of a homogeneous commodity.[7] Unlike neoclassical economics which discusses competition using assumptions which "*if* they were true of the real world, would make it wholly uninteresting and useless" because if everybody knew about data, then competition would result in a wasteful method of co-ordination among individuals, Hayek proposes to consider competition as a "discovery procedure" (Hayek, 1978, p. 179).

Mainstream economic theory cannot understand the true function of competition, because its starting point is a *given* supply of scarce goods (Hayek, 1978, p. 181). However, the discoveries of what and how much to produce; the discovery of "which goods are scarce goods, or which things are goods, and how scarce and valuable they are" (Hayek, 1978, p. 182); or the discovery of "minimum cost of production", or of the desires and attitudes of unknown customers (Hayek, 1946, pp. 100–101; 1978, p. 182); are all precisely what the market is supposed to find out. Note that, this "finding out" by the market is at the same time a material force. Scarcity is a produced result of market interaction, not a presupposition, as the process of competition on the market creates needs and wants. Unlike the classical political economy tradition, prices are not only the expression of past activity, but are the information signals that excite future activity, that allow individuals to focus their attention on what is worth producing and what is not. The price system is a communication system. Knowledge which is widely dispersed through society can thus become effectively utilized (Hayek, 1978, pp. 181–182, 188), not simply as *know-how* necessary for the production of individual commodities, but as a social force that makes it *necessary* to produce in certain ways and for certain purposes.

This compulsory aspect embedded within Hayek's liberal philosophy of freedom acquires a systemic character, and pervades the context within which he argues that private individuals can exercise their liberty. By letting themselves be guided by these common indicators (Hayek, 1978, p. 60) private individuals have learnt to substitute abstract rules for 'the needs of known fellows' and for coercive, imposed ends (ibid, p. 61). In this condition, the relation of the individual relation with the "other" is not direct, but mediated by "a system of abstract relations" in which "individual man can be directed by the private knowledge of his own purposes, and not by the knowledge of other people's needs, which is outside the range of his perceptions" (Hayek, 1978, p. 268).

The order brought about by the market is one that never reaches the equilibrium position that neoclassical economists talk about, but in a sense only always approximates it. This because individual plans never finish mutually adjusting through a series of negative feedback signals, the same ones that Smith defined under the category of the invisible hand and that regulate prices in a market (Hayek, 1978, p. 184). Mutual adjustment of expectation is only one of the unintended outcomes of the market order. The other is efficiency. The market in fact "also secures that whatever is being produced will be produced by people who can do so more cheaply than (or at least as cheaply as) anybody who does not produce it ... and that each product is sold at a price lower than that at which anybody who in fact does not produce it could supply it" (Hayek, 1978, p. 185).

These aggregate demand and supply curves of economic analysis therefore, are not, in reality, pre-given, "but results of the process of competition going on all the time" (Hayek, 1978, p. 187). Thus the formation of prices resembles the incessant and continuous process of formation of socially necessary time that Marx (1867) is referring to (De Angelis forthcoming). As any disciplinary process must (Foucault, 1977), this one too embeds the duality of rewards and punishments. Thus doing, Hayek presents the social setting as a drawing that awaits the coloring of flesh and blood power relations. The forces of social change are portrayed in their strategic setting, but the power relations within which these forces are embedded are completely invisible. Power is left only as an implicit issue. Changes may occur only if

> the few willing and able to experiment with new methods *can make it necessary for the many* to follow them, and at the same time to show them the way (Hayek, 1978, p. 187; my emphasis).

The ways to "make necessary" the "required changes in habits and customs" are of course in principle endless, and all have to do with a form of power.

But implicit to Hayek's point is that ultimately, there are two camps: those who are for change and those who are not because it is not in their interests. Competition creates a continuous compulsion and resistance to this compulsion:

> The required discovery process will be impeded or prevented, if the many are able to keep the few to the traditional ways. Of course, it is one of the chief reasons for the dislike of competition that it not only shows how things can be done more effectively, but also confronts those who depend for their incomes on the market with the alternative of imitating the more successful or losing some or all of their income. Competition produces in this way a kind of impersonal compulsion which makes it necessary for numerous individuals to adjust their way of life in a manner that no deliberate instructions or command could bring about (Hayek, 1978, p. 189).

But why is continuous "change" necessary? In the presence of Hayek's rejection of a "hierarchy of ends" to evaluate human societies, the criteria brought forward by Hayek that justify this continuous compulsion are the identification of an abstractly defined "progress" as an end in itself: "Progress is movement for movement's sake" (Hayek, 1960, p. 41). This idealization of movement for movement's sake, irrespective of the direction of the movement, its social outcome, what is produced and how needs are formed and met, and irrespective of the nature of social interaction, makes Hayek the quintessential capitalist apologist.[8]

There are two implications of this. First, "competition is valuable *only* because, and so far as, its results are unpredictable and on the whole different from those which anyone has, or could have, deliberately aimed at." Second, "that the generally beneficial effects of competition must include disappointing or defeating some particular expectations or intentions" (Hayek, 1978, p. 180). The latter means that in the functioning of the market order (Hayek, 1978, p. 185), "a high degree of coincidence of expectation is brought about by the systematic disappointment of some kind of expectations". The market order rewards some, punishes someone else. The continuous process of compulsion and series of rewards and punishments "going on all the time", that is, the process of competition, has the property identified by Foucault (1977) as that of a "disciplinary mechanism." Bentham's panopticon is also one of these devices.[9]

Panopticism

A *"new mode of obtaining power"*
Bentham certainly does not claim the panopticon to be an emergent order. *Prima facie*, in his model of the "inspection house" there is little rhetoric of the evolution of freedom. The panopticon is unmistakably an institution of confinement, intended to facilitate the extraction of labor, and one designed precisely for this double purpose.

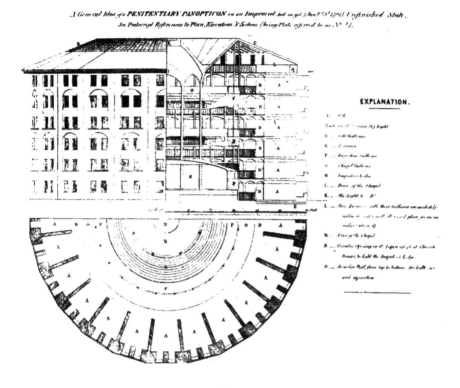

Jeremy Bentham's plan of the Panopticon (Bentham, 1787).

The panopticon is a circular building with at the center a watchtower with large windows. The peripheral ring is subdivided into cells, each of which has a window facing the outside and one facing the tower. The light coming from the outside window therefore, allows the occupants of each cell to be seen as if in many little shadow theatres (Foucault, 1977). Meanwhile the inspectors in the central tower, protected by blinds and by an opposite source of light, are at any time invisible to the eye of the occupant of each cells.

The cover of the 1787 project document boasts the general principle of the panopticon (here called, following Foucault (1977), *panopticism*). Its applicability, according to Bentham, is generalizable to any circumstance in which, to use Hayek's terms, individual plans are not matching. As described on the front cover, the panopticon contains

the Idea of a New Principle of Construction applicable to any Sort of Establishment, in
which Persons of any Description are to be kept under Inspection. And in Particular to
Penitentiary-Houses, Prisons, Houses of Industry, Work-Houses, Poor-Houses,
Manufactories, Mad-Houses, Hospitals, and Schools.

What prisoners, workers, poor people, "mad" persons, patients, and students
have in common is the fact that they need to be put under inspection, because
their individual "plans" do not match the plan that Bentham has in mind for
them. To a variety of degrees, they all share the same desire of *escaping* from
the particular confinement in which they are put, and of *exercising less effort*
in the work that they are asked to perform. Inspection fulfils this double role
of maximization of security and minimization of shirking. The innovation is
in Bentham's opinion that the principle of panopticism is generalizable to any
situation in which "persons of any description" would tend to follow or make
plans that do not conform to a given norm, and therefore require to be kept
under inspection. The Penitentiary-House is just an application of the
panopticon principle, in fact one "most complicated" in which "the objects of
safe-custody, confinement, solitude, forced labour, and *instruction,* were all of
them to be kept in view" (Bentham, 1787, p. 3). In the preface, Bentham
promises the solution of all problems pertaining to different spheres (health,
education, production, economy, crime management, and public finance)
through the application of "a simple idea of Architecture!", that is by a spatial
configuration of *relations* between bodies, through the arrangement of bodies
in space:

Morals reformed – health preserved – industry invigorated – instruction diffused – public
burthens lightened – Economy seated as it were upon a rock – the Gordian knot of
the Poor-Laws not cut but untied – all by a simple idea of Architecture! (Bentham, 1787,
p. iii).

This is a principle for the management of power relations, and nothing else. In
particular, it is a principle to increase the power of the "inspectors" over
the power of the "inspected" and thus allowing the latter to be put into "useful
use". The norm is usefulness of the inspected body. Without proper application
of the principle of the panopticon, "persons of any description" would tend
not to conform to a given norm, and therefore require to be kept under
inspection. This "new mode of obtaining power, of mind over mind, in a quantity
hitherto without example," offered by the panopticon, is based on a simple
principle: "the *centrality* of the inspectors' situation, combined with the well
known and most effectual contrivances for *seeing without being seen*" (Bentham,
1787, p. 21).

Immediately, this introduces a quality in the relation of power. Power is exercised not so much by the actual presence of the inspector over the inspected. The inspected does not need to *have full knowledge* of being inspected and the inspector *does not have* full knowledge of the plans and behavior of the inspected. In fact, this "ideal perfection" is not possible, because it "would require that each person should actually be ... constantly ... under the eyes of the persons who should inspect them." Thus, "this being impossible, the next thing to be wished for is, that, at every instant, seeing reason to believe as much, and not being able to satisfy himself to the contrary, he should *conceive* himself to be so" (Bentham, 1787, p. 3).

This situation would enable "the *apparent omnipresence* of the inspector ... combined with the extreme facility of his *real presence*" (Bentham, 1787, p. 25). The *conception*, rather than the reality, of constant surveillance is what gives the inspector a god-like character (omnipresence). To paraphrase Hayek, Bentham knows that the individual in authority – in the name of the inspector - cannot have full knowledge of the inspected, his actions, and his plans. But Bentham uses an architectural design to reverse this potential ignorance and turn it into a potential knowledge to the advantage of the inspectors.

Modularization and Productivity of Power

Another aspect of the generalizable character of the panopticon principle is in the modularization of its constituent parts: the peripheral ring, the central Tower, and the relations among them. This meant that the principle of the panopticon could cover "an area of any extent." For example,

> If the number of rotundas were extended to *four*, a regular uncovered area might in that way be enclosed: and, being surrounded by covered galleries, would be commanded in this manner from all sides, instead of being commanded only from one.

> The area thus enclosed might be either *circular* like the buildings, or *square*, or *oblong*, as one or other of those forms were best adapted to the prevailing ideas of beauty or local convenience. A chain of any length, composed of inspection-houses adapted to the same or different purposes, might in this way be carried round an area of any extent (Bentham, 1787, p. 18).

The panopticon therefore does not need a *singular center*; it may well be constituted by a series of centers, as long as they are *integrated*.

Another aspect of the panopticon is that it leads to an emergent property, that of economy of scale in the production of inspection, the "*inspection force*":

> On such a plan, either one inspector might serve for two or more rotundas, or, if there were one to each, *the inspective force*, if I may use the expression, would be greater in such a compound building than in any of the number, singly taken, of which it was composed: since each inspector might be relieved occasionally by every other (Bentham, 1787, p. 19).

It must be pointed out that this increased productivity of inspection depends on the increased pervasiveness of the panopticon principle, to *see without been seen*, once more "rotundas" are integrated. In other words, the greater the number or integrated rotundas, the more efficiently power can be organized through a panopticon principle. This panoptical's "efficiency of scale" of inspections is therefore an important quality that allows to extend the panopticon beyond the confinement of one institution.

Unwaged Work of Inspection

As part of the increased efficiency of inspection, the Panopticon also allows the co-optation of the inspector's family unwaged labor. Provided "that room be allotted to the lodge . . . for the principal inspector . . . and his family, . . . the more numerous . . . the family, the better; since, by this means, there will in fact be as many inspectors as the family consists of persons, though only one be paid for it" (Bentham, 1787, p. 23).

Bentham is very clear on why this should be the case, why the members of the family of the head inspector would want to perform the duties of the family head. It is an utterly *free* choice, but one which arises out of a *context* that has been entirely engineered, planned, designed.

> Neither the orders of the inspector himself, nor any interest which they may feel, or not feel, in the regular performance of his duty, would be requisite to find them motives adequate to the purpose. Secluded oftentimes, by their situation, from every other object, they will naturally, and in a manner unavoidably give their eyes a direction conformable to that purpose, in every momentary interval of their ordinary occupations. It will supply in their instance the place of that great and constant fund of entertainment to the sedentary and vacant in towns, the looking out of the window. The scene, though a confined, would be a very various, and therefore perhaps not altogether an unamusing one (Bentham, 1787, p. 20).

Here, what from the perspective of the family members appears as leisure, entertainment, is turned into surveillance work from the perspective of the mechanism of the panopticon. This free-choice co-optation of the inspector's family work is very similar in context to what we will see later as the free-choice co-optation of the prisoners' work.

The Rest of the World

The principle of modularization of the Panopticon can also be seen in another aspect. The Panopticon, a discrete building, can be interfaced with the outside world through an administrative device, bookkeeping and its publicity. In letter 9 Bentham envisages high rewards for those who will manage the panopticon. The chosen contractor will be the one who offers "the best terms." The contractor will be given "all the *powers* that his interest could prompt him to wish for, in order to enable him to make the most of his bargain; with only some reservations . . ." (Bentham, 1787, p. 39). "On pain of forfeiture or other adequate punishment . . . and that upon oath," the contractor would have to publicize the panopticon's accounts, "the whole process and details of his management", as well as "all history of the prison" (ibid.).

The advantage of having this information is the institution of a mechanism that signals profits and losses to the rest of the world, and therefore enables a form of competition to take place. Bad management is demonstrated by loss of profit "for it is one advantage of this plan, that whatever mischief happens must have more than eat out all *his* profits before it reaches *me*" (Bentham, 1787, p. 41). The publication of the accounts is a way to increase the productivity of surveillance, its effectiveness, to maximize to the limit the panopticon principle. It is the means through which the disciplinary mechanism set in place can operate efficiently:

> After such publication, who should I have then? I should have every body: every body who, by fortune, experience, judgement, disposition, should conceive himself able and find himself inclined, to engage in such a business: and each person, seeing what advantage had been made, and how, would be willing to make his offer in proportion. What situation more favourable for making the best terms? (Bentham, 1787, p. 42).

Collateral Advantages

The panopticon also offers a series of important "collateral" advantages. The first one is that the number of inspectors required is relatively less than a comparable establishment (Bentham, 1787, p. 25). Second, the principle of the panopticon also applies to all layers of the staff forming the inspection force:

> the *under* keepers or inspectors, the servants and subordinates of every kind, will be under the same irresistible control with respect to the *head* keeper or inspector, as the prisoners or other persons to be governed are with respect to *them* (Bentham, 1787, p. 26).

This allows the panopticon be beneficial not only for the maximization of the discipline of the inmates, but also of the discipline of the inspectors, because "in no instance" (Bentham, 1787, p. 26) could they either perform or depart from their duty." The panopticon therefore provides a satisfactory answer "to one of the most puzzling of political questions, *quis custodiet ipsos custodes?*" Inspectors and inspected are both locked into a mechanism of surveillance. The panopticon is "no less beneficial to what is called *Liberty* than to necessary coercion; no less powerful as a control upon subordinate power, than as a curb to delinquency; as a field to innocence than as a scourge to guilt" (Bentham, 1787, p. 27). The panopticon principle disciplines everyone, free and un-free.

The third advantage is a sanitized exercise of power, through the elimination of "disgust" and risks of infection due to face-to-face interactions by making sure that the job of inspection is replaced by an impersonal mechanism. Through this device, those who exercise power can minimize their contact with their subordinates.[10]

Fourth and finally, the panopticon ought to be open to visitors so as to give rise to a *system* of inspection. Again, Bentham here is referring to the ability of the system to capitalize on the *unintended* results of the action of the visitors. The visitors, "without intending perhaps, or even without thinking of any other effects of their visits, than the gratification of their own particular curiosity" (Bentham, 1787, p. 29) do contribute to the system of competition. A multi-layer system of inspection could emerge, in which "these spontaneous visitors" play the unintended role of "superintendent, assistants, deputies" of the inspectors "in so far as he is faithful" or "witnesses and judges, should he ever be unfaithful, to his trust." The motives of the visitors are for this purpose "perfectly immaterial; whether the relieving of their anxieties by the affecting prospect of their respective friends and relatives thus detained [over time], or merely the satisfying that general curiosity, which an establishment on various accounts so interesting to human feelings, may naturally be expected to excite" (Bentham, 1787, p. 29).

The motivations of individual agents is irrelevant. What counts is their role within a system of inspection. Whatever their intentions and motivations to visit the establishment, by so doing they become *integrated* within the purpose of a system of inspection.

III. MARKET AND PANOPTICISM: TWO OVERLAPPING ORDERS

There are striking similarities and complementarities between Hayek's and Bentham's systems. These are summarized in Box 1 and discussed below.

1. Origins
In the first place, and very briefly, there are, quite surprisingly, some similarities of origination between the two mechanisms. While for Bentham the construction of this mechanism resides squarely on the ingeniousness of the planner of the panopticon, for Hayek, the market would be an emergent order *if* it were not for those like Keynesians and socialists, who put limits to the market evolution. But in Hayek, the policy implication is the same as in Bentham: the role of the state is not that of co-ordinating individual action, but one of allowing

---

Box 1.

Market and Panopticism: Two Overlapping Orders

1. Origins. The "planner" plays an important role in the design of the parameters of the order/mechanism.

2. Impersonality and efficiency. The impersonal mechanism of co-ordination of individual subjectivities (plans) is functional to the maximisation of extraction of labour (Bentham) or maximisation of efficiency (Hayek).

3. Extension and integration. The order/mechanism can be generalised through the social field by means of the modular properties of the panopticon (Bentham) or commodification of new areas of life.

4. Imperfect knowledge. There is the recognition that power (inspectors in Bentham's panopticon or the state in Hayek's market) has imperfect knowledge of individual plans.

5. Freedom of private, not social, individuals. The order/mechanism relies on freedom of private individuals (given a menu). The consequent strategic intent of power is the emphasis on co-optation of unintended consequences of individual freedom.

6. Role of "enclosures." Individual confinement is a condition of individual freedom. In Bentham, the confinement is created by the cell's walls, while in Hayek, it is created through property rights, which turn individuals into private individuals.

7. Disciplinary order. The mechanism of co-ordination (watchtower or competition) distributes punishments or rewards and is "invisible" to individuals. In Bentham, this is the power behind the watchtower, in Hayek it is the emergent and ongoing compulsion of the competitive process.

8. Fetishism and signalling. Both mechanisms function through "shadowy projections" of real life activities. In the panopticon these are light signals, in competitive market these are price signals.

---

the emergence of an order in which individual actions are coordinated spontaneously. Similarly, the belief that the market is a spontaneous order implies that the state ought to *promote* policies that create and facilitate the market as *condition* in which private individuals operate.[11]

2. Impersonal Mechanism of Coordination

Both systems are impersonal mechanisms of co-ordination of individual subjectivities that give form to social labor. The impersonal aspect of the co-ordinating mechanism is enthusiastically boasted by Bentham and it is a quality that makes it suitable to be applicable to a large variety of social subjects "in need" of inspection. As we have seen, in Hayek's market the emphasis is on abstract rules of conduct, which bind together private individuals so that there is no need for them to develop common aims.[12] As an impersonal mechanism, the market frees individuals from the "need of known fellows" and yet allows them to socially co-operate in their labor. There are also some important parallels in the "aims" of this impersonal mechanism. For Bentham we are clearly and explicitly talking about a mechanism aimed at extraction of labor and maximization of profit (see letter 13 on "the means of extracting labour" and the discussion below on individual freedom). We can discern the same preoccupation in Hayek once we look at the mode of functioning, the *process* of the market order, rather than its end result.

For Hayek in fact, the end result of the market order (say a particular distribution of income, or any other particular "still picture" of the socio-economic condition) cannot be judged "by criteria which are appropriate only to a single organised community serving a given hierarchy of ends," because such a hierarchy of ends is not relevant to the "complex structure composed of countless individual economic arrangements" (Hayek, 1978, p. 183). The word "economy" is in fact inadequate to describe a multitude of individual ends because it refers to "an organisation or arrangement in which someone deliberately allocates resources to a unitary order of ends." Instead, the market order, or catallaxy, does not have any particular end. But if this is the case, "what, then, do we mean when we claim that [it] produces in some sense a maximum or optimum?" If the market order cannot be said to have a purpose,

> it may yet be highly conducive to the achievement of many different individual purposes non-known as a whole to any single person, or relatively small groups of persons. Indeed, rational action is possible only in a fairly orderly world. Therefore it clearly makes sense to try to produce conditions under which the chances for any individual taken at random to achieve his ends as effectively as possible will be very high – even if it cannot be predicted which particular aims will be favoured, and which not (Hayek, 1978, p. 183).

The catallactic order of the market is for Hayek the optimum condition within which individual freedom can be organized. It is not possible to predict the result of this discovery process because "the only common aim which we can pursue by the choice of this technique of ordering social affairs is the general kind of pattern, or the abstract character, of the order that will form itself" (Hayek, 1978, p. 184).

If the market order cannot be judged by its ends, we can develop an understanding of its rationale by regarding it an incessant *process* in which social labor is caught up. As we have seen, this process never reaches the equilibrium position that neoclassical economists talk about, because there is no pre-established equilibrium to reach. While in orthodox welfare economics, the role of the market is that of a "social computational device" (Kirzner, 1973, p. 214) – which computes pre-established hidden prices given perfect information – in Hayek the role of the market, as a discovery mechanism that communicates information, is to *create* reality.

Continual mutual adjustment of expectations brought about by this discovery procedure allows the market order to generate efficiency by securing that "whatever is being produced will be produced by people who can do so more cheaply than (or at least as cheaply as) anybody who does not produce it" (Hayek, 1978, p. 185).

Thus, if the market cannot be said to have a "unitary order of ends", it prioritizes a unitary rationale for human social interaction: the endless promotion of efficiency, the endless unqualified "progress", the never ending rat race, the competitive compulsion that "goes on all the time." This is not an external "end product" of Hayek's market order, but its *raison d'être*.

3. Extendibility of the System

Another similarity is in the potential spatial realm of the two mechanisms. It is true that *prima facie* Bentham's panopticon is a closed system, clearly limited in space, while Hayek's market order is an open one, which spans over the social field without inherent limit. Yet, Bentham micro-technology of power is generalizable thanks to the *modular* properties of the panopticon, which allow a series of watchtowers to be integrated so as to control larger areas (Bentham, 1787, p. 18). Hayek's market on the other hand, is the representation of a social organism, but one whose dynamics of interactions among individuals is particularizable to any area of the social field, as long as individuals are turned into private individuals with "no need of known fellow." The last three centuries of commodification of many spheres of social life are a clear extension of Hayek's market principle. Therefore, though their starting sphere of application is different, the two systems can be imagined as 'convergent'.

4. Authority's Imperfect Knowledge of Individual Plans

In both Bentham's and Hayek's order, power's knowledge of individual actions and plan is not perfect, and the rationale of both orders is to tap into human knowledge held by private individuals. In both cases, this co-optation of knowledge and tacit plans is at the basis of the system's maximization of efficiency. Within their respective orders, power's acknowledgement of its imperfect knowledge becomes an opportunity to channel individual actions into the efficiency of an order, and therefore, given the structure of power relations embedded in that order, to promote profit.

5. Freedom of Private Individuals

It follows from 4. that both orders rely on freedom of *private* individuals understood as free choice of options from a *given* menu. While this is obvious in Hayek's market order, it is not immediately so in Bentham.

We have discussed how Bentham thinks to co-opt the free choice and intentionality of the inspector's family members and those of visitors to the systemic work of inspection of the panopticon. This unwaged work by the inspectors' family members is one which is unintended, exercised by free individuals operating within a *context* that has been designed for the purpose of surveillance *and* labor extraction.[13] A similar principle applies to the inmates.

Letter 13 is titled "on the means of extracting labour." These means are based on putting the prisoners in a condition to exercise a *choice* and therefore to reap a reward.[14] Here, individual freedom of choice is disconnected, as in Hayek, from the collective freedom to choose the constraints of that choice. This choice amounts to a *means* to extract labor![15] And what an efficient mechanism of labor extraction is this:

> What hold can any other manufacturer have upon his workmen, equal to what my manufacturer would have upon his? What other master is there that can reduce his workmen, if idle, to a situation next to starving, without suffering them to go elsewhere? What other master is there, whose men can never get drunk unless he chooses they should do so? And who so far from being able to raise their wages by combination, are obliged to take whatever pittance he thinks it most for his interest to allow? (Bentham, 1787, p. 76).

In Hayek, the question of freedom is at the core of his investigation, and it assumes not so much the connotation of a moral theory (Gamble, 1996, p. 41), but one of politics. The notion of freedom informs the strategic horizon of his legacy. For example, he writes:

> My aim will not be to provide a detailed program of policy but rather to state the criteria by which particular measures must be judged if they are to fit into a regime of freedom. . . . Such a program . . . must grow out of the application of a common philosophy to the problem of the day (Hayek, 1960, p. 5).

Here Hayek's strategic horizon is clearly *deployed*. His philosophy of freedom is a weapon that serves as a yardstick to make judgements, to measure concrete instances and to evaluate them in order to see whether they conform to a "regime of freedom" understood in liberal terms. In a word, it is a liberal *line in the sand*. In this sense, Hayek is one of those economists who provide a flexible and adaptable conceptual grid, and is aware of this role. This conceptual grid represents the glasses through which liberal and neo-liberal economists in different contexts and times can filter out their reality, circumstances and historical contexts, and adapt their basic principles to these realities with policies.

This filter sees freedom as a relation between individuals as defined by private property. For Hayek, liberty has nothing to do with social individuals being able to define the conditions of their interaction. Freedom is defined negatively, as the state of independence of the arbitrary will of another' (Hayek, 1960, p. 12). Freedom is taken away from an individual when "in order to avoid greater evil, he is forced to act not according to a coherent plan of his own but to serve the ends of another" (Hayek, 1960, p. 12). In this sense, freedom is to be free to choose from a given menu, in which the emphasis is not so much on the range of choices listed on the menu, but on the "given character" of the menu:

> 'freedom' refers solely to a relation of men to other men, and the only infringement on it is coercion by men. This means, in particular, that the range of physical possibilities from which a person can choose at a given moment has no relevance to freedom (Hayek, 1960, p. 12).

Coercion exists in Hayek when a specific individual bends another to his will; when it is done by impersonal market forces, it is not coercion, by definition. But the "given character" of the menu is a form of coercion. The fact that some choices are not contemplated – such as the freedom to choose the kind of rules of social interaction, the freedom to choose not to be governed by abstract rules, but by mutual recognition, or solidarity for example – is a way to force people into choosing the remaining options. Let us briefly explore this.

There are five fundamental freedoms in Hayek including ownership of property. These are "legal status as a member of the community; immunity from arbitrary arrest; the right to work at any trade; the right to free government and the right to own property" (Steele, 1993, p. 33). Gamble (1996) and others have noticed that the freedom represented by ownership of property, is positively, rather than negatively, defined.[16] This implies that as far as property is concerned, the negative, relational definition of freedom arises out of property monopoly. In other words, constriction arises from monopolizing the means of existence, as revealed by his often-noted spring in the desert monopoly case (Hayek, 1960,

p. 136).[17] In this case coercion arises when ownership of means existence reaches an extent that it prevents *others* access to the means of existence.

In both Hayek and Bentham we have a clear emphasis on the emergence of unintended consequences out of given parameters, or rules. Whether these are embedded in a designed architecture (Bentham) or are the (naïvely believed) product of a evolutionary order (Hayek), the point that interests both is the resulting system-like mechanism of co-ordination. The system-like co-ordination can emerge only if the individuals are allowed a sphere of freedom within which to operate. For both Bentham and Hayek this mechanism is rooted on a system of individual free-choice, but individual free-choice always comes with a rigid *given* set of "constraints." In the microcosm of Bentham's panopticon, this constraint is the result of an ingenious project. In the organic system of Hayek's market, constraints are believed to be a naturally evolutionary result. Yet, in both cases, individual freedom is the main condition for the system to operate at maximum efficiency and to turn "individual plans" into social efficiency.

6. Individual Confinement as Systemic Condition of Individual Freedom
Another similarity is that in both cases we have individual confinement as a presupposed basis of the extent of their freedom. In the case of the individuals of the panopticon, the walls of the cells are the physical barriers that allow the creation of confinement. The purpose of "safe confinement" is to prevent escape and enforce labor. Safe confinement *isolates* the inspected from each other in order to dash their *hope*, and dangerous *"concert among minds"* (Bentham, 1787, p. 32) which would overpower the guards. In the case of Hayek, the barriers are social, and constructed in the forms of *property rights.* In both cases however, the very existence of these barriers are *naturalised.*

7. Mechanism of Coordination is "Invisible" to Individuals
Another similarity is the notion that the co-ordinating power, the one that distributes punishments and rewards to individual singularities, is invisible. In both cases, there is an automatic mechanism that co-ordinates individual subjectivities, and in both cases the latter do not relate to each other *directly* but through the mediation of other things. In the case of the panopticon, it is the central power of the inspectors' apparatus that mediates between individuals and thus co-ordinates the division of labor of a multitude. In Hayek's case, it is money as expression of relative prices that does the mediation.

8. The Role of "Shadowy Projections"
Finally, both these mechanisms use projections of real life activity as data to feed the mechanism of control and co-ordination. In Bentham's panopticon,

they are the mechanical products of an ingenious architectural design. In Hayek, prices fulfil the same role. There is of course an important difference between the two mechanisms. The knowledge embedded by market pricing in Hayek is knowledge that all individuals can in principle use (Gray, 1998, p. 38), while the one yielded by the shadowy projections of the panopticon do not. But this difference is ultimately the difference in how the "watchtower" is constituted in the two systems. We have to understand the watchtower as the center of disciplinary power, as the dispenser of punishment and rewards. While in Bentham the watchtower is a material physical presence, that is pre-supposed and stands outside individuals subjectivities, in Hayek' market order the center of disciplinary power is the emergent property of individual competitive inter-action. The knowledge embedded in Bentham's shadowy projections gives the inspectors in the watchtower the same thing that market prices give to competing agents on the market: "systemic or holistic knowledge, knowledge unknown and unknowable to any of the elements of the market system, but given to them all by the operation of the system itself" (Gray, 1998, p. 38).

IV. CONCLUSION: THE MARKET ORDER AS A FRACTAL-PANOPTICON

The overlap between Bentham's and Hayek's apparently opposite systems of co-ordination of social labor opens up an understanding of the current global market order under construction as imbued with the property of *panopticism*. This is not the place to investigate this further. Suffice it to say that following Bentham, it is possible to understand panopticism as a modality of power that rests on the principle of "to see without being seen", made possible by a flow of information that turns real subjects and activities into *data*, shadowy projections of real subjects. Combining these principles of panopticism with its property of *modularisation* and Hayek's characterization of the market as co-ordinating mechanism of the action of private individuals, we can understand the rationale of the neoliberal project as one aiming at the construction of a system of interrelated virtual "inspection houses", which I called elsewhere, "fractal panopticon" (De Angelis, 2001). In this project, individuals and networks of individuals, such as firms, industrial sectors, cities, nations, regions, etc. relate to a "watchtower" that emerges out of the process of competition and that sees, classifies, strikes, punishes and rewards. The panopticon of the global market is "fractal", in that each level of social aggregation is "self-similar" to others: the disciplinary process of competition become socially pervasive and touches areas not previously organized by the market. The watchtower of this fractal-panopticon of the neoliberal age is invisible because decentered. and is constituted by pervasive market-like interactions. However, its effects are tangible and operate through the disciplinary processes of competition. In this sense, the watchtower is an emergent property of competitive markets, in which Hayek's "competition that goes on all the time" embeds the systemic compulsory functions of Bentham's central tower. It must be pointed out that as in Bentham's panopticon, the role of the planner in the fractal-panopticon is to provide the design of a mechanism, which is then left to operate out of its internal logic of power between inspectors and inspected. Neoliberal policies can thus be regarded as attempts to define the *conditions* of interaction among private individuals, by extending and defending the realm of enclosures and competitive interaction.

Bentham however gives us a further insight. His panopticon is a place of safe custody, i.e. safe confinement preventing escape, and of labor. (Bentham, 1787, p. 31). Safe confinement is due to the fact that inmates are *isolated* from each other and communication among them is prevented. As we have seen, there are two interrelated reasons for Bentham's strategic choice of power's control of communication, and these are the ability to frustrate the *hope* of the inmates to escape from their condition, and power's attempt to avoid dangerous *"concert among minds"*.[18] In the condition of the neoliberal fractal-panopticon, the reduction of hope brought about by the *penseé unique* of our age seems to have received the first blows by new counter-globalization movements that have begun to question competition as mechanism of co-ordination and instead explore new forms of communication and "concert among minds." By building bridges across political issues and subjectivities, women, labor, environmentalists, farmers, indigenous and other movements are increasingly faced by the problem of exploring and thinking about new ways of social co-ordination that move beyond the one inspired by the combination of Hayek's market order and Bentham's panopticon. To do so however, they will face the greatest challenge of all, and this is to redefine for themselves a practice of freedom that breaks with the one that simply sees it as making free choices from a *given* menu. It is time now to talk about what to put on the menu and who decides it!

NOTES

1. Many thanks to an anonymous referee of this journal for the useful comments. The usual caveats apply.
2. Hayek (1988, p. 52) writes: "Long before Auguste Compte introduced the term 'positivism' for the view that represented a 'demonstrated ethics' (demonstrated by reason, that is) as the only possible alternative to a supernaturally 'revealed ethics' ... Jeremy Bentham had developed the most consistent foundations of what we now call legal and moral positivism: that is, the constructivistic interpretation of systems of law

and morals according to which their validity and meaning are supposed to depend wholly on the will and intention of their designers. Bentham is himself a late figure in this development. This constructionism includes not only the Benthamite tradition, represented and continued by John Stuart Mill and the later English Liberal Party, but also practically all contemporary Americans who call themselves 'liberals' ".

3. On this point see Gray (1998, p. 151) and on the role of the state in shaping markets see the classic statement by Polanyi (1944). See Chapters 26 to 33 of Marx's *Capital* (Marx, 1867) for a historical and theoretical discussion of the emergence of capitalist markets with emphasis on power and expropriation in complete opposition to Hayek's belief in spontaneous order.

4. Order on the other hand is defined as "a state of affairs in which a multiplicity of elements of various kinds are so related to each other that we may learn from our acquaintance with some spatial or temporal part of the whole to form correct expectations concerning the rest, or at least expectations which have a good chance of proving correct. It is clear that every society must in this sense possess an order and that such an order will often exist without having been deliberately created" (Hayek, 1973, p. 36).

5. Note that precisely because the starting point is private individuals, the problem of co-ordination of individual plans is often the problem of co-ordinating of conflicting plans. Let us take a classic example, the co-ordination problem arising out of two social figures, capitalists and workers. The workers have a plan, to get a wage. They have knowledge of how poor life is without it. The employers have knowledge of the conditions of the market. The mechanisms that co-ordinates their conflicting knowledge rooted in conflicting standpoints within society, is one that enables them to co-ordinate their actions without challenging the *premises* that are at the basis of their actions.

6. Incidentally, therefore, the problem of social order in Hayek overlaps with the question of forces of production in a society.

7. Thus "it need hardly be said, no products of two producers are ever exactly alike, even if it were only because, as they leave his plant, they must be at different places. These differences are part of the facts which create our economic problem, and it is little help to answer it on the assumption that they are absent" (Hayek, 1946, p. 98).

8. This philosophical stand is in fact the closest to what Marx identifies as the nature of capitalist movement, i.e. "production for production sake" or "accumulation for accumulation sake." The continuous process of accumulation implies the continuous need for individual private agents to blindly adapt to its movement.

9. It has been correctly argued that Hayek emphasis on progress for progress' sake internalizes also an important contradiction between "a conservative attachment to inherited social forms and a liberal commitment to unending progress" (Gray, 1998, p. 156). This contradiction is mostly revealed when the "unending progress" do actually destroys the authoritarian basis which helped to establish the premises of its movement, by, for example, destroying social cohesion through the undermining of patriarchal relations.

10. "Another advantage ... is the great load of trouble and disgust, which it takes off the shoulders of those occasional inspectors of a higher order, such as *judges*, and other *magistrates*, who called down to this irksome task from the superior ranks of life, cannot but feel a proportionable repugnance to the discharge of it" (Bentham, 1787, p. 27). The technology of power given by the panopticon, makes it possible to avoid entering the cells one by one to inspect. Thus, "by this new plan, the disgust is entirely removed; and the trouble of going into such a room as the lodge, is no more than the trouble of going into any other" (Bentham, 1787, pp. 27–28).

11. For example, since "rational action is possible only in a fairly orderly world", then "it clearly makes sense to try to produce conditions under which the chances for any individual taken at random to achieve his ends as effectively as possible will be very high – even if it cannot be predicted which particular aims will be favoured, and which not" (Hayek, 1978, p. 183). The production of these conditions, in the world of Hayek, is the state creation of markets. The story of markets as spontaneous order turns therefore into a self-fulfilling prophecy. Because markets are believed to be emerging spontaneously, the state must promote the conditions for their emergence, which, even if the thesis of spontaneous order is proven wrong, would result in any case in the creation of markets.

12. On Hayek's abstraction see Gamble (1996, pp. 44–46).

13. "Neither the orders of the inspector himself, nor any interest which they may feel, or not feel, in the regular performance of his duty, would be requisite to find them motives adequate to the purpose. Secluded oftentimes, by their situation, from every other object, they will naturally, and in a manner unavoidably give their eyes a direction conformable to that purpose, in every momentary interval of their ordinary occupations. It will supply in their instance the place of that great and constant fund of entertainment to the sedentary and vacant in towns, the looking out of the window. The scene, though a confined, would be a very various, and therefore perhaps not altogether an unamusing one" (Bentham, 1787, p. 20).

14. "If a man won't work, nothing has he to do, from morning to night, but to eat his bad bread and drink his water, without a soul to speak to. If he will work, his time is occupied, and he has his meat and his beer, or whatever else his earnings may afford him, and not a stroke does he strike but he gets something, which he would not have got otherwise" (Bentham, 1787, p. 67).

15. The British Library copy of the 1787 edition has a stamp of the "Patent Office" right above the title of this letter "on the means to extract labour." It would be interesting to uncover the history of this "intellectual property right."

16. Gamble (1996, p. 42) rhetorically asks: "In a society in which the opportunities to own and acquire property were limited not by the arbitrary decision of rulers but by laws which allowed only members of one minority group to hold property, would it be justifiable to advocate the redistribution of property to increase the total sum of liberty?"

17. See Gamble (1996, p. 42). See also the discussion in Kuhathas (1989).

18. "Overpowering the guard requires an union of hands, and a concert among minds. But what union, or what concert, can there be among persons, no one of whom will have set eyes on any other from the first moment of his entrance? Undermining walls, forcing iron bars, requires commonly a concert, always a length of time exempt from interruption. But who would think of beginning a work of hours and days, without any tolerable prospect of making so much as the first motion towards it unobserved?" (Bentham, 1787, p. 32) In letter 8 Bentham addresses the issue of how can this confinement be applicable "to the joint purposes of *punishment, reformation,* and *pecuniary economy?*" Because it may be disputable that solitude may serve a purpose to reformation. But "In the condition of *our* prisoners . . . you may see the students paradox, *nunquam minus solus quam cùm solus* [never less alone than when alone] realized in a new way; to the keeper, a *multitude,* through not a *crowd;* to themselves, they are *solitary* and *sequestered* individuals" (Bentham, 1787, p. 35).

REFERENCES

Bentham, J. (1787). *Panopticon: or the Inspection-House.* Dublin: Thomas Byrne.

De Angelis, M. (2001). Hayek, Bentham and the Global Work Machine: the Emergence of the Fractal-Panopticon. In: A. Dinestern & M. Neary (Eds), *The Labour Debate. An Investigation into the Theory and Reality of Capitalist Work.* Aldershot: Ashgate.

De Angelis, M. (Forthcoming). Defining the Concreteness of Abstract Labour and its Measure. In: A. Freeman & A. Kliman (Eds), *Current Issues in Marxian Economics.* Edward Elgar.

Foucault, M. (1977). *Discipline and Punish: The Birth of the Prison.* A. Sheridan (Trans.). London: Penguin Books.

Gamble, A. (1996). *Hayek. The Iron Cage of Liberty.* Cambridge: Polity.

Gray, J. (1998). *Hayek on Liberty.* London: Routledge.

Hayek, F. (1945). The use of Knowledge in Society. *American Economic Review, 4,* 519–530. Reprinted in: F. Hayek (1948). *Individualism and economic order.* Chicago: Chicago University Press.

Hayek, F. (1946). The meaning of competition. In: F. Hayek (1948), *Individualism and Economic Order.* Chicago: Chicago University Press.

Hayek, F. (1960). *The Constitution of Liberty.* London: Routledge.

Hayek, F. (1970). The errors of constructivism. In: F. Hayek (1978/1985), *New Studies in Philosophy, Politics, Economics and the History of Ideas* (pp. 8–9). Chicago: Chicago University Press.

Hayek, F. (1973). *Law, Legislation and Liberty, Vol. 1: Rules and Order.* Chicago: University of Chicago Press.

Hayek, F. (1978). *New Studies in Philosophy, Politics, Economics and the History of Ideas.* Chicago: Chicago University Press.

Hayek, F. (1988). The Fatal Conceit: the Errors of Socialism. In: W. W. Bartley, III (Ed.), *The Collected Works of F. A. Hayek* (Vol. I). Chicago: University of Chicago Press.

Kirzner, I. M. (1973). *Competition and Entrepreneurship.* Chicago and London: University of Chicago Press.

Kuhathas, C. (1989). *Hayek and modern liberalism.* Oxford: Clarendon Press.

Marx, K. (1844). Economic and Philosophical Manuscripts. In: *Early Writings.* New York: Vintage Book, 1975.

Marx, K. (1867). *Capital.* Vol. 1. London: Penguin, 1976.

Perelman, M. (2000). *The Invention of Capitalism.* Durham, NC: Duke University Press.

Sciabarra, C. M. (1995). *Marx, Hayek and Utopia* (p. 31). State University of New York Press.

Polanyi, K. (1944). *The Great Transformation. The Political and Economic Origins of our Time.* Boston: Beacon Press.

Steele, G. R. (1993). *The Economics of Friedrich Hayek.* London: Macmillan.